MW01245420

European Monetary Unification

European Monetary Unification: Theory, Practice, and Analysis

Barry Eichengreen

The MIT Press
Cambridge, Massachusetts
London, England

Second printing, 1998

© 1997 Massachusetts Institute of Technology

All rights reserved. No part of this book may be reproduced in any form by any electronic or mechanical means (including photocopying, recording, or information storage and retrieval) without permission in writing from the publisher.

This book was set in Palatino on the Monotype "Prism Plus" PostScript Imagesetter by Asco Trade Typesetting Ltd., Hong Kong.

Printed and bound in the United States of America.

Library of Congress Cataloging-in-Publication Data

Eichengreen, Barry J.
  European Monetary Unification: theory, practice and analysis / Barry Eichengreen.
      p.   cm.
  Includes bibliographical references and index.
  ISBN 0-262-05054-4
  1. Monetary unions—European Union countries. 2. Monetary policy—European Union countries. I. Title.
HG3942.8.E45   1997
332.4'566'094—dc21   97-7565
                                                                         CIP

Contents

1   Introduction

The contents of this book were written between 1989 and 1997, a critical period in the history of European integration. That period is delimited on one end by the Delors Report, the document that launched the current drive for economic and monetary union, and on the other by the deadline for determining which European Union (EU) states will be founding members of Europe's monetary union. The chapters appear in roughly the order they were written, although I have taken some chronological liberties to group together chapters addressing similar themes. Presenting them in order is designed to convey a sense of the development of a rapidly evolving academic literature and also of the changing preoccupations of policymakers.[1]

My approach is unabashedly empirical. The analysis is informed by theory—by the theoretical literatures on optimum currency areas (OCAs), fiscal federalism, and the time inconsistency of optimal monetary policy—for this is what academics bring to such discussions. Ultimately, however, European monetary unification raises issues of practical policy that can only be settled on empirical grounds.

An obvious question is what an American can add to a European policy debate. One answer is the perspective that distance provides. From across the ocean it is sometimes possible to see more clearly the broad contours of the policy debate. Another answer is that a resident of the United States is uniquely situated to weigh in on issues of monetary unification by virtue of firsthand knowledge of the operation of a currency and customs union, namely his own. Thus, individual chapters use the experience of the United States as a metric by which to assess the operation of a European monetary union (EMU).

The theory of optimum currency areas, initiated by Robert Mundell (1961), is the organizing framework for the analysis. In Mundell's paradigm, policymakers balance the savings in transactions costs from the creation of a single money against the consequences of diminished policy autonomy. The diminution of autonomy follows from the loss of the exchange rate and of an independent monetary policy as instruments of adjustment. That loss will be more costly when macroeconomic shocks are more "asymmetric" (for present purposes, more region- or country-specific), when monetary policy is a more powerful instrument for offsetting them, and when other adjustment mechanisms like relative wages and labor mobility are less effective.

Chapter 2, "One Money for Europe? Lessons from the U.S. Currency and Customs Union," shows how these ideas can be operationalized through the use of U.S.-European comparisons.[2] This chapter employs data for Puerto Rico, part of the U.S. currency and customs union (for which balance-of-payments data are conveniently gathered), to analyze external adjustment with a single currency. It shows that capital flows react more quickly in Puerto Rico than in Portugal; although Portugal belongs to the EU, it retains its national money, subjecting investors to currency risk that limits the responsiveness of capital flows. The analysis uses data on state bond yields to ask whether market discipline helps to prevent over-borrowing by subcentral governments in a monetary union; it finds some support for the hypothesis. It examines the impact on fiscal behavior of the debt and deficit limits under which state governments operate in the United States, which subsequently proved a popular basis for speculating about the likely effects of the Maastricht Treaty's Excessive Deficit Procedure (a provision designed to prevent overborrowing by EU members). It shows that unemployment differentials tend to persist even in the integrated labor markets of the United States, which serves as a warning that Europe's regional problems might worsen in the absence of exchange-rate adjustments (given its lower levels of labor mobility). It documents that labor market adjustment across EU states is slower than across U.S. regions.

Many of these issues are analyzed more fully in subsequent work, including subsequent chapters of this book. "One Money for Europe?" helps establish this research agenda. Chapter 3, "Is Europe an Optimum Currency Area?" elaborates several of its themes. It compares the variability of real exchange rates across EU member states and U.S. regions on the grounds that movements in relative price levels are required to maintain internal and external balance when shocks are asymmetric. It documents higher levels of real-exchange-rate variability between EU member states than between U.S. regions, suggesting that shocks are more asymmetric in Europe and pointing to problems from eliminating the exchange rate as an instrument for adjusting relative prices. (Real exchange rates could still move, of course, as a result of changes in price levels, but price levels cannot jump, making them imperfect substitutes for exchange-rate adjustments and implying that, in the absence of the latter, asymmetric shocks may show up as larger regional unemployment differentials.) I also examine co-movements in equity prices in Paris, Düsseldorf, Toronto, and Montreal as a way of gauging the symmetry of disturbances to profitability. Again, the comparison indicates a higher correlation of shocks across regions within North America than Europe. Finally, I look more closely at the roles of labor mobility and fiscal federalism in accommodating disturbances to U.S. regions, using as a case study the automobile-producing state of Michigan following the oil-price shocks of the 1970s. Again, I find that both mechanisms are more highly developed in the United States, suggesting difficulties with the operation of a European monetary union.

Most empirical work quantifies the asymmetric shocks of the theory of optimum currency areas in relatively primitive ways, utilizing, for example, cross-country differences in rates of economic growth. Chapter 4, "Shocking Aspects of European Monetary Unification," develops a more refined measure. (One indication of the skepticism with which North American-based research is received in Europe is that the German news weekly *Die Zeit*, overlooking the pun, cited this title as evidence of the unsympathetic attitude of American researchers toward the EMU project.) Using an econometric methodology developed by Olivier Blanchard and Danny Quah, chapter 4 distinguishes aggregate-supply and aggregate-demand disturbances from the adjustment process through which equilibrium is restored. The model is estimated for eleven European countries (the twelve member states prior to the last enlargement, minus Luxembourg) over the period 1960–88. The results distinguish an EU core, made up of Germany, France, Belgium, the Netherlands and Denmark, in which supply shocks are small and well correlated across countries, and an EU periphery, comprised of the United Kingdom, Italy, Spain, Portugal, Ireland, and Greece, in which supply shocks are larger and less well correlated.[3]

Chapter 4 compares the size and symmetry of disturbances to Europe's economies with those to U.S. regions. It finds that supply shocks to U.S. regions are more symmetric than supply shocks to European countries. Only if the European core is compared to the whole of the United States is the magnitude and symmetry of disturbances comparable. These results, when they were published, provided perhaps the first scholarly support for the strategy of two-speed EMU with membership initially limited to Europe's core countries.

When supply and demand shocks are identified and removed, what remain are responses. These indicate that U.S. regions adjust more quickly than European countries despite lacking an independent exchange rate. This plausibly reflects greater factor mobility and flexibility in the United States, pointing to now-familiar obstacles to the construction of a well-functioning European monetary union.

Can the theory of optimum currency areas be operationalized to rank the readiness of EU member states for monetary unification? Chapter 5, "Ever Closer to Heaven? An Optimum Currency Area Index for European Countries," attempts to do just that. It develops a procedure for applying the theory's core implications to a panel of industrial countries, asking whether those implications explain cross-country differences in the degree of exchange-rate variability.[4] The results reported in this chapter are consistent with the implications of the theory, namely, that the variability of bilateral exchange rates depends on the asymmetry of shocks, on country size (small countries benefiting the most from the enhanced transactions services of a common currency), and on trade dependence (since two countries that trade heavily will prefer a stable bilateral rate).[5] The econometric relationship can be used to assess which countries are best prepared to be founding EMU members. The results broadly coincide with popular handicapping of the Maastricht stakes, with Germany, Austria, the Benelux countries, and Ireland high on the list, and the United Kingdom, Denmark, and Finland lagging behind.[6] Strikingly, the estimates for France suggest that its structural characteristics and cyclical performance are not consistent with a high level of exchange-rate stability vis-à-vis Germany. This supports the view that France's desire for monetary unification is driven at least partly by noneconomic factors and that the success of the project may turn on whether the country succeeds in surmounting these structural obstacles and meeting the Maastricht Treaty's criteria for participation.

I pursue the factor-mobility side of the optimum currency area (OCA) equation in chapter 6, "Labor Markets and European Monetary Unification," which compares migration and labor-market flexibility in Britain, Italy, and the United States. In contrast to "One Money for Europe?" which asked how quickly equilibrium between national unemployment rates is restored, this chapter disaggregates Europe's national markets into regions and asks how quickly equilibrium relationships are restored across regions. The dispersion of shocks to regional labor markets is found to be broadly similar in the three countries, but the migration response is greater in the United States. Estimates of the elasticity of migration with respect to interregional unemployment differentials point to greater unemployment responsiveness in the United States. Compared to Americans, not only are Europeans less likely to migrate between EU member states, but they are less likely to migrate even between regions of their own country. Removing legal barriers to labor mobility within the European Union therefore may not be enough to raise migration to U.S. levels.

These findings reflect the state of the literature circa 1992, by which time there was considerable similar research underway.[7] But history is not always kind to academic agendas. And so the 1992–93 crises in the European Monetary System (EMS) forced that agenda to be recast. These crises drove the U.K. and Italy from the Exchange Rate Mechanism (ERM) of the EMS and forced Portugal, Spain, and Ireland to realign their currencies. They culminated in the summer of 1993 with a fierce attack on the French franc and the decision by European officials to widen the ERM's fluctuation bands from $2\frac{1}{4}$ to 15 percent. This raised questions in the minds of market participants about the viability of a protracted three-stage transition to EMU, in which countries were required to hold their currencies within their ERM bands without "severe tensions" for up to two years.

It is important for the architects of Europe's monetary union to understand the causes of the crisis in order to predict whether similar events might again disrupt the transition to EMU. Chapter 7, "The Unstable EMS," was perhaps the first systematic attempt to provide such an analysis. It set the stage for the subsequent debate by showing how two models of speculative attacks on pegged exchange rates might be applied to the crisis. In the first model, created by Paul Krugman (1979), attacks result when fundamentals (inflation, the real exchange rate, the budget and current account) are out of line. Deteriorating competitiveness causes the central bank's foreign reserves to fall to the point where a speculative attack is launched, exhausting remaining reserves and forcing the authorities to abandon their currency peg. In the second model, created by Robert Flood and Peter Garber (1984b) and Maurice Obstfeld (1986a), attacks can occur and succeed even in the absence of any ex ante imbalance in fundamentals. If the government and central bank respond to the crisis by abandoning their defense of the currency peg and relaxing policy, then a speculative attack can prove self-fulfilling.

In chapter 7, Charles Wyplosz and I argue that the 1992 crisis cannot be understood purely in terms of the Krugman model. Italy, to be sure, had experienced excessive inflation that damaged its competitiveness. For other countries whose currencies were attacked, however, evidence of inadequate competitiveness was less clear. Aside from the lira, the movement of forward exchange rates does not suggest the kind of progressive deterioration of market confidence one would expect in response to gradually worsening fundamentals.[8]

Since the point is sometimes misunderstood, it is important to stress that the argument is not that fundamentals played no role. Rather, problems with fundamentals and self-fulfilling dynamics reinforced one another. Consider the plight of a government seeking to defend its currency in the face of high unemployment.[9] Officials are willing to trade the costs of unemployment now for the benefits of qualifying for monetary union later. But if the currency is attacked, making it necessary to raise interest rates still further and in turn aggravating unemployment, the benefits may no longer dominate the costs. The fact of an attack may then induce the government, which had been willing previously to maintain the currency peg indefinitely, to abandon its defense and shift to a more expansionary policy. This shift is more likely if the country has already developed a problem with fundamentals (in this case, excessive unemployment), for the worse the fundamentals, the more likely is an attack of given size to cause the authorities to abandon their previous policy. Thus, explanations based on fundamentals and self-fulfilling dynamics are complements, not incompatible alternatives.

This tale of self-fulfilling prophecies rests on two preconditions: high capital mobility and limited foreign support. Chapter 7 emphasizes that in a world of high capital mobility, the resources of the markets far exceed those of individual central banks. When pressure comes, defending a pegged currency can require the central bank to raise interest rates to politically insupportable levels, as Sweden found out in 1992 and Ireland learned in 1993.

The only escape from this dilemma is foreign support for the currency under attack. In fact, the EMS Articles of Agreement contain a clause committing strong-currency countries to support their weak-currency counterparts through interventions "unlimited at the compulsory intervention rates" (that is, at the edge of the ERM fluctuation bands). Some commentators concluded that this provision ruled out self-fulfilling attacks.[10] But the provision in question was not incentive compatible. As explained in this chapter, already in 1978 the German Bundesbank had obtained a letter from the Government of the Federal Republic authorizing it to opt out of its commitment to intervene if it thought that price stability was threatened. The markets drew the relevant conclusion.

A prediction of chapter 7, published in the spring of 1993, was additional currency crises. It identified greater exchange-rate flexibility, restraints on capital mobility, and a forced march to EMU as the viable alternatives to the narrow-band EMS, whose pegged rates were indefensible under these conditions. At the end of July 1993, another crisis forced the issue, and European policymakers opted for the first of these alternatives.[11]

The Maastricht Treaty specifies not just exchange-rate stability but price stability, interest-rate stability, and fiscal stability as preconditions that must be met by candidates for EMU. Although the exchange-rate condition was the focus of attention during this episode of EMS turbulence, the fiscal criteria have proven even more controversial. Chapter 8, "The Political Economy of Fiscal Restrictions: Implications for Europe from the United States," analyzes them by again drawing on the experience of the United States. U.S. experience indicates that statutory and constitutional restrictions on the fiscal position of state governments significantly limit the size of deficits, suggesting that the restrictions of the Maastricht Treaty, insofar as they are similar, should be enforceable. But if rigorously enforced, the Maastricht criteria threaten to weaken the automatic stabilization capacity of Europe's national budgets; this is suggested by the fact that U.S. state governments operating under stringent balanced-budget rules provide less automatic stabilization over the cycle.[12] Having tied their monetary hands behind their back, Europe's governments, if they apply the Maastricht criteria too rigidly, will also lose the freedom to use fiscal policy to counter shocks.

These themes are developed further in chapter 9, "Fiscal Policy and Monetary Union: Is There a Tradeoff between Federalism and Fiscal Restrictions?" which considers the treaty's Excessive Deficit Procedure.[13] The principal motivation for this procedure is the fear that member states that borrow excessively will fall prey to a debt crisis, to which the European Central Bank (ECB) will feel compelled to respond with an inflationary bailout. The Excessive Deficit Procedure is designed to contain this tendency to overborrow and remove the pressure for the central bank to intervene.

If overborrowing and debt bailouts are serious problems, we should expect to see fiscal restrictions in existing monetary unions. Strikingly, we do not. Nor do countries with a federal structure generally limit the fiscal freedom of subcentral governments. Such restraints prevail only where the central or federal government collects the bulk of the tax revenues itself. When subcentral governments do not control their own taxes, there exist only two responses to a debt run—bailout and default. Since default has political and economic costs, the pressure for a bailout will be intense. But when subcentral governments possess a third option, namely raising their own taxes to close the debt-servicing gap, central banks can insist that they solve their own problem. The monetary authorities are better able to resist the pressure for a bailout.

The implication for Europe is clear. The member states control the majority of the EU's taxes. They can therefore use their own resources to solve their own fiscal problems. From this point of view, the Excessive Deficit Procedure is redundant.

Chapter 9 takes this argument a step further. It argues that pressure for the central government to provide tax-smoothing and automatic-stabilization services through a system of fiscal federalism will be greater where restrictions on borrowing by subcentral governments prevent the latter from providing those services themselves. This suggests that the Excessive Deficit Procedure may spur the creation of a system of fiscal federalism in which Brussels collects taxes and provides transfers to member states in amounts that increase with, say, the level of unemployment. And because the member states will resist giving up their tax revenues as quickly as they demand additional services from the EU, the financial position of the latter will deteriorate. Restraints on the budgetary freedom of subcentral governments may thereby increase the demand for central government borrowing, ultimately weakening the financial stability of the center.

Taken together, these arguments suggest that the Excessive Deficit Procedure should be weakened or abandoned. Since member states and not the EU control the bulk of Europe's taxes, that procedure is super-fluous. It will hamstring automatic stabilization. It may exacerbate the very problem of bailouts that it is designed to avert. And by encouraging the concentration of fiscal functions in Brussels, it will tend to create the kind of political superstate that many Europeans fear.

I consider this and other arguments that monetary integration requires political integration in chapter 10, "A More Perfect Union? On the Logic of Economic Integration." Clearly, no such implication follows on fiscal grounds if one concludes that the budgetary restrictions of the Maastricht Treaty are redundant. A stronger justification for political integration is to

render the ECB accountable to its constituencies. Democratic accountability is not, however, the only source of legitimation for a central bank.
Increasingly countries are buttressing the independence of their national
central banks and insulating them from political pressures. Monetary
policymakers are appealing less, not more, to democratic legitimation.
Publics accept independent central banks because they perceive them as
efficient—as insulated from political pressures that would otherwise
bias policy excessively toward short-term goals. The implication is that
the ECB need not be answerable to a powerful parliament so long as
Europeans are confident of the central bank's commitment to its mandate.

Chapter 11, "How Will Transatlantic Policy Interactions Change with
the Advent of EMU?" turns to EMU's implications for the international
monetary system and the rest of the world. EMU will alter interactions
not just between members of the monetary union but also between those
countries and the rest of the world. Chapter 11 analyzes these questions
in a formal framework under alternative assumptions about fiscal policy.
While in standard models fiscal retrenchment reduces output and employment, the possibility has been raised in the current European context that
fiscal consolidation can be expansionary. Under this "anti-Keynesian"
assumption, it turns out that EMU may actually enhance monetary and
fiscal discipline and stabilize employment. While governments will wish
the ECB and its foreign counterparts to coordinate national monetary
policies, the central banks will not share their interest in international
cooperation. And there is reason to think that fiscal-policy coordination
can be counterproductive under EMU. Thus, the implications of EMU for
the interaction of the Euro zone with the rest of the world are anything
but intuitive.

European monetary unification is a process, not a grand achievement or
a great blunder. That process will end neither when Stage III begins on
January 1, 1999, nor when the Euro replaces national currencies in 2002.
Rather, Europe's monetary union will continue to develop. The incidence
of supply and demand shocks will change as the continent's financial and
commodity markets are restructured by the fact of monetary unification.
Adjustment within the Euro zone will change as labor grows more
mobile. The stringency with which the Excessive Deficit Procedure is
enforced will decline once the ECB demonstrates its unwillingness to
succumb to pressure for a debt bailout. And the prospects for monetary
policy coordination between Europe, the United States, and Japan will
grow once the institutions and arrangements of international cooperation
are adapted to the reality of a European Central Bank. None of this will

occur overnight. In the meantime, economists concerned with the implications will continue to draw evidence from Europe's history and from the experience of monetary unions like that of the United States.

I acknowledge at the beginning of each chapter the friends and colleagues who commented on preliminary drafts and otherwise contributed to the analysis. My greatest debt, however, is to Tam Bayoumi, Fabio Ghironi, Jürgen von Hagen, and Charles Wyplosz for co-authoring chapters. Much of what I know about EMU grows out of joint work with these scholars. Their collaboration may even free me of the criticism of having failed to appreciate British, Italian, German, and French sensibilities.

At MIT Press, Terry Vaughn provided much valued support, and Kathleen Caruso shepherded the manuscript into print. In Berkeley, Kira Reoutt solved a variety of logistical problems with efficiency, humor, and grace. Erwin Cho-Woods helped prepare the index and references.

I dedicate the book to Michelle. Her patience with my absences on research trips is appropriately rewarded, I hope, by the accumulation of frequent flyer miles.

Notes

1. Thus, although I have updated references and notes and eliminated the first half of chapter 2 (on the grounds that Stage I of the Maastricht process, with which it is concerned, is now far behind), the chapters otherwise appear as originally published. In particular, I have not changed European Community to European Union or twelve EU members to fifteen in order to provide the reader with a clear sense of the historical context in which they were written.

2. This was not the first attempt to employ evidence from the United States in analyzing balance-of-payments adjustment and monetary unification. James Ingram's 1962 book had already utilized data for Puerto Rico and the rest of the United States to analyze balance-of-payments adjustment in a monetary union. And a first draft of Xavier Sala-i-Martin and Jeffrey Sachs's influential piece on fiscal federalism and monetary union, using data for U.S. states, had been presented to the National Bureau of Economic Research Summer Institute in 1989.

3. Bayoumi and Eichengreen (1993a) extends these results to the then-EFTA countries, showing that Austria belongs with the core, Finland belongs with the periphery, and Sweden lies in between. The reason for concentrating on supply shocks is that demand shocks are more likely to change with the advent of EMU. This is not to deny that supply shocks will also be affected, although there is dispute in the literature about whether they will become more or less symmetric. I review this debate in Eichengreen (1993b). It is worth noting that demand shocks are also smaller and better correlated in the core than the periphery, although the difference is relatively small.

4. Mundell (1961), in his seminal article, suggested that the same factors that determine whether two countries should adopt a common currency should also affect their decision of whether or not to stabilize the exchange rate between their separate national monies.

5. Labor mobility, which is also emphasized in the theory of optimum currency areas, has not played a significant role in adjustment to shocks that vary across countries (as shown in chapter 2). Because this analysis uses the nation as the unit of observation, labor mobility is not considered.

6. Note that the list of prime candidates is largely the same as in chapter 4 and in the companion paper (Bayoumi and Eichengreen 1993a) that considered also the EFTA countries. Ireland has joined the prime candidates, however, because this analysis considers also factors other than asymmetric shocks (country size, for example), and because it focuses on the relatively recent period over which Ireland has converged with the EU core.

7. "Shocking Aspects of European Monetary Unification" appeared as an NBER Working Paper that year, although it was only published in 1993.

8. These conclusions have been reinforced by the more sophisticated analyses of this phenomenon that followed subsequently, using models of exchange-rate target zones (Rose and Svensson 1996) and options pricing (Campa and Chang 1996). We also report a survey of foreign exchange dealers that suggests that traders were prompted to act not just by the deterioration of fundamentals but also by the perception that other traders were selling the currency and by questions about the capacity of central banks to stem the tide.

9. This example is drawn from Eichengreen (1993a). I choose it over the rationale for self-fulfilling attacks emphasized in chapter 7 (having to do with some peculiar incentives associated with provisions of the Maastricht Treaty) to highlight the complementarity of fundamentals-based and self-fulfilling attacks.

10. See, for example, Kenen (1988).

11. In retrospect, it must be admitted that we underestimated the willingness of European officials to turn to wide bands. But, then, so did everyone else, including the officials themselves, who were forced into this expedient by the speculative attack on the French franc and their inability to agree on another solution.

12. In comparison with states whose fiscal position is substantially constrained. Evidence to this effect is developed more fully in Bayoumi and Eichengreen (1995).

13. This chapter is an expanded version of von Hagen and Eichengreen (1996).

2

**One Money for Europe?
Lessons from the U.S.
Currency Union**

2.1 Introduction

To an American observer, a European central bank and a common currency are radical ideas. But imagine 50 US states with 50 different currencies, responds the European to the sceptical American. A common currency, like permanently fixed exchange rates, encourages flows of commodities, capital and labour between states by eliminating exchange-rate uncertainty and reducing transactions costs. By encouraging factor mobility, a common currency and an integrated market enhance the capacity of European Community member states to accommodate balance-of-payments disturbances. More controversial is the assertion that these gains are obtained at a cost that is dwarfed by the benefits. A permanently fixed exchange rate requires those who join the currency union to sacrifice autonomy of monetary policy and possibly fiscal autonomy as well. No longer can exchange-rate changes be used to resolve conflicts between internal and external balance. Here the sceptical European responds that the 50 US states evince no desire for independent macroeconomic policies. Neither does one hear talk of balance-of-payments "problems" among the states, or of regional problems severe enough to induce them to secede from the Federal Reserve System.

For evidence on these questions, Sections 2.2 and 2.3 examine US experience with customs and monetary union. I take seriously the analogy between the United States of America and the "United States of Europe." In Section 2.2 I first consider the institutional mechanisms designed to resolve regional conflicts over economic policies within the US. I then assess the notion that the single US market differs fundamentally from its

Originally published, in slightly longer form, in *Economic Policy* 10 (1990): 118–87. Reprinted with permission.

more balkanized EC counterpart in its capacity to accommodate disturbances and in the constraints it imposes on member states. It is a common observation that balance-of-payments problems do not arise within
the US. In Section 2.3 I use some unusual data to analyse exactly how
interregional payments balance is maintained. This enables us to ask
whether or not the conditions for replicating the American situation are
present in Europe.

To assess the notion that the creation of a European monetary union
will require not only the harmonization of national monetary policies but
close coordination of fiscal policies as well, I analyse state budget balances
within the US. A related assertion is that following the elimination of
controls on short-term capital flows and long-term foreign investment it
will not be possible to sustain corporate tax rates that differ significantly
across states. Hence, the imperative of fiscal harmonization will equalize
not only the level of deficit spending but the level of government expenditure throughout Europe. I assess this proposition by analysing variations in tax rates and levels of public expenditure within the US. A final
assertion is that inter-regional movements of capital and labour largely
eliminate the problems of depressed regions that would otherwise arise
in the US currency/customs union. I examine data on regional unemployment in the US as a way of gauging the likely European response.

Heroic assumptions are required to export the lessons of US experience
to Europe. The concluding section, therefore, speculates about the extent
to which US experience is an export good.

2.2 Policy Formulation in the US Currency Union

US experience cannot be applied mechanically to Europe. The United
States of America and a "United States of Europe" would differ in both
economic and political structure. Table 2.1 displays some economic similarities and differences. Per capita income in 1987 remained more than
50% higher in the US, whether market exchange rates or purchasing
power parity conversions are used. The degree of openness of the two
economies was comparable (only slightly higher in the EC) once intra-EC
trade is netted out. Not only was average unemployment higher in
Europe in 1986, so was its variability across locations whether measured
by the standard deviation or coefficient of variation. The share of labour
in agriculture in Europe remains considerably higher than in the US, and
not only because of Greece, Portugal and Ireland. The share of labour in

Table 2.1
The US and the EC12
(Data for Most Recent Year Available)

Item	US	EC12
Population (1,000s)	241,600 (1)	322,668 (1)
Area (1000 km^2)	9,363 (1)	2,259 (2)
GDP per capita, US$, current exchange rates	16,936 (3)	10,752 (3)
Standard deviation of GDP per capita (above)	3,674	4,073
GDP per capita using EC purchasing power parity adjustment	18,338 (4)	11,729 (4)
External trade (exports + imports as % of GDP) (excluding trade within EC12)	14.7 (5)	18.4 (5)
Unemployment rate (%)	6.95 (6)	10.9 (7)
Standard deviation of unemployment rate (%)	2.23	4.93
Share of labour force in agriculture (%)	4.1 (8)	9.1 (9)
		7.4 (10)
Standard deviation of share of labour force in agriculture (%)	2.9	9.2
		3.8
Share of labour force in service sector (%)	13.9 (11)	56.2 (12)
	44.2	57.4 (13)
Standard deviation of share of labour force in services (%)	2.1	10.2
	2.9	7.3

Source: (1) *World Development Report 1988.* Data are for mid-year 1986. (2) *World Development Report 1988*, except for Luxembourg which is from *Eurostat 1987.* (3) US figure is from the Advisory Committee on Intergovernmental Relations, *Significant Features of Fiscal Federalism*, 1988. The figure shown differs slightly from the US GDP per capita for 1986 from the source used for Europe ($17,349). The ACIR figure was used in order to obtain individual state figures. The European figure is from *OECD Main Economic Indicators* for 1986 at current prices and exchange rates in billions of US dollars. Population figures for Europe are from *World Development Report.* (4) *OECD National Accounts*, Volume 1, 1960–87. GDP per capita uses current prices at current PPP in US dollars for 1987. (5) External trade = exports plus imports. *OECD Monthly Trade Statistics*, 1987. Data in US dollars. *OECD Main Economic Indicators for 1987* GDP in US dollars. (6) *Statistical Abstract of the United States.* Data are for 1986. (7) *Eurostat Yearbook 1987.* Data are for April 1986. (8) *Geographic Profile of Employment and Unemployment.* United States Department of Labor, Bureau of Labor Statistics, 1987. Table 15, p. 64. (9) *Eurostat 1987*, data are for 1983. For Greece, Ireland and Portugal, source is *World Development Report*, data for 1980. (10) Same as (9) except Greece, Portugal and Ireland are excluded. (11) The first figure and corresponding standard deviation pertain to the BLS definition. This number is far out of line with the European figures, as the BLS definition of services is very restrictive. The expanded definition of "Services" includes: technicians and related support, sales and administrative support, including clerical. (12) Same as sources in note 9. (13) Same as sources in note 9 except Greece, Portugal and Ireland are excluded. The data represent the sum of "market" and "non-market" services.

services is higher in Europe than in the US, even, when a generous measure of US service sector employment is applied.

2.2.1   The Institutional Framework for Monetary Policymaking

Regional monetary policy preferences are reconciled by placing on the Board of Governors of the Federal Reserve System representatives of Federal Reserve Districts organized along geographic lines. The Federal Open Market Committee comprises the seven members of the Board of Governors (appointed by the President and confirmed by the Senate), plus five Reserve Bank presidents (one of whom is president of the Federal Reserve Bank of New York, the others of whom rotate). This geographic form was adopted to allay fears of Westerners that the newly created central bank would adopt an overly deflationary policy, and fears of Easterners that the Fed would be overly inflationary. (Europeans reading this passage may be tempted to replace "Westerners" and "Easterners" with "Southerners" and "Northerners.") Considerable autonomy to regulate local banks and allocate discounts across borrowers was delegated to the district reserve banks. The Federal Reserve Act empowered them "to establish from time to time, subject to review and determination of the Federal Reserve Board, rates of discount...for each class of paper." From the beginning the Federal Reserve Board exercised "considerable influence on the district banks in the direction of equalizing rates" (Myers, 1970, p. 275).

In its early years this arrangement did not succeed in alleviating regional conflicts completely. That a reasonable degree of cooperation quickly developed among the regional reserve banks is attributed to the fact that the nation was engaged in a war which rendered "apparent to all the necessity of subordinating considerations purely of sectional advantage" (Reed, 1922, p. 9). But as soon as the war ended, representatives of the East and West found themselves at loggerheads over Fed policy. In the postwar agricultural depression (starting in the summer of 1920), western and southern periodicals published scathing attacks on the Federal Reserve System for pursuing a tight-money policy that favoured metropolitan financial interests. It was complained that the Federal Reserve Bank of New York, set in the international financial centre of the US, exercised disproportionate influence over the formulation and implementation of financial and monetary policies.

Decentralization gave rise to uncertainties about the locus of power that undermined the capacity of the newly established central bank to maintain monetary stability. According to Friedman and Schwartz (1963), the power struggle between the New York Fed and the Washington, D.C.-based Board of Governors, where the western reserve banks exercised more influence, immobilized the Fed when the money supply collapsed in the early stages of the Great Depression. According to Wigmore (1988), the run on the dollar in 1933 forced the US to abandon the gold standard because of the unwillingness of interior Reserve Banks, concerned about their own balance sheets, to rediscount on behalf of the Federal Reserve Bank of New York.

How divergent regional preferences over monetary policy will be reconciled by a European central bank remains to be seen. Proposals for a European central bank closely resemble the Federal Reserve System in structure. They stress the need to ensure the independence of the governing body from national political bodies as well as from other EC institutions. German officials, used to functioning under a decentralized Bundesbank system with 11 Land Central Banks and a Board of Governors in Frankfurt, propose organizing the European central bank along federal lines (Poehl, 1988). US experience in the early years of the Federal Reserve System suggests that this guarantees neither effective cooperation among members of the monetary union nor the alleviation of regional conflicts over monetary policy.

2.2.2 The Institutional Framework for Fiscal Policymaking

Federal fiscal policy in the US is formulated by a convoluted process involving Congress, the Executive Branch and the electorate. The President, with the help of his Office of Management of the Budget, submits a budget to Congress in January of each year. This budget is scrutinized by House and Senate Committees. Concurrent resolutions lead to the passage of a reconciliation bill. The President can influence the process only by pressuring Congress and threatening to veto appropriation bills. This is in contrast with parliamentary systems, where either the legislature accepts the government's budget or the government falls. In the US the President's budget is merely a recommendation to Congress.

Regional conflicts continue to feature prominently in the US fiscal debate. Representatives of agricultural regions lobby for farm programmes, those from regions with insolvent banks for bank bailout schemes. Regional interests make difficult reductions in spending on existing programmes. An illustration is military base closures. Every regional representative has a strong interest in opposing base closures in her own district, and a diffuse interest in supporting specific base closures else-where. The US has found it next to impossible to succeed in closing redundant bases. (The European analogy might be spending on the CAP.) Clearly, centralizing the budgetary process and allowing it to be deter-mined by proportional representation has not sufficed to alleviate regional conflicts.

The EC budget is determined in a broadly similar fashion, but with one important difference. In contrast to the US, where the President can veto Congress's budget, in Europe it is the EC Parliament which can veto the Council of Ministers' budget. Expenditures are divided into two cate-gories. The so-called compulsory expenditures, which have traditionally comprised about two-thirds of total spending, are determined by the Council of Ministers. The so-called non-compulsory expenditures are voted directly by Parliament. Compulsory spending results from the Treaty and associated Acts and includes such items as expenditures on the purchase of agricultural surpluses, grants to improve farm structures, interest rebates on EMS loans, and aid to developing countries. Since this portion of the budget is decided by the Council of Ministers (in this case, finance minis-ters), representing their national governments, the process is broadly sim-ilar to that portion of the American budget over which the Executive branch has control or influence. The CAP accounts for the largest share. Other items include outlays on energy, research, transport, administrative costs and salaries and pensions of EC employees. Since Members of the European Parliament are directly elected, this component of spending is subject to the same kind of pressures as in the US. If the Parliament finds components of the budget—presumably compulsory expenditures—unsatisfactory, it can reject it if a majority of voting members and two-thirds of all Members of the European Parliament so decide. This occurred in 1980. Until the dispute is resolved, the EC proceeds on the basis of the previous year's budget.

2.2.3 Fiscal Federalism

In the US, the 50 states retain fiscal independence. They decide their own levels of spending, taxation and borrowing. The EC, in contrast, foresees a situation in which the Community will exercise increasing influence over the fiscal policies of member states. A number of critics (e.g. Padoa-Schioppa, Emerson, King, Milleron, Paelinck, Papademos, Pastor, and Scharpf, 1987) have questioned the viability of the EC's model and have suggested emulating the US example.

A central feature of the American budgetary process is fiscal federalism. Tax revenues are raised by local, state and national governments, with the states redistributing a portion of the receipts to localities, just as the national government redistributes a portion of the revenues to the states. One rationale for this arrangement is that some effects of government spending spill across state and local borders. Standard examples are spending on education, environmental quality, health and public welfare. Because local governments have no reason to internalize these externalities, spending would remain at suboptimal levels. Only federal authorities are in a position to internalize these externalities. They can do so through transfers to state and local jurisdictions, generally in the form of matching grants. If the external benefits of additional provision of these items are especially high when undertaken by jurisdictions in which incomes are especially low, then there may be a case for a continuous net transfer of resources from high to low-income jurisdictions.

A second rationale for fiscal federalism views intergovernmental transfers as insurance. If economic conditions are imperfectly correlated across member states, then all can benefit from a programme of fiscal insurance through which resources are transferred from jurisdictions in which income is temporarily high to those in which income is temporarily low. This rationale is especially relevant to a monetary union. Normally, a decline in the demand for a region's exports requires a decline in spending (to reduce the demand for imports from other regions) and a fall in real wages (to help restore the competitiveness of exports to other regions). In a country with its own currency, devaluing the exchange rate can accomplish both ends. In a country that belongs to a monetary union and cannot devalue, all wages and prices, upon which production and spending decisions depend, must change to bring about adjustment. Inward transfers to the depressed region reduce the need for these difficult forms of adjustment to restore external balance.

Both arguments have been applied to the EC. Padoa-Schioppa et al. (1987, p. 162) argue for Community support for general education in low-income states, citing the benefits to the entire Community from a more educated labour force, and the special problems facing countries like Portugal and Ireland due to emigration of their workers to higher income states. Sala-i-Martin and Sachs (1992) suggest that without simultaneously creating a fiscal union responsible for the insurance function, a viable monetary union in Europe may not be possible.

In the US, the dominant form of intergovernmental transfers is federal grants-in-aid. An increasing number of federal grant programmes have

Table 2.2
US Intergovernmental Revenue as Percentage of Recipients' Expenditures

	State receipts from federal government as percentage of state expenditures	Local receipts from federal and state governments as percentage of local expenditures
1902	1.6	5.8
1922	7.4	7.1
1932	8.0	12.8
1942	16.6	25.4
1958	18.3	24.9
1964	21.2	27.0
1967	23.2	30.3
1972	24.5	33.5
1974	23.9	39.0
1976	23.2	38.4
1978	24.6	39.8
1980	24.0	39.3
1982	21.3	37.2
1984	21.7	35.3
1986	21.8	34.4
1987	20.9	33.7

Source: Break (1967), p. 5, for 1902–64. Advisory Committee on Intergovernmental Relations, *Significant Features of Fiscal Federalism 1989*, vol. 1, for 1967–87.

incorporated explicit equalizing formulas, which allocate a higher proportion of the available funds to low-income states or increase the federal share of total programme costs in states with low per capita incomes (Break, 1967, p. 121). Public assistance programmes account for the largest segment of the equalization group. Intergovernmental grants comprise a high and rising share of state and local government spending (Table 2.2). Federal intergovernmental spending approached 2% of GNP in the 1960s. Receipts from the Federal government accounted for nearly a quarter of state spending in the 1960s and 1970s, and for nearly 40% of local spending. In the 1980s, with the rise of the deficit problem, these ratios have begun to decline, though both remain substantial.

Sala-i-Martin and Sachs (1992) have attempted to quantify the extent to which transfers function as insurance. They estimate that a one-dollar decline in income in the average US region leads to a rise in federal transfers of 6 to 10 cents. (Transfers include social security and other retirement plans, income maintenance payments, veterans' benefits and payments to non-profit institutions.) The more important source of regional insurance is on the tax side. Sala-i-Martin and Sachs estimate that a one-dollar decline in income in the average US region leads to a decline in Federal tax payments on the order of 30 cents. Thus, the magnitude of insurance on the tax side is three to five times as important as that on the expenditure side. Together, tax and transfer adjustments eliminate as much as 40% of the decline in regional incomes.

Does there exist scope in Europe for replicating US arrangements? This really is two questions: first, whether there exist institutions with the relevant structure; second, whether they operate on the relevant scale. On the transfer side, the EC has created a series of structural funds to discharge redistributive functions and deal with regional problems. A Social Fund was introduced to deal with the labour market adjustment problems brought about by economic integration. A Regional Fund was created to address their uneven geographical incidence. The Integrated Mediterranean Programmes were created to deal with the special problems of the southern members of the Community. Yet the scope for redistribution on the American scale will remain limited so long as the Community budget barely exceeds 1% of EC GNP. Estimates of the national incidence of the Community budget appear in table 2.3. Important redistributive vehicles such as the regional fund receive less than 10% of the Community budget. Since a non-negligible share of these expenditures is allocated to projects in high-income states (Croxford, Wise, and Chalkley 1987), their redistributive impact is smaller still. In 1987 the Commission began to propose increasing expenditure on these structural programmes, but even at projected levels intergovernmental transfers would remain minute by US standards.

As to scale, imagine a severe recession, say a decline in income of 10% affecting half of the EC. In order to emulate US adjustment, using the estimates of Sala-i-Martin and Sachs, transfers to the depressed regions should amount to 0.5% of EC GNP. Spending on EC programmes is currently in the range of 1% of EC GNP. Thus, raising EC spending by 0.5% of EC GNP, under the favourable assumption that the entire increase goes to the depressed regions, implies at least a 50% increase in spending. It is hard to imagine that existing programmes are able to respond on such a scale. Thus, replicating the US situation would require a significant increase in the scale of the EC budget.

The EC derives most of its revenue from VAT, customs duties and agricultural levies. VAT contributions are roughly proportional to GDP, all member states contributing between 0.4 and 0.6% of GDP to the

Table 2.3
Net National Contributions and Receipts from EC Budget

	1982–84 Average		1985–87 average	
	% GDP	ECUs per capita	% GDP	ECUs per capita
Germany	−0.41	−45	−0.44	−59
France	−0.09	−9	−0.05	−5
Italy	0.27	17	0.04	3
Netherlands	0.18	17	0.20	23
Belgium–Luxembourg	−0.52	−45	−0.28	−37
UK	−0.23	−19	−0.35	−29
Ireland	3.77	206	4.75	260
Denmark	0.52	60	0.41	53
Greece	2.12	81	3.31	70
EC10	−0.07	−6	−0.13	−13
Spain[a]	N/A	N/A	0.08	3
Portugal[a]	N/A	N/A	1.01	12
EC12	N/A	N/A	−0.14	−10

Sources: Ardy (1988) for 1982–84, and author's calculations, following Ardy, for 1985–87 based on: Contributions/Receipts: E.C. Court of Auditors *Annual Report 1988*; Population: *OECD Main Economic Indicators*; ECU/local currency rates: IMF *International Financial Statistics*; Deflators: *OECD National Accounts 1960–87*; GDP: *OECD National Accounts.*
Notes: All magnitudes are in 1982 prices. Minus sign indicates contributions exceed receipts.
[a] Data for Spain and Portugal are 1986 and 1987 only. Consequently EC12 average for 1985–87 is actually for 10 countries and 1986–87 for Portugal and Spain.

Community (Ardy, 1988, Table 2). If VAT is levied at a constant ad valorem rate, a $1 decline in income in an EC member state would lead to a 0.4 to 0.6¢ decline in VAT payments. The actual situation is more complicated, since VAT is remitted on exports and investment, while government expenditure is VAT exempt. (Other spending is taxed at 1.4%, although 10% of revenue collected is remitted to member states to defray collection costs.) Since investment and exports are more cyclically volatile than other components of national income, a fall in national income of $1 is likely to reduce that portion of GDP subject to VAT by less than $1 and, therefore, to reduce VAT payments by even less than 0.4 to 0.6¢. Customs duties are about half as important on the revenue side as VAT, and they are likely to respond proportionately to changes in national income, or by the logic of the preceding paragraph, somewhat less. At most, a $1 fall in national income would lead to a 0.2 to 0.3¢ fall in this tax. The cyclical volatility of the agricultural and sugar levies is by far the most difficult to estimate. Insofar as the production and consumption of foodstuffs are relatively unresponsive to changes in prices and income, and since receipts from these levies are only $\frac{1}{3}$ as important as receipts from customs duties, at most a $1 fall in national income would reduce receipts by 0.07 to 0.1¢.

Combining estimates for the three principal categories of receipts, a $1 fall in national income would reduce tax payments to the EC by no more than 1¢. This is in contrast to Sachs and Sala-i-Martin's estimate that federal tax payments by US states would fall by on the order of 30¢.

Steps are underway to augment the budgetary resources of the EC. In February 1988 contributions based on each country's GNP were added as a "fourth resource" to agricultural import levies, customs duties and VAT. But emulating the stabilizing regional impact of the US fiscal system would require very substantial changes in the scale and responsiveness of this fourth resource.

Some observers argue that the case for fiscal federalism will be rendered redundant by the elimination of capital controls. Europeans will be able to protect themselves against the impact on their incomes of region-specific shocks by holding diversified portfolios of financial claims on firms in other regions. However, US experience suggests that freedom to invest in other regions weakens at most slightly the rationale for fiscal federalism. The majority of Americans hold most of their wealth in human capital, the returns on which (labour income) depend on region-specific factors, and in real estate (their homes). The incomes and net asset positions of Texans decline significantly when the Texas economy falls on hard times even while the rest of the American economy remains prosperous, despite the fact that Texans are free to diversify away this risk by accumulating financial claims on other states and countries.

2.3 Operation of the US Currency Union

2.3.1 Balance-of-Payments Adjustment

According to its proponents, establishment of a currency/customs union transforms the balance-of-payments adjustment process. The mechanisms remain the same as between any countries with fixed exchange rates, but they operate more smoothly and powerfully, facilitating adjustment.

The first such mechanism is international capital flows. Imagine that a country suffers a temporary decline in competitiveness leading to a deterioration in its balance of payments. The cause might be a fall in the demand for its exports, leading to a trade deficit. Capital should flow in to allow residents to alleviate their temporary difficulties. If the domestic central bank (or in the US case, the regional reserve bank) raises its discount rate, any incipient rise in local market interest rates will be arbitraged away by capital inflows. According to proponents of monetary union, stabilizing capital flows will operate more powerfully in the presence of a common currency or immutably fixed exchange rates. There is no danger that balance-of-payments problems will lead to devaluation and capital losses for foreign investors. The incipient rise in interest rates, therefore, provides an irresistible incentive to investors. Stabilizing capital flows will be even more important than under fixed but adjustable exchange rates.

If the shock is permanent, eventually domestic wages and spending will have to fall to restore competitiveness. Exports have to be raised and/or imports reduced to make it profitable for domestic firms to employ the labour supplied and in order to generate the earnings needed to service the additional external debt. If wages and costs fail to decline, unemployment results. According to proponents of union, labour-market adjustment is smoother when factor markets are integrated. Rather than being forced to accept lower earnings or higher unemployment, some residents of the region whose competitiveness has declined can migrate to other regions experiencing an increase in the demand for their goods and enjoying higher living standards. This raises the capital-labour ratio at home, minimizing the fall in real wages required of workers who remain. Thus, labour mobility like capital mobility facilitates balance-of-payments adjustment.

The US provides a clear example of a credible customs/currency union. Adequate balance-of-payments statistics are not gathered on a state or Federal Reserve District level, however. There exist state data on exports to other countries, but no official statistics on state of origin of those goods or on interstate trade. Interstate trade in commodities can be inferred only on the basis of restrictive assumptions about within-state consumption. The Interdistrict Settlement Fund of the Federal Reserve System provides summary data on flows of funds between Federal Reserve Districts but omits cheque clearings that go directly through correspondent banks and important inter-district currency flows. Moreover, it is impossible to break down the gross flows into components. Fortunately, the requisite data are gathered for Puerto Rico, a fact exploited by Ingram (1962) nearly three decades ago.[1]

2.3.2   The Example of Puerto Rico

Puerto Rico is a semi-autonomous Commonwealth associated with the US and a full-fledged member of the US customs/currency union. The American dollar is the sole local currency. There are no barriers to trade or factor mobility between Puerto Rico and the mainland. That Puerto Rico is an island makes it possible for the authorities to estimate the value of transactions with mainland US with accuracy that would be impossible for most states.

Two qualifications to this general statement are in order. The US has maintained quotas on sugar shipments from Puerto Rico, while Puerto Rico has made extensive use of excise taxes (which have the same effects as tariffs in the absence of local production). In addition, US companies investing in Puerto Rico have traditionally enjoyed tax advantages. (This may affect the level of investment but not the responsiveness of investment flows to interest-rate changes and other shocks, which is the main focus of the analysis to follow.)

Puerto Rico is a special region of the US. The dominant language differs from the mainland's. The economy is relatively underdeveloped. But the presence of a distinct language and a distinct regional culture makes Puerto Rico's experience all the more apposite for Europe. The income differential suggests that lessons of Puerto Rican experience may be relevant to Spain or Portugal. Table 2.4 compares Puerto Rico and Portugal with the US and the EC, respectively. Per capita income and crude birth rate ratios of Puerto Rico versus the US and Portugal versus the EC are quite similar. Puerto Rico and Portugal are more open, more rural and more agricultural than the US and the EC. On the other hand, external trade is considerably more important to Puerto Rico than to Portugal. Table 2.5 summarizes the balance-of-payments experience of Puerto Rico. Clearly, foreign investment and remittances are extremely important. Transfers from the Federal government (and miscellaneous transfers from other state governments) represent a particularly important element of the current account.

Balance-of-payments adjustments in Puerto Rico and Portugal are analysed with the help of simulations. Based on historical statistical relationships between the relevant variables, I simulate the response to a (one standard deviation) shock to investment of: the terms of trade, the balance of trade, the value of remittances, and net international capital flows (all variables but the terms of trade expressed as ratios to GDP).[2] The first

Table 2.4
A Comparison of Four Economies

Item	Puerto Rico	US average	Portugal	EC average
Income per capita ($)	4,519 (a)	17,417 (a)	2,886 (b)	10,752 (b)
Birthrate (per 000)	19.4 (c)	16.0 (d)	14.2 (e)	11.9 (e)
% Urban (f)	66.8	74.0	31.0	78.0
Imports/GDP (%)	67.4 (g)	9.1 (i)	36.6 (j)	22.2 (j)
	26.0 (h)		13.4 (k)	9.3 (k)
Share of labour force in agriculture (%)	5.4 (l)	2.7 (m)	26.0 (n)	9.1 (o)
Unemployent (%)	21.0 (p)	7.0 (p)	8.7 (q)	10.9 (q)

Sources: (a) *Statistical Abstract of the United States,* 1985. (b) *OECD Main Economic Indicators* for GDP in 1986, US$, current exchange rates. Population figures from *World Development Report.* (c) *Informe de Recursos Humanos,* Junta de Planificacion de Puerto Rico, June, 1986. (d) *World Development Report.* Year is 1986. (e) *Eurostat 1987.* Year is 1986. (f) *World Development Report 1988.* Data are for 1985. EC average not including Luxembourg is constructed using population weights from *World Development Report.* Data for Puerto Rico are from *Statistical Abstract of the United States, 1988,* p. 18. Year is 1980. (g) *Statistical Abstract of the United States 1988.* Data are for 1985 and include trade with the rest of the U.S. (h) Same source as (g). Excludes trade with the rest of the US. (i) Trade data from *OECD Monthly Statistics of Foreign Trade.* Data are for 1987. GDP from *OECD Main Economic Indicators,* also for 1987. (j) Same source as (i). Figures include trade within the EEC. (k) Same source as (i). Figures net out trade within the EEC. (l) *Informe de Recursos Humanos.* Figures are for 1984. (m) *Statistical Abstract of the United States.* Figures are for 1985. (n) *World Development Report 1988.* Figure is for 1980. (o) *World Development Report 1988* for Greece, Portugal and Ireland. Figures are for 1980. *Eurostat 1987* for the rest. Figures are for 1983. Average is obtained by weighting by population as per *World Development Report.* (p) *Statistical Abstract of the United States.* Figures are for 1986. (q) *Eurostat 1987.* Rates are for 1986.

part of Figure 2.1 shows the simulation results for Puerto Rico. The behaviour of the trade balance and terms of trade document Puerto Rico's dependence on imported capital goods. The balance of trade turns negative in the wake of the investment boom. Puerto Rico's terms of trade weaken, suggesting a shift of expenditure from domestic to imported goods.

Since savings minus investment equals the current account, a positive shock to investment should bring about a balance-of-payments deficit that must be financed or eliminated. It is financed; in the short run, the rise in investment is financed almost entirely by overseas capital as opposed to domestic saving. Note that this is not due to the response of "foreign aid" (transfers from the Federal government), since this item is not included in capital flows. In the second year, the capital inflow falls to zero, indicating presumably that the induced rise in GDP augments saving by a sufficient

Table 2.5
Balance of Payments for Puerto Rico: 1960–83
(Annual Averages in Millions of 1947 Dollars)

Item	1960–69	1970–79	1980–83
Merchandise exports	733.8	1,474.4	2,315.5
Merchandise imports	−1,010.5	−2,024.4	−2,406.5
Transport (net)	−78.1	−138.6	−102.3
Travel (net)	30.4	57.5	75.1
Income on investments	13.9	65.3	193.0
Outlays on investment (including net interest of Commonwealth and municipal governments)[a]	−190.0	−696.6	−1,346.1
Miscellaneous Services (net) (including outlays of federal agencies)	76.3	59.6	49.3
Remittances (net) (including transfers from non-residents)	33.1	30.0	60.8
Transfers from Federal Government	119.8	534.2	871.1
Total current account	−271.8	−638.6	−290.0
Long-term external investments			
In Puerto Rico	295.1	662.6	585.5
Obligations of Government Sector[b]	91.8	208.6	152.6
Direct Investments	146.1	418.8	406.0
Other[c]	57.1	35.3	26.9
Long-term External Investments of Puerto Ricans	−30.0	−30.8	−34.8
Short-term Capital Movements (net)	2.5	5.6	−254.0
Total capital account	267.6	637.4	296.7
Errors and omissions[d]	3.7	1.0	−6.6

Source: Balanzo de Pagos, 1983. Junta de Planificacions de Puerto Rico, San Juan. Data are converted to constant prices using *Statistical Yearbook of Puerto Rico* (various issues) and *Informe Economica al Gobernador* (Governor of Puerto Rico, 1984, various issues).
[a] Data on net interest of the Commonwealth and municipal governments not available until 1971.
[b] Includes Federal Agencies mortgages and loans.
[c] Includes Home Mortgages and loans and investments in local corporations.
[d] Note that *Balanzo de Pagos* shows 12.6 for errors and omissions for 1980–83. However, there are several errors in the summations of various capital sub-categories. I have assumed that the individual line items are correct and have used "errors and omissions" to adjust so that the accounts balance.

amount to finance the additional investment.[3] Overall, these results are consistent with the important role of capital flows in bringing about balance-of-payments adjustment within the US hypothesized by previous authors (e.g., Hartland, 1949). High capital mobility between Puerto Rico and the mainland implies that capital flows almost exactly match the initial domestic investment disturbance.

Labour mobility seems to play a less important role. The net change in remittances is small relative to capital flows which suggests that the amount of return migration induced by the investment surge is too small to play much role in adjustment to the shock. Despite the absence of barriers to labour mobility between Puerto Rico and the mainland, and the inducement to mobility provided by a common currency and the absence of exchange risk, adjustment to a domestic shock appears to occur mainly through changes in domestic costs rather than out migration.

2.3.3   Comparison between Puerto Rico and Portugal

How much difference does Puerto Rico's membership in the US customs/currency union make? The comparison between Puerto Rico and Portugal appears in Figure 2.1. The effects of the investment shock in Portugal are broadly consistent with those for Puerto Rico. The investment boom leads to a deterioration in the trade balance and a weakening of the terms of trade.[4] The investment boom is partly financed by a capital inflow. As in Puerto Rico, there is little short-run movement of remittances, although eventually remittances fall, suggesting some repatriation of guest workers abroad in response to the investment surge.

While the patterns are broadly similar, the magnitudes and timing are strikingly different. Whereas in Puerto Rico the first year of the investment boom is completely financed by overseas capital, in Portugal only a tenth of the short-run rise in investment is financed out of foreign sources. This is reflected in the relatively small short-run deterioration in the trade balance. The mechanism works through interest rates. In Puerto Rico, which enjoys a very responsive supply of overseas capital, the investment boom has little effect on interest rates. But in Portugal, where the supply of external capital is less responsive, the investment surge puts upward pressure on interest rates. Some investment is crowded out and domestic saving is stimulated. A further consequence is that the short-run deterioration in the terms of trade is smaller because of a more limited rise in the demand for traded goods.

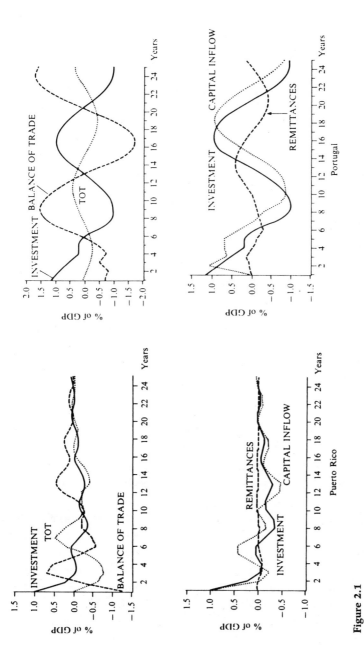

Figure 2.1

Response to an investment shock.

Note: Annual simulations based on VAR of the following data: Puerto Rico: 1950–84; Portugal: 1956–86; gross fixed domestic investment, balance of trade, terms of trade, remittances and net international capital flows (all but terms of trade as ratios to GDP). VAR
with 3 lags of all variables, a time trend and a constant. Variables ordered as listed above.

The contrast with Puerto Rico suggests that membership in a currency
union does in fact enhance the facility with which capital mobility accom-
modates domestic investment fluctuations in the short run. In contrast to
Puerto Rico, where investment and capital inflows are roughly in phase, in
Portugal capital movements lag behind investment fluctuations, which
appears to contribute to the longer periodicity of investment cycles in
Portugal. As in Puerto Rico, remittances and, by implication, labour mobility play a relatively minor role in adjustment although, curiously, remittances seem to be more responsive in Portugal. In part this may reflect
differences in data: the series for Portugal also includes other unrequited
transfers. In part it may reflect the greater tendency of Puerto Rican
workers to migrate together with their families and hence their lower tendency to remit earnings.

2.3.4   The Extent of Fiscal Autonomy

Does membership in a currency area provide US states with the leeway
to run independent fiscal policies? State budget deficits as a share of
expenditure typically are small. Surpluses are more common than deficits:
states attempt to accumulate an ending balance of 5% of total expenditures "to provide cash flow during the year, to accommodate the cyclical
nature of revenue collections and disbursements, and most particularly,
to provide sufficient revenues at the change of a fiscal year without disruption in service" (Howard, 1989). Yet occasionally individual states
have run quite substantial budget deficits. Louisiana's state deficit
amounted to nearly 5% of expenditures in 1986, nearly 12% in 1987, and
more than 18% in 1988, for example.

2.3.4.1 Balanced budget requirement.   Behind the preponderance of surpluses in Table 2.6 is the fact that, but for Vermont, all 50 states possess
either statutory or constitutional balanced budget requirements. Not all
these restrictions are binding, however. In fully 25 states the governor
only has to submit a balanced budget, the legislature only has to pass a
balanced budget, and/or the state may carry over a deficit but is formally
obliged to correct it in the next fiscal year (Table 2.7). In all these states,
there is scope for at least temporary budget deficits.

2.3.4.2 Rising costs of debt financing?   Those deficits are financed by issuing debt, as shown in Table 2.8. The critical question is whether states

Table 2.6
State Budget Balances by Region

	Dollar amount (millions)			As a % of expenditures		
Region	1986	1987	1988	1986	1987	1988
US overall	5,398	6,586	7,066	4.21	3.76	4.55
New England	430	291	266	3.18	5.73	5.01
Middle Atlantic	887	1,239	838	3.00	4.07	2.59
East North Central	1,175	725	939	3.28	2.30	2.95
West North Central	658	465	931	6.33	4.41	9.14
South Atlantic	1,126	1,151	1,331	5.03	5.06	5.10
East South Central	414	353	349	4.28	4.03	3.55
West South Central	−433	−1,430	−1,301	−1.88	−5.42	−4.55
Mountain	322	260	306	7.00	3.64	4.64
Pacific	819	672	805	3.18	6.97	7.38
Standard deviation	494	777	761	2.55	3.57	3.82

Source: National Governors' Association, 1988.

seeking to finance deficits face higher interest rates as they attempt to increase their borrowing, and actually may be unable to borrow beyond some point. I am unaware of previous studies that have asked this question. The closest approximation is provided by studies which seek to explain the Moody's credit rating of US cities. These credit ratings have a decided influence on the interest rates cities are required to pay when floating bonds. Most studies are unable to replicate Moody's ratings using readily observable economic and social characteristics of cities.

Those previous studies do not isolate how particular variables affect the costs of borrowing of local governments. To that effect, I use regression analysis in an attempt to explain the required yields upon issue on state bonds. Table 2.9 reports the results. There is weak evidence that higher debt burdens increase the cost of borrowing. The debt-state product ratio in the first two regressions enters positively. This remains true when dummy variables for time of issue or years to maturity are added. The squared term is consistently negative, which is inconsistent with the view that high-debt states get rationed out of the market. Interest rates continue to rise until the debt ratio reaches 20 to 25%. This suggests that most states face rising costs of borrowing. The third and fourth columns measure debt on a per capita basis rather than relative to state GNP, producing no discernible change in the results.

Table 2.7
State Balanced Budgets: Statutory (S) or Constitutional (C) Requirements

States	(1) Governor only has to submit a balanced budget	(2) Legislature only has to pass a balanced budget	(4) May carry over a deficit but must be corrected in next fiscal year	(6) State cannot carry over a deficit into next biennium	(8) State cannot carry over a deficit into next fiscal year	Degree of stringency scale (high—10; low—1)
New England						
Connecticut	S*	S	S			5
Maine					S	9
Massachusetts	C					3
New Hampshire	S					2
Rhode Island					C	10
Vermont		No Requirement*				0
Mideast						
Delaware	C	C			C*	10
Maryland		C	C			6
New Jersey	C				C	10
New York	C					3
Pennsylvania	S,C	S	S,C			6
Great Lakes						
Illinois	C	C				4
Indiana					C*	10
Michigan			C			6
Ohio					S,C	10
Wisconsin			C*			6

Plains					
Iowa				C	10
Kansas				C	10
Minnesota			S,C		8
Missouri			C	C	10
Nebraska				C	10
North Dakota					8
South Dakota				S,C	10
Southeast					
Alabama				C	10
Arkansas				S	9
Florida				S,C	10
Georgia				C	10
Kentucky			C*	S	10
Louisiana	C				4
Mississippi				S	9
North Carolina		S,C		S,C	10
South Carolina		C		C	10
Tennessee			S,C	C	10
Virginia					8
West Virginia				C*	10
Southwest					
Arizona			C	C	10
New Mexico				C	10
Oklahoma				C	10
Texas	C				8

Table 2.7 (continued)

States	(1) Governor only has to submit a balanced budget	(2) Legislature only has to pass a balanced budget	(4) May carry over a deficit but must be corrected in next fiscal year	(6) State cannot carry over a deficit into next biennium	(8) State cannot carry over a deficit into next fiscal year	Degree of stringency scale (high—10; low—1)
Rocky Mountain						
Colorado	C				C	10
Idaho					C	10
Montana		C			C	10
Utah				C	S,C	10
Wyoming				C		8
Far West						
California	C		C*			6
Nevada	S	C				4
Oregon	S			C		8
Washington				S,C		8
Alaska	S		C			6
Hawaii	S,C			C		10

Source: ACIR staff compilation based on 1984 surveys of executive and legislative fiscal directors, and *Limitations on State Deficits,* Council of State Governments, Lexington, Kentucky, May 1976.

Note: There exist additional complications regarding California, Connecticut, Delaware, Indiana, Kentucky, Vermont, West Virginia and Wisconsin. Details are provided in the source document.

Table 2.8
State Debt by Region

	Number of states	Total state debt (millions of current dollars)			Ratios of state debt/state product means (standard deviations)		
		1984/85	1985/86	1986/87	1984/85	1985/86	1986/87
US Overall	50	210,285	248,337	265,705	0.0731 (0.0542)	0.0822 (0.0610)	0.0811 (0.0578)
New England	6	23,394	27,036	28,536	0.1280 (0.0472)	0.1337 (0.0410)	0.1232 (0.0313)
Middle Atlantic	3	53,010	61,071	66,936	0.0833 (0.0335)	0.0907 (0.0398)	0.0910 (0.0372)
East North Central	5	28,499	35,490	37,330	0.0451 (0.0152)	0.0518 (0.0145)	0.0517 (0.0120)
West North Central	7	11,165	12,817	13,853	0.0506 (0.0344)	0.0582 (0.0406)	0.0622 (0.0464)
South Atlantic	8	24,600	28,384	31,448	0.0671 (0.0518)	0.0780 (0.0710)	0.0776 (0.0696)
East South Central	4	9,792	11,200	11,980	0.0510 (0.0220)	0.0557 (0.0241)	0.0571 (0.0256)
West South Central	4	17,692	20,828	21,948	0.0552 (0.0391)	0.0652 (0.0503)	0.0736 (0.0567)
Mountain	8	8,048	10,880	11,216	0.0506 (0.0186)	0.0629 (0.0260)	0.0601 (0.0194)
Pacific	5	34,085	40,625	42,445	0.1389 (0.0999)	0.1517 (0.1170)	0.1458 (0.1116)
Standard deviation among regions		13,422	15,514	16,925	0.03345	0.03404	0.03003

Sources: For Gross State Product: *ACIR, Significant Features of Fiscal Federalism* (various issues). For Debt: Moody's *Governments Manual* (various issues).

Table 2.9
State Debt and the Cost of Borrowing: Regression Results
(Dependent Variable Is Yield on Most Recent General Obligation Bond)

Explanatory variables	(1)	(2)	(3)	(4)
Constant	−3.03	−3.12	−2.78	−3.14
	(2.70)	(2.73)	(2.72)	(2.74)
Yield on Composite Portfolio	1.19	1.17	1.18	1.15
	(0.35)	(0.35)	(0.35)	(0.36)
Debt/State product	12.51	13.43	—	—
	(9.35)	(9.51)		
Debt/State product squared	−28.65	−31.77	—	—
	(24.39)	(24.98)		
Debt per capita	—	—	0.65	0.89
			(0.63)	(0.67)
Debt per capita squared	—	—	−0.10	−0.14
			(0.11)	(0.12)
Measure of financial stringency	—	0.03	—	0.04
		(0.04)		(0.04)
R^2	0.31	0.32	0.30	0.32
Number of observations	33	33	33	33

Source: See text.
Note: Standard errors in parentheses.

Specialists in state and local public finance view the differences in bond yields—that I interpret as evidence of a increasing costs of borrowing—as evidence of differences across states in tax treatment of state bonds. Generally, state bonds are tax exempt only for state residents. (Some states also extend this treatment to residents who hold bonds of certain other states.) A high yield is taken to reflect a high state marginal tax rate. These considerations may have grown less important since the tax reforms of the second half of the 1980s. Nonetheless, to explore the hypothesis, I added to all the regressions in Table 2.9 the US Advisory Commission on Intergovernmental Relations's (ACIR) estimate of the highest marginal tax rate for each state. It appears to play no significant role.

Even in the absence of exchange risk, state governments in the US face increasing costs of debt finance. Since European governments can still change their minds about never devaluing and, therefore, cannot totally eliminate exchange risk, it is tempting to infer that they should face even more steeply increasing borrowing costs of debt finance. A possible caveat

Table 2.10
Measures of State Tax Burdens
(Taxes as % of Personal Income)

	Effective individual income tax rate	Effective corporation tax rate	Sum of Effective individual and corporate rates	Total tax revenue
New England	2.2	0.9	3.0	6.7
Middle Atlantic	2.7	0.6	3.3	6.5
East North Central	2.0	0.6	2.6	6.5
West North Central	2.0	0.4	2.4	6.3
South Atlantic	1.8	0.4	2.2	7.0
East South Central	1.1	0.4	1.6	6.9
West South Central	0.5	0.1	0.6	6.8
Mountain	1.5	0.3	1.8	7.6
Pacific	2.2	0.7	3.0	9.8
Mean	1.8	0.5	2.3	7.1
Standard deviation	0.6	0.2	0.8	1.0
Coefficient of variation	0.34	0.43	0.35	0.14

Source: ACIR, *Significant Features of Fiscal Federalism* (various issues); *Statistical Abstract of the United States* (various issues).

is that in the US, where many states function under statutory balanced-budget requirements, a deficit is taken as a signal of serious fiscal difficulties. Such states may face increasing borrowing costs of debt finance even steeper than their European counterparts. The argument presumably applies mainly to states with stringent balanced-budget requirements. I therefore interacted the ACIR's index of fiscal stringency (which ranges from zero for states with no statutory or constitutional balanced-budget requirements to 10 for states with strict constitutional requirements) with the debt-income ratio and the debt-income ratio squared. The two interaction terms were uniformly insignificant, had extremely small coefficients, and had little impact on the results, suggesting that the signaling argument has little force.

2.3.4.3 Taxes and firms' location. Are US states forced to levy identical tax rates to prevent footloose capital from fleeing to low-tax jurisdictions? In fact, there is considerable geographical dispersion of tax rates. Table 2.10 shows average effective personal income and corporation tax rates by census region. Total state tax revenue (essentially the sum of individual and corporation tax revenues) relative to state personal income has a mean of 7.1% and a standard deviation of 1.0%. The coefficient of variation of

0.141 is 52% of the comparable measure for Europe (total taxes exclusive
of social security contributions), suggesting that mobility within the US
may have imposed more tax harmonization on the American states.
(When social security taxes are included for Europe, the coefficient of variation for US regions is still smaller than that for European countries, but
by a considerably smaller margin.)

A variety of studies have attempted to estimate directly the impact of
interstate tax differentials on firms' location decisions. McGuire (1986) has
surveyed these studies, concluding that tax differentials do affect location
decisions, although the magnitude of the effect is not large. Bartik (1985),
for example, finds that corporate income tax differentials have a significant impact on location decisions for new branch plants, but with limited
responsiveness. Papke and Papke (1986) similarly report that a measure of
sales, property and corporate income taxes is a significant determinant of
capital investment per worker. Yet none of these effects seems to be sufficiently large to force US states to closely harmonize their taxes.

A popular approach to estimating the degree of tax autonomy US
states possess is to examine revenue spill-overs. The question is the
extent to which changes in tax rates in one state affect the tax revenues of
another. The overall effect is ambiguous in sign. Higher tax rates in one
state can increase revenues of its neighbours through the substitution
effect, as residents cross the border to purchase or produce goods in the
lower-tax jurisdiction. Conversely, higher tax rates in one state can reduce
the revenues of its neighbours insofar as lower disposable incomes reduce
spending on both sides of the border. If the substitution effect dominates,
states setting tax rates non-cooperatively will tend to set them at lower
levels than they would cooperatively, because they neglect the tendency
of their lower rates to reduce the revenues of their neighbours. Insofar as
tax revenues determine levels of spending on public goods, tax competition arising from revenue spill-overs will produce a suboptimal level of
public spending. If the income effect dominates, states setting tax rates
non-cooperatively will tend to set them at higher levels than they would
under cooperation, because they neglect the tendency of their higher tax
rates to reduce the revenues of their neighbours. Public spending will be
too high.

Hewett and Stephenson (1983) studied state tax revenues under competition in the case of Iowa and the surrounding region (defined to
include Illinois, Kansas, Minnesota, Missouri, Nebraska, South Dakota and
Wisconsin) in the years 1950–79. They found that the income effect
dominated for most taxes: higher sales tax and income tax rates in the

surrounding region significantly reduced Iowa's tax revenues. Only in the case of gasoline taxes did higher rates in the surrounding region significantly increase Iowa's revenues.

The sign and magnitude of spill-overs may depend on the size of the regions considered. Fox (1986) in a study of moderately-sized metropolitan regions on state borders found in two of three cases that changes in state and local sales tax rates tended to reduce the level of retail activity on that side of the border. He found state income taxes to have little impact on the location of retail activity. Stephenson and Hewett (1985) analysed changes in not only own tax rates and tax rates in the surrounding region, but also tax rates in individual neighbouring states. (They considered the impact of changes in Iowa's taxes on Missouri and vice versa, as well as analysing separately income, sales and gasoline tax receipts.) One would expect that when the impact on Iowa of Missouri alone rather than of the group of seven neighbouring states is considered, both income and substitution effects would be weaker, but that the sign of the spill-over would remain ambiguous. Most of the results are consistent with this prior. Higher gasoline tax rates in either state raise gasoline tax receipts in its neighbour. Higher sales tax rates in either state reduce sales tax revenue in its neighbour. Higher income tax rates in Iowa reduce income tax revenues in Missouri, although paradoxically higher income tax rates in Missouri seem to raise income tax revenues in Iowa.

The only consistent conclusion to emerge from these studies is that the sign and magnitude of spill-over effects depends on the size of the region and the tax instrument studied. For groups of US states like those studied by Hewett and Stephenson that approximate the size of EC member states, they suggest that the dominant forms of taxation in the EC, income and sales taxes, exhibit negative spill-overs due to the predominance of income effects. Assuming these results apply to Europe, then absent cooperation, continued integration may leave EC members with tax rates above optimal levels.

2.3.5   Does Factor Mobility Prevent Depressed Regions?

2.3.5.1   Sources of concern.   The prospect of a European customs/currency union creates two kinds of worry about the emergence of depressed regions or countries (Servais, 1988). A customs union which permits increased competition among producers located in different European nations will push the least efficient competitors out of business, forcing European nations to specialize in those industries and product lines in which they have a comparative advantage. Resources will have to be shifted out of industries previously protected by import barriers and into other sectors. Workers in traditionally sheltered industries may suffer transitional unemployment, where the length of the transition—according to pessimists—may be substantial. If expanding industries pay lower wages than contracting ones, workers may be forced to accept wage cuts in order to gain employment. The strains of unemployment and reductions in living standards may fuel political opposition to the customs union. Alternatively, the removal of barriers to the migration of capital and labour may permit resources to be redeployed rapidly from regions and nations where their marginal productivity and the demand for their services are low to other regions and nations where productivity and factor demands are high.

The second worry is that currency union will require nations that have traditionally relied on the inflation tax for government revenues to reduce public spending. The decline in public spending will raise their unemployment rates relative to those in the rest of Europe. Alternatively, the free mobility of capital and labour across national borders within Europe may conceivably prevent sustained differentials in unemployment rates from emerging. The elimination of exchange risk will enhance international capital mobility within the union, so that any potentially depressed area will immediately receive an injection of investible funds.

2.3.5.2 Unemployment in the US and in the EC. The dispersion of state unemployment rates within the US provides a benchmark for these arguments. Europeans and Americans can debate which continent is more homogeneous culturally, socially and economically and, therefore, whether US unemployment differentials are likely to over- or underestimate European unemployment differentials following the completion of the internal market and establishment of a European central bank. Distances are shorter in Europe, but a common language, a common national media and a footloose tradition all suggest that mobility in the US exceeds the degree of labour mobility that is likely to obtain in Europe.

Table 2.6 summarizes raw unemployment differentials within the EC and US. Both the standard deviation and the coefficient of variation of unemployment rates is higher in the EC than the US. This is consistent with the view that the existence of a US currency/customs union facilitates capital and labour flows which minimize regional problems. But it may be that the EC has recently suffered region-specific shocks larger than those experienced by the US. A snapshot of unemployment differentials in 1986 may say little about how quickly local labour markets within the two unions respond to region-specific shocks. Figure 2.2 therefore displays alternative measures of the dispersion of unemployment rates in the nine US regions and the EC9. All of the measures of US unemployment dispersion rise over time. The trend is most pronounced in the absolute difference in unemployment rates between each year's highest unemployment region and lowest unemployment region, least pronounced in the standard deviation of regional unemployment rates. The alternative measures for Europe paint a less consistent picture. When measured by the absolute differential between highest and lowest unemployment rate countries, there has been for Europe, as for the US, a tendency for unemployment dispersion to rise over time. The trend in the standard deviation is less pronounced, rising only slightly in the 1980s, while the coefficient of variation falls steadily until 1982–83, suggesting that, at least until recent years, any rise in the cross-country standard deviation of European unemployment rates has been dwarfed by the rise in the average level of European unemployment.

The most dramatic difference between the US and the EC is the average level of all the dispersion measures. Where the absolute difference in US regional unemployment rates rises from less than 2% in the early 1960s to more than 5% in the 1980s, that for Europe rises from 4 to 10%. Where the US standard deviation rises from less than 1% in the 1960s to less than 2% in the 1980s, the standard deviation for Europe is consistently between 2 and 3%. The alternative measures suggest that the dispersion of regional unemployment rates is 50 to 100% higher in Europe than in the US. A possible implication is that local labour markets are slower to adjust to regional disturbances in Europe than in the US. This could reflect greater labour mobility within the US than the EC. It also could reflect the greater integration of commodity and capital markets in the US, the first of which minimizes region-specific demand-side shocks, the second of which evens out the effects of those shocks which occur. Alternatively, it is possible instead that European labour markets respond as quickly as their American counterparts but have been consistently subjected to larger region-specific shocks.

To begin to distinguish between these alternatives, I measured how correlated are unemployment rates in the current year and in the following year, for every year starting in 1960 in the nine US census regions, and in Europe for every year starting in 1958 (using the Spearman rank correlation coefficient). The correlations are consistently higher for Europe. (The unweighted average is 0.88 for the US and 0.91 for Europe.) The

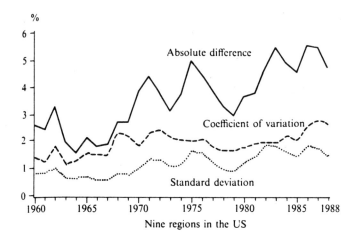

Nine regions in the US

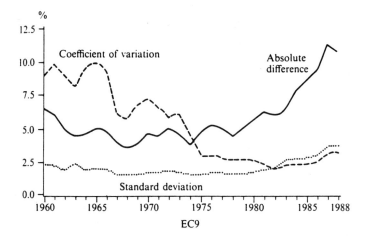

EC9

Figure 2.2
Dispersion of unemployment rates.
Sources: US: author's calculations of state unemployment rates; EC: Commission's *Annual Economic Reports,* various issues.

difference grows more pronounced when the ranking of unemployment rates in the current year is compared with the ranking five years later and 10 years later. The longer the interval, the greater the disparity between the US and Europe. (Unweighted averages for five-year intervals are 0.49 for the US and 0.72 for Europe. For 10-year intervals they are 0.17 for the US and 0.66 for Europe.) The implication is that the location of depressed regions in the US tends to vary over time, but the same European countries tend to suffer high unemployment and enjoy low unemployment persistently. For the incidence of shocks rather than faster labour-market adjustment in the US to explain the difference, one would have to argue that shocks in Europe were not only larger but more persistent, which does not seem particularly plausible.

2.3.5.3   Adjustments in the labour markets.   Convincingly distinguishing between these alternatives requires measuring how quickly labour markets adjust to disturbances. To carry out such an estimation, we need to assess the nature of the long-run relationship among regional labour markets. A strong assumption would be that labour migrates from high to low-unemployment regions until regional unemployment differentials are eliminated. There is a large literature for the US, however, starting with Hall (1972), suggesting that significant local unemployment differentials persist. There is little agreement on the reasons for these differentials. Murphy and Hofler (1984), for example, suggest that regional unemployment differentials reflect differences in the sectoral composition of employment (as between construction, agriculture and manufacturing) and differences in the education of the work force. Topel (1984) focuses on the role of experience, suggesting that more experienced workers have more invested in region-specific skills and are therefore less likely to migrate, so that regions in which experienced workers dominate are likely to experience relatively persistent unemployment differentials.

Given this evidence on the persistence of regional unemployment differentials, it is inappropriate to assume that unemployment rates simply converge to the same level. Instead, I entertain the more general assumption that there is some stable long-run relationship between unemployment in each US region (each EC member) and the overall US (EC) unemployment rates. Technically, this amounts to assuming that regional and overall unemployment rates are cointegrated. The analysis was conducted using the annual data summarized in Figure 2.2. Results are summarized in Table 2.11. The first column reports the test for a stable long-run relationship. Such a relationship is not rejected for only four of

Table 2.11
Speed of Labour-Market Adjustment in EC9 and Nine US Regions

	Test for cointegration		Speed of adjustment
	(1)	(2)	(3)
Denmark	0.54	2.49	−0.42
			(0.16)
Germany	0.71	2.73	−0.36
			(0.15)
France	0.32	2.78	−0.45
			(0.16)
Ireland	0.34	0.91	−0.11
			(0.16)
Italy	0.17	0.39	−0.27
			(0.25)
Netherlands	0.32	0.99	−0.43
			(0.20)
Belgium	0.29	0.80	−0.13
			(0.13)
Luxembourg	0.61	3.00	−0.39
			(0.13)
UK	0.51	1.26	−0.48
			(0.20)
EC9 Average	—	—	−0.34
Middle Atlantic	0.30	1.90	−0.40
			(0.12)
New England	0.21	2.12	−0.47
			(0.15)
East North Central	0.44	2.86	−0.34
			(0.15)
West North Central	0.71	2.86	−0.64
			(0.19)
South Atlantic	0.52	1.54	−0.43
			(0.17)
East South Central	0.25	1.56	−0.22
			(0.14)
West South Central	0.23	1.46	−0.50
			(0.21)
Mountain	0.74	3.65	−0.48
			(0.18)
Pacific	0.27	1.49	−0.28
			(0.16)
US Average	—	—	−0.42

Source: See text.
Note: Standard errors in parentheses. Critical value of Durbin–Watson test for cointegration (column 1) is 0.386 (for 100 observations). Critical value of Engle–Yoo t-test for the three-variable case (column 2) is 4.11 (5% significance level for 50 observations) (see Engle and Yoo, 1987).

nine European countries. Two of these are small, highly open economies (Luxembourg and Denmark) whose labour-market outcomes might be expected to be particularly closely tied to those in the EC as a whole. But two are relatively large economies (Germany and the UK), to which this argument does not apply. Overall, there appears to have been only a weak tendency for stable long-run equilibrium relationship between national and EC9 unemployment rates to hold over the last three decades. Strikingly, however, the same is true for the US. In only four of nine cases can we accept the existence of a stable long-run relationship between regional unemployment rates. It is commonly suggested that completion of the internal market will attenuate problems of regional unemployment as labour-market integration in Europe achieves US levels. Despite the fact that regional unemployment rates are less disperse in the US than in Europe, the remarkable fact is that regional unemployment rates in the US appear to be only weakly related to one another.

It is not possible to estimate the response to a shock to regional unemployment rates if there is no stable relationship among them. A solution to this problem is to investigate whether shifts in the presumed relationship are explained by changes in some other factors. If changes in domestic market structures and/or international competitive conditions in the 1980s permanently raised unemployment in some regions relative to others, for example, one could add to the equation a dummy variable for the 1980s. A more general version of this approach is to add a time trend which allows unemployment in some regions to rise steadily relative to the average and unemployment in other regions to fall. With this amendment, the second column of Table 2.11 shows that the existence of a stable long-run relationship between unemployment rates is accepted in all cases, both in the US and in the EC. This does not change the conclusion that regional unemployment rates seem only weakly related to the overall rate, but it permits estimation of the speed of adjustment.

I can then ask how quickly these long-run relationships responded to disturbances. (In technical terms, I estimate the error correction model associated with the cointegrating regression). The speed of adjustment to shocks to the relationship between regional and overall unemployment rates is shown in the third column of Table 2.11. Overall, the speed of adjustment is nearly 25% higher in the US than in the EC. The individual country estimates for Europe are plausible, given the literature on labour-market institutions and labour-market adjustment. Speed of adjustment is lowest for Ireland, Italy and Belgium. It is highest for France, the Netherlands and the UK.

These results confirm at least some of the intuition of proponents of labour-market integration. Regional unemployment differentials are smaller in the US than in the EC. The speed of adjustment to region-specific labour-market shocks is faster in the US than in the EC. The decline of statutory barriers and cultural impediments to labour mobility within the EC could go some way toward attenuating the regional problems that might otherwise arise in the course of increasing monetary and fiscal harmonization. At the same time, many of the conditions for labour-market integration in the US will be difficult to replicate in Europe. In the absence of fiscal federalism on the scale of the US system, region-specific shocks are likely to remain larger in Europe than in the US. In the absence of the same degree of cultural and linguistic homogeneity as in the US, adjustment through intra-EC-member labour flows is likely to remain slower than comparable adjustment within the US. Thus, US experience provides an upper bound on the extent to which labour-market integration can ameliorate Europe's regional problems. Moreover, US experience suggests that the links between regional unemployment rates even in a highly integrated continental labour market are weak at best. Significant and persistent regional unemployment differentials have consistently characterized US experience over the last three decades. In the US, regional pressures have not led to effective pressure to "devalue the West South Central dollar" or to impose tariffs on goods entering the West South Central region. In part this reflects the federal system of taxes and transfers, which has led to a significant transfer of resources toward high-unemployment regions. In part it reflects the broader political context in which US economic policy is formulated. Neither of these forces operates as powerfully in Europe. Even if the EC manages to replicate the degree of economic integration enjoyed in the US, significant regional imbalances will continue to arise.

2.4 Lessons for Europe

What lessons emerge from viewing the operation of the US currency/customs union in the light of recent European experience? The comparison suggests that the creation in Europe of a customs/currency union along American lines will fundamentally alter policy formulation and market outcomes. The elimination of capital controls dictates increasingly close monetary harmonization. There will remain some scope for independent fiscal policies; both theory and US experience suggest that member states will be able to pursue divergent fiscal policies for limited periods. EC members with high debt-to-GNP ratios and low levels of reserves will have particularly little fiscal autonomy. Moreover, since EC members, like US states, will retain sufficient sovereignty to at least contemplate the option of default on their debts, they will face an increasing borrowing cost of external finance, which will further limit the length of time for which fiscal independence and monetary union are compatible.

US experience confirms that the elimination of restrictions on the mobility of capital, labour and commodities will create pressure for the harmonization of tax rates across EC member states. It is unlikely to require tax equalization at the lowest prevailing levels, however. While US factors of production are footloose, they are not sufficiently footloose to flee local jurisdictions in response to small tax differentials. Still, some pressure exists: the variability of state tax rates in the US is about 40% less than in EC member states. US evidence suggests that high taxes at home will depress economic activity across the border, a negative externality that needs to be internalized through the international coordination of revenue policies. This evidence suggests that if they set domestic taxes non-cooperatively, failing to take into account the effect of domestic taxes on their neighbours, EC member states will tend to set tax rates too high.

Creating a European central bank and a common currency will fundamentally alter the balance-of-payments adjustment process. US evidence suggests that, in the absence of devaluation risk and exchange controls, capital should flow more freely among member states to finance payments imbalances. A temporary rise in investment or fall in saving should be almost completely financed by accommodating capital inflows. US evidence also implies, however, that labour mobility among member states will be a less important element of the adjustment process than sometimes posited in discussions of integration. Moreover, the increased scope for capital mobility within a currency union is a two-edged sword. Just as capital inflows can finance a temporary surge in investment, the capital outflows induced by a fall in investment can prevent the excess of domestic savings over domestic investment from reducing local interest rates and thereby moderating the investment slump. The enhanced capital mobility likely to characterize monetary union may ease external adjustment at the cost of greater domestic instability.

Critics might object that this analysis, based on the experience of Puerto Rico, a distinctive part of the US, understates the scope for labour mobility within a customs/currency union to eliminate depressed local conditions. Evidence on regional unemployment differentials within the

US confirms this intuition, but at the same time suggests that the capacity of labour mobility to eliminate regional unemployment differentials should not be exaggerated. Historically, the dispersion of unemployment rates within the US is only half that within the EC9. The adjustment to regional labour-market shocks is about 20% faster in the US than in the EC9. But a striking feature of US experience is the extent to which regional un-employment differentials persist. The tendency for US regional labour-market conditions to converge is surprisingly weak. Given the extent of social, cultural and linguistic diversity in Europe, the tendency for labour mobility to produce convergent labour-market outcomes is likely to remain weaker than in the US even if the internal market is completed and a common currency is established.

What do these findings imply for the role of monetary union in the completion of the internal market? There is no reason to doubt that sig-nificant regional problems will continue to arise after the elimination of statutory barriers to labour and commodity movements across national borders. Reflationary initiatives by the depressed regions will be limited by the external constraint. Even in a currency union, member states will face sharply rising costs of debt finance.

Regional problems could be attenuated by fiscal federalism. In the US the political pressures to which divergent regional labour-market out-comes give rise are ameliorated by a system of interregional fiscal transfers which limits regional unemployment differentials by offsetting a portion of the decline in regional income and helping to relax the external con-straint. Fiscal federalism thereby cements the political consensus for inte-gration. There exists a system of fiscal transfers within the EC, but it too would have to be very considerably expanded before it could have a noticeable impact. Since regional problems are likely to be significantly greater in the "USE" than in the USA, the extent of fiscal transfers in Europe would have to significantly exceed their extent in the US.

Notes

I thank Carolyn Werley, Noelle Knox and Kris Mitchner for research assistance; Jeff Frankel and Securities Data Company for data; Margo Sercarz of the Institute of Business and Eco-nomic Research of the University of California at Berkeley and Richard Grossman for logis-tical support; and John Black, Olivier Blanchard, Menzie Chin, Bill Dickens, Albert Fishlow, Maury Obstfeld, Richard Portes, John Quigley and Charles Wyplosz for advice.

1. Ingram had data on Puerto Rico's external transactions only for the first post-World War II decade. We now possess time series for the entire period 1948–83. That Puerto Rican experience encapsulates both the costs and benefits of membership in a currency union has been argued previously by Tobin, Donaldson, Gordon, Lewis, Robbins, and Treiber (1975, p. 58):

Puerto Rico benefits greatly from its position within the common financial and monetary system of the United States. Its ability to tap Mainland credit markets has been important for the Commonwealth's growth and development. The absence of foreign exchange risk and the guaranteed right to transfer funds freely have made Puerto Rico much more attractive to Mainland investors than other overseas economies.

At the same time, membership in the US financial system has limited Puerto Rico's freedom of action. The mobility of funds makes an independent monetary policy impossible. Without a national currency of its own, the Puerto Rican government cannot monetize its debt, but must borrow in the market at competitive rates.

2. The simulation technique requires orthogonalizing the estimated equations, attributing common variance among the residuals in the various equations to one of the variables. Since I am interested in the response of the system to a shock to investment, I chose investment as the "most exogenous variable" by attributing common variance to it. (Movements in investment are effectively assumed to precede movements in other variables.)

Different orderings made some difference for the precise effects, but had no impact on the direction or in general on the relative sizes of the responses.

3. This interpretation is confirmed by alternative regressions and simulations, in which all variables were expressed in levels rather than relative to GDP, GDP was included as an additional element, and a time squared term was added to pick up growth.

4. Differences in the magnitude of the terms of trade effects may simply reflect differences in data, since for Portugal I use export and import prices, whereas for Puerto Rico I am forced to use relative CPIs, which contain also some non-traded goods prices.

3   Is Europe an Optimum Currency Area?

3.1 Introduction

An optimum currency area (OCA) is an economic unit composed of regions affected symmetrically by disturbances and between which labour and other factors of production flow freely (Mundell, 1961). Insofar as regions within the OCA experience the same shocks, there is no obvious advantage to altering relative prices between them. Insofar as localized concentrations of unemployment nonetheless remain, the free mobility of labour from high- to low-unemployment regions can eliminate the problem. It is hence optimal to dispense with one of the principal instruments—changes in the exchange rate—traditionally used to effect relative price adjustments, and to reap the benefits, in terms of convenience and efficiency, of a common currency.

The question of whether Europe is an OCA is not one, unfortunately, that admits of a simple "yes" or "no" answer. Given the rapid progress of the EC92 programme and the timeliness of the question, it is all the more unfortunate that the OCA literature does not provide a formal test through whose application the hypothesis can be accepted or rejected. Whatever evidence is considered, some standard of comparison is required.

A number of authors have used other continental economies already possessing a common currency and a free internal market as precisely such a standard. In Eichengreen (1990b) I analyzed balance of payments adjustment and regional labour market dynamics within the United States. Boltho (1989) compared regional income and growth rate disparities within the United States and the European Community. Poloz (1990) contrasted the variability of relative prices across Canadian regions and the variability of real exchange rates across four European countries.

Originally published, as chapter 8, in *The European Community after 1992*, ed. Silvio Borner and Herbert Grubel (London: Macmillan, 1992), 138–61. Reprinted with permission.

This chapter presents further variations on this theme. I ask whether Europe is (and is likely to remain) further than the United States and Canada from satisfying Mundell's (1961) criteria for an OCA: free mobility of labour within the area and stability of relative prices.

Previous comparisons along these lines have been surprisingly ambiguous. Poloz (1990) found that real exchange rates between Canadian provinces were actually more variable than real exchange rates between France, Italy, the United Kingdom and Germany. In Eichengreen (1990b), in contrast, I found evidence of faster labour market adjustment between US regions than between EC members, although the difference was not large.

The evidence presented in this paper is less ambiguous. It uniformly points to the conclusion that Europe is less of an optimum currency area than its North American counterparts. Arguing that real exchange rate variability among Canadian provinces, and for that matter among France, Italy, the United Kingdom and Germany, is a special case, I instead analyze real exchange rate variability among all EC members and among the principal regions of the United States. I find that real exchange rates within the Community have been more variable than real exchange rates within the United States, typically by a factor of three to four. In a second approach to analyzing the extent to which disturbances affect regions symmetrically, I examine the comovement of securities prices on the Paris and Düsseldorf Stock Exchanges with the prices of shares traded in Toronto and Montreal. Once again, the comparison points to the existence of a much higher correlation of shocks in North America than in Europe.

Finally, direct evidence points to significantly lower labour mobility within Europe than within the United States. Of course, with the removal of legal restrictions in conjunction with the EC92 programme, it is likely that labour mobility within Europe with increase. It is important to bear in mind, however, that the absence of legal restrictions is necessary but not sufficient for high levels of labour mobility. I use a case study of the US North and South, between which a high degree of labour mobility has not always prevailed, to shed light on factors that help break down persistent regional labour market segmentation.

The bulk of the evidence thus suggests that the establishment of a currency union in Europe will be associated with non-negligible regional problems. This makes it all the more essential to develop the political and economic institutions necessary for the smooth operation of a currency union. Sala-i-Martin and Sachs (1992) and Eichengreen (1990b) have considered the role of fiscal federalism in the United States as a regional shock absorber. Whether the absence of comparable institutions in Europe is a serious challenge to the case for an OCA turns out to be a complicated question. I focus on this issue in the penultimate section of the chapter, approaching it both abstractly and using a case study approach.

3.2 Relative Price Disturbances and Region-Specific Shocks

3.2.1 Real Exchange Rates

In the OCA literature it is argued that exchange rate changes may be desirable to facilitate adjustment between regions experiencing large changes in relative prices, assuming that wages and other nominally-denominated costs are slow to adapt. A rise in German productivity relative to French productivity or a shift in demand from French to German goods will require a fall in French costs and prices relative to German, or unemployment will result. Devaluation of the franc may circumvent the problem of coordination failure that impedes the adjustment of costs and thereby accelerate the transition to the new steady state.

Thus, the more variable real exchange rates, the stronger the case for exchange rate flexibility. Poloz (1990) has shown that regional real exchange rates within Canada are more variable than national real exchange rates between France, the United Kingdom, Italy and Germany. The implication is that Europe is every bit as much an OCA as Canada. Quebec nationalists aside, few observers question that Canada is a viable currency area. Hence, the inference runs, Europe must be one as well.

There are good reasons to argue, however, that the United States versus the Community is a more appropriate standard of comparison than Canada versus France, the United Kingdom, Italy and Germany. Canadian provinces are highly specialized in production. Alberta and Saskatchewan specialize in primary commodities, Ontario in manufactured goods. It is not surprising that real exchange rates between them are highly variable. France and Germany are diversified economies. Both possess substantial manufacturing, agricultural and service sectors. It is not surprising that real exchange rates between them are relatively stable.

Moreover, any case on these grounds for a floating exchange rate for Alberta or Saskatchewan is undermined by the small size of provincial populations and the thinness of provincial financial markets. Models in the OCA literature balance the benefits of devaluation by a region suffering a deterioration in its terms of trade against the loss of liquidity services it suffers with an independent currency and a variable exchange rate. The loss of liquidity services is modelled as a decreasing function of the size of the domestic economy and the depth of its financial markets. Even if Alberta has a more variable real exchange rate vis à vis Ontario than France has vis à vis Germany, such models do not suggest that it would be more desirable for Alberta than for France to maintain a flexible exchange rate.

It may be more illuminating, therefore, to compare the different regions of the United States with all 10 EC members. Population size and the average degree of sectoral diversification are more directly comparable. So are the depth and breadth of regional financial markets in the United States with national financial markets in Europe.

The results of such a comparison appear in Table 3.1. Regional consumer price indices are calculated by the Bureau of Labor Statistics for the North East, North Central, South and West of the United States. The resulting real exchange rates can be compared with relative CPIs within the Community, converted into DM by period average market exchange rates. For the 1970s, the standard deviations of European real exchange rates, on a quarterly basis, range from 5.4 to 14.0 percent, averaging 8.9 percent for the period. For the four US regions, standard deviations for the same period range only from 2.0 to 2.7 percent. For the 1980s, with the decline of oil and commodity price shocks, the variability of US regional real exchange rates fell to still lower levels, to the range of 1.3 to 1.5 percent. The variability of intra-EC real exchange rates fell as well, to 1.0 to 9.6 percent, but still averaged 5.7 percent.

This comparison is likely to be biased by the variability of nominal exchange rates in Europe in the 1970s and 1980s. Edwards (1989) has shown for developing countries, as have Mussa (1986) and Eichengreen (1991) for industrial countries, that the variability of real exchange rates increases with the variability of nominal rates. The exceptional variability of the sterling-DM real exchange rate in the 1980s is consistent with this presumption. If the United Kingdom, Ireland, Portugal and Greece are excluded on the grounds that they were members of the European Monetary System for at most part of the period, the average variability of intra-EC real rates in the 1980s falls to 4 percent.

Another way to think about this point is that real exchange rates between European countries in the 1970s and 1980s have been perturbed both by real and by monetary disturbances; in the United States, in con-

Table 3.1
Summary Statistics for Regional Real Exchange Rates, Other EC Members against Germany
1971.1–1979.4, 1971.1 = 100

	Minimum	Maximum	Standard deviation
Belgium/Germany	92.71	111.62	5.55
France/Germany	99.84	122.28	5.40
Greece/Germany	100.00	122.28	5.40
Ireland/Germany	100.00	138.39	10.75
Italy/Germany	100.00	145.40	14.02
Netherlands/Germany	88.76	104.31	4.62
Portugal/Germany	86.11	118.06	9.46
Spain/Germany	83.77	117.68	7.42
UK/Germany	100.00	150.94	13.74

1980.1–1987.4, 1971.1 = 100

	Minimum	Maximum	Standard deviation
Belgium/Germany	92.99	108.29	4.88
France/Germany	97.75	122.15	3.64
Greece/Germany	105.07	133.54	9.57
Ireland/Germany	87.91	114.83	6.28
Italy/Germany	104.79	126.19	5.67
Netherlands/Germany	89.45	93.48	1.05
Portugal/Germany	89.60	114.87	5.95
Spain/Germany	78.48	95.22	4.62
UK/Germany	82.40	116.04	9.22

Other US regions against the US North East
1973.12–1979.12, 1977.12 = 100

	Minimum	Maximum	Standard deviation
North Central/North East	97.253	103.730	2.06
South/North East	96.016	102.653	2.02
West/North East	94.024	103.731	2.74

1980.1–1987.12, 1977.12 = 100

	Minimum	Maximum	Standard deviation
North Central/North East	98.926	104.835	1.54
South/North East	99.195	104.444	1.32
West/North East	100.805	106.174	1.30

Source: See discussion in text.
Note: US data are computed as quarterly averages of monthly consumer prices. Consumer prices are gathered by the US Bureau of Labor Statistics for roughly 100 countries in each of the 4 regions of the USA.

trast, monetary disturbances are common to the nation as a whole and should not have an equally dramatic effect on real exchange rates between US regions. The data for the 1970s and 1980s are best interpreted, therefore, as an upper bound on the US–European differential that would obtain if Europe possessed a common currency.

3.2.2   Real Security Prices

A second comparison is based on regional stock price differentials. In theory, the prices of equities should reflect the present value of current and expected future profits. If shocks are asymmetrical, profits will rise in one region relative to the other. Hence the more closely real share prices move across regions, the more symmetrical the disturbances and the more rapid the reallocation of factors of production from regions experiencing negative shocks to regions experiencing positive ones.

I compare the differentials between averages of the prices of securities traded on two regional Canadian Stock Exchanges (Toronto and Montreal) with differentials between Paris and Düsseldorf. Consistent with arguments presented in Section 3.2.1 above, it would have been preferable to conduct this analysis for the United States instead of Canada. Though there are Stock Exchanges in a number of different regions of the United States (the most prominent subsidiary exchanges including Chicago, San Francisco, Philadelphia and Boston), the shares of many of the same companies are bought and sold on each of them, contaminating their share price indices with common observations (Berlin, 1990). The two Canadian exchanges, in contrast, have non-overlapping listings, the Montreal index specializing in enterprises located in Quebec, the Toronto index listing firms headquartered elsewhere in Canada. If the dispersion of regional shocks is smaller within Canada, we would expect prices in Toronto and Montreal to move together more closely than prices in Paris and Dusseldorf.

Share price indices were gathered for the last Friday in each quarter from issues of the *Financial Times*. (The Commerzbank and Herstat Bank Index for Düsseldorf is used in lieu of other German share price indices because it is the only index provided by the *Financial Times* for the entire period.) Since stock prices are nominally denominated, they must be adjusted for international price and exchange rate differentials. Share prices in Toronto are deflated by the Toronto CPI, share prices in Montreal by the Montreal CPI. (Unpublished CPI data were provided by Statistics Canada.) For Europe I provide two versions of the calculations, one

Table 3.2
Summary Statistics for Real Share Price Indices
Canada and Europe
(1980.4 = 1.00)

	Coefficient of Variation		Paris/Düsseldorf
	Toronto/Montreal	Paris/Düsseldorf	(Exchange rate corrected)
1971.1−1987.4	0.0451	0.2314	0.3421
1971.1−1979.4	0.0305	0.2851	0.3901
1980.1−1987.4	0.0350	0.1435	0.1841

Source: See discussion in text.
Note: Real share price indices are constructed as share price indices normalized by consumer price indices for the relevant region. Coefficient of variation is standard deviation divided by the mean. Constituent series are all normalized to 1980.4 = 1.

in which franc prices are deflated by the French CPI and German prices are deflated by the German CPI, and a second, which is more appropriate if purchasing power parity does not hold, in which real French securities prices are converted into DM by the nominal exchange rate.

This is not a test of the degree of capital mobility between regions. If we thought that perfect capital mobility equalized the return on baskets of securities traded on the exchanges (which might not be an appropriate assumption if the two baskets had different risk characteristics), we would expect holding period returns, or the *rate of change* of prices plus dividends, to be equal across exchanges. Price *levels* on different exchanges would move independently, reflecting changes in expected future profitability, so as to permit the preceding condition to obtain.

Table 3.2 displays the results for the last two decades and for the same subperiods considered in Table 3.1. Share prices in Toronto and Montreal move much more closely together than share prices in Dusseldorf and Paris. Since the respective indices are deflated by domestic prices, inflation differentials do not account for the difference. Adjusting for exchange rate changes between France and Germany does not alter the finding. (The exchange rate adjustment increases the variability of the Paris/Düsseldorf ratio because the exchange rate is more variable than the ratio of real share prices and its covariance with the share price ratio is virtually zero.) There is strong evidence of convergence between Paris and Düsseldorf over time when the 1970s is compared with the 1980s. But even in the 1980s, the ratio of real share prices between Paris and Düsseldorf is five times as variable as the comparable ratio between Toronto and Montreal.

The strong implication of this analysis is that region-specific shocks are greater in Europe than in Canada. There are good reasons, however, to treat this comparison, like the previous one focusing on real exchange rates, with considerable caution. Firms headquartered in Quebec do business in Ontario, just as firms headquartered in Ontario do business in Quebec. The same is true of firms headquartered in France and Germany, but the degree of interpenetration is likely to be greater at the moment in Canada than in Europe. European commodity prices will move more closely together as border taxes are eliminated, and interest rates and other financial determinants of share prices will move more closely together with the elimination of capital controls. Hence real share prices in different European markets are likely to move more closely together in the future than they do now. It is appropriate to assume that these results provide an upper bound on the North American–European differential.

3.3   Labour Mobility

3.3.1   The Argument and the Evidence

The more mobile factors of production within a region, the more likely that region is, ceteris paribus, to constitute an OCA. Consider again the mental experiment of a decline in labour productivity in France relative to Germany, or a shift in demand from the products of French firms to those of their German competitors. Assume that neither a decline in French labour costs nor a change in the nominal exchange rate is feasible. It is still possible for unemployment to be avoided if French labour can migrate freely to Germany, where a notional excess demand for labour exists.

Direct evidence on the extent of interregional labour mobility is hard to obtain. The one systematic comparison of which I am aware (OECD, 1986) concluded that mobility within the United States was two to three times as high as mobility within European states. Table 3.3 shows that in 1980, for example, 6.2 percent of the US population changed its county of residence, 3.3 percent its state of residence. In contrast, 1.1 percent of Englishmen and Welshmen moved between regions, and 1.3 percent of Germans moved between states. (These comparisons must be treated cautiously in light of the different definitions of regional units used in different countries.)

But the contrast seems to be too pronounced to be explicable on these grounds. Nor is it plausible that the difference reflects legal barriers to

Table 3.3
Geographic Mobility—Proportion of Population Who Changed Region of Residence, %

Country	Regional units (no. of regions)	Reference population	Multi-year period data			1970	1975	1980	1981	1982	1983
			1965–70	1970–5	1975–80						
Australia	Inter-states (8)	Pop. 15 yrs+				1.7	1.9[c]	1.8	1.8	1.1	1.1
	Inter-states	Labor force[a]				5.6[b]	5.0[c]				4.9
	Inter-states	Labor force[a]				21.6[b]	18.7[c]				17.6
Canada	Inter-provinces (12)	Total population	4.3	4.3	5.1	1.9	1.9	1.8	1.9		
	Inter-provinces	Labor force			6.0						
	Intra-provinces	Total population	14.0	16.5	15.1						
		Labor force			16.7						
USA	Inter-states (51)	Total population	8.6		9.7	3.4		3.3			
	Inter-counties	Total population	17.1		19.5	6.5		6.2			
Japan	Inter-prefectures (47)	Total population			7.7	3.6		2.6			
	Inter-prefectures	Total population			24.1	3.7		6.9			
England and Wales	Inter-regions (8)	Total population				1.5		1.1			
Finland	Inter-counties (12)	Total population				2.5	1.7[c]			1.5	
	Inter-communes	Total population				5.8	4.4[c]	4.1	4.0	3.9	
France	Inter-regions (21)	Total population	6.5[d]	8.7[e]	7.9[f]						
	Inter-regions	Labor force	6.4[d]	8.9[e]	8.3[f]						
W. Germany	Inter-Länder (11)	Total population				1.8	1.3	1.3	1.3		
Norway	Inter-counties (19)	Total population				3.0	2.5	2.3	2.2	2.1	2.0
Sweden	Inter-counties (24)	Total population				2.4[g]	2.4	2.1	1.7	1.7	1.7
	Inter-communes	Total population				4.8[g]	4.7	4.0	3.5	3.5	3.5
Switzerland	Inter-cantons (26)	Total population	7.6	6.3							

Source: Organisation for Economic Cooperation and Development (1986).
[a] Employed population at the time of the survey who changed jobs during the previous year and changed usual residence when changing jobs.
[b] 1972.   [c] 1976.   [d] 1962–8.   [e] 1968–75.   [f] 1975–82.   [g] 1973.

movement, since such barriers do not exist within European countries. Public policy (the council house problem in the United Kingdom, or the need to establish residence before qualifying for unemployment benefits, for example) may play a role, but the dominant explanation is that America's shared immigrant past, in contrast to the tradition of ties to one's locality in Europe, continues to influence behaviour.

The problem with this evidence is that relatively low levels of labour mobility within Europe may reflect a lesser incentive to move rather than a lower level of intrinsic mobility. At the international level, less labour may move between European countries, not only because of border controls but also because adjustment can take place along a number of other margins (by changing nominal exchange rates, for example). At the national level, less labour mobility may occur within European countries not because Europeans are less mobile intrinsically but because of a lower incidence of asymmetric regional shocks.

To address this possibility, a number of authors have considered the behaviour of variables that contain information about the incentive for migration. Boltho (1989), for example, examined evidence on regional income differentials in the United States, in the Community, and within various European countries. For 1983, the coefficient of variation of *per capita* incomes was 0.25 for 12 EC members, but only 0.10 for 9 US census regions. This would appear at first glance to be strong evidence of the effects of greater factor mobility within the United States. When the same statistic is calculated for only 9 EC members (excluding Greece, Portugal and Spain), however, it falls to 0.16. Still, a noticeable differential remains.

It is not obvious, however, whether this evidence for 1983 reflects legal barriers to migration between EC countries or cultural impediments. Here evidence on inequality within European countries is useful. The standard deviation of *per capita* incomes in 1983 was 0.21 for 31 regions of Germany, 0.25 for 20 regions of Italy, 0.21 for 19 regions of Spain, but only 0.16 for 48 US states, as if factor mobility were greater in the United States than within any of these European countries. On the other hand, the comparable measures for 21 regions of France and 35 regions of the United Kingdom were only 0.15 and 0.12, respectively. (So much for the "council house" explanation.) The argument that the less footloose nature of Europeans leads to greater income inequality in Europe does not appear uniformly to apply.

The problem with such evidence is that simple tabulations still do not distinguish the disturbances from the response. Interregional income differentials reflect both the extent of asymmetric shocks affecting incomes in different regions differently, and the elasticity of factor flows with respect to regional income differentials. Tabulations of migration rates reflect changes over time or across locations in the shocks that provide the incentive to migrate as well as in the speed of the migratory response. Disentangling the impulse from the response requires a model. In Eichengreen (1990b) I therefore estimated time-series models of regional unemployment differentials for both Europe and the United States.

I examined the speed with which unemployment in various EC countries, when perturbed, converged to its long-run equilibrium relationship to EC-wide unemployment, and compared that with the speed which regional unemployment rates in the United States converged to the national average. (No assumption was imposed about the nature of the long-run equilibrium relationship.) The results suggest that regional unemployment rates adjust to one another about 20 percent more rapidly in the United States than national unemployment rates adjust to one another within the Community. While this conclusion points in the same direction as the evidence cited above, it is still surprisingly weak evidence of slow adjustment in Europe. It thus appears that greater labour mobility leads to faster adjustment to regional shocks in the United States than in Europe. But the differential is surprisingly small. A possible interpretation is that the mobility of other factors of production, such as capital, substitutes for labour mobility.

3.3.2 Breaking Down Barriers to Labour Mobility: An Historical Interlude

A presumption in this discussion, as in much current policy analysis, is that, with the removal of legal restrictions, labour mobility within Europe is sure to increase. By how much is a matter for debate. The absence of legal restrictions is necessary but not sufficient for labour to move freely between regions. The historical experience of the US South, documented by Wright (1986), from whose analysis my discussion is drawn, illustrates the point and identifies factors that help to overcome a legacy of regional labour market segmentation.

The origins of a separate Southern labour market are not difficult to understand. Slavery was only the most visible manifestation of the social, cultural, political and economic institutions that differentiated South from North in the United States. After the Civil War, race relations continued to take on very different forms in the American South and North. Southern labour was provided with significantly lower levels of education than its Northern counterpart.

The result was strikingly low level of labour mobility between the US North and South in the 75 years from the American Civil War to the Second World War. For fully three-quarters of a century, farm wage rates without board, a proxy for the wages of unskilled labour, in states like Mississippi and North Carolina averaged only half their equivalent in states like Ohio and Iowa.

It is important to note what does not explain these differentials. Low Southern wages were not due to the absence of a properly functioning regional labour market. Wage rates for unskilled workers in different Southern states converged steadily over the period. Wage differentials within the South were never significantly larger than wage differentials within the North. Nor do low Southern wages appear to have been due to racial discrimination. Though there is ample evidence of firm level and occupational segregation, competitive pressures drove the wages of black and white farm labourers to equality. Given the size of the agricultural sector, this dictated the wages that industrial employers could pay for unskilled labour. If they attempted to pay less, workers would simply return to agriculture. Hence the competitiveness of the unskilled agricultural labour market equalized wages for unskilled black and white workers in industry.

Low Southern wages are sufficient to explain why neither Northerners nor Europeans migrated to the South. What then prevented low-paid Southern workers from migrating to the North? In part, the region's history of labour market segmentation perpetuated itself. The information and reception migrants require is provided typically by family or neighbours who had made the trip in years past. Southerners lacked transplanted relatives and friends in the North to extend these services. In contrast, European migrants followed their relatives and former neighbours to ports of entry like New York and then to cities in the Middle and Far West. When additional employment opportunities appeared in the North, these were filled not by Southerners but by European immigrants. Wright concludes that the Northern labour market was more integrated with that of Europe than with that of the South.

One would think nonetheless that a few hearty souls would have somehow travelled North, paving the way for others. Additional factors must have contributed, therefore, to the isolation of the Southern labour market. Those additional factors, Wright suggests, were political as well as economic. Large Southern employers and landowners discouraged Northern labour recruiters who might have wished to appropriate their low wage labour. These same individuals discouraged the provision of education on the grounds that educated workers were more likely to emigrate than others. Since literacy and numeracy enhance mobility, the existence of a substantial wage gap meant that that the South would have been unable to appropriate the benefits of additional educational spending. Agriculture and low wage industries such as textiles and timber benefited from the elastic supply of low wage labour, and the disproportionate political power of large landowners and industrialists prevented institutions and markets from responding so as to arbitrage the wage gap between North and South.

If Southern labour failed to move out so as to eliminate inter-regional wage differentials, why did Northern capital fail to move in to take advantage of cheap Southern labour? To some extent it did, as Wright shows. But Northern capital had to hurdle three barriers. First, capital and labour mobility were complementary, so barriers to one also posed barriers to the other. The difficulties of effectively monitoring investment from afar meant that capital tended to migrate across states only when its owners accompanied it, or followed quickly. Hence obstacles to the immigration of persons also impeded the immigration of capital. Second, the predominance of unskilled, relatively uneducated labour in the South dictated the adoption of technologies and production processes very different from those appropriate to skilled labour in the North: Northern investors had little prior opportunity to acquire familiarity with Southern methods. Finally, wealthy Southerners discouraged outside investment, which threatened to drive down the rate of return on their own capital and undermine their political control.

What was responsible ultimately for breaking down the barriers between Southern and Northern labour markets? Wright points to simultaneous supply and demand shocks in the 1940s. On the demand side, the Second World War created new employment opportunities in the North and West. That the demand for labour rose in the North during wartime meant that, for once, the supply of immigrants from Europe was relatively inelastic. But similar opportunities for Southerners had opened up in the North during the First World War without permanently eliminating regional labour market segmentation. Wright suggests that the Second World War had more profound effects because its demand-side shock reinforced equally profound supply-side disturbances. The NIRA had reduced labour hours and established minimum wages that were binding for much of Southern industry. The Fair Labor Standards Act of 1938 made wage minima permanent. Federal incentives for agricultural mechanization further reduced opportunities for farm employment for unskilled labour. Unskilled blacks priced out of employment naturally began to seek opportunities elsewhere. The result was massive outmigration by unskilled workers once employment opportunities opened up in the North.

What are the implications of this tale for labour mobility in Europe? A first implication is that the removal of legal restrictions does not automatically produce an integrated labour market. Regional labour market segmentation can be remarkably persistent, especially if distinctive cultural and social factors are embedded in a political system that vests power in individuals with an interest in the maintenance of segmentation. A second implication is that investment in education is important for promoting interregional mobility. A third implication is that breaking down barriers to worker mobility requires policies targeted at both the demand and supply sides of the labour market.

3.4   Regional Self-Insurance

3.4.1   The Argument and the Evidence

A popular explanation for the tolerance in currency areas like the United States and Canada of region-specific shocks is that their federal fiscal systems provide regional insurance. If incomes in a US state decline by $1, federal tax payments by residents of that state decline by 30 cents, while transfers from Washington, D.C., mostly in the form of federally-funded unemployment insurance benefits, rise by 10 cents (Sala-i-Martin and Sachs, 1992). The impact of regional shocks on interregional income differentials is thereby attenuated. Insofar as the locus of regional shocks shifts over time, all regions are rendered better off by risk sharing achieved via the federal fiscal system (Eichengreen, 1990a).

It is important to be clear on the nature of this argument. It is not that fiscal federalism is a necessary prerequisite for monetary unification. Historically, most federal unions established common currencies before adopting extensive systems of fiscal federalism; the United States and Canada are two obvious cases in point. The argument is rather that monetary union accompanied by fiscal federalism is likely to operate more smoothly than monetary union without it, insofar as regional problems that otherwise might arise are mitigated by interregional transfers.

Interregional transfers accomplished through federal taxes and expenditures are justifiable only if insurance cannot be provided by the market. In principle, a lumberjack or an aerospace worker in Washington state should be able to write a contract selling part of his expected labour income to an auto worker in Michigan or to an investment banker in New York City. In practice, problems of moral hazard and adverse selection prevent such diversification of human capital portfolios. Alternatively, individuals should be able to diversify away regional risk by purchasing financial assets, the returns on which are imperfectly correlated with their income streams. Most individuals seem to do so only to a limited extent, a fact for which there are two plausible explanations.

The first one is liquidity constraints. For most workers, financial wealth is a small share of undiversifiable, largely illiquid, human capital. The second one is that much of the financial wealth workers possess may be tied up in their homes, the epitome of an indivisible, regional-specific asset. The large literature on state and local public finance is predicated in part on the presumption that there are intrinsic reasons why markets fail to resolve the problem, creating a role for government intervention.

But it does not follow that intervention can occur only at the federal level. Because they possess powers of taxation, state governments can compel their residents to participate in the regional insurance scheme, solving the adverse selection problem. States can borrow on the OCA-wide capital market when regional incomes decline and repay when incomes rise. This would seem to be a perfectly adequate substitute for a system of fiscal federalism.

The capacity to borrow of members of a currency area may, however, be limited. The debt they can incur today is limited by the present value of the taxes they can collect tomorrow (taxes which will be used to service the accumulated debt). This is evident in the experience of US states, which are forced to pay sharply rising interest rates as they continue to borrow. Given the high mobility of factors of production within the United States, individual states cannot credibly promise to raise future taxes significantly above those prevailing elsewhere in the currency and customs union, since footloose factors of production will flee to lower tax jurisdictions. Moreover, problems of moral hazard remain. States that borrow on the OCA-wide capital market have an incentive to default when the time comes to repay the loans.

As Bulow and Rogoff (1989) have noted, reputational considerations may not help. Hence states that run budget deficits are likely to face

Table 3.4
US Inter-governmental Revenue as Percentage of Recipients' Expenditures

Year	State receipts from federal government as % of state expenditures	Local receipts from federal and state governments as % of local expenditures
1902	1.6	5.8
1922	7.4	7.1
1932	8.0	12.8
1942	16.6	25.4
1958	18.3	24.9
1964	21.2	27.0
1967	23.2	30.3
1972	24.5	33.5
1974	23.9	39.0
1976	23.2	38.4
1978	24.6	39.8
1980	24.0	39.3
1982	21.3	37.2
1984	21.7	35.3
1986	21.8	34.4
1987	20.9	33.7

Source: Break (1967), p. 5, for 1902–64. Advisory Committee on Inter-governmental Relations, *Significant Features of Fiscal Federalism 1989*, vol. 1, for 1967–87.

sharply rising supply curves of external funds. As the costs of fiscal self-insurance rise, state governments may find themselves rationed out of the capital market. These factors are likely to be particularly important for EC members already burdened by high levels of public debt. Belgium, Ireland and Italy all possess public debts that approach or exceed 100 percent of GNP. These are large debts by Latin American standards. In a recession, when the budget deficit grows and GNP shrinks, this debt-to-income ratio may rise dramatically, exacerbating the difficulties of borrowing.

These, then, are the grounds for institutionalizing interregional transfers at the federal level. Table 3.4 summarizes the extent of fiscal transfers among governments in the United States. Clearly there does not exist the possibility of fiscal federalism on this scale in Europe, where the Community budget is on the order of 1 or 2 percent of GNP.

Sceptics counter that factor mobility is lower in Europe than in the United States. Hence members of the Community have more latitude to vary future taxes relative to those prevailing elsewhere in the currency union. As noted above, this may be a mixed blessing: while it enhances a country's capacity to borrow, it also increases the need to borrow in a recession.

A second counterargument to the case for fiscal federalism is that fiscal transfers into a depressed region from elsewhere in the federal system discourage factors of production from moving out—that is, from reallocating themselves to other areas where their productivity is higher. This is not an argument against fiscal transfers, however, but a caution against transfers so generous as seriously to distort economic incentives. Here the optimal adjustment assistance literature, in which the marginal utility households derive from income transfers is balanced against the marginal costs of discouraging adjustment, provides guidance on how to structure a tax and transfer programme.

A final counterargument (the idea for which I owe to Jacques Melitz) is that fiscal federalism, like any form of insurance, creates still other problems of moral hazard which are likely to manifest themselves in labour militancy. Consider the following example. National labour unions seeking to maximize the wage bill set the level of real wages, subject to which firms then choose the level of employment. Assume that there exist transfers from employed workers to their unemployed brethren (unemployment insurance benefits, for example). In general, the union will set wages that are above market-clearing, socially-efficient levels. If the union is region-specific (a French union within a single European market, for example), and if the cost of financing unemployment benefits is shifted from French taxpayers to the Community as a whole, the French union has an incentive, ceteris paribus, to raise the wage it sets, creating more socially-inefficient unemployment. The same holds, *ceteris paribus*, for unions in other countries. Not only does the provision of insurance thereby encourage the outcome—unemployment—whose effects it is designed to mitigate, but the magnitude of the distortion increases with the extent of fiscal federalism.

In the United States, a variety of incentive mechanisms built into the administration of unemployment insurance minimize these forms of moral hazard. Each state administers its own unemployment insurance trust fund. In addition, states pay a fraction of the payroll taxes levied to finance the programme into a Federal Unemployment Trust Fund, which is administered by the secretary of the Treasury. States whose own trust funds move into deficit are able to borrow from this federal fund. Significantly, however, states must pay interest on the monies they borrow from the federal trust fund. Except insofar as those interest rates are set below market levels, states are unable to shift the burden of financing their unemployment programmes. Proposals for federal reinsurance of state unemployment insurance programmes have been mooted in recent years; under these proposals states would pay unemployment-insurance-related payroll taxes into a federal trust fund in proportion to the value of state payrolls but draw from that fund in proportion to the level of state unemployment. Such a programme might well reintroduce the moral hazard problems of which some observers warn.

3.4.2   Fiscal Federalism in Practice: An Historical Interlude

To illustrate the importance of the mechanisms described above in adjust-ment to regional shocks in the United States, I consider the case of Michigan's adjustment to a region-specific shock at the end of the 1970s. Michigan is the most cyclically-sensitive state economy in the United States (Bretzfelder, 1973). When America sneezes, the popular saying goes, Michigan catches pneumonia. The case of pneumonia I consider here is the recession that followed the 1979 oil shock. Unemployment rose nationwide following the oil shock and the adoption of disinflationary policies, but as Figure 3.1 makes clear it rose especially dramatically in Michigan. At its peak in 1982, the differential between unemployment in

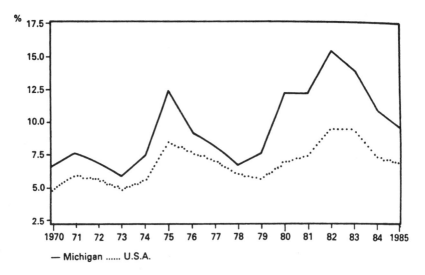

Figure 3.1
Michigan and national unemployment rates, 1970–85.

Michigan and the national average approached six percentage points. The rise in energy prices had a disproportionate impact on production costs in cold-winter states heavily reliant on space heating. It depressed the demand for motor vehicles as consumers substituted toward more fuel-efficient Japanese imports. Rising interest rates on consumer instalment loans and lagging incomes reinforced the slump in the automobile industry.

Figure 3.2 displays one mechanism by which Michigan adjusted to this shock, namely outward labour mobility. The differential between the Michigan and national unemployment rates is compared with the rate of emigration from Michigan. The two lines in Figure 3.2 must be compared cautiously, since their numerators differ. (Persons unemployed are expressed as a percentage of the labour force, while emigration is expressed as a percentage of state population.) Nonetheless, Figure 3.2 shows that interregional labour mobility was one significant form of regional adjustment.

Figure 3.3 shows the swing in the state budget balance and in net federal transfers to Michigan. Since the state is bound by its constitution to run a balanced budget, the government accumulates a reserve in its Budget Stabilization Fund in good times in order to incur expenses in excess of current revenues in slumps without showing a deficit on its books. It is not the level of the state deficit or surplus that is relevant, but the swing between peak and trough.

Figure 3.2
Michigan unemployment differential and emigration, 1970–85.

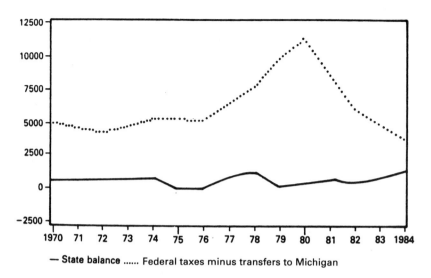

Figure 3.3
Michigan state budget balance and net federal tax payments.

The series shown is total state revenues including those transferred to local governments minus state government expenditures. (Were transfers to local government netted out and revenues for which the state government is final receipient used instead, the line would shift down but its contours would remain the same.) At its peak, the state deficit measured on this basis would have been $422 million rather than $1 million in 1975.

Also displayed is a measure of net transfers to Michigan from the federal government. This series is estimated by the Tax Foundation, a non-profit research organization, and published in the *Michigan Statistical Abstract* (Verway, 1987). Constructing it requires assumptions about the incidence of federal taxes. To obtain a continuous time series, I have interpolated linearly where there are missing data. The series shows that the swing in net federal transfers after 1976 was large compared to the shift in the state government's budgetary position. Federal expenditures in Michigan fell short of federal tax payments by Michigan residents according to these calculations. The main reason for the disparity is the low rate of federal defence spending in the state (Erdevig, 1986).

A dramatic decline in the differential is evident after 1980. Most of the swing is on the disbursement side: federal expenditure in Michigan rose by 12 percent between 1979 and 1980 and by an additional 44 percent between 1980 and 1981, largely reflecting transfers to support the unemployed. (Unemployment insurance and employment training, community and urban development, and Medicaid were the three categories of federal programmes to show the largest increases in outlays in Michigan between 1980 and 1981.) Though the federal fiscal shift was large compared to the change in the state's budgetary position, it occurred with a lag. Unemployment started rising in 1979, yet a significant swing in federal transfers began only in 1981, once the position of the state's unemployment insurance trust fund had eroded. Although the largest swing in the state's budgetary position took place in 1978–9, it was another two years before federal transfers responded.

Though it operates with significant lags, the American system of fiscal federalism plays an important role in regional adjustment within the United States. So does the high level of labour mobility. Neither mechanism can be expected to operate as powerfully in Europe. The implication is that serious thought must be given to the cultivation of other mechanisms to facilitate regional adjustment.

3.5 Conclusion

This paper has argued that Europe remains further than the United States and Canada from the ideal of an OCA. Real exchange rates are more variable in Europe than in the United States, suggesting a greater prevalence of region-specific shocks and a case for nominal exchange rate changes to coordinate price level adjustments between regions. Real securities prices are more variable within Europe, confirming the importance of region-specific shocks. Although regional disparities within Europe will decline with the completion of the internal market, the extent remains a subject for debate. The extent of regional problems within existing currency and customs unions like the United States underscores the need for regional shock absorbers, such as fiscal federalism, to accommodate asymmetrical disturbances.

Note

I thank Kris Mitchner and Carolyn Werley for research assistance, Statistics Canada for data, and the National Science Foundation, the German Marshall Fund of the United States, and the Institute of International Studies of the University of California at Berkeley for financial support.

4

Shocking Aspects of
European Monetary
Unification

4.1 Introduction

From all appearances the process of European monetary unification continues to gather momentum. Nearly four years have passed since the last significant realignment of exchange rates of members within the European Monetary System (EMS).[1] All significant controls on capital movements among member countries have been removed. Discussions of the establishment of a European central bank and a single currency are proceeding apace. If the current timetable is observed the transition will have been completed by the end of the decade.

At the same time there remain serious questions about the advisability of a European Monetary Union (EMU) voiced, in the most recent round of discussions, by the governments of the United Kingdom and Spain. By definition, EMU involves a sacrifice of monetary autonomy. In response to country-specific shocks, governments will no longer have the option of pursuing a monetary policy which differs from that of the union as a whole. Insofar as monetary policy is useful for facilitating adjustment to disturbances, adjustment problems may grow more persistent and difficult to resolve.

These concerns are reinforced to the extent that it is believed that completion of the internal market will place new limits on the use of fiscal policy. Not only will individual governments have lost autonomy over the use of seigniorage to finance budget deficits but, insofar as the 1992 process renders factors of production increasingly mobile, constraints will be placed on their ability to impose tax rates significantly different from

Originally published, as chapter 7, "Shocking Aspects of European Monetary Integration," in *Growth and Adjustment in the European Monetary Union*, ed. Francisco Torres and Francesco Giavazzi (Cambridge: Cambridge University Press (1993), 193–229, with Tamim Bayoumi. Reprinted with permission.

those of their neighbours. Limits on their ability to tax in the future will limit their ability to run budget deficits in the present; hence all important fiscal instruments may be constrained.[2] The sacrifice of monetary autonomy is potentially all the more serious.

The weight that should be attached to these arguments depends on the incidence of shocks. If disturbances are distributed symmetrically across countries, symmetrical policy responses will suffice. In response to a negative aggregate demand shock that is common to all EMU countries, for example, a common policy response in the form of a common monetary and fiscal expansion should be adequate. Only if disturbances are distributed asymmetrically across countries will there be occasion for an asymmetric policy response and the constraints of monetary union may then be felt. This has been widely understood, of course, since the seminal work on the theory of optimum currency areas by Mundell (1961).

In light of the attention attracted by EMU, we possess remarkably little evidence on the incidence of shocks to the European economy. In this chapter, therefore, we analyse data on output and prices for 11 European Community (EC) member countries in order to extract information on aggregate supply and aggregate demand disturbances. We use the structural vector auto regression approach for isolating disturbances developed by Blanchard and Quah (1989) and extended by Bayoumi (1991). We examine the time-series behaviour of real gross domestic product (GDP) and the price level. To recover aggregate supply and demand disturbances, we impose the identifying restrictions that aggregate demand disturbances have only a temporary impact on output but a permanent impact on prices, while aggregate supply disturbances permanently affect both prices and output.

To assess the magnitude of disturbances to the European economy, a standard of comparison is required. The United States of America is the obvious possibility. It is a smoothly functioning monetary union. Its local authorities possess fiscal autonomy. It can be divided into regions that are approximately the economic size of Community countries, and supply and demand disturbances to each region can be calculated. If it turns out, for example, that supply shocks are less correlated across US regions than across the member countries of the Community, then there can be no presumption that asymmetric shocks will necessarily threaten the success of EMU. If, on the other hand, shocks to EC countries are significantly more asymmetric than shocks to US regions, then adoption of a single currency could give rise to serious problems.

The empirical framework allows us not just to identify aggregate supply and demand disturbances but to examine the economy's speed of adjustment. Comparing the responses of US regions and EC countries provides suggestive evidence on the structural implications of the Single Market. If the responses of US regions are more rapid than those of European countries, this would suggest that the creation of a unified internal market in Europe will encourage factor mobility and create other mechanisms which will facilitate the Community's adjustment to shocks. Evidence from the USA is useful, therefore, for gauging the extent to which monetary unification and the rest of the 1992 programme is likely to accelerate the response to shocks, as argued by the Commission of the European Communities (1990).[3]

The remainder of this chapter is organized as follows. In Section 4.2 we review the theoretical literature on optimum currency areas and what it says about asymmetric shocks. Previous empirical work on the issue is also surveyed. In Section 4.3 the framework used to identify supply and demand disturbances is set out. A description of our data and its properties is given in Section 4.4, while Section 4.5 contains the results of the statistical analysis. Our conclusions are given in Section 4.6.

4.2 Optimum Currency Areas: Theory and Evidence

The point of departure for the literature on optimum currency areas was Mundell (1961).[4] Mundell observed that an exchange rate adjustment which permitted the pursuit of different monetary policies in two countries (say, the USA and Canada) was of little use if the disturbance in response to which the policies were adopted depressed one region within both countries (say, western Canada and the western United States) while simultaneously stimulating other regions within both (say, eastern Canada and the eastern United States). In this case, there is an efficiency argument for forming one currency area comprised of the two western parts and a second currency area made up of the eastern parts. In response to this disturbance, the western regions can then adopt one policy, the eastern regions another, and the exchange rate between them can adjust accordingly, while preserving the advantages of a common currency in the form of reduced exchange rate risk and lower transaction costs within the eastern and western regions. In Mundell's framework, then, the incidence of disturbances across regions is a critical determinant of the design of currency areas.[5]

One strand of subsequent literature explored the determinants of the incidence of shocks. Kenen (1969) highlighted the degree of industry or product diversification as a determinant of the symmetry of disturbances. When two regions are highly specialized in the production of distinct goods the prices of which are affected very differently by disturbances, he argued, asymmetric shocks are more likely than when the two regions have the same industrial structure and produce the same goods.[6]

A second direction taken by the subsequent literature analysed mechanisms other than exchange-rate-cum-monetary policy that might facilitate adjustment. Following Meade (1957), Mundell emphasized labour mobility. The greater the propensity for labour to flow from depressed to prosperous regions, he argued, the less the need for different policy responses in the two regions to prevent the emergence of pockets of high unemployment. Ingram (1973) noted that even where labour remains imperfectly mobile, capital mobility has typically reached high levels.[7] Hence capital flows can substitute for labour migration as a mechanism for reallocating resources across regions. But physical capital mobility eliminates the need for labour mobility only under restrictive assumptions.[8]

Given that the markets for labour and physical capital do not respond instantaneously to region-specific shocks, a number of authors have analysed market mechanisms and the policy measures that can insure against region-specific risk. Atkeson and Bayoumi (1993) explore the extent to which financial capital mobility can substitute for physical capital mobility. In their model, agents can diversify away the risk of region-specific shocks by holding financial assets the returns on which are uncorrelated with region-specific sources of labour and capital income. Sala-i-Martin and Sachs (1992) have suggested that regional problems can be alleviated through transfers of purchasing power from booming to depressed regions accomplished by federal fiscal systems. This creates a presumption that currency areas should coincide with fiscal jurisdictions.

This predominantly theoretical literature suggests an agenda for empirical research: (i) identifying the incidence of shocks, (ii) isolating their determinants, and (iii) analysing the market and policy responses. A remarkable feature of the scholarly literature—and of the debate over EMU—is how little empirical analysis has been devoted to these questions.

One approach to gauging the extent of asymmetric shocks has been to compute the variability of real exchange rates, since changes in relative prices reflect shifts in demand or supply affecting one region relative to another. Poloz (1990) compared regional real exchange rates within Canada with national real exchange rates between France, the UK, Italy and Germany. He found that real exchange rates between Canadian provinces were more variable than those between the four EC countries. Since Canada runs a successful monetary union, the implication is that the Community should be able to do likewise. Eichengreen (1992a) extended Poloz's analysis, using consumer price indices, to four US regions (North East, North Central, South and West) and ten Community countries. He found that real exchange rates within the EC have been more variable than real exchange rates within the US, typically by a factor of three to four. De Grauwe and Vanhaverbeke (1993) similarly considered real exchange rates of regions within individual European countries. Using data on unit labour costs for different regions within Germany, France, Spain, the UK and the Netherlands in the period 1977–85, they found that real exchange rates were significantly less variable within European countries than between them. One interpretation is that the European Community as a whole is significantly further from being an optimum currency area than are the individual countries makings up the Community.

In a related analysis, Eichengreen (1992a) analysed the covariance of real share prices in Toronto and Montreal and in Paris and Düsseldorf. In theory, the prices of equities should reflect the present value of current and expected future profits. If shocks are asymmetric, profits will rise in one market relative to the other. Real share prices in Toronto and Montreal were found to move more closely together than real share prices in Düsseldorf and Paris. There was evidence of convergence between Paris and Düsseldorf over time, but even in the 1980s the ratio of real share prices between Paris and Düsseldorf was five times as variable as the ratio for Toronto and Montreal.

A limitation of approaches which focus on relative prices, as pointed out by Eichengreen (1992a), is that they conflate information on the symmetry of shocks and on the speed of adjustment. If real share prices in two regions move together, this may indicate either that the two regions experience the same shocks or that capital is quick to flow from the region where the rate of return has fallen to the one where it has risen. Similarly, if the relative prices of the products of two regions show little variability, this may reflect either that their product markets experience the same supply and demand disturbances or that factors of production are quick to flow out of the region where prices have begun to fall and into the region where they have begun to rise, thereby minimizing relative price variability.

This has led other authors to focus on the behaviour of output rather than prices. Cohen and Wyplosz (1989) were first to use the time series of output to investigate the asymmetry of shocks.[9] They transform data on real GDP for France and Germany into sums and differences, interpreting movements in the sum as symmetric disturbances, movements in the difference as asymmetric disturbances. They remove a trend component from the sum and the difference using a variety of time-series techniques, and interpret the standard deviation of the de-trended series relative to the standard deviation of the original as a measure of the contribution of temporary disturbances to overall variability. They find that symmetric shocks are much larger than asymmetric shocks. (In other words, the variability of the sum is larger than the variability of the difference.) By their interpretation, symmetric shocks are predominantly permanent, while asymmetric shocks are predominantly temporary. (De-trending the sum eliminates much of its variability, while de-trending the difference has a smaller effect.)

The limitation of this approach is much the same as the one that focuses on prices. Observed movements in real GDP reflect the combined effects of shocks and responses. Using this methodology it is impossible to distinguish their separate effects.[10]

Independent evidence on the response to disturbances may permit information about the symmetry and magnitude of shocks to be extracted. Recent investigations have focused on the responsiveness of labour markets. The Organisation for Economic Cooperation and Development (OECD 1986) assembled data comparing inter-regional labour mobility within the USA and within EC countries. The tabulations suggest that mobility within the US has been two or three times as high as mobility within European countries. De Grauwe and Vanhaverbeke (1993) found a much higher degree of inter-regional labour mobility in northern European countries such as Germany, the UK and France than in southern countries like Spain and Italy. While they do not provide comparisons with the US, their numbers are consistent with those of the OECD study.

The problem with such evidence, again, is that a high degree of observed labour mobility may reflect either an exceptionally responsive labour market or exceptionally asymmetric regional labour market shocks. Eichengreen (1990b) therefore estimated time-series models of regional unemployment differentials for both Europe and the United States. He examined the speed with which rates of unemployment in individual EC countries converged to their long-run relationship to the EC average and compared his findings with data showing the speed at which regional unemployment rates in the US converged to the average for the USA as a whole. The results suggest that regional unemployment rates adjust to one another about 20% more rapidly in the United States than national unemployment rates adjust to one another within the EC.

Given the costs of migration, the movement of labour is a plausible mechanism mainly for adjusting to permanent shocks. Work on responses to temporary disturbances has focused on portfolio diversification and fiscal redistribution. Using data for US regions, Atkeson and Bayoumi (1993) estimate that recipients of capital income succeed in using portfolio diversification to insure against a significant proportion of region-specific income fluctuations, but that recipients of labour income do so only to a very limited extent.

On the effects of fiscal federalism, Sala-i-Martin and Sachs (1992) conclude that the US fiscal system offsets about one-third of a decline in regional personal incomes relative to the national average. In other words, when incomes in one US region fall by $1 relative to incomes in the nation as a whole, the fall in tax payments by that region to Washington, DC plus inward transfers from other regions via the expenditure side of the government budget is about 33 cents. Disposable income therefore falls by only 67 cents.[11]

These studies uniformly point to the conclusion that adjustment to region-specific shocks, whether by markets or by policy, is faster in the USA than in Europe. Hence, the smaller variability of output and prices across regions in the US than across countries in Europe may reflect the fact that the US exhibits either a faster response to larger, more asymmetric shocks or a faster response to smaller, less asymmetric shocks. The approaches utilized in previous studies thus fail to provide enough information to distinguish disturbances from responses.

4.3   Methodology

It is for this reason that we take an alternative approach to identifying disturbances. Our point of departure is the familiar aggregate demand and aggregate supply diagram, reproduced as the top panel in Figure 4.1. The aggregate demand curve (labelled AD) is downward sloping in the price/output plane, reflecting the fact that lower prices, by raising money balances, boost demand. The short run aggregate supply curve ($SRAS$) is upward sloping, reflecting the assumption that wages are sticky and hence that higher prices imply lower real wages. The long run supply curve ($LRAS$) is vertical, since real wages adjust to changes in prices in the long run.[12]

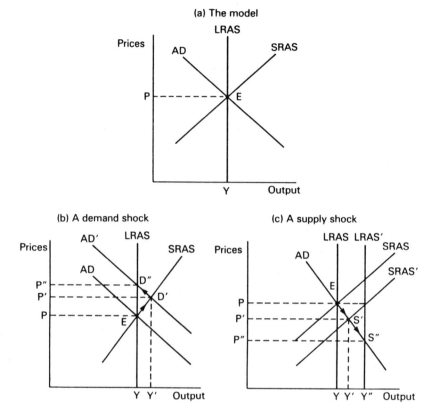

Figure 4.1
The aggregate demand and supply model.

The effect of a shock to aggregate demand is shown in the left half of
the lower panel. The aggregate demand curve shifts from *AD* to *AD'*,
resulting in a move in the equilibrium from initial point *E* to the new
intersection with the short run curve, *D'*. This raises both output and
prices. As the aggregate supply curve becomes more vertical over time, the
economy moves gradually from the short run equilibrium *D'* to its new
long run equilibrium, *D"*. This movement along the aggregate demand
curve involves the return of output to its initial level, while the price level
rises to a level which is permanently higher. (Depending on the price
mechanism, there could be cycling around the new long run equilibrium.)
Hence the response to a permanent (positive) demand shock is a short
term rise in output followed by a gradual return to its initial level, and a
permanent rise in prices.

The effect of a supply shock is shown in the right-hand bottom panel of Figure 4.1. Assume that the long run level of potential output rises, say because of a favourable technology shock. The short and long-run supply curves move rightwards by the same amount, as shown by $SRAS'$ and $LRAS'$. The short run effect raises output and reduces prices, shifting the equilibrium from E to S. As the supply curve becomes increasingly vertical over time, the economy moves from S' to S'', implying further increases in output and reductions in prices. Unlike demand shocks, supply shocks result in permanent changes in output. In addition, demand and supply have different effects on prices; positive demand shocks raise prices while positive supply shocks reduce them.

This model is estimated using a procedure proposed by Blanchard and Quah (1989) for decomposing permanent and temporary shocks to a variable using a vector auto regression (VAR) and extended by Bayoumi (1991).[13] Consider a system where the true model can be represented by an infinite moving average representation of a vector of variables, X_t, and an equal number of shocks, ε_t. Formally, using the lag operator L, this can be written as:

$$X_t = A_0 \varepsilon_t + A_1 \varepsilon_{t-1} + A_2 \varepsilon_{t-2} + A_3 \varepsilon_{t-3} \cdots$$

$$= \sum_{i=0}^{\infty} L^i A_i \varepsilon_t \tag{1}$$

where the matrices A_i represent the impulse-response functions of the shocks to the elements of X.

Specifically, let X_t be made up of the change in output and the change in prices, and let ε_t be demand and supply shocks. Then the model becomes

$$\begin{bmatrix} \Delta y_t \\ \Delta p_t \end{bmatrix} = \sum_{i=0}^{\infty} L^i \begin{bmatrix} a_{11i} & a_{12i} \\ a_{21i} & a_{22i} \end{bmatrix} \begin{bmatrix} \varepsilon_{dt} \\ \varepsilon_{st} \end{bmatrix} \tag{2}$$

where y_t and p_t represent the logarithm of output and prices, ε_{dt} and ε_{st} are independent supply and demand shocks, and a_{11i} represents element a_{11} in matrix A_i.

The framework implies that while supply shocks have permanent effects on the level of output, demand shocks only have temporary effects. (Both have permanent effects upon the level of prices.) Since output is written in first difference form, this implies that the cumulative effect of demand shocks on the change in output (Δy_t) must be zero. The model implies the restriction,

$$\sum_{i=0}^{\infty} a_{11i} = 0. \tag{3}$$

The model defined by equations (2) and (3) can be estimated using a
VAR. Each element of X_t can be regressed on lagged values of all the elements of X. Using B to represent these estimated coefficients, the estimating equation becomes,

$$X_t = B_1 X_{t-1} + B_2 X_{t-2} + \cdots + B_n X_{t-n} + e_t$$

$$= (I - B(L))^{-1} e_t$$

$$= (I + B(L) + B(L)^2 + \cdots) e_t$$

$$= e_t + D_1 e_{t-1} + D_2 e_{t-2} + D_3 e_{t-3} + \cdots \tag{4}$$

where e_t represents the residuals from the equations in the *VAR*. In the
case being considered, e_t is comprised of the residuals of a regression of
lagged values of Δy_t and Δp_t on current values of each in turn; these
residuals are labelled e_{yt} and e_{pt}, respectively.

To convert equation (4) into the model defined by equations (2) and (3),
the residuals from the *VAR*, e_t, must be transformed into demand and
supply shocks, ε_t. Writing $e_t = C\varepsilon_t$, it is clear that, in the two-by-two case
considered, four restrictions are required to define the four elements of the
matrix C. Two of these restrictions are simple normalizations, which
define the variance of the shocks ε_{dt} and ε_{st}. A third restriction comes from
assuming that demand and supply shocks are orthogonal.[14]

The final restriction, which allows the matrix C to be uniquely defined,
is that demand shocks have only temporary effects on output.[15] As noted
above, this implies equation (3). In terms of the *VAR* it implies,

$$\sum_{i=0}^{\infty} \begin{bmatrix} d_{11i} & d_{12i} \\ d_{21i} & d_{22i} \end{bmatrix} \begin{bmatrix} c_{11} & c_{12} \\ c_{21} & c_{22} \end{bmatrix} = \begin{bmatrix} 0 & \cdot \\ \cdot & \cdot \end{bmatrix} \tag{5}$$

This restriction allows the matrix C to be uniquely defined and the
demand and supply shocks to be identified.[16]

Clearly, interpreting shocks with a permanent impact on output as
supply disturbances and shocks with only a temporary impact on output
as demand disturbances is controversial. Doing so requires adopting the
battery of restrictions incorporated into the aggregate-supply-aggregate-
demand model of Figure 4.1. It is possible to think of frameworks other

than the standard aggregate-supply-aggregate-demand model in which that association might break down. Moreover, it is conceivable that temporary supply shocks (for example, an oil price increase that is reversed subsequently) or permanent demand shocks (for example, a permanent increase in government spending which affects real interest rates and related variables) dominate our data. But here a critical feature of our methodology comes into play. While restriction (5) affects the response of output to the two shocks, it says nothing about their impact on prices. The aggregate-supply-aggregate-demand model implies that demand shocks should raise prices while supply shocks should lower them. Since these responses are not imposed, they can be thought of as "over-identifying restrictions" useful for testing our interpretation of permanent output disturbances in terms of supply and temporary ones in terms of demand. Only if this over-identifying restriction is satisfied can we be confident of our interpretation of disturbances with permanent and temporary effects on output as supply and demand disturbances, respectively.

4.4 Data

Annual data on real and nominal GDP spanning the period 1960–88 were obtained from the OECD annual *National Accounts* for the 11 principal members of the European Community. This same source provided an aggregate measure of output and price performance for the EC as a whole.[17] These same data were collected for 11 additional OECD countries: six members of the European Free Trade Area (EFTA)—Sweden, Switzerland, Austria, Finland, Norway and Iceland—plus the United States, Japan, Canada, Australia and New Zealand. For each country growth and inflation were calculated as the first difference of the logarithm of real GDP and the implicit GDP deflator. The GDP deflator was used to measure prices since it reflects the price of output rather than the price of consumption. This distinction is particularly important for regional US data since the integration of the domestic goods markets minimizes differences in regional consumer price indices.[18]

For US regions, annual data on real and nominal gross product for the separate states were collected for 1963–86. The gross product series for the states, produced by the US Department of Commerce, is described in the *Survey of Current Business* (May 1988). It measures gross output produced by each state and hence represents the regional equivalent of the gross domestic product series in the OECD data. The data were aggregated into the eight standard regions of the United States used by the

Bureau of Economic Analysis, namely New England, the Mid-East, the Great Lakes, the Plains, the South East, the South West, the Rocky Mountain states and the Far West. As is the case for EC countries, these regions differ considerably in size; the Rocky Mountain region is the smallest, with under 3% of US population, while the Mid-East, South East and Great Lakes each contain around 20% of the US population. Growth and inflation for each region were calculated in the same way as for the OECD series, namely as the first difference in the logarithm of real gross product for the state and of the state's gross product deflator.

Before analysing these data, we consider them in their unprocessed form. Table 4.1 shows standard deviations and correlation coefficients for the logarithm of the growth in output and of inflation across eleven countries of the Community and the eight regions of the United States for the full data period.[19] The correlations are measured with respect to Germany in the case of the European Community and the Mid-East for the US.[20] The standard deviations indicate that output fluctuations have generally been somewhat smaller across EC countries than across US regions, while inflation variability has been higher in Europe. The correlation coefficients indicate that output growth is generally more highly correlated across US regions than EC countries, although two regions (the South West and the Rocky Mountains) show relatively idiosyncratic behaviour. For inflation, the correlation coefficients are much more highly correlated across US regions than EC countries, presumably reflecting the existence of a common currency.

In Tables 4.2 and 4.3 the analysis of correlations is extended. The share of the variance of output growth and inflation explained by the first principal component (the orthogonal component most correlated with the underlying series) is shown for different groups of countries or regions over several time periods. The results confirm the greater coherence of price and output movements among US regions than among EC countries. For the full period, the first principal component explained 74% of the variance in output movements for US regions but only 57% for EC countries. For inflation the comparable figures are 92% and 59% respectively.

For both the USA and the European Community the first principal component explained the largest share of the variance in output in the 1970s and the smallest share in the 1960s. This presumably reflects the fact that all countries and regions experienced an unusually severe recession following the first oil shock. For both the US and the EC the first

Table 4.1
Standard Deviations and Correlation Coefficients with Anchor Areas
(Logarithms of Raw Data)

	Growth of real GDP		Inflation	
	Standard deviation	Correlation	Standard deviation	Correlation
EC countries				
Germany	0.022	1.00	0.017`	1.00
France	0.018	0.74	0.031	0.47
Belgium	0.022	0.73	0.024	0.57
Netherlands	0.022	0.79	0.028	0.68
Denmark	0.025	0.67	0.023	0.69
United Kingdom	0.021	0.54	0.052	0.48
Italy	0.023	0.52	0.054	0.33
Spain	0.027	0.56	0.044	0.26
Ireland	0.022	0.09	0.050	0.49
Portugal	0.034	0.57	0.074	−0.07
Greece	0.035	0.66	0.067	0.00
US regions				
Mid-East	0.025	1.00	0.020	1.00
New England	0.031	0.94	0.020	0.98
Great Lakes	0.040	0.88	0.022	0.98
Plains	0.027	0.85	0.023	0.94
South East	0.027	0.76	0.022	0.72
South West	0.022	0.40	0.035	0.89
Rocky Mountains	0.024	0.27	0.024	0.84
Far West	0.033	0.66	0.018	0.96

Source: See text.
Note: All variables are measured in logarithms, so that 0.027 indicates a standard deviation
of approximately 2.7 percent.

86 Chapter 4

Table 4.2

Percentage of Variance Explained by the First Principal Component across Different Groups of Countries: Raw Data

	European Community (11 countries)	Other 11 OECD countries	EC core	EC periphery	EFTA	Control group
Growth of real GDP						
Full period	57	42	73	49	43	49
1963–71	40	39	73	35	51	49
1972–79	62	39	82	49	43	53
1980–88	44	46	54	42	42	57
Inflation						
Full period	59	54	64	70	53	57
1963–71	44	37	46	38	42	36
1972–79	39	46	58	52	44	59
1980–88	73	61	82	69	68	58

Notes: (a) Since the percentage of variance explained varies with the number of countries in the group, it is not useful to compare the results from the first two columns with those in the subsequent columns. The control group comprises USA, Japan, Canada, Australia, New Zealand and Iceland.
(b) The European Community excludes Luxembourg.

Table 4.3

Percentage of Variance Explained by the First Principal Component Across Different Groups of US Regions

	Eight US regions	Six "core" regions	Six "peripheral" regions
Growth of real GDP			
Full period	74	85	73
1966–72	79	88	78
1973–79	92	94	92
1980–86	78	92	74
Inflation			
Full period	92	93	92
1966–72	84	90	83
1973–79	70	77	67
1980–86	98	99	98

Note: The core regions comprise the Mid-East, New England, Great Lakes, Plains, South East and Far West while the peripheral regions are the Mid-East, Plains, South East, South West, Rocky Mountains and Far West.

principal component explained the largest share of the variance in inflation in the 1980s, presumably reflecting the extent to which price-level
trends in both the US and Europe were dominated by disinflation after
1980.

In Table 4.2, contrasts in the behaviour of output and prices in the EC
and in the 11 other industrial economies in our sample are shown.
Although the first principal component explained a larger share of the
variance of output in the EC than in the other industrial countries, this
appears to be because of the similar reaction of EC members to the oil
shock and to other events in the 1970s, rather than to the EMS and the
first steps toward completion of the internal market in the 1980s. In contrast, there is weak evidence of the effects of the EMS in the larger share
of the variance of inflation explained for the EC than for the other economies in the 1980s.

The failure to discern a large difference in the coherence of output
movements between the Community countries and the other industrial
economies reflects divergent movements not among what might be
regarded as the "core" members of the EC (Germany, France, Belgium,
Luxembourg, the Netherlands and Denmark)[21] but between the core and
the EC "periphery" (the UK, Italy, Ireland, Greece, Portugal and Spain). In
each sub-period, the first principal component explained much less of the
variance in output growth among peripheral countries, and generally less
for inflation. The coherence of price and output trends among the EFTA
countries was similar to that among the members of the EC periphery.
The final column of Table 4.2 shows the results for a control group, made
up of the five countries in our sample which are not members of the EC or
of EFTA plus Iceland. Iceland, an EFTA member, is included in the control
group in order to make the number of countries in each group equal.[22]
Again, the behaviour of this control group was not dissimilar to that of
the EC periphery.

Table 4.3 shows an analogous breakdown for the United States. The
second column, which excludes the South West and Rocky Mountains,
can be thought of as the US "core."[23] The third column, which excludes
the Great Lakes and New England, is intended to simulate a US "periphery." The second column confirms that output movements were more
closely synchronized, most notably in the 1980s, when the South West
and Rocky Mountains were removed. This presumably reflects the very
different composition of production in these two regions (dominated by
oil in the South West and by other minerals and raw materials in the

Rocky Mountain states). There is less difference in the behaviour of inflation, as if the integration of product markets encompasses even those
regions where the composition of local output is different.

The third column confirms that the picture is reversed when the Great
Lakes and New England are removed. Compared with Table 4.2, however, the contrast between columns is quite small, substantiating the view
of greater coherence of price and output trends among US regions than
within the EC and among other countries.

4.5 Results

To recover disturbances, we estimated bivariate *VAR*s for each country
and region in the sample. In all cases, the number of lags was set to 2,
since the Schwartz Bayesian information criterion indicated that all of the
models had an optimal lag length of either one or two.[24] A uniform lag of
two was chosen in order to preserve the symmetry of the specification
across countries. For the EC and other countries, the estimation period
was 1963–88, while for US regions it was 1966–86. For the OECD
countries, the estimation period includes a potential change in regime,
namely the break-up of the Bretton Woods fixed exchange rate system in
the early 1970s. Chow tests of the structural stability, however, produced
no evidence of a shift in the early 1970s. Limited analysis using data sets
which excluded the Bretton Woods period showed similar results to those
reported.

In nearly every case, the estimation and simulation results accord with
the aggregate-demand-aggregate-supply framework discussed in Section
4.3. The "over-identifying restriction" that temporary shocks, in order
to be interpreted as demand disturbances, should be associated with
increases in prices while permanent shocks, in order to be interpreted as
supply disturbances, should be associated with falls in prices was generally observed. In only three of the 30 cases, namely Norway, Ireland
and the Rocky Mountain region of the United States, was it impossible to
interpret the results using the aggregate-demand-aggregate-supply framework. Henceforth, we therefore refer to the permanent and temporary
shocks as supply and demand disturbances.

In Figure 4.2 some illustrative results are displayed. Output and price
impulse-response functions are shown for the EC and for the US as a
whole.[25] The impulse-response functions for output shown in panels (*A*)
and (*B*) illustrate the restriction that aggregate demand shocks have only
temporary effects on the level of output while supply shocks have per-

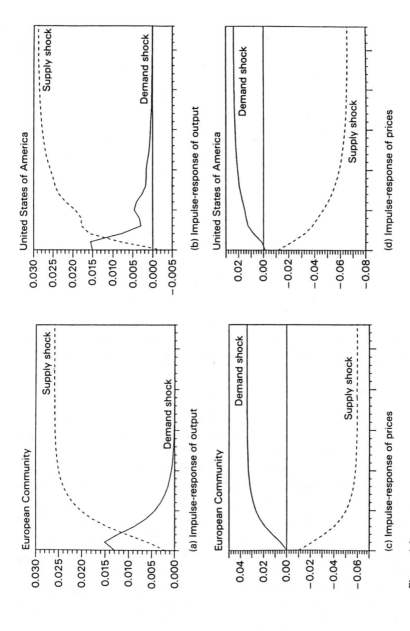

Figure 4.2
Impulse-response functions for the European Community and the United States.

manent output effects. Positive demand shocks produce a rise in output initially, which then reverts to its baseline level; the return to zero is imposed by the methodology, but the smooth adjustment path is not. By comparison, positive supply shocks produce a steady rise in output to a new higher equilibrium level. The impulse-response functions for prices in panels (C) and (D) show that the "over-identifying restriction" is satisfied. While both permanent and temporary shocks have long-run effects on the price level, temporary ("demand") shocks produce a gradual rise in prices over time, while permanent ("supply") shocks produce a steady decline in prices, as predicted by the aggregate-demand-aggregate-supply framework.

Three additional features of the impulse-response functions stand out.

(i) Demand shocks are more important than supply shocks for output in the short run. (By construction, they become progressively less important over time.) No such regularity holds for prices.

(ii) The impulse-response function for the US appears to show a faster response to shocks than that for the EC.

(iii) In contrast to the results for speed of response, the magnitude of response is remarkably similar for the US and for the EC, implying that the underlying shocks may be of a similar magnitude. (These are all issues to which we return later.)

In Figure 4.3 the underlying demand and supply shocks for the EC and US aggregates are shown. In the case of the EC, large negative disturbances to supply are evident in 1973–75 and 1979–80, corresponding to the two oil shocks, along with a large negative supply shock in 1968 which is more difficult to interpret. The demand disturbances illustrate the different response of the EC to the first and second oil crises; there was a large positive demand shock in 1976, while from 1980 onwards demand shocks were negative. In the case of the US the effects of the oil crises are also clearly evident, while the rapid recovery of the 1980s seems to be associated with a series of positive supply shocks (perhaps reflecting tax cuts which were supply-side friendly). There was a major negative demand shock in 1982, corresponding to the policy of disinflation pursued by the Federal Reserve System.

We now turn to the results for individual EC countries and US regions. We first examine the correlation of aggregate demand and supply shocks across EC members and standard US regions in order to identify similarities and differences between the two groups. We next consider com-

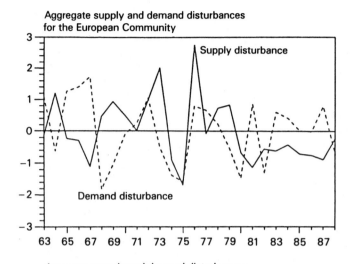

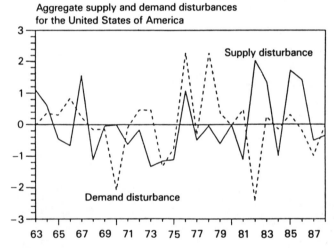

Figure 4.3
Aggregate demand and supply shocks for the European Community and the United States.

parisons over time in order to study whether the shocks to the EC have become more correlated as a result of the convergence of macroeconomic policy. Finally, we compare the magnitude of underlying demand and supply disturbances in Europe and the US and contrast their speed of adjustment.

4.5.1 Correlations

The first column of data in Table 4.4 shows correlation coefficients measuring the association of supply shocks in Germany with those in other EC countries. German supply shocks were highly correlated with those experienced by four of its close neighbours: France, the Netherlands, Denmark and Belgium. All four had correlation coefficients of 0.5 to 0.65, while the other six EC countries had lower correlations, in the order of −0.1 to +0.3.[26]

Table 4.4
Correlation Coefficients between Anchor Areas and Other Regions: Underlying Shocks

	Supply shocks	Demand shocks
EC countries		
Germany	1.00	1.00
France	0.54	0.35
Belgium	0.61	0.33
Netherlands	0.59	0.17
Denmark	0.59	0.39
United Kingdom	0.11	0.16
Italy	0.23	0.17
Spain	0.31	−0.07
Ireland	−0.06	0.08
Portugal	0.21	0.21
Greece	0.14	0.19
US regions		
Mid-East	1.00	1.00
New England	0.86	0.79
Great Lakes	0.81	0.60
South East	0.67	0.50
Plains	0.30	0.51
South West	−0.12	0.13
Rocky Mountains	0.18	−0.28
Far West	0.52	0.33

Note: The correlation coefficients refer to the entire data period: 1962–88 for the European Community and 1965–86 for the regions of the United States.

The bottom half of the table shows the same results for US regions (with the Mid-East being taken as the US centre analogous to Germany in the EC). The data display a similar pattern but with higher correlations than those of EC countries. The three US regions neighbouring the Mid-East (New England, the Great Lakes and the South East) had correlations of over 0.65, while the other four regions had lower correlations. The correlation between the Far West and the Mid-East was still relatively high (over 0.5), but that between the South West and the Mid-East was negative (presumably reflecting the importance of the oil industry in states like Texas and Oklahoma).

In effect, then, both the EC and the US appear to divide themselves into a "core" of regions characterized by relatively symmetric behaviour and a "periphery" in which disturbances are more loosely correlated with those experienced by centre. As in Europe, the US "core" is made up of areas that are neighbours of the centre region (the only exception being the Far West).

The results for demand disturbances, reported in column 2, are more difficult to characterize. All of the correlations for EC countries were in the range −0.1 to +0.4. As with supply disturbances, there is some evidence that demand disturbances are more highly correlated across core countries than among the members of the EC periphery. The simple arithmetic means of the respective sets of correlation coefficients are 0.31 and 0.10. The "core-periphery" distinction is less strong, however, for the demand shocks than for the supply shocks.

The correlation of regional demand disturbances for the US was higher than the analogous correlation for Europe. This is what could be expected in that US regions are members of a monetary union and should therefore experience similar monetary and (perhaps) fiscal shocks. The other three members of the US core all had correlation coefficients with the Mid-East in excess of 0.5. The Far West and the Plains had correlation coefficients of more than 0.33, while the two remaining regions had more idiosyncratic demand shocks.

In Figure 4.4 the correlation coefficients of demand shocks (on the vertical axis) and the correlation coefficients supply shocks (on the horizontal axis) are juxtaposed. (The top panel is for Germany and the other EC countries, while the lower panel is for the Mid-East and other US regions). While the distinction between "core" (with highly correlated supply shocks) and "periphery" is evident in both panels, it is also clear that the US regional data are characterized by higher correlations.

Chapter 4

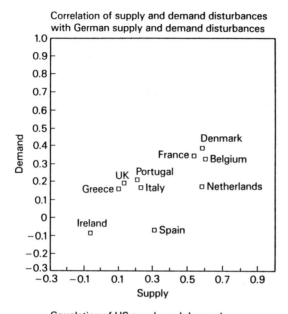

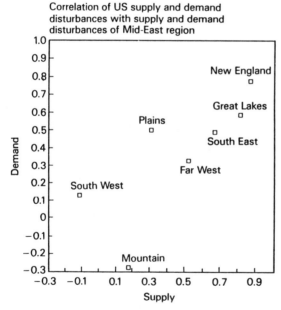

Figure 4.4
Correlation of demand and supply shocks with anchor areas.

Table 4.5
Percentage of Variance Explained by the First Principal Component for Geographic Groupings

Regions	European Community[a]	Other 11 OECD countries	EC core	EC periphery	Control group[b]	USA
Supply shocks						
Full period	33	26	54	32	33	49
1963–71	34	33	39	40	42	53
1972–79	44	41	63	41	51	65
1980–88	35	37	62	41	47	68
Demand shocks						
Full period	31	26	53	36	41	51
1963–71	30	34	58	30	37	44
1972–79	40	38	50	49	48	49
1980–88	40	34	54	43	56	75

[a] The European Community excludes Luxembourg.
[b] The control group comprises USA, Japan, Canada, Australia, New Zealand and Iceland. The sample period is 1962–88.

In Table 4.5 the correlations between demand and supply shocks are summarized using principal components analysis. Results are reported for three successive sub-periods as a way of exploring the extent to which supply and demand shocks in EC member countries have grown more similar over time. The first two columns compare the 11 member countries of the EC with the 11 other industrial economies. For the full sample period, aggregate supply and aggregate demand shocks for the EC countries were more correlated. The first principal component explained 31–33% of the variance for the 11 EC countries; for the others it explained only 26%. This pattern of higher correlations among EC countries generally held for sub-periods. There is, however, little or no evidence of convergence over time. There is no apparent tendency for the difference in the percentage of the variance explained for the EC and for the other 11 industrial countries to increase over time.

In columns 3–5 the results are extended to distinguish the EC core (Germany, France, Belgium, the Netherlands, Denmark and Luxembourg), the EC periphery (the UK, Italy, Spain, Portugal, Ireland and Greece), and a control group of other countries (the US, Japan, Canada, Australia, New Zealand and Iceland). The countries of the EC core had more correlated supply and demand shocks than either the periphery or the control group.

The difference is most striking for supply shocks: the first principal component explained 54% of the variance for the core EC countries, compared to 32% for the periphery, and 33% for the control group. In facts the first principal component actually explained a slightly lower percentage of variance for the EC periphery than for the control group. This is true for both supply and demand shocks and for the full data period. There is little indication, moreover, of convergence by newcomers to the EC—in other words, of a tendency for the correlation of disturbances among members of the EC periphery to rise over time compared to the correlation of disturbances among members of the control group.

The sixth column shows the results for the eight US regions. Their correlations are similar to those for the EC core but noticeably higher than those for the EC periphery and the control group. The correlations were considerably higher when the South West and Rocky Mountains were excluded than when all eight US regions were included. When the Great Lakes and New England were excluded, the correlations fell. Thus, the correlation of supply and demand disturbances across US regions is highly sensitive to the regions included. The core EC countries were consistently near the bottom of the range defined by the correlations for these sub-sets of US regions.

To summarize, the results for both the US and EC suggest that it is possible to distinguish core regions for which supply and demand shocks are highly correlated, and a periphery in which the correlation of shocks is less pronounced. Whether the eight US regions are compared with the 11 EC members or whether the comparison is limited to the EC and US core countries/regions, disturbances tended to be more highly correlated in the US.[27] Only if the core EC countries are compared with all eight US regions are the correlations of similar magnitude, although it should be recalled that in the case of demand shocks the higher US correlations may reflect the impact of uniform economic policies.

4.5.2   Size of Shocks

In addition to looking at the symmetry or correlation of shocks across regions, our methodology can also be used to estimate their relative size. The larger the size of the underlying shocks, the more difficult it may be to maintain a fixed exchange rate, and the more compelling may be the case for an independent economic policy response. This is particularly true of supply shocks, which may require more painful adjustment.

Table 4.6
Standard Deviations of Aggregate Supply and Aggregate Demand Shocks

	Supply shocks	Demand shocks
EC countries		
Germany	0.017	0.014
France	0.012	0.012
Belgium	0.015	0.016
Netherlands	0.017	0.015
Denmark	0.017	0.021
United Kingdom	0.026	0.017
Italy	0.022	0.020
Spain	0.022	0.015
Ireland	0.021	0.034
Portugal	0.029	0.028
Greece	0.030	0.016
US regions		
Mid-East	0.012	0.019
New England	0.014	0.025
Great Lakes	0.013	0.033
Plains	0.016	0.022
South East	0.011	0.018
South West	0.019	0.018
Rocky Mountains	0.018	0.015
Far West	0.013	0.017

Note: All variables are measured in logarithms, so that 0.027 indicates a standard deviation of approximately 2.7 percent.

In Table 4.6 the standard deviations of the aggregate demand and aggregate supply disturbances are given for the EC countries and the US regions. For the EC, the magnitude of supply shocks, like the correlation of supply shocks, suggests the existence of two distinct groups of countries. The core countries all have standard deviations in the range of 0.01 to 0.02 (1–2% per annum). The standard deviations for the periphery all range from 0.02 to 0.04 (2–4% per annum). Broadly speaking, then, the peripheral countries experience supply shocks twice as large as the core countries.

The supply shocks to US regions are similar to those experienced by the EC core and uniformly lower than those of the EC periphery. The standard deviation for the US South West, which at 0.019 is the largest for any US region, is still lower than that for any of the members of the EC periphery. There is also some indication that the US regions, particularly those in the core, experience smaller supply shocks than member

countries of the EC core; five of the eight US standard deviations are
below 0.15, compared to only one of five for the EC core countries.

The results for demand shocks, shown in the right hand column, are
quite different. Demand shocks in the EC core countries are slightly
smaller than those of the EC periphery. Germany and France, for example,
have the lowest standard deviations. More striking, however, is the comparison between the US and the EC. In contrast to the results for supply
shocks, the US regions actually have somewhat larger standard deviations
than the EC countries.

This finding is not a reflection of larger aggregate disturbances to the
US as a whole; the standard error for the US aggregate, using OECD
data, is 0.153—lower than that for most EC countries. The high variability of demand affecting US regions may therefore reflect the greater
specialization of industrial production in the US (for data on the concentration of industry within the US, see Krugman (1991a), Appendix D).
The large region-specific demand disturbances would then reflect shifts in
demand from the products of one region to those of another region. This
supposition is supported by the ranking of the size of demand disturbances across US regions. The largest demand disturbances are those
for the Great Lakes, Mid-East, Plains and New England regions, all of
which are relatively specialized while the South East and Far West, which
are more sectorally diversified, have lower variability. If this interpretation is correct, the evidence suggests that completion of the internal
market in Europe may well magnify aggregate demand disturbances by
leading to increased specialization.[28]

In Figure 4.5 (A)–(D) the size of disturbances against their correlation
with that of the centre country or region is juxtaposed. The vertical axis
measures the standard deviation of the disturbance, while the horizontal
axis shows the correlation. Panel A shows the results for supply shocks in
EC countries, B the results for supply shocks in US regions. Panels (C) and
(D) show the results for the demand disturbances. The panels are plotted
using the same scales to aid comparison. The supply disturbance panels
vividly illustrate the different behaviour of the core and periphery for
both the EC and the US. It is also clear, however, that the shocks affecting
the US periphery were much smaller than those affecting the EC periphery, making the lack of correlation with the anchor region somewhat less
of an issue. The data for the demand disturbances, on the other hand,
show relatively little pattern, although the relatively large shocks experienced by US regions are evident.

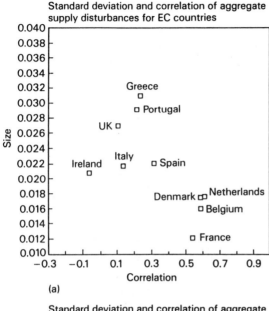

(a)

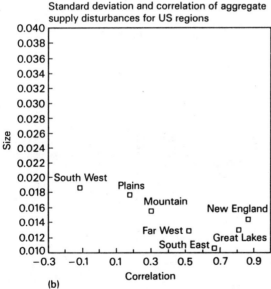

(b)

Figure 4.5(a, b)
The size and correlation of the demand and supply disturbances.

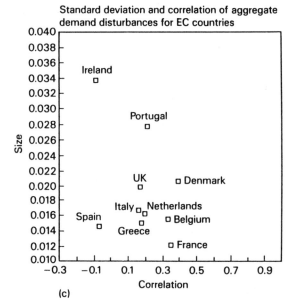

(c)

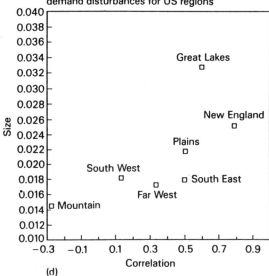

(d)

Figure 4.5(c, d)
The size and correlation of the demand and supply disturbances.

4.5.3   Speed of Adjustment to Shocks

In addition to isolating underlying disturbances, our procedure permits the responses of economies to shocks to be analysed. This can be done by looking at the impulse-response functions associated with the structural *VARs*. Two issues of interest can then be addressed. How does speed of adjustment by EC countries characterized by relatively low factor mobility but adjustable exchange rates compare with speed of adjustment by US regions characterized by high factor mobility but fixed exchange rates? Is there evidence of consistent differences among EC countries associated with openness or other structural characteristics?

In Figures 4.6 and 4.7 the impulse-response functions for output are displayed for the EC countries and for US regions. In Figure 4.6 the responses to supply shocks are shown; the top panel displays the impulse-responses for the core EC countries, the middle panel the responses for the remaining EC economies, and the bottom panel the responses for US regions.[29] A noticeable feature is the faster speed of adjustment for the US regions despite the lack of an exchange rate instrument within the US currency area. The bulk of the adjustment by the US regions to supply shocks occurred within three years; for EC countries it typically took substantially longer. A simple measure of the speed of adjustment is the ratio of the impulse-response function in the third year to its long run level; a high value indicates a fast adjustment, a low value a relatively slow adjustment. The average value of this statistic across US regions was 0.94, as opposed to 0.72 across EC countries. Interestingly, the average value for the EC core was also somewhat higher than that for the periphery.

The impulse-response functions to demand shocks shown in Figure 4.7 show a similar pattern. Again, the US regions appear to exhibit significantly faster responses than EC countries. One measure of the speed of this adjustment is to take the value of the impulse-response function after five years; a low value will now represent speedy adjustment. The values of the statistic were generally lower across US regions than EC countries, confirming the visual impression.

These *VAR* decompositions have allowed the analysis to proceed considerably further than simple comparisons of growth and inflation rates permit. The distinction between EC core and periphery is much less clear when the raw data are analysed. For example, the standard deviations of untransformed GDP growth rates for Italy and the UK were quite similar to those for Germany and France, while US regions tended to show relatively large variability in output growth. Our decomposition, by

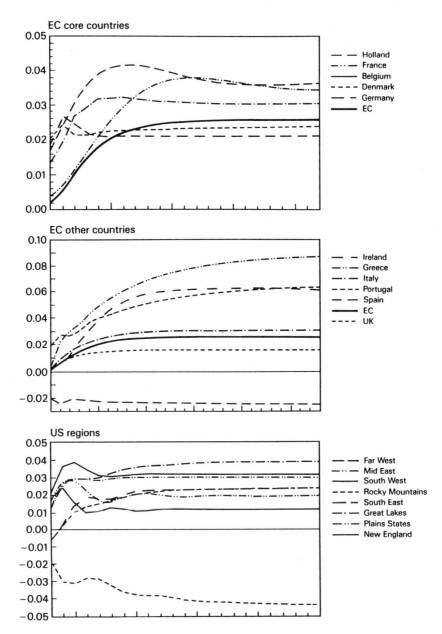

Figure 4.6
Impulse-response functions to a supply shock.

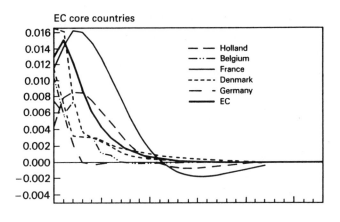

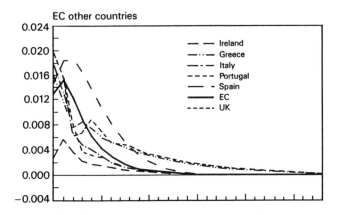

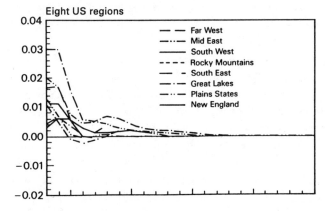

Figure 4.7
Impulse-response functions to a demand shock.

differentiating supply and demand disturbances from responses, allows the sources of this variability to be identified more precisely. Differences among countries and regions in the extent to which output variability and its sources are correlated with analogous variables in the centre country or region are less striking in the raw data than in the transformed series, rendering the former more difficult to interpret. Moreover, the calculations of the impulse-response functions allowed us to analyse the different set of issues revolving around speed of adjustment to shocks which cannot be addressed using the raw data.

4.6 Summary and Implications

In this chapter we have used structural vector auto regression to identify the incidence of aggregate supply and demand disturbances in Europe and to analyse the response of the economies of the European Community. A strong distinction emerges between the supply shocks affecting the countries at the centre of the European Community—Germany, France, Belgium, the Netherlands and Denmark—and the very different supply shocks affecting other EC members—the United Kingdom, Italy, Spain, Portugal, Ireland and Greece. Supply shocks to the core countries were both smaller and more correlated across neighbouring countries. The demand shocks experienced by the core countries were also smaller and more inter-correlated, although the difference on the demand side was less dramatic. There was also little evidence of convergence in the sense of the core-periphery distinction becoming less pronounced over time.

Our analysis of the American monetary union similarly suggests the existence of an economic core comprised of the Eastern Seaboard, the Mid-West and the Far West, along with a periphery comprised of the Rocky Mountain states and the South West. Shocks to the US core and periphery showed considerably more coherence than shocks to the analogous European regions. Only if the EC core is compared with the entire US (core and periphery together) were the magnitude and coherence of aggregate supply and demand disturbances comparable. The US does, however, contain two (relatively small) regions, the South West and the Rocky Mountains, where the underlying disturbances were relatively idiosyncratic.

Our impulse response functions indicate that the US regions adjust to shocks more quickly than do EC countries, in spite of the lack of the exchange rate instrument. This finding, which holds for both aggregate demand and aggregate supply shocks, plausibly reflects greater factor mobility in the United States than in Europe.

What are the implications of this analysis for the debate over EMU? Our finding that supply shocks are larger in magnitude and less correlated across regions in Europe than in the United States underscores the possibility that the European Community may find it more difficult, initially, to operate a monetary union than the United States. Large idiosyncratic shocks strengthen the case for policy autonomy and suggest that significant costs may be associated with its sacrifice. Our finding that the adjustment to shocks is faster in the US than in Europe emphasizes this point.

The strong distinction that emerges in our analysis between on the one hand, a core of EC member countries that experienced relatively small, highly-correlated aggregate supply disturbances, and on the other, a second group of countries, in which supply disturbances were larger and more idiosyncratic, is consonant with arguments that have been advanced for a two-speed monetary union (e.g., Dornbusch 1990). Information on other dimensions of the performance of these economies will be required, however, before we are in a position to pass judgement on the case for and against a two-speed EMU. Nevertheless, our analysis of disturbances suggest that for the time being, Germany and its immediate EC neighbours (the EC core) come much closer than the Community as a whole to representing a workable monetary union along American lines.

The conclusions reached in the preceding two paragraphs on the outlook for monetary unification in the EC reflect the fact that the results are based on historical data. The incidence of supply and demand shocks could well change with the completion of the 1992 programme and the transition to EMU. As market structures grow more similar across European countries, the incidence and correlation of supply disturbances should also become more similar. As factor mobility increases, the speed of adjustment to shocks should rise, approaching, if not necessarily matching, US levels. On the other hand, demand disturbances may grow less correlated across European countries as market integration leads to increased regional specialization.[30] Changes on the supply side will make monetary union easier to operate, while those on the demand side will introduce further difficulties; but both set of changes will work to make the incidence of supply and demand shocks across European nations resemble more closely those experienced in the United States. Thus, the comparative evidence for the US reported in this chapter remains a logical benchmark for those seeking to forecast the performance of the European economy once the transition to monetary and economic union is complete.

Notes

We wish to thank Peter Kenen, Jeff Frankel and our conference discussants, Giorgio Basevi and Patrick Minford, for helpful comments on earlier drafts. The text does not necessarily reflect the views of the Bank of England.

1. As of early 1991.

2. The argument that deficit spending will be constrained follows from the observation that investors will hesitate to purchase the additional bonds issued by a jurisdiction running a budget deficit if the implied debt service exceeds its capacity to raise revenues. The force of this argument is disputed. For reviews of the debate see Eichengreen (1992a), Bayoumi (1992) and Goldstein and Woglom (1991).

3. This change in response could take place through a number of different mechanisms. Horn and Persson (1988) suggest that EMU, by increasing the credibility of policy-makers' commitment to price stability, might enhance wage flexibility. The Commission of the European Communities (1990) argues similarly that EMU, by increasing the credibility of fiscal authorities' commitment not to bail out depressed regions, will encourage workers in such areas to moderate wage demands. Marsden (1989) suggests that increased product market integration, by reducing product market power at the national level, will make the derived demand for labour more price elastic, rendering wage setting more responsive to market conditions. Bertola (1988) presents arguments suggesting that once exchange rates are immutably fixed, workers will respond by adjusting on other margins, notably inter-regional migration. We discuss some potential limitations of the US-European comparisons below.

4. Here we review only selected aspects of the optimum currency area literature as they bear on the issues. A more comprehensive survey is given in Ishiyama (1975).

5. Symmetry of shocks is not the only criterion for the choice of an optimal currency area. Other factors such as the cost of operating an independent currency, size of trade with other regions, and (possibly) similarity of public preferences are also important. When comparing the current EC with the US, however, many of these differences are relatively small. In particular, both regions represent continent-wide industrial areas with a high degree of internal trade and similarly sized populations. Accordingly, this chapter will focus on the issue of the symmetry and size of the underlying shocks in EC countries as compared with those across US regions.

6. The Commission of the European Communities (1990) presents evidence on the similarity of industrial structure across EC countries and argues that product market integration will increase the scope of intra-industry trade, rendering national industrial structures increasingly similar over time. Krugman (1991a, 1993) suggests in contrast that completion of the internal market may lead to greater regional specialization and thereby magnify geographical differences in industrial structure. We return to this issue later.

7. The essence of this argument appears also in Scitovsky (1967).

8. If technology exhibits increasing returns, a shock which requires the expansion of one sector at the expense of another may require the inter-sectorial reallocation of both factors of production for full efficiency to be achieved. See Eichengreen (1990b). A taxonomy of cases is provided by Helpman and Krugman (1985).

9. Weber (1990) has extended their analysis of other EC countries.

10. De Grauwe and Vanhaverbeke (1993) study the variability of output across regions *within* European nations, arguing that this holds economic policies constant. But since it fails to hold the responsiveness of market adjustment mechanisms constant (such as, for example, internal migration and wage flexibility), which may themselves vary across regions, it remains difficult to distinguish disturbances from market responses. Eichengreen (1993c) estimated models of internal migration for the United Kingdom, Italy and the United States and similarly found support for the hypothesis of greater labour mobility in the US.

11. Using different econometric methods, von Hagen (1992) has suggested that regional co-insurance in the US is closer to one-tenth than one-third. More recently, Bayoumi and Masson (1995) have arrived at estimates which are close to those of Sala-i-Martin and Sachs. In any case, fiscal redistribution across US regions is much more extensive than across EC member countries. In terms of the automatic stabilizer response to cyclical movements within regions, Atkeson and Baymoui (1993) present evidence that the behaviour of US regions and EC countries is similar.

12. Although this is usually thought of as a closed economy model, it is readily extended to include trade and the exchange rate. Textbook descriptions of the model include Dornbusch and Fischer (1986) Ch. 11, and Hall and Taylor (1988) Ch. 4–5.

13. Quah (1991) discusses the issue of identifying restrictions for *VARs*. An important assumption which is required to ensure uniqueness of the decomposition is that the underlying series (growth and inflation in this case) are fundamental in a Wold sense, as pointed out by Lippi and Reichlin (1993).

14. The conventional normalization is that the two variances are set equal to unity, which together with the assumption of orthogonality implies $C'C = \Sigma$, where Σ is the variance-covariance matrix of e_y and e_p. When we wish to calculate the variance of the shocks themselves, however, we report results using the normalization $C'C = \Gamma$, where Γ is the correlation matrix of e_y and e_p. (See Bayoumi, 1991, for a discussion of this decomposition.) These two normalizations gave almost identical paths for the shocks, except for a scaling factor, and hence are used inter-changeably.

15. This is where our analysis, based on the work of Blanchard and Quah (1989), differs from other *VAR* models. The usual decomposition assumes that the variables in the *VAR* can be ordered such that all the effects which could be attributed to (say) either a_t or b_t are attributed to whichever comes first in the ordering. This is achieved by a Choleski decomposition.

16. Note from equation (4) that the long run impact of the shocks on output and prices is equal to $(I - B(1))^{-1}$. The restriction that the long run effect of demand shocks on output is zero implies a simple linear restriction on the coefficients of this matrix.

17. Two different measures of the EC aggregate are available from the OECD, one based on conversions of local currency data using 1985 dollars, and a second based on a weighting of the EC real GDP and GDP deflator indices. Since the two data sets gave very similar results, only those based on 1985 dollar exchange rates are reported.

18. For evidence and comparisons with Europe, see Eichengreen (1992a).

19. Since the data are in logarithms, a standard deviation of 0.012 implies an average deviation of 1.2%.

20. Germany is the largest economy in Europe, and has played the anchor role in the Exchange Rate Mechanism, making it the obvious standard for comparison. The Mid-East, which is the most important region in the US financially and, arguably, economically, is

taken as the analogous 'anchor' region of the US. These choices are retained in all subsequent analysis. Patrick Minford, in his comments, raised the question of whether our results for Europe are sensitive to the choice of Germany as the anchor area. In fact, this turns out not to be the case, as we elaborate below.

21. Luxembourg (which is otherwise excluded from the analysis because of its small size) was included in this part of the analysis in order to make the number of countries equal in each group. It should be stressed that the results from principal components analysis depend upon the number of series involved in the comparison. Hence it is not useful to compare the results for the EC 11 with (say) those for the six members of the EC periphery. Note that we have arbitrarily divided the EC countries and US regions into a core and periphery on the basis of our priors and by eyeballing correlation coefficients. In future work we plan to use cluster and discriminant analysis to sort these countries more systematically into groups, thereby getting at the issue known in Europe as 'variable geometry'.

22. We include six regions in each column and therefore render our principal-components analysis as consistent as possible. Since growth and inflation rates are relatively variable in Iceland, and since its supply and demand shocks are fairly loosely correlated with those of other countries, its inclusion will tend to make shocks to other countries appear coherent compared to the control group.

23. We show later that the two excluded regions respond differently to shocks from the rest of the US.

24. We also estimated VARs with three lags because, in contrast to the Schwartz Bayesian statistic, the Akaike information criterion showed the optimal lag to be above 2 in some of the models; this specification produced very similar results.

25. These results were obtained by estimating VARs on aggregate data for the US and EC, not by aggregating results obtained using regional US and national European data.

26. The same result holds when another member of the "core," say France, is substituted for Germany as the anchor area. The result for the "periphery" also continues to hold: on average, the peripheral countries do not exhibit a higher correlation with the other members of the core than they do with Germany. Nor do the peripheral countries exhibit as high a correlation with one another (or with a hypothetical anchor area like the UK or Italy) as do the countries of the core.

27. This is particularly true if account is taken of the fact that several of the peripheral US regions are quite small. Together the Rocky Mountains and South West contain less than 12% of the US population.

28. Our results concerning the magnitude of disturbances are broadly consistent with the more impressionistic evidence presented by Krugman (1993). Both studies suggest that market integration of the type that characterizes the US leads to regional specialization and large region-specific shocks. The main difference is that Krugman, basing his interpretation on Blanchard and Katz (1992), argues that these region-specific disturbances are permanent, whereas our evidence suggests that the component of disturbances associated with US-style market integration is largely temporary. One explanation for this difference in interpretation is the following. Blanchard and Katz identify a single regional disturbance the long-run effect of which on activity (measured by employment) is slightly larger than its initial impact; hence the view that disturbances have permanent effects. We identify two disturbances with permanent and temporary effects on activity. The permanent disturbance typically has a long-run effect which is much larger than its impact effect, while the temporary disturbance has no long-run effect (see Figures 4.6 and 4.7). A weighted average of these two paths can

give an aggregate response of the type identified by Blanchard and Katz, while still implying a large role for temporary disturbances in regional activity. Hence we believe our results are not inconsistent with those in the work of Blanchard and Katz; rather they result from a more detailed disaggregation of the underlying data.

29. The larger scale required for the EC periphery is another illustration of the relatively large shocks they experience.

30. Note that our estimates for successive sub-periods (in Table 4.5), including pre- and post-EMS decades, suggest that market integration works only slowly to alter the incidence of supply and demand disturbances.

5

Ever Closer to Heaven? An Optimum Currency Area Index for European Countries

5.1 Introduction

Like it or not, the theory of optimum currency areas (OCAs) remains the workhorse for analyses of European monetary unification. Indeed, many economists do not like it very much. OCA theory, with its focus on asymmetric shocks, labor mobility, and the transactions value of a single currency, subsumes but a subset of considerations relevant to the decision of whether to fix the exchange rate or form a monetary union. The theory has advanced only minimally since the seminal contributions of Mundell (1961), McKinnon (1963), and Kenen (1969). It remains difficult to move from theory to empirical work and policy analysis. A popular device is to conclude a review of the theoretical literatures by stating that "Europe is not an optimal currency area," without providing much analysis of how this situation is changing or of the comparative prospects of different countries.

In this chapter we develop a procedure for applying the core implications of the theory of optimum currency areas to cross-country data. We demonstrate that these implications find strong empirical support. The relationship between the characteristics of countries to which OCA theory points and the observed behavior of exchange rates seems sufficiently stable and robust to support simple forecasting. Extrapolating the independent variables, we therefore use our exchange-rate equations to predict which countries will be best able to support stable exchange rates in the future—equivalently, which are likely to be best prepared to be among the founding members of Europe's monetary union.

Originally published in *European Economic Review* (1997), with Tamim Bayoumi. Reprinted with permission.

5.2   Operationalizing the Theory of Optimum Currency Areas

The key to our approach to operationalizing the theory of optimum currency areas is to analyze the determinants of nominal exchange-rate variability. By contrast, most earlier analysis of the choice of exchange-rate
regime has used relatively judgmental categorizations of exchange-rate
arrangements.[1] The variability of real and nominal exchange rates is itself
the outcome of the choice of exchange-rate regime and as such should
contain information about the decision of which arrangement to adopt.
Actual exchange-rate behavior may in fact convey more information
about underlying economic determinants than the putative exchange-rate
regime. Countries not only have to adopt an exchange-rate arrangement,
in other words; they also have to maintain it. Thus, the limited dependent
variable on which most previous investigators focus does not make use
of all the information available in the variability of the exchange rate.
Throughout, we analyze annual data on bilateral exchange rates for twenty-
one industrial countries.[2]

OCA theory focuses on characteristics that make stable exchange rates
and monetary unification more or less desirable. The most important of
these are asymmetric disturbances to output, trade linkages, the usefulness
of money for transactions, the mobility of labor, and the extent of automatic stabilizers. While the last two characteristics are clearly important
for behavior across regions within a country, they have not played a significant role in responding to shocks that are felt asymmetrically across
countries, at least over our sample period. Consequently, our empirical
work focuses on capturing the first three factors.[3]

We measure output disturbances as the standard deviation of the
change in the log of relative output in the two countries. Thus, for countries in which business cycles are symmetric and national outputs move
together, the value of this measure will be small.[4] We add the dissimilarity
of the commodity composition of the exports of the two countries as a
second proxy for the asymmetry of shocks on the grounds that industry-
specific shocks will be more symmetric when two countries have a revealed comparative advantage in the same export sectors.[5]

We measure the importance of trade linkages using data on bilateral
trade, computing the average value of exports to the partner country,
scaled by GDP (gross domestic product), for the two countries concerned.
The costs of a common currency, in terms of macroeconomic policy independence foregone, should be balanced against the benefits, which will be

greatest for small economies where there is least scope for utilizing a separate national currency in transactions. That is, small countries should benefit the most from the unit of account, means of payment, and store of value services provided by a common currency. We measure the benefits from a more stable currency by including the arithmetic average of (the log of) real GDP in U.S. dollars of the two countries as a measure of country size.[6]

The estimating equation is therefore

$$SD(e_{ij}) = \alpha + \beta_1 \, SD(\Delta y_i - \Delta y_j) + \beta_2 \, DISSIM_{ij} + \beta_3 \, TRADE_{ij} + \beta_4 \, SIZE_{ij},$$

$$(1)$$

where $SD(e_{ij})$ is the standard deviation of the change in the logarithm of the end-year bilateral exchange rate between countries i and j, $SD(\Delta y_i - \Delta y_j)$ is the standard deviation of the difference in the logarithm of real output between i and j, $DISSIM_{ij}$ is the sum of the absolute differences in the shares of agricultural, mineral, and manufacturing trade in total merchandize trade, $TRADE_{ij}$ is the mean of the ratio of bilateral exports to domestic GDP for the two countries, and $SIZE_{ij}$ is the mean of the logarithm of the two GDPs measured in U.S. dollars.[7] In each case, the independent variables are measured as averages over the sample period. We focus on the variability of nominal rates rather than their real counterparts because nominal rates provide an easier benchmark for comparison to a single currency—with a single currency the variability of the nominal exchange rate is zero. In related work (Bayoumi and Eichengreen 1996a), we have found that equations of the type reported in the text generated similar results for both nominal and real exchange rates.

For 1983–92, estimation yielded the following (with standard errors in parentheses):

$$SD(e_{ij}) = -0.09 + 1.46 \, SD(\Delta y_i - \Delta y_j) + 0.022 \, DISSIM_{ij}$$
$$\quad\quad\;\; (0.02)\;\;(0.21) \quad\quad\quad\quad\quad (0.006)$$

$$\quad\quad - 0.054 \, TRADE_{ij} + 0.012 \, SIZE_{ij},$$
$$\quad\quad\;\; (0.006) \quad\quad\quad\quad (0.001) \quad\quad n = 210, R^2 = 0.51, S.E. = 0.027$$

$$(2)$$

Thus, all four variables have the anticipated signs and coefficients that differ from zero at the one percent confidence level. We take this as strong support of the empirical implications of the theory of optimum currency areas.

5.3 Prediction and Forecasting

Out-of-sample forecasting is problematic if the relationship of structural characteristics to exchange-rate behavior is not stable over time. We therefore ran the above regression for successive moving averages of ten-year periods: 1973–82, 1975–84, 1977–86, 1979–88, 1981–90, and 1983–92. The coefficients on the two trade-related variables (the similarity of exports and the importance of bilateral trade) prove quite stable. In contrast, the two output-related variables (economic size and relative output variability) tend to increase after 1975–84. This may reflect the ERM, through whose operation European countries were increasingly able to stabilize their exchange rates in the face of structural differences and cyclical disturbances. The estimated equation for the most recent period is broadly consistent with those for earlier years, supporting its use for forecasting purposes.

To forecast the dependent variable, it is necessary to construct projections of the independent variables. To project asymmetric shocks, we calculated $SD(\Delta y_i - \Delta y_j)$ over a ten-year period centered on the current year. This variable was then regressed on a constant term and a time trend for the period 1971–87, and the results were used to project for the period 1988–95. The coefficient on the trend was negative, suggesting that asymmetric shocks have been diminishing; hence, this is our implicit assumption about the effect of continued European integration.[8] To project the similarity of export structures, we extrapolated the change over the two most recent three-year periods. For economic size and the export ratio, we used actual data.

Table 5.1 shows forecasts of the dependent variable, which we refer to as the OCA index, vis-à-vis Germany in 1987, 1991, and 1995.[9] (See also figure 5.1.) 1987 is the last year with full data on all variables (for subsequent years it is necessary to base our measure of asymmetric shocks on projections). 1995 reflects the current state of affairs, while 1991 gives some sense of trends over time. The countries divide into three groups: prime candidates for EMU, those which are converging to EMU, and those for which the index shows little convergence. More work will, of course, be needed to test the robustness of our results to alternative empirical approaches.

In the first group are Austria, Belgium, and the Netherlands, joined recently by Ireland and Switzerland. All these countries have indices in 1995 under 0.025 (less than one standard error for the regression as a

Table 5.1
OCA Indexes versus Germany, 1987–95

	1987	1991	1995
France	0.068	0.067	0.074
Italy	0.070	0.065	0.059
U.K.	0.099	0.094	0.089
Austria	0.008	−0.004	0.008
Belgium	0.003	−0.008	0.013
Denmark	0.063	0.060	0.074
Finland	0.098	0.095	0.087
Greece	0.053	0.054	0.054
Ireland	0.043	0.036	0.021
Netherlands	0.003	−0.008	0.007
Norway	0.078	0.078	0.077
Portugal	0.068	0.066	0.062
Spain	0.088	0.082	0.073
Sweden	0.068	0.063	0.056
Switzerland	0.038	0.030	0.023

Note: For details on the construction of the OCA indexes, see the text.

whole).[10] There is striking conformance between the makeup of this group and press commentary, circa mid-1996, on the leading candidates for Stage III, except for the presence of Switzerland, which is not an EU member, and the absence of France, whose participation is widely regarded as essential to the political viability of the enterprise. Austria and the Benelux countries have been closely linked to the German economy for many years. The result for Ireland is interesting, since our index of its convergence in economic structure and cyclical position corresponds to the convergence observed under the Maastricht criteria.[11] For the sample as a whole, however, there is strikingly little correlation between the deficit ratio and our OCA index (see figure 5.2).

The second group, countries for which there is little convergence, includes the United Kingdom, Denmark, Finland, Norway, and France. In all cases, the forecast standard deviation of the exchange rate in 1995 using the OCA index equation is large (greater than 0.07, over $2\frac{1}{2}$ times the standard error of the regression) and shows little tendency to decline over time. These results suggest structural reasons for the decisions of the U.K. and Denmark to demand opt-out clauses from EMU and for

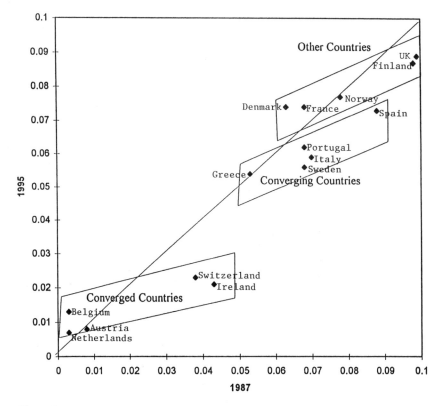

Figure 5.1
Movements in OCA indexes over time.

Norway's decision to opt out of EMU by opting out of the EU. While the Maastricht criteria show Finland converging over time, this is not evident in our OCA index. The most striking result is that our analysis places France in the group of countries for whom there is little evidence of convergence, despite its recent history of low exchange-rate variability vis-à-vis Germany.

The final group, countries that are gradually converging toward EMU, includes Sweden and the EU's southern tier: Italy, Greece, Portugal, and Spain. In all cases these countries' OCA indices are declining over time. They average 0.06 for 1995. Spain's is the largest, at 0.072, not dissimilar from that of some of the nonconvergers. Assuming for sake of argument that their OCA indices continue to trend downward at the same rate through 1999, they will remain around 0.05 in most cases, still relatively large by the standards of the first group.

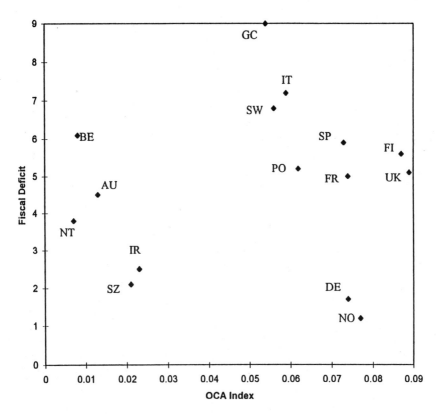

Figure 5.2
Fiscal policy and OCA indexes, 1995.

Cross-country differences in the average level of the OCA index are driven mainly by relative size (which does not vary over time) and the importance of bilateral trade. Thus, the poor average OCA index for France reflects the fact that it is large and relatively closed (by European standards), so that while it trades a lot with its EU partners, bilateral trade as a share of GDP is rarely very high. Changes over time in the index are dominated by changes in the intensity of bilateral trade and asymmetric output movements. The first of these findings suggests that an important factor driving convergence is the role of the EU in promoting intra-European trade. Insofar as European integration has worked to encourage trade among EU members, there may have been a tendency to encourage monetary integration.[12] This supports the argument of the European

Table 5.2
OCA Indexes for Specific Relationships, 1987–95

	1987	1991	1995
France—Italy	0.060	0.059	0.052
France—Spain	0.064	0.060	0.048
France—Portugal	0.053	0.055	0.053
Sweden—Finland	0.032	0.035	0.027
Sweden—Norway	0.039	0.043	0.046
Italy—Greece	0.057	0.043	0.027
Spain—Portugal	0.037	0.024	0.013

Note: For details on the construction of the OCA indexes, see the text.

Commission that perfecting the Single Market, which can be expected to promote trade, is essential for a successful transition to EMU.

While we have focused on structural relationships vis-à-vis Germany, the same approach can be used to analyze other bilateral relationships and shed light on other issues. In table 5.2 we show our OCA index for some other bilateral exchange rates. These suggest that Italy and Spain's enthusiasm for EMU may hinge on France's participation, while that of some smaller countries will depend on the participation of larger neighbors; they suggest, for example, that Finland's interest in EMU may hinge on Swedish participation.[13] Similar considerations are evident in the cases of Portugal and Spain and of Greece and Italy. These results suggest significant interdependencies when the time comes to constitute and enlarge the monetary union.[14]

5.4   Conclusion

Our goal in this chapter has been to operationalize the theory of optimum currency areas by constructing an OCA index based on a particular empirical specification that summarizes countries' readiness for EMU, as predicted by the core implications of that theory. The results show European countries dividing into three groups: those exhibiting a high level of readiness, those with a tendency to converge, and those in which little or no convergence is evident. The makeup of the groups tends to coincide with popular handicapping of the Maastricht stakes with one notable exception: France. Our estimates of France's OCA index does not indicate that the country's structural characteristics and cyclical performance are consistent with a high level of bilateral exchange-rate stability vis-à-vis

Germany or an easy transition to monetary union. This finding supports the view that the desire for monetary unification in France is driven by political rather than economic considerations.

A further finding is the symbiotic relationship between economic integration and monetary integration. Countries among whom the completion of the Single Market has led to the greatest increase in bilateral trade have experienced the greatest increase in their readiness for monetary integration according to our OCA index. Economic integration has thus increased countries' readiness for monetary integration. Conversely, insofar as stable exchange rates encourage trade, monetary integration in the form of the EMS has also helped advance economic integration. Together, these findings support the notion that EMU and the Single Market can constitute a virtuous, self-reinforcing circle.

Notes

We thank Andrew Hughes-Hallett and others at the European Economic Association in Istanbul, August 22–24, 1996, for useful comments and suggestions. None of the views expressed are necessarily the positions of the IMF.

1. These previous studies follow the IMF's *Exchange and Trade Restrictions* volumes in characterizing exchange rates as pegged or flexible, or as pegged, displaying limited flexibility and displaying greater flexibility. See Savvides (1993) for a review of the literature.

2. These are the principal European economies plus the United States, Canada, Japan, Australia, and New Zealand. This focus on industrial countries distinguishes our work from previous studies of the determinants of exchange-rate variability. While we focus here on nominal exchange rates, results for real exchange rates were quite similar.

3. In related work (Bayoumi and Eichengreen 1996a) we look at a somewhat more general specification, including non-OCA variables such as the depth of financial systems. The results are similar to those reported here.

4. It would be preferable to decompose relative output movements into relative supply shocks, relative demand shocks, and the respective economies' response to each. Elsewhere (Bayoumi and Eichengreen 1993b), we have applied a methodology for distinguishing supply and demand shocks, but this is infeasible to implement with the relatively short time series utilized here.

5. To construct this variable, we collected data on the shares of manufactured goods, food, and minerals in total merchandise trade for each country. Manufactured goods are defined as the total of basic manufactures, chemicals, machines and transport equipment, miscellaneous manufactured goods, and other goods. Food is the sum of food and live animals, beverages and tobacco, and animals, vegetable oils, and fats. Minerals amalgamate data on crude materials excluding fuel with mineral fuels, etc. The dissimilarity of the commodity composition of two countries' exports was then defined as the sum of the absolute values of the differences in each share (with higher values indicating less similarity in the composition of commodity exports between the two countries).

6. An alternative, suggested by McKinnon, is to use openness to international trade as a measure of the benefits from stabilizing the exchange rate. However, economic size would appear to be a better measure of the benefits from a stable currency, as a comparison between the benefits provided by the national currencies of Germany (a large and relatively open economy) and Spain (a smaller and more closed economy) should make clear.

7. A potential technical concern with this specification is that not all of the entries for the dependent variable are independent of each other. However, while it is true that *changes* in bilateral rates are not independent (the change in the bilateral rate between the dollar and the yen is equal to the change between the dollar and the deutsche mark and between the deutsche mark and the yen), the *standard deviations* of these rates are independent as the covariances can differ across pairs of countries.

8. Bini-Smaghi and Vori (1993) and Frankel and Rose (1996) similarly argue that European integration should increase the symmetry of shocks.

9. We consider indices for bilateral rates against Germany because that country is widely viewed as the core member of EMU to which other potential participants need to converge. The value of 0.074 for France in 1995 is the standard deviation of the logarithm of the nominal bilateral exchange rate predicted by the equation. Since the data are in logs, this is approximately $7\frac{1}{2}$ percent per annum.

10. By way of contrast, the OCA indexes between the three largest industrial countries, the United States, Germany, and Japan, vary between 0.09 and 0.15.

11. The relationship between structural characteristics of countries, as suggested by OCA theory, and the convergence criteria of the treaty is the subject of De Grauwe (1996). Ireland's OCA index with the United Kingdom, a country with which it has traditionally had close monetary ties but with whom these ties have been waning, remains below that of Germany.

12. This finding could simply reflect the existence of the ERM, but the rolling regressions tend to refute this interpretation.

13. In contrast, Norway's OCA index vis-à-vis Sweden is rising over time, indicating a diminishing pull to EMU, which plausibly reflects in the impact on its external economic relations of the decision to stay out of the EU.

14. For a theoretical discussion of these interdependencies, see Bayoumi (1994).

6   Labor Markets and European Monetary Unification

6.1   Introduction

Monetary unification promises to revolutionize the conduct of macro-economic policy in Europe. Countries previously free to pursue independent monetary policies will be forced to toe a common line. New constraints will be placed on the conduct of fiscal policy, whether the monetary union treaty incorporates explicit ceilings on budget deficits or governments are simply precluded from printing money to finance public spending.[1] Economic and Monetary Union, or EMU, insofar as it entails a loss of policy autonomy, may involve real economic costs as well as the convenience and efficiency gains of transacting in one rather than several national currencies.

In his seminal article on optimum currency areas, Mundell (1961) identified two criteria useful for evaluating such costs. The first is the incidence of shocks. If disturbances are distributed symmetrically across countries, a common policy response will suffice. In response to a negative aggregate demand shock, for example, that is common to all EMU countries, a common policy response in the form of a simultaneous monetary and/or fiscal expansion may be all that is required. Only if disturbances are distributed asymmetrically across countries will there be occasion for an asymmetric policy response and may the constraints of monetary union bind.

The second criterion identified by Mundell is the extent of labor mobility. The more mobile is labor the less is the need for different policy responses to prevent the emergence of regional problems. Labor can simply move from the depressed to the booming region, eliminating the need

Originally published, as chapter 6, in *Policy Issues in the Operation of Currency Unions*, ed. Paul Masson and Mark Taylor (Cambridge: Cambridge University Press, 1993), 130–62. Reprinted with permission.

for an asymmetric policy response. When labor mobility is limited, in contrast, regional unemployment problems may persist unless the depressed region is allowed to pursue independent policies and, if necessary, to depreciate its currency.

Recent researchers have devoted considerable attention to the incidence of shocks.[2] Bayoumi and Eichengreen (1993a, 1993b), for example, found that shocks to eleven EC member countries have been more asymmetrically distributed than shocks to the eight census regions of the United States. Whereas common factors account for 49 percent of the variance of supply shocks to US regions from the 1960s through the 1980s, they explain only 33 percent of the variance of supply shocks to EC countries.[3] In the case of demand shocks, common factors account for 51 and 33 percent of the variance for the US and Europe, respectively. According to Mundell's first criterion, then, the EC is less of an optimum currency area than the United States.

In comparison, little systematic attention has been directed toward the analysis of labor mobility. Previous studies cited in Eichengreen (1992a) indicate that observed migration rates are lower in Europe than in the US. Not only are migration rates between European nations relatively low, but so are migration rates within those nations. Americans move between US states about three times as frequently as Frenchmen move between *départements* and Germans move between *lander*. If Europeans move little among regions of European nations within which culture and language are relatively minor barriers to mobility, they can hardly be expected to move between European nations once statutory barriers to migration are removed. On the basis of this evidence, Mundell's second criterion also suggests that the EC is less of an optimum currency area than the United States.

One problem with simple comparisons of migration rates is that the geographic units of analysis may not be strictly comparable. Another is that the economic determinants of labor mobility are not held constant. Labor may move less within European countries not because it is less mobile intrinsically but because it has less incentive to move. While previous work on the incidence of disturbances has shown shocks to European countries to be distributed asymmetrically, it still could be that shocks to regions within individual European countries are relatively symmetric.[4] Hence labor may not move between regions within European countries because it has no reason to do so, not because it is unwilling or unable.

If labor really is mobile within European countries, then it may become almost as mobile among them once remaining statutory barriers to migration come down.[5] Relinquishing the exchange rate as a policy instrument may then be of no more consequence than it is for the regions of the United States. Asymmetric policy responses will not be required in response to asymmetric shocks, since labor can simply move from depressed to booming regions. The benefits of EMU are then likely to dominate the costs.

This chapter presents a preliminary exploration of the implications of European labor-market performance for EMU. The analysis comes in three parts. The first part investigates shocks to regional labor markets in Great Britain, Italy, and the United States. Britain and Italy are two countries where the regional problem is prominent, while the US is the obvious basis for comparison. The second part of the analysis considers the migratory response in the three countries. Migration is not the only way in which regional labor-market disequilibria can be eliminated, of course; others include adjustments in regional wages and prices, inter-regional capital movements and inter-regional fiscal transfers. The third part of the analysis therefore asks directly how quickly regional labor-market equilibrium is restored. This three-part analysis is preceded by an overview of regional labor-market conditions and followed by a brief conclusion.

The results are striking. First, the dispersion of shocks to regional labor markets is quite similar across the three countries. The variability of the response of regional unemployment to changes in national unemployment is smaller in the US than in Britain, and smaller in Britain than in Italy, but the differences are minor. Moreover, the variability of the response of regional unemployment to changes in the nation's real exchange rate is the same for Italy and the US and somewhat lower for Britain. On the basis of these results, there is little reason to think that labor-market disturbances are more asymmetrically distributed within Britain and Italy than within the United States.

Second, the responsiveness of migration to regional labor-market disequilibria is greater in the US than in either Britain or Italy. The elasticity of migration with respect to inter-regional wage differentials is at least five times as large for the US as for Britain. The estimated wage elasticity for Italy is smaller still. International variations in the elasticity of migration with respect to inter-regional unemployment differentials are less pronounced, but they too point to the greater responsiveness of labor flows in the United States. The implication is that labor mobility works less powerfully in Europe than in the US to eliminate regional labor-market disequilibria.

The third finding is surprising in light of the previous two. Despite that shocks to regional labor markets in the US and Europe are of comparable magnitude and that migration in the US responds more powerfully to those shocks, it is not obvious that deviations from the long-term relationship among regional unemployment rates are more persistent in Europe than in the US. Though the evidence on this question is not clearcut, it appears that, when disturbances cause regional unemployment rates within European countries to diverge, other mechanisms, perhaps including relative wage adjustments, labor-force participation rates, interregional capital mobility, and government policy, substitute adequately for Europe's limited labor mobility in order to bring them back into line.

6.2   An Overview of Regional Labor Markets

The last decade and a half in the industrial economies has been characterized by volatile unemployment fluctuations at both the national and regional levels. This section sketches the outlines of those fluctuations and provides some discussion for Britain, Italy, and the United States.

Unemployment in Britain, displayed in figure 6.1, is dominated by the steady rise after 1974, reflecting first the oil shock and then the Thatcher disinflation.[6] Figure 6.2 shows the very different rates of unemployment that prevailed in different regions at the end of the period.[7] Prominent in that figure is the north–south divide, with unemployment well below the national average in the South and East Anglia, slightly below average in the East Midlands, and above average in the West Midlands, the North, Wales, and Scotland.

In part, the varying fortunes of different regions reflect the composition of economic activity. Wales for example relies for much of its income and employment on metal manufacturing and on the energy sector (coal mining and oil refining), which fell on hard times in the 1980s. The North and Yorkshire–Humberside are similarly oriented toward energy and heavy manufacturing, particularly minerals, metals, and chemicals. Unemployment in the West Midlands is associated with a higher share of employment in the manufacturing sector than any other Britain region, and with the fact that it depends on a relatively narrow range of industries centering on engineering and motor vehicles which were depressed for most of the 1980s.

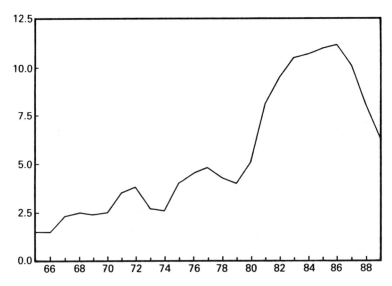

Figure 6.1
UK unemployment rate, 1966–88.

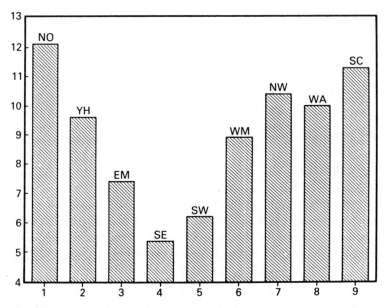

Figure 6.2
UK regional unemployment rates, 1988.

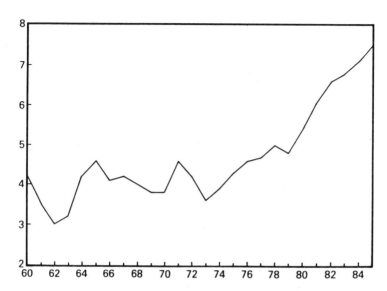

Figure 6.3
Italian unemployment rate, 1960–84.

Sectors dependent on light manufacturing and services were less severely affected by the post-1979 slump. Employment in the South East, dominated by London, is concentrated in banking, insurance, finance, business services, and leasing. The South West relies on public administration, agriculture, and defense. In the East Midlands, a higher-than-average share of regional GDP is generated by manufacturing industry (31 percent in 1986 compared to a UK average of 25 percent); those industries are predominantly engaged in light manufacturing, of products such as textiles, clothing, and footwear. East Anglia was similarly insulated by its specialization in light manufacturing (primarily food and beverages) and agriculture.

Figure 6.3 for Italy shows a dramatic increase in unemployment in the mid seventies, followed by a further increase through the first half of the 1980s. Figure 6.4 shows the different levels of unemployment prevailing in different Italian regions in 1988.[8] Their standard deviation is 6.40, or nearly twice the comparable figure for Britain (3.46), despite that the average unemployment rate for 1988 was almost exactly the same. The dominant feature of the figure is the north–south divide: unemployment was above 15 percent in Sardinia, Campania, Sicily, and the rest of the south; at roughly the national average of 11 percent in Lazio (which

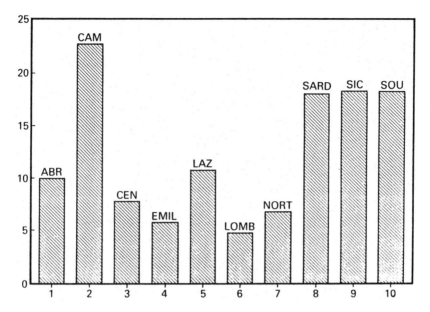

Figure 6.4
Italian regional unemployment rates, 1988.

includes Rome) and Abruzzi; but below 10 percent elsewhere in the center and in the north.

In Italy as in Britain, differences across regions in the sectoral composition of employment go some way toward explaining these regional unemployment disparities. The north, defined here to include Piedmont, Liguria, Veneto, and Emilia-Romagna, accounts for 70 percent of Italy's manufacturing employment.[9] Piedmont and Liguria specialize in heavy industries such as motor vehicles, iron and steel, and shipbuilding, Veneto in light industries such as footwear and apparel. Small and medium-size firms producing labor-intensive, high-value added products such as ceramics, furniture, scientific instruments, and automotive parts are increasingly evident in Emilia-Romagna.[10] Lombardy has the most broadly based industrial structure, featuring both traditional staples such as textiles, food processing, metal working and engineering, and also newer light industries, such as electronics. Its capital, Milan, has a highly developed service sector: it is the seat of the Italian stock exchange, the site of the country's leading trade fair, and the host of the head offices of most important Italian corporations.

The situation is different in Campania, Sicily, Sardinia, and the rest of the Mezzogiorno. Along with agriculture, these regions rely on heavy

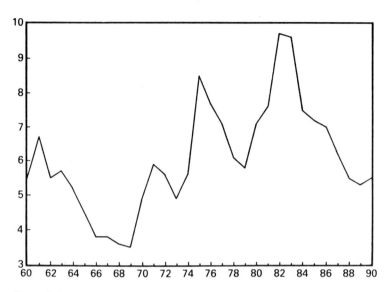

Figure 6.5
US unemployment rate, 1960–90.

industries such as petroleum, petrochemicals, and steel, whose location in the south and whose capital intensity have been encouraged by regional policy. These industries operated at only a fraction of capacity for much of the 1980s, making for high unemployment.

Central Italy (Marche, Umbria, Tuscany, and Lazio) combines elements of the north and south. The region relies heavily on the tertiary sector. Textiles, chemicals, metallurgy, and motor vehicles are all represented in Lazio. The "Emilian model" of small-scale, labor-intensive, high-value-added light industry is increasingly evident as well.

One way to gauge the seriousness of unemployment problems in Britain and Italy is to view them through the lens provided by the experience of the United States. Figure 6.5 depicts the time-series behavior of US unemployment. It is dominated by a dramatic upward movement in the wake of the two oil shocks, but also by a dramatic decline in US unemployment after 1981. This last movement is in contrast with the persistence of high unemployment in the eighties in both Italy and Britain.

In the United States, as in Britain and Italy, regional disparities in unemployment are of long-standing concern. Figure 6.6 displays regional unemployment rates in 1988.[11] These vary from a low of 3.1 percent in New England to a high of 7.8 percent in the West South Central region. The standard deviation of the regional figures—1.45 percent—is consid-

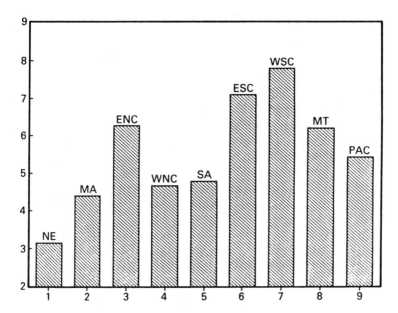

Figure 6.6
US regional unemployment rates, 1988.

erably smaller than the analogous standard deviations for Britain and Italy (3.46 and 6.40 percent, respectively). In part this reflects a lower national unemployment rate (5.5 percent), but even when coefficients of variation rather than standard deviations are compared, the inter-regional variation in unemployment rates is lower in the US. What inferences should be drawn from this fact is unclear, for the uniformity of regional unemployment rates in the US could reflect either a greater symmetry of shocks to regional labor markets or a more powerful response. The next three sections of the paper are designed to help distinguish these alternatives.

6.3 Shocks to Regional Labor Markets

To analyze the incidence of shocks to regional labor markets, I estimate a variant of the model developed by Branson and Love (1988). I regress regional unemployment on unemployment nationwide, on the real exchange rate, and on the real price of energy. I then examine the dispersion of regional responses to shocks to the common explanatory variables. Following Branson and Love, a time trend is included where necessary to pick up secular trends not captured by the other variables. Regressions are estimated using ordinary least squares.[12]

The dependent variable is the number of workers unemployed (in thousands). Regional and national unemployment are expressed in logs. Insofar as the cyclical sensitivity of regional unemployment exceeds (falls short of) the cyclical sensitivity of national unemployment, the coefficient on the log of national unemployment should exceed (fall short of) unity. The coefficient on the real exchange rate should be positive (negative) for regions specializing in the production of non-traded (traded) goods, since a decline in the real rate signals an appreciation. The coefficient on the real energy price should be positive for energy-using regions, negative for energy-producing regions.

Table 6.1 reports regression results for Britain for the period starting in 1974.[13] The elasticity of regional unemployment with respect to national unemployment varies from a low of 0.85 in the North to a high of 1.21 in the South East. Scotland has a relatively low cyclical sensitivity, the East and West Midlands relatively high ones. Industrial composition goes some way toward explaining these regional characteristics. The tendency for employment to hold up relatively well in Scotland, for example, reflects the economy's diversification out of traditional staples (textiles, shipbuilding, and metals) into electronics and services.[14] The cyclical sensitivity of unemployment in the Midlands reflects the importance of manufacturing industries (motor vehicles and engineering in the West Midlands, textiles in the East Midlands).[15] The standard deviation of the table 6.1 coefficients on national unemployment for British regions is 0.13.[16]

These results differ from those reported in previous studies of cyclical sensitivity. For example, Armstrong and Taylor (1985) found, by regressing regional unemployment on national unemployment, that cyclical sensitivity was lowest in the North West, South East, and East Anglia, highest in the North, Wales, and the West Midlands. Differences between their results and mine are attributable to the fact that previous studies fail to control for determinants of regional unemployment other than unemployment nationwide, whereas the results in table 6.1 are partial correlations controlling for the real exchange rate and the real price of energy.

Only one of the ten coefficients on the real price of energy, that for the North West, differs significantly from zero at the 90 percent level. Although this plausibly reflects the energy-using character of the region's industries, it is not clear why the same relationship is not evident for other industrial areas like Yorkshire and the Midlands.

Table 6.1
Covariates of Regional Unemployment in Britain, 1974–87
(Unemployment in Logs)

Region	Constant	National unemploy-ment	Real exchange rate	Real energy price	R^2
East Anglia	−5.299	1.147	0.003	0.001	0.99
	(16.68)	(44.39)	(2.87)	(0.13)	
East Midlands	−3.800	1.146	−0.001	−0.001	0.99
	(13.54)	(50.25)	(1.06)	(0.96)	
West Midlands	−3.652	1.186	−0.002	0.001	0.99
	(7.51)	(29.98)	(1.40)	(0.24)	
North	−0.719	0.849	−0.002	0.001	0.99
	(1.98)	(28.73)	(1.43)	(0.31)	
North West	−1.293	0.946	0.001	0.001	0.99
	(12.22)	(109.87)	(0.07)	(1.98)	
York & Humberside	−2.899	1.112	−0.002	−0.002	0.99
	(9.15)	(43.44)	(1.71)	(1.61)	
South East	−4.036	1.206	0.005	0.001	0.99
	(13.60)	(49.96)	(5.17)	(1.13)	
South West	−2.912	0.971	0.005	0.001	0.99
	(5.62)	(23.02)	(2.86)	(0.45)	
Wales	−1.740	0.914	−0.001	0.001	0.99
	(7.07)	(45.68)	(1.27)	(0.62)	
Scotland	−0.830	0.910	−0.001	−0.001	0.99
	(1.63)	(21.95)	(0.45)	(0.60)	

Source: See text.
Note: t-statistics in parentheses.

Three of the ten coefficients on the real exchange rate in table 6.1 differ significantly from zero at the 90 percent confidence level, and a fourth, that for Yorkshire and Humberside, comes close to significance at that level. Six of the ten coefficients are negative, four positive, indicating considerable regional heterogeneity in the unemployment response to real exchange-rate shocks. Thus, even after controlling for the business cycle and the relative price of energy, the real exchange rate significantly affects regional unemployment differentials in Britain.

The signs of the coefficients on the real exchange rate can be interpreted in terms of sectoral composition: employment in regions with positive coefficients is concentrated disproportionately in sheltered sectors (services in the South East, public administration and defense in the South

Table 6.2
Covariates of Regional Unemployment in Britain, 1974–87, Including Trend
(Unemployment in Logs)

Region	Constant	National unemployment	Real exchange rate	Real energy price	Time	R^2
East Anglia	−6.187	1.335	0.003	−0.002	0.021	0.99
	(33.55)	(45.71)	(6.09)	(3.23)	(6.94)	
East Midlands	−3.427	1.067	−0.001	−0.001	0.009	0.99
	(9.26)	(18.21)	(0.96)	(0.15)	(1.44)	
West Midlands	−4.564	1.379	−0.003	−0.002	0.021	0.99
	(8.13)	(15.51)	(1.92)	(0.92)	(2.34)	
North	0.171	0.660	−0.001	0.003	0.021	0.99
	(0.54)	(13.20)	(1.84)	(2.47)	(4.02)	
North West	−1.192	0.924	0.001	−0.001	0.002	0.99
	(8.11)	(39.68)	(0.17)	(2.21)	(1.00)	
York & Humberside	2.195	0.970	−0.002	−0.001	0.016	0.99
	(6.91)	(19.28)	(2.02)	(0.32)	(3.19)	
South East	4.688	1.344	0.005	−0.001	−0.015	0.99
	(15.57)	(28.20)	(6.71)	(0.24)	(3.12)	
South West	−4.25	1.255	0.005	−0.002	−0.031	0.99
	(10.51)	(19.58)	(4.57)	(1.71)	(4.76)	
Wales	−1.800	0.927	−0.001	0.001	−0.001	0.99
	(5.01)	(16.29)	(1.23)	(0.39)	(0.24)	
Scotland	0.086	0.716	−0.001	0.001	0.021	0.99
	(0.14)	(7.50)	(0.30)	(0.50)	(2.19)	

Source: See text.
Note: t-statistics in parentheses.

West, agriculture and light manufacturing in East Anglia). The positive coefficient for the North West is an anomaly, but unlike the other three positive coefficients it differs insignificantly from zero.

Table 6.2 adds a time trend to the basic regression. Six of the ten coefficients on the real exchange rate now differ from zero at standard confidence levels. Their magnitude remains basically unchanged from table 6.1. The positive coefficient for the North West turns negative, reassuringly, although that for Scotland turns positive, albeit insignificantly so.

For Italy, there exist separate definitions of unemployment for the pre- and post-1975 periods. Surveys for the post-1975 period added a third category of unemployed workers to the two categories reported previously.[17] Insofar as the national unemployment rate included as an ex-

Table 6.3
Covariates of Regional Unemployment in Italy, 1960–84, Pre-1978 Definitions of Unemployment
(Unemployment in Logs)

Region	Constant	National unemployment	Real exchange rate	Real energy price	R^2
Piedmont, Valle	−4.067	1.182	0.005	−0.001	0.97
d'Aosta, Liguria	(6.67)	(14.33)	(1.76)	(0.74)	
Lombardy	−3.215	1.275	−0.009	0.001	0.86
	(2.41)	(7.09)	(1.45)	(0.003)	
Tre Venezie	−1.476	1.095	−0.011	−0.001	0.77
	(1.03)	(5.67)	(2.36)	(0.02)	
Emilia-Romagna,	−0.049	0.889	−0.012	−0.001	0.87
Marche	(0.61)	(8.19)	(2.98)	(0.34)	
Tuscany, Umbria,	−1.732	0.990	0.007	−0.001	0.97
Alto Lazio, Lazio	(3.07)	(12.98)	(2.60)	(0.65)	
Meridionale, Campania					
Abruzzi, Molise	−2.389	0.800	0.004	−0.001	0.92
	(3.96)	(9.28)	(1.45)	(1.52)	
Puglia, Basilicata,	−1.259	0.817	0.006	−0.001	0.88
Calabria	(1.28)	(6.14)	(1.25)	(0.008)	
Sicily	−1.596	0.828	0.001	0.003	0.97
	(2.72)	(10.47)	(0.27)	(3.33)	
Sardinia	−5.459	1.231	0.005	0.002	0.94
	(5.07)	(8.46)	(0.87)	(1.11)	

Source: See text.
Note: *t*-statistics in parentheses.

planatory variable in the regressions is an aggregation of the dependent variable for the individual regions, the coefficient on unemployment nationwide may capture any implications of the shift. This is not true, of course, to the extent that the change in definition affected measured unemployment differently in different regions. I therefore estimated two variants of the basic equation, one which included among the unemployed only the two categories of workers considered before 1975, the other which included also the third category of unemployed workers for the post-1975 years.

The variation across regions in the cyclical sensitivity of local unemployment to national unemployment is almost exactly the same for Italy as for Britain. In table 6.3, which uses only pre-1975 categories of unemployment, the elasticity of regional unemployment with respect to

Table 6.4
Covariates of Regional Unemployment in Italy, 1960–84, Post-1977 Definitions of Unemployment
(Unemployment in Logs)

Region	Constant	National unemployment	Real exchange rate	Real energy price	R^2
Piedmont, Valle	−3.880	1.148	0.006	−0.001	0.98
d'Aosta, Liguria	(8.69)	(18.71)	(1.90)	(1.06)	
Lombardy	−2.692	1.228	−0.012	−0.001	0.94
	(3.02)	(10.01)	(1.94)	(0.06)	
Tre Venezie	−1.214	1.041	−0.016	0.001	0.89
	(1.25)	(7.77)	(2.34)	(0.22)	
Emilia-Romagna,	−1.176	0.940	−0.007	0.001	0.95
Marche	(2.19)	(12.75)	(1.94)	(1.03)	
Tuscany, Umbria,	−1.533	0.978	0.006	−0.001	0.98
Alto Lazio, Lazio	(4.04)	(18.73)	(2.19)	(0.66)	
Meridionale, Campania					
Abruzzi, Molise	−3.452	0.937	0.007	−0.002	0.97
	(7.45)	(14.71)	(2.07)	(1.93)	
Puglia, Basilicata,	−1.353	0.827	0.006	0.001	0.94
Calabria	(2.04)	(9.08)	(1.32)	(0.47)	
Sicily	−2.301	0.907	0.003	0.003	0.99
	(5.77)	(16.53)	(1.17)	(3.27)	
Sardinia	−5.114	1.198	0.003	0.001	0.97
	(6.88)	(11.71)	(0.65)	(0.91)	

Source: See text.
Note: t-statistics in parentheses.

national unemployment ranges from a high of 1.28 for Lombardy to a low of 0.80 for Abruzzi and Molise, with a standard deviation for the nine regions of 0.16. In table 6.4, which uses the alternative definition of unemployment, this elasticity ranges from 1.23 (again for Lombardy) to 0.83 (this time for Puglia, Basilicata, and Calabria), with a standard deviation of 0.14.[18] Recall that for Britain the comparable high and low values of this elasticity were 1.21 and 0.85, with a standard deviation of 0.13. Thus, the variability in regional responses to the business cycle is almost exactly the same across the two countries.

Only for Sicily and for Abruzzi-Molise is there evidence of a differential response to real energy prices. In contrast, four of the nine coefficients on the real exchange rate in table 6.3 differ significantly from zero at the 90 percent level; in table 6.4, six of the nine are statistically significant. (The pattern of signs is identical across the two tables.) Of the six significant coefficients in table 6.4, three are positive, three negative, again suggesting considerable regional heterogeneity in unemployment responses to changes in the real exchange rate.

The signs of the coefficients are generally plausible, although there are anomalies. The negative real exchange-rate coefficients are for Lombardy, Veneto, and Emilia-Romagna, which produce a variety of manufactures and thus should be adversely affected by a real appreciation.[19]

How does the regional variation in the response of unemployment to real exchange-rate shocks differ between Italy and Britain? Regional disparities created by real exchange-rate shocks are more important for Italy. The standard deviation of the real exchange-rate coefficients is 0.028 for Britain but 0.0074 for Italy when table 6.3 data are used and 0.0087 for Italy when table 6.4 data are used. Thus, while roughly comparable regional unemployment disparities emerge in the two countries in response to business cycle fluctuations (holding the real exchange rate constant), larger regional unemployment differentials emerge in Italy than Britain in response to real exchange-rate fluctuations (holding aggregate unemployment constant).

Table 6.5 summarizes the results for the United States. The dispersion of regional unemployment responses to national unemployment is remarkably similar to those for Britain and Italy. The elasticity of regional unemployment with respect to national unemployment ranges from 1.12 for the East North Central (home of the cyclically sensitive motor vehicle complex), to 0.81 for the Mountain states. The standard deviation for the nine regions is 0.12. Recall that the analogous estimates for Britain and Italy were 0.13 and 0.14–0.16, respectively, only slightly larger.

There is evidence of a tendency for higher energy prices to raise regional unemployment only for the East North Central (again reflecting the importance of the motor vehicle production) and the East South Central (which traditionally relies on the energy-using steel sector and other industries that act as suppliers to the automotive complex). The negative coefficient for the West South Central borders on significance, reflecting the tendency for higher energy prices to reduce unemployment in oil-patch states like Texas and Oklahoma.

Six of the nine coefficients on the real exchange rate differ significantly from zero at the 95 percent level or better. Three of the six significant coefficients are positive, three negative, again indicating considerable diversity of regional response to real exchange-rate shocks. Of all nine coefficients, four are positive.

Table 6.5
Covariates of Regional Unemployment in the United States, 1960–89
(Unemployment in Logs)

Region	Constant	National unemploy- ment	Real exchange rate	Real energy price	Time	R^2
New England	−4.073 (3.50)	1.104 (6.70)	0.014 (3.26)	−0.572 (1.46)	−0.032 (5.46)	0.78
East North Central	−2.931 (5.91)	1.119 (16.22)	−0.002 (0.97)	0.330 (1.98)	0.001 (0.22)	0.98
East South Central	−1.379 (1.59)	0.849 (6.90)	−0.011 (3.42)	0.882 (3.03)	0.012 (2.69)	0.95
Middle Atlantic	−2.389 (4.97)	1.034 (15.20)	0.008 (4.25)	0.189 (1.17)	−0.027 (11.06)	0.96
South Atlantic	−2.691 (7.33)	1.021 (19.64)	0.005 (3.42)	0.184 (1.49)	−0.001 (0.17)	0.99
West North Central	−0.726 (1.99)	0.816 (15.80)	−0.008 (6.22)	0.212 (1.73)	0.007 (3.85)	0.98
West South Central	−0.783 (0.74)	0.942 (6.31)	−0.013 (3.19)	−0.566 (1.61)	0.028 (5.19)	0.93
Mountain	−1.700 (3.08)	0.807 (10.33)	−0.002 (0.75)	−0.057 (0.31)	0.025 (8.94)	0.98
Pacific	−0.800 (1.02)	0.874 (7.86)	0.002 (0.64)	−0.345 (1.30)	0.009 (2.13)	0.94

Source: See text.
Note: *t*-statistics in parentheses.

The standard deviation of the nine estimated coefficients for the real exchange rate is 0.0089, matching almost exactly the table 6.4 estimate for Italy. Thus, holding the economy-wide level of unemployment constant, a real exchange-rate shock has the same tendency to create regional unemployment disparities in Italy as in the US. In contrast, Britain is less vulnerable to regional problems caused by real exchange-rate disturbances than the United States.

Overall, then, the dispersion of shocks to regional labor markets is remarkably similar across countries. The variability of the response of regional unemployment to changes in national unemployment is smaller in the US than in Britain, and smaller in Britain than in Italy, but the differences are minor. The variability of the response of regional unemployment to changes in the real exchange rate is the same for Italy and the US, and somewhat lower for Britain than for the other two countries.

On the basis of these results, then, there is no reason to think that labor-market disturbances are more asymmetrically distributed within Britain and Italy than within the United States. On the contrary, the regional variability of shocks looks remarkably similar across countries. This creates a presumption that observed high rates of inter-regional migration in the US reflect higher labor mobility, not a similar response to dissimilar shocks. The next section asks whether this presumption can be documented systematically.

6.4 The Migratory Response

To analyze the migratory response to regional labor-market disturbances, I estimate a variant of the model of inter-regional migration utilized by previous authors in studies of Britain and Italy. Given the persistence of regional problems in Europe, there exists an extensive literature on the subject. For Britain, a first generation of studies used aggregate Census data to measure the capacity of regional and local labor-market variables to explain migration patterns.[20] More recent studies utilize micro-data. Hughes and McCormick (1981), for example, considered the impact of council housing policies on the propensity for individuals to migrate between regions. They found that council tenants are less likely to relocate than other renters, presumably reflecting their fear of losing the benefits of sub-market rents.

A particularly simple and intuitive model is that applied to British data by Pissarides and McMaster (1990). Pooling data for nine British regions for the years 1961–82, they relate net immigration (as a share of population) in each region at each date to the natural logarithm of the relative wage of that region (its wage divided by the average wage in Great Britain), and to the unemployment ratio of that region (its unemployment rate divided by the British unemployment rate). Both variables are entered with one-year lags to permit the relationship to be estimated by ordinary least squares, while the log of relative wages is entered in first-difference form.[21] In-migration is hypothesized to rise with the relative wage and fall with the relative unemployment rate.

For Italy, a number of migration models have been estimated using data disaggregated to the regional level. Salvatore (1981) estimated a time-series model relating the number of emigrants from the south to the north to unemployment rates, the growth of the non-agricultural labor force, and the real industrial wage in each region. Low unemployment, rapid labor force growth and high wages locally all were found to discourage emigration. A'Hearn (1991) estimated similar equations using pooled data for a larger set of Italian regions, relating migration to the level and change in relative wages, relative unemployment rates, and relative consumption levels. Both unemployment and wages (the level of the local–national differential but not the change) had statistically significant effects on migration.

Attanasio and Padoa-Schioppa (1991) estimate a model for Italy broadly similar to the Pissarides–McMaster model for Britain. Using annual data for six geographic regions for the years 1960–86, they relate net immigration to the log of local wages, the log of national wages, local unemployment, and national unemployment.[22] Comparisons with the Pissarides–McMaster model are complicated by the fact that Attanasio and Padoa Schioppa enter log wages in level rather than first-difference form, do not hypothesize that local and national conditions affect migration symmetrically, and estimate contemporaneous rather than lagged effects.

Moreover, there does not appear to exist a comparable model for the United States. There is an extensive literature on inter-regional migration in the US (see the survey by Greenwood, 1975), but to date most of it has utilized micro-data or Census data disaggregated to the metropolitan level. Two exceptions are Miller (1973) and Barro and Sala-i-Martin (1991). Miller used state-level data from the 1960 Census, where median family income was his proxy for regional wages. Despite little correlation between migration rates and family income, upon controlling for other determinants of migration propensities (extent of previous migration and college attendance, among other variables), he identified a consistently significant relationship. Using annual data for 1950 through 1987, Barro and Sala-i-Martin similarly find a strong relationship between inter-state migration and personal income. International comparisons are again difficult, however, by virtue of the fact that local economic conditions are measured differently than in the studies of Britain and Italy described above (personal income rather than wages is used to measure compensation, while unemployment rates are not considered).

I have therefore estimated migration equations for the three countries, attempting to make the data and specification as closely comparable as possible. My point of departure is the Pissarides–McMaster model, since theirs is a particularly parsimonious specification. The first column of table 6.6 reports the results of my effort to replicate their basic regression. As in their paper, immigration responds positively to changes in local wages relative to national wages, negatively to local unemployment relative to national unemployment. There is considerable persistence in migratory

Table 6.6
Basic Migration Models for Britain, the US, and Italy
(Dependent Variable Is Immigration Scaled by Population)

	(1) Britain (1961–82)	(2) US (1962–88)	(3) Italy (1962–85)
Constant	0.12	1.50	0.01
	(2.32)	(5.76)	(0.06)
Change in log wages lagged	0.42	15.13	0.23
	(1.76)	(2.52)	(0.30)
Unemployment lagged	−0.17	−0.37	−0.04
	(2.87)	(1.92)	(0.48)
Migration lagged	0.58	−0.05	0.73
	(9.56)	(0.77)	(21.82)
Number of obs.	180	243	144

Source: See text.
Note: t-statistics in parentheses. Change in wages and unemployment variables both denote ratio of local value to national average. Dummy variables for regions are included in each regression but not reported.

patterns, as reflected in the coefficient on the lagged dependent variable of 0.61.[23]

The second column presents comparable estimates for the nine Census regions of the United States. Most of the coefficients have the same signs and the same significance levels as in the Pissarides–McMaster study of Britain. The economic implications are different, however. The elasticity of immigration with respect to the change in relative wages is an order of magnitude larger.[24] The elasticity with respect to relative unemployment rates is twice as large, although the magnitude of the standard errors suggests caution when comparing elasticities. In contrast to the result for Britain, there appears to be little persistence in US migratory patterns after controlling for wage and unemployment differentials. (The coefficient on the lagged dependent variable is essentially zero.) This is systematic evidence, then, that migration is more sensitive to current economic conditions in the US than in Britain.

The Pissarides–McMaster specification performs poorly on data for six Italian regions.[25] Neither the change in the relative wages of industrial and agricultural workers nor relative unemployment rates appears to have much impact on Italian migration, which displays even more persistence than in Great Britain. It could be that Italian labor simply does not respond to these variables. But Attanasio–Padoa-Schioppa and A'Hearn

Table 6.7
Alternative Migration Models for Italy
(Dependent Variable Is Immigration Scaled by Population)

	First wage series (1)	Second wage series (2)	Second wage series (3)
Constant	0.18	0.01	0.37
	(1.49)	(5.76)	(2.70)
Level of log wages lagged	1.35		1.07
	(3.71)		(4.43)
Change in log wages lagged		0.22	
		(0.45)	
Unemployment lagged	−0.11	−0.04	−0.20
	(1.27)	(0.50)	(2.31)
Migration lagged	0.63	0.73	0.62
	(15.37)	(21.98)	(16.01)
Number of obs.	144	144	144

Source: Author's estimates, as described in the text.
Note: t-statistics in parentheses. Sample period is as in table 6.6. Change in wages and unemployment variables both denote ratio of local value to national average. Dummy variables for regions are included in each regression but not reported. Column 1 utilizes the same definition of wages as in the previous table, while columns 2 and 3 use the alternative definition.

have shown that the explanatory power of Italian migration equations can be enhanced by substituting the level of the wage differential for its first difference. The first column of table 6.7 displays the results of estimating this variant of the model. When the log of the local–national wage differential is entered in levels rather than changes, it has a statistically significant positive impact on immigration. Still, the wage elasticity of migration is only half that for Britain and less than a tenth that for the United States. The unemployment differential enters with the anticipated sign, but its coefficient is small relative to that in the US and British equations and remains statistically indistinguishable from zero.

The second and third columns of table 6.7 substitute an alternative definition of Italian wages. Previous regressions used the effective daily wage paid to industrial and agricultural employees, a series that excludes the service sector and includes only firms covered by the provisions of the public insurance system. The alternative series used in the second and third columns of table 6.7 is the compensation of all employees, inclusive of social security contributions. When this series is entered in difference form, the results are essentially identical to those in table 6.6. When it is entered in level form, its point estimate is slightly smaller; in addition, however, the unemployment differential is statistically different from zero at standard confidence levels. The point estimate on the unemployment differential is comparable to that for Britain, which means that it is little more than half the size of that for the United States.

The models estimated here confirm the tendency for inter-regional labor flows to respond to economic conditions. In all three countries, immigration is encouraged by relatively high wages and relatively low unemployment. But the elasticity of migration with respect to wage differentials is very much larger in the United States. Similarly, US labor exhibits a greater tendency to move in response to regional unemployment differentials. This, then, is systematic evidence in support of the presumption of greater labor mobility in the US.

6.5   Restoring Regional Labor-Market Equilibria

Migration is not the only mechanism whereby divergences among regional unemployment rates can be eliminated. Even if labor fails to flow from high to low unemployment regions, capital may flow in the other direction to make use of idle labor. The increase in capital/labor ratios in depressed regions should enhance the productivity of labor there, reducing unemployment. Alternatively, wages may fall in high unemployment regions, pricing unemployed labor back into the market.[26] A third possibility is that labor–leisure choice responds elastically to regional unemployment, with labor supply rising in low unemployment regions, thereby increasing the pool of individuals seeking work, and conversely in high unemployment regions. Finally, fiscal transfers to depressed regions, operating through either the federal fiscal system or explicit regional policies, may boost purchasing power and labor demand. Thus, it need not follow from the fact that European labor is less mobile between regions that regional problems are more persistent than in the United States.

To analyze the speed with which regional labor-market disequilibria are eliminated, I extend the approach taken in chapter 2. Given large literatures for all three countries suggesting that local unemployment differentials persist, it is inappropriate to assume that unemployment rates converge to the same level. Instead, I adopt the more general assumption that there is a stable long-run relationship between unemployment in a region and the average unemployment rate in the nation of which that region is a part. In other words, regional and national unemployment rates are cointegrated. I therefore estimate for each region a cointegrating regression of the form:

$$U^R = a + bU^N \tag{1}$$

where U^R is the regional unemployment rate, U^N is the national unemployment rate, and a and b are parameters to be estimated. If regional and national unemployment rates are cointegrated, then the associated error correction form can be used to identify the speed of adjustment of regional unemployment rates:

$$dU^R = a + bdU^N + ce_{t-1} \tag{2}$$

where d is the difference operator, e is the residual from equation 1 above, and a, b, and c are again parameters to be estimated. c captures the speed with which regional labor markets respond to divergencies between local and national unemployment rates.

For Britain and Italy, the analysis is straightforward. Despite the notoriously low power of tests for the cointegration of short time series, for all nine British regions it is impossible to reject the null that regional unemployment rates are cointegrated with the national rate.[27] Cointegration obtains for five of the six Italian regions, and for the sixth (the Italian North) the Durbin–Watson statistic falls just short of the critical value provided by Dickey and Fuller. Results are summarized in table 6.8. For the nine British regions, the unweighted average of the error correction term c is 0.47. The analogous average for Italy is 0.34. This means that about a half of any divergence between regional and national unemployment rates in Britain, and about a third in Italy, is eliminated in the next year.

Analyzing the US data is more complex, for evidence of cointegration ranges from weak to non-existent. Of nine US regions, unemployment rates in only three (East North Central, South Atlantic, and Mountain) ares clearly cointegrated with the national rate. This fact was previously noted in chapter 2 and, using another approach, by Hall (1972). Following chapter 2, I therefore add additional regressors to the right-hand side of equation 1 in order to produce a cointegrated vector. Specifically, I add the real energy price and real exchange-rate variables used section 6.3.

With the addition of these variables, the hypothesis of cointegration can no longer be rejected for any of the nine US regions.[28] Equation 2 can then be estimated, including on its right-hand side all of the differenced variables. As shown in the first column of table 6.9, the error correction

Table 6.8
Cointegration and Error Correction Parameters for Britain and Italy

	Cointegrating regression			
	Constant	Slope	Durbin–Watson statistic	Error correction term
UK				
North	0.94	1.32	0.67	−0.30
	(5.43)	(48.73)		(1.94)
Yorkshire–Humberside	−0.50	1.15	1.19	−0.97
	(2.36)	(34.92)		(5.96)
East Midlands	−0.47	0.95	1.15	−0.87
	(9.18)	(120.28)		(3.85)
South-East–East Anglia	−0.73	0.92	0.52	−0.34
	(2.86)	(22.91)		(2.08)
South-West	0.77	0.76	0.45	−0.21
	(4.34)	(27.34)		(1.50)
West Midlands	−1.37	1.31	0.51	−0.46
	(10.24)	(62.84)		(2.66)
North-West	−0.37	1.30	0.59	−0.15
	(3.23)	(72.73)		(0.92)
Wales	0.76	1.15	0.83	−0.57
	(5.92)	(57.19)		(2.75)
Scotland	1.31	1.09	0.46	−0.32
	(6.28)	(33.49)		(1.89)
Italy				
North-East	−0.01	0.71	0.92	−0.54
	(0.70)	(14.43)		(3.15)
North	0.01	0.61	0.30	−0.17
	(1.37)	(5.09)		(1.73)
East-Central	0.01	0.53	0.67	−0.29
	(3.99)	(8.13)		(2.04)
Lazio	0.04	0.54	0.46	−0.23
	(4.95)	(3.66)		(1.72)
South-East	−0.01	1.18	1.07	−0.58
	(0.47)	(17.95)		(2.92)
South	−0.01	1.69	0.70	−0.26
	(3.56)	(20.57)		(1.88)

Note: t-statistics in parentheses. Samples are as in table 6.6.

Table 6.9
Error Correction Parameters from Augmented Specification

United States		Great Britain		Italy	
NE	−0.26	NO	−0.44	NE	−0.65
	(3.08)		(2.57)		(3.23)
MA	−0.24	YH	−1.14	NO	−0.21
	(2.16)		(5.72)		(1.60)
ENC	−0.31	EM	−0.99	CE	−0.39
	(2.37)		(4.02)		(2.13)
WNC	−0.19	SE	−0.56	LA	−0.25
	(1.44)		(2.73)		(1.55)
SA	−0.43	SW	−0.72	SE	−0.69
	(3.13)		(4.49)		(3.21)
ESC	−0.31	WM	−1.06	SO	−0.43
	(2.99)		(4.51)		(2.37)
WSC	−0.19	NW	−0.22		
	(2.03)		(0.97)		
MT	−0.40	WA	−0.71		
	(2.38)		(3.33)		
PA	−0.18	SC	−0.69		
	(1.42)		(3.93)		

Source: See text.
Note: t-statistics in parentheses. Sample periods are as in table 6.6.

terms again vary across regions. They are largest, plausibly, for three regions whose unemployment rates were cointegrated with the national average even before the additional regressors were added to equation 1.

The unweighted average of the error correction terms for the nine US regions is 0.26, smaller than the comparable averages for Britain and Italy. This suggests that some other mechanism besides labor mobility works to restore regional labor-market equilibrium in the European countries.

To check the robustness of these results, I re-estimated the cointegrating regressions and error correction forms for Britain and Italy including also the real energy price and real exchange rate. With the addition of these variables, the hypothesis of cointegration could not be rejected for any Italian region. In the case of Britain, in contrast, the addition of the real energy price (alone or in conjunction with the real exchange rate) caused the hypothesis of cointegration to be rejected for York, where it had been accepted before.

Estimates of the error correction term from the augmented model are summarized in the last two columns of table 6.9. Compared to the first column for the US, they continue to show relatively rapid adjustment. The unweighted average for Britain is 0.73, for Italy 0.44.[29] This confirms the results reported above.

This section, along with its substantive results, also suggests an agenda for research. That regional unemployment rates are cointegrated with the national rate in Britain and Italy but not in the United States warrants further analysis. The idea that one US region's unemployment rate can diverge indefinitely from the national average is not plausible. Eventually that differential must become so conspicuous that some adjustment mechanism will begin to bring it back into line. That the US data appear inconsistent with the hypothesis of cointegration may simply reflect that existing time series are short and that regional unemployment differentials in the US show relatively little variation. More data acquired with the passage of time may allow the hypothesis of cointegration to be resurrected.[30]

Even so, the absence of cointegration for the United States is indicative of more than data problems. Within European nations, regions characterized by unusually high unemployment in one year (or one decade) also tend to be characterized by unusually high unemployment in the next. The hypothesis of cointegration is readily accepted for Italy and Britain because unemployment rates in high unemployment regions tend to maintain a relatively stable relationship to unemployment rates nationwide, and similarly for low unemployment regions. In the US in contrast, one decade's high unemployment regions can become the next decade's low unemployment regions.[31] The transformation of New England, for example, from a textile- and boot-and-shoe-based economy in the 1960s and early 1970s to a center of high-technology industries in the 1980s converted it from a relatively high to a low unemployment region. With unemployment rates in New England moving from well above the national average to well below it over the sample period, it is not surprising that the hypothesis of cointegration is rejected. Why the identity of relatively high and relatively low unemployment regions should persist in Europe but shift repeatedly in the United States remains inadequately understood.

The other item for research is to identify and analyze the mechanisms that substitute for labor mobility in bringing Britain and Italy's regional labor markets back into line. What we know about wage flexibility and private investment suggests that neither one furnishes the critical mechanism. Most observers believe that wages are less, not more, flexible in

Europe than in the US. Similarly, policy-makers complain of the dearth of private capital flows to depressed regions to make use of idle labor. It could be that individuals enter the labor force in disproportionate numbers in regions where unemployment is low, augmenting the stock of idle workers, and that they exit the labor force in regions where unemployment is high, reducing numbers measured as out of work. Alternatively, fiscal transfers to depressed regions within Britain and Italy may be sufficiently flexible and generous that region-specific shocks are eliminated as quickly as in the US. But again, further analysis is required.

6.6 Conclusion

The literature on optimum currency areas points to the symmetry of shocks and the mobility of factors of production as two criteria for evaluating the costs of EMU. This chapter has analyzed both criteria from a labor-market perspective. Since the United States forms a currency area, the evidence for Britain and Italy is compared systematically with evidence for the US. The dispersion of shocks to regional labor markets was found to be similar across countries. But the responsiveness of migration to regional labor-market disequilibria was found to be much greater in the US. International variations in the elasticity of migration with respect to inter-regional unemployment differentials, while less pronounced, point similarly to the greater responsiveness of labor flows in the United States.

Yet despite that shocks to regional labor markets in the US and Europe are of comparable dispersion, and that US migration responds more powerfully to those shocks, it is not obvious that deviations from the long-term relationship among regional unemployment rates are more persistent in Europe than in the US. When disturbances cause regional unemployment rates within European countries to diverge, it appears that other mechanisms, perhaps including relative wage adjustments, inter-regional capital mobility, and government policy, substitute adequately for Europe's limited labor mobility in order to bring them back into line. Further analysis of those alternative mechanisms forms the obvious agenda for research.

Data Appendix

1   Post-war Britain

Data on British unemployment were drawn from Department of Employment and Productivity (1971), supplemented by various issues of the Department of Employment *Gazette*. The regions distinguished by the Department of Employment are the South East, East Anglia, South West, West Midlands, East Midlands, Yorkshire (including Humberside), North West, North, Wales, Scotland, and Northern Ireland. (Given changes in regional definition in 1974, for that portion of the analysis (tables 6.6–6.9) where longer time series are important, East Anglia and the South East were combined.) I excluded Northern Ireland on the grounds that its labor market is very imperfectly integrated with that of Great Britain, although in principle Irish data could be used.

Data on number of migrants as a share of regional population were constructed as described in Pissarides and McMaster (1990).

To construct a time series for the real exchange rate, nominal exchange rates and consumer price indices were first gathered for Britain's ten leading trading partners. Trade was measured as the sum of imports and exports in 1980. A consumer price index for Saudi Arabia is not available for the early part of the sample period; I therefore dropped Saudi Arabia from the initial list of ten trading partners. (Since British imports from Saudi Arabia are almost entirely oil, the impact of conditions there on the British economy should be captured by real energy prices.) I then computed the real exchange rate as the trade-weighted arithmetic average of foreign consumer prices, converted into sterling using the spot rate, relative to the British consumer price index. For energy prices I drew the prices of fuel purchased by manufacturing industry from the *Annual Statistical Abstract of the United Kingdom*, deflated by consumer prices, from Feinstein through 1965, from Mitchell (1988) for 1966–70, and from *IFS* thereafter.

2 Italy

The surveys used to gather labor market statistics for Italy were revised in 1977 to reflect new definitions of unemployment. For prior years, two categories of unemployed persons were distinguished: persons separated from a previous position, and new entrants to the labor force in search of their first position. Much of the rise in Italian unemployment in the 1970s is concentrated in the second category, reflecting legally mandated severance pay provisions which discouraged layoffs and made it more difficult for recent school leavers to find a first position. The revised surveys after 1976 distinguish persons recently separated from a previous position, new entrants in search of a first position, and other persons in search of work. These data are drawn from *Annuario Statistico del Lavoro*. Problems of comparability between pre- and post-1975 data are discussed and an attempt to reconcile the two is made by Massarotto and Trivellato (1983).

The Italian real exchange rate was calculated identically to that for Britain, except that Saudi Arabia and Libya were excluded from the initial list of ten leading trade partners due to the absence of a continuous consumer price index.

No energy price index appears to be available for Italy for the entire period. I spliced the following series: the price of fuel oil in Turin for 1958–62, the arithmetic average of separate indices for crude petroleum and for petroleum products for 1963–74, and the published index for crude oil and petroleum products for 1975–84. All series were taken from the *Annuario Statistico Italiano* (various issues). The resulting index was deflated by Italian consumer prices as published in *IFS*.

Data on domestic migration were drawn from *Popolazione e Movimento Anagrafico dei Comuni* (various issues). The net migration rate was calculated as the percentage of the total resident population per administrative region tabulated in the *Ricostruzione della Popolazione Residente per Sesso, Eta' e Regione* (1960–72), *Popolazione e Bilanci Demografici per Sesso, Eta' e Regione* (1973–81), *Popolazione Residente per Sesso, Eta' e Regione* (1982–5), and *Statistiche Demografiche* (1986–7).

Two series are used for nominal wages by region. The first is the effective daily wage paid to the injured-at-work employees of industry and agriculture, which appears in the *Notiziario Statistico* (various issues). This series excludes the service sector and includes data only for firms complying with the rules of the public insurance system. The second series is the compensation of employees, inclusive of social security contributions, drawn from the *Annuario di Contabilita' Nazionale* (1974, 1986). There are two regional series, one for 1961–70 and one for 1970–84, but they are not homogeneous. See Attanasio and Padoa-Schioppa (1991) for details about the construction of consistent series.

3   United States

Data for the US on unemployment by state, based on the Current Population Survey, have been published by the US Department of Labor since the early to mid 1970s (depending on the state and the size of the CPS sample). These data appear in the Labor Department's *Geographic Profile of Employment and Unemployment* (various issues). For prior years I rely on the estimates of state agencies, as tabulated in the *Manpower Report of the President* (various issues).

The real exchange rate for the US was constructed to be comparable to those for Britain and Italy, starting with consumer price indices and exchange rates for the country's ten leading trade partners in 1980, excluding Saudi Arabia for lack of a continuous consumer price index, and using trade weights to aggregate. The real price of energy is computed as the consumer price index for energy relative to the consumer price index for all items, both from Council of Economic Advisors (1991).

Series P-20 of Current Population Reports, which provides direct data on domestic migration patterns, distinguishes four regions only. For finer geographic breakdowns like those utilized here, one has to rely on residual computations. Total population change was first calculated taking mid-year population estimates for each region. Natural population change was then computed as the average of births minus deaths for end-year observations, since births and deaths are over the entire year whereas population is computed at mid year. The difference between total and natural migration was attributed to net migration.

Data on population are based on the *Current Population Survey*, while data on births and deaths were drawn from the *Vital Statistics of the U.S.*.

Average hourly earnings of production workers in manufacturing industries were drawn from the *Employment and Earnings*. Since these data were provided by state, we constructed a weighted average for each division; the weight used for each state was the number of employees in non-agricultural establishments, whose source was again *Employment and Earnings*.

Notes

I thank Orazio Attanasio and Christopher Pissarides for help with data and Luisa Lambertini for expert research assistance. Financial support was provided by the Center for German and European Studies of the University of California at Berkeley.

1. The extent to which fiscal convergence is a necessary concomitant of monetary union remains a debated point. See Eichengreen (1992a), Bayoumi (1992), and Goldstein and Woglom (1991).

2. Early contributions include Cohen and Wyplosz (1989) and Weber (1990). For a more detailed review of the literature than is presented here see chapter 4.

3. Common factors are measured by the share of the cross-country variance explained by the first principal component.

4. De Grauwe and Vanhaverbeke (1993) examine growth rates of output and employment for a number of European countries, and find that they vary more at the regional than at the national level. From this they conclude that shocks are more asymmetric at the regional than at the national level. They do not, however, provide systematic comparisons between Europe and the United States.

5. Those impressed by the importance of cultural and linguistic differences would probably anticipate that migration between European countries will remain lower than migration within them even after statutory barriers are removed.

6. The data upon which these and subsequent figures are based are described in the data appendix.

7. The labels denote, reading left to right, North, Yorkshire–Humberside, East Midlands, South East, South West, West Midlands, North West, Wales, and Scotland.

8. The labels denote, reading left to right, Abruzzi, Campania, Center, Emilia, Lazio, Lombardy, North, Sardinia, Sicily, and South.

9. Following King (1985), I also include as part of the North Val d'Aosta, Trentino-Alto, Adige, and Friuli-Venezia Giulia.

10. See Bianchi and Gualtieri (1990).

11. The labels denote, reading left to right, New England, Middle Atlantic, East North Central, West North Central, South Atlantic, East South Central, West South Central, Mountain, and Pacific.

12. Endogeneity of the explanatory variables, notably the real exchange rate, is unlikely to be a problem insofar as explanatory variables are measured for the entire economy while the dependent variables are for relatively small regions. Any one region's unemployment is unlikely to have a discernible impact on real wages economy-wide and hence on the nation's real exchange rate, for example. An exception to this statement is when workers in the industries that dominate economic activity in a particular region set the tone for wage negotiations economy-wide.

13. Standard definitions of regions used by the Ministry of Labour were revised in 1974, rendering problematic the use of pre- and post-1974 data together. There were also a variety of procedural changes in the measurement of British unemployment in the 1980s, which inevitably complicates the interpretation of its time series behavior.

14. North Sea oil provided an additional boost to Scottish employment in the early 1980s. Townsend (1983, p. 98).

15. Townsend (1983, pp. 118–19).

16. All subsequent comparisons across countries also refer to table 6.1 estimates for Britain.

17. See the data appendix for further discussion.

18. The relatively low coefficients for Abruzzi, Calabria, and the rest of the South are consistent with the results of Caroleo (1990), who regressed unemployment in the Mezzogiorno on national unemployment and a time trend, obtaining coefficients on national unemployment in the neighborhood of 0.8.

19. Insofar as workers in these manufacturing industries set the tone for wage negotiations nationwide, a rise in their unemployment may put downward pressure on real wages, leading to real exchange-rate depreciation. This positive correlation between unemployment and the real exchange rate is the opposite of the sign of the estimated coefficient on the real exchange rate, suggesting that the estimated effect represents a lower bound on the real exchange-rate effect. On the other hand, reverse causation may help to explain the positive coefficient for Piedmont-Liguria, the home of much of Italy's heavy industry.

20. See for example Creedy (1974), Hart (1970), and Langley (1974).

21. A lagged dependent variable and regional dummy variables are also included.

22. First and second lags of the dependent variable are also included. I refer in the text to the equations reported in their table 6.2.

23. The only respect in which my estimates differ from Pissarides and McMaster is in the coefficient on relative wages. My point estimate is smaller than theirs and it is statistically different from zero at the 90 rather than the 95 percent level.

24. According to my point estimates, the elasticity for the US is about 25 times as large as for Britain. If that of Pissarides and McMaster is used instead, the US wage elasticity is still larger by a factor of five.

25. For the remainder of this chapter I follow Attanasio and Padoa Schioppa's scheme for consolidating Italian regions. The six regions are Northeast (Tre Venezie: Veneto, Trentino-Alto, Adige, Friuli-Venezia Giulia), Northwest (Piedmonte, Valle d'Aosta, Lombarida, Liguria), Center (Emilia-Romagna, Toscana, Umbira, Marche), Lazio, Southeast (Abruzzo, Molise, Puglia), and Southwest (Calabria, Basilicata, Campania, Sicilia, and Sardegna).

26. Alternatively, wages may rise in the booming region, pricing its labor out of the market and thereby eliminating the differential.

27. After the first draft of this chapter was written, I came across Chapman (1991), who undertakes a similar cointegration analysis of regional and national unemployment rates for the UK. Despite slight differences in implementation, his results are consistent with mine: unemployment rates in the UK are cointegrated, although "regional and national unemployment are not as closely related as might have been supposed..." Chapman (1991, p. 1059).

28. I used the test statistics developed by Engle and Yoo (1987).

29. As further sensitivity analysis, I re-estimated these models adding the real exchange rate or the real energy price, but not both, to the basic cointegrating regression and the associated error correction from. For Italy, the results were essentially unchanged. (The average value of the error correction term was 0.39 when the real energy price was added, 0.41 when the real exchange rate was added instead.) For Britain, the error correction terms tended to shrink noticeably (to 0.56 and 0.55, respectively) but remained larger than the corresponding values for the United States.

30. See Frankel (1991) for a discussion of the sensitivity of such tests to the limited availability of data.

31. For further discussion, again see Eichengreen (1990b).

7   The Unstable EMS

From the standpoint of European monetary affairs, 1992 opened with a bang and closed with a whimper. In January, the European Monetary System (EMS) celebrated five years of exchange rate stability: sixty full months without a realignment. The month before, the representatives of European Community (EC) member-states initialed the Treaty on Economic and Monetary Union concluded at Maastricht in the Netherlands. The transition to European monetary union (EMU) was fully underway.

By the end of the year, the European monetary system had endured —indeed, was continuing to experience—the most severe crisis in its fourteen-year history. Two of ten currencies, the Italian lira and the British pound, had been driven from the system. (Of the twelve EC countries, Greece is not a member of the Exchange Rate Mechanism (ERM), while Luxembourg's franc is set at par to Belgium's franc.) Other currencies, including the Spanish peseta and the Portuguese escudo, had been devalued involuntarily.[1] Some of the affected countries reimposed capital controls. British Prime Minister John Major and others complained of "fault lines" running through the European Monetary System.[2] The EC's Monetary Committee, the body responsible for coordinating the operation of the system, held three meetings in the final months of the year in a fruitless effort to identify and repair the system's flaws. Clearly, the process that was supposed to culminate in monetary union had suffered a serious setback.

As we explain in this chapter, until the summer of 1992, anticipations of a smooth transition to monetary union had stabilized expectations and hence the operation of the EMS. At that point, the protracted process of negotiation and ratification allowed doubts to surface about whether the

Originally published in *Brookings Papers in Economic Activity* 1 (1993): 51–143, with Charles Wyplosz. Reprinted with permission.

treaty would ever come into effect. This altered the costs and benefits of the policies of austerity required of countries seeking to qualify for European monetary union, leading the markets to anticipate that those policies would ultimately be abandoned.

Certain perverse incentives built into the treaty complicated the situation further. One of the four convergence criteria required of countries qualifying for European monetary union is that they maintain exchange rate stability: they must keep their currencies within their EMS fluctuation bands "without severe tensions" for at least two years before inaugurating monetary union. A speculative attack forcing a devaluation that prevents a country from satisfying this requirement might, by eliminating the lure of membership in the monetary union, induce its government to abandon its current policy regime. Because the country, once driven out of the EMS, might no longer qualify for EMU membership, it would have no incentive to continue pursuing the policies of austerity necessary to gain entry. Thus a speculative attack could prove self-fulfilling.

We develop this hypothesis by contrasting two models of balance-of-payments crises. The first, following Paul Krugman[3] and Robert P. Flood and Peter M. Garber,[4] relates speculative attacks to economic fundamentals. Countries experience balance-of-payments crises because they run unsustainable monetary and fiscal policies or their competitiveness otherwise deteriorates. Krugman's own formulation requires current policies to be inconsistent with the exchange rate peg; we discuss a variant of the model in which an attack can occur even when current policies are consistent with the peg, but future policies are expected with certainty to shift in a direction inconsistent with its maintenance.

The second model, following Flood and Garber[5] and Maurice Obstfeld,[6] allows purely self-fulfilling speculative attacks to occur. In the absence of an attack, monetary policies remain unchanged and the exchange rate peg is maintained forever. If and only if an attack occurs, monetary policy will shift in a less restrictive direction, causing the exchange rate to depreciate. In the first model, the speculative attack merely anticipates events that would eventually occur; in the second model, in contrast, the attack provokes events that would not occur in its absence. For this model to be compelling, there must be an intrinsic reason why monetary policy would shift only in the event of an attack. As explained above, the Maastricht treaty provides such a reason. It makes exchange rate stability a precondition for participation in European monetary union. Once driven out of the EMS, a country could no longer qualify for EMU membership and hence would no longer have an incentive to pursue the policies of austerity required for entry. The force of this explanation is illustrated by the behavior of the United Kingdom, which, after having pursued high interest rate policies for more than two years, cut its discount rate in half as soon as it was driven out of the EMS—despite no other obvious change in economic circumstances, no change in government, and not even a change in the identity of the Chancellor of the Exchequer.

In the second section of our chapter, we review recent EMS history; in the third, we analyze the requirements for operating pegged exchange rate systems. We then discuss four distinct explanations for the September 1992 crisis, working from the simplest to the increasingly complex. The first explanation, considered in the fourth section, is that persistent high inflation and rising labor costs in some EMS countries eroded their competitiveness and created balance-of-payments problems. For the vast majority of EMS countries, we find little support for this view in the data. Except in Italy, there is little evidence that wage inflation was inadequately compensated for by increases in labor productivity.

In the fifth section, we analyze a second explanation. Starting in 1990, EMS countries suffered a massive asymmetric shock: German economic and monetary unification (GEMU). While this explanation also focuses on competitiveness, unlike its predecessor it emphasizes that evidence of competitive difficulties will not be easy to detect in relative prices. As an asymmetric shock, GEMU required a change in relative prices and costs. Maintaining the historical relationship of unit labor costs between Germany and the rest of the EMS was not enough; prices and costs in other EMS countries actually had to decline relative to those prevailing in Germany. We analyze profitability in manufacturing and the current account of the balance of payments to ascertain whether the requisite adjustment took place; again, we conclude that in most cases it did. By the time the crisis erupted, most EMS countries had successfully carried out the changes in relative prices and costs required to maintain their EMS parities.

The sixth and seventh sections then introduce the two models that we believe best fit the facts: the Krugman model with speculative attacks driven by inevitable future policy shifts; and the Obstfeld model with multiple equilibria, contingent policy shifts, and self-fulfilling attacks.

Given four different interpretations of the crisis, it is natural to ask foreign exchange traders what they actually thought. Thus in the eighth section, we report the results of an extensive mail questionnaire administered to European foreign exchange dealers, which provides some support for our interpretation. The ninth section explains why governments and central banks found it so costly to defend their pegged rates once speculative attacks were underway, while the tenth section assesses the political economy of the crisis from the German Bundesbank's perspective.

The last two sections consider options for the future. We list the alternatives for completing the transition to European monetary union. These include attempting to proceed as before, but realigning more frequently; arranging a merger between the Bundesbank and the Bank of France; establishing an early two-speed EMU within the framework of the Maastricht treaty; and enhancing exchange rate flexibility. We conclude that none of these alternatives is viable.[7] This leaves the option of providing pecuniary disincentives against speculative attacks. Either levying a Tobin tax on foreign exchange transactions or requiring purchasers of foreign exchange to make non-interest-bearing deposits at the central bank would serve this purpose. It would thereby stabilize the EMS during the transition. Our recommendation is consistent with the provisions of the Single European Act and the Maastricht Treaty. We recognize that both a Tobin tax and deposit requirements have disadvantages: they reduce the liquidity of the foreign exchange markets, which may discourage foreign investment and hinder efforts to develop financial markets. But it is not enough to point to these disadvantages. Critics must also offer a viable alternative.

The Three Stages of the New EMS

EMS histories abound. Most conclude around 1987 or so, however, immediately before the system was dramatically transformed. This section provides a capsule history of the new EMS, the modified system that came into operation in 1987. Our account distinguishes three stages in its development.[8]

No Realignments after 1987

In the first phase of the new EMS, realignments were eliminated. From the inception of the EMS in 1979 through January 1987, there were eleven realignments—more than one a year, on average. By contrast, from January 1987 until the 1992 crisis, no further realignments occurred. Table 7.1 presents the dates of these realignments and their composition.[9]

Table 7.1
Exchange-Rate Realignments within the EMS, 1979–87[a]
(Percent)

Date of realignments	Deutsche mark	Dutch guilder	French franc	Bel./Lux. franc	Italian lira	Danish krone	Irish punt
September 24, 1979	2.0	...	...	...	...	−2.9	...
November 30, 1979	...	...	...	...	...	−4.8	...
March 23, 1981	...	...	...	...	−6.0	...	...
October 5, 1981	5.5	5.5	−3.0	...	−3.0	...	...
February 22, 1982	...	...	...	−8.5	...	−3.0	...
June 14, 1982	4.3	4.3	−5.8	...	−2.8	...	...
March 21, 1983	5.5	3.5	−2.5	1.5	−2.5	2.5	−3.5
July 22, 1985	2.0	2.0	2.0	2.0	−6.0	2.0	2.0
April 7, 1986	3.0	3.0	−3.0	1.0	...	1.0	...
August 4, 1986	...	...	...	...	...	...	−8.0
January 12, 1987	3.0	3.0	...	2.0	...	...	...

Source: Fratianni and von Hagen (1992, p. 22).
[a] The numbers are percentage changes of a given currency's bilateral central rate against those currencies whose bilateral parities were not realigned. A positive number denotes an appreciation, a negative number a depreciation. On March 21, 1983, and on July 22, 1985, all parities were realigned.

The need for realignments reflected the persistence of inflation differentials across EMS countries. Paul De Grauwe has noted that the standard deviation of inflation rates across EMS countries actually rose in the first four years of the EMS, compared to the preceding period.[10] Indeed, inflation differentials in this period were larger across EMS countries than across EC countries that did not participate in the system. The situation began to change in 1983, although inflation differentials remained substantial, narrowing only after 1987. Even thereafter, however, substantial differentials still remained between Italy, the United Kingdom, and Spain on the one hand and Germany on the other.

By 1987, it seemed that realignments had become a thing of the past.[11] What led policymakers to ignore continuing inflation differentials and adopt the no-realignment strategy? The answer is particularly interesting in light of the 1992 crisis. The January 1987 realignment, the last one to occur under the old EMS, was widely viewed as unprecedented. It was attributed not to imbalances within the EMS but to extraneous factors. The leading culprits—a declining dollar and self-fulfilling speculative expectations—were precisely the same as in 1992! This interpretation

led to revisions of EMS arrangements designed to strengthen intervention and encourage policy coordination (the Basle-Nyborg Agreement of
1987).[12] Credit facilities were extended for longer periods. For the first
time, countries were permitted to draw on credits before a currency
reached the limit of its EMS band. Imbued by confidence because of these
innovations, policymakers discarded the realignment option.

No Capital Controls after 1990

Intervals of exchange rate stability punctuated by occasional realignments
were possible because controls protected central banks' reserves against
speculative attacks. Inflation differentials continued to offer exchange
market participants a one-way bet: given Italy's tendency to run a looser
monetary policy than Germany, for example, it was easy to anticipate that
the lira would have to be devalued sooner or later. When the time came,
huge quantities of financial capital flowed from Milan to Frankfurt, threatening the Banca d'Italia's reserves and the EMS itself. Capital controls
provided insulation from these pressures. They allowed monetary authorities to retain some policy autonomy for limited periods. Different inflation rates were thereby reconciled with pegged yet adjustable exchange
rates.

As table 7.2 shows, these controls took a variety of forms, ranging
from taxes on holdings of foreign currency assets to restrictions on the
ability of banks to lend abroad. Controls were eliminated as an adjunct to
the 1992 program to complete the internal market. It was hardly feasible
to restrict the freedom of Italians to open bank accounts in Germany, for
example, while eliminating all controls on intra-EC movements of portfolio capital and direct foreign investment—not to mention labor and commodities. Hence controls were a casualty of the Single European Act,
which mandated their elimination by July 1, 1990 (except in Spain and
Ireland, which were exempted until December 31, 1992, and Portugal and
Greece, which were exempted until December 31, 1995).[13] Most EMS
members had removed their capital controls by the beginning of 1990,
while Spain and Portugal had significantly relaxed their controls before
the crisis struck.

For a time, the no realignment–no controls strategy seemed to work
even in the face of persistent inflation differentials. The question is
what tied down nominal exchange rates when real exchange rates were
diverging.

Table 7.2
Capital Controls for EMS Countries by Type of Transaction, 1988
(Type of control[a])

	Securities		Loans		Other	
Country	Primary market	Secondary market	Trade related	Other	Deposit accounts	Other[b]
Belgium[c]	F/A	F	F	F	F	F
Denmark	F	F	A	A	A	A
France	R/A	F	R	R	F/R	F
Germany	F	F	F	F	F	F
Ireland	A	F/R	F/A	F/A	F/P	F/P
Italy	A/P	F/R	F/A	A	F/P	F/P
Luxembourg[c]	F/A	F	F	F	F	F
Netherlands	F	F	F	F	F	F
United Kingdom	F	F	F	F	F	F
Greece	A/P	A/P	A	A	R/P	R/P
Portugal	R/A	R/A	A	A	A	A
Spain	A	F/R	A	R/A	F/A	A

Source: Morgan Guaranty Trust Co. (1988, p. 5).
[a] The first code refers to capital inflows, while the second code refers to outflows. If only one code is listed, we infer that the code applies to both inflows and outflows. The controls are coded as follows:
F = Free of controls.
A = Subject to authorization.

No Stability after 1991

The answer, as revealed by the third stage in the evolution of the new EMS, was nothing more than self-validating expectations of continued stability. As soon as doubts began to surface, the viability of the new EMS was threatened.

The lira was the first ERM currency to weaken in the second quarter of 1992. Observers cited a declining U.S. dollar, which undermined Italian international competitiveness; the possibility of an extraordinary tax on bank deposits and government bonds; the country's large budget deficit; its high public debt; the ongoing government crisis associated with the inconclusive debate over deficit reduction; and the negative outcome of the Danish referendum on Maastricht. The Banca d'Italia intervened extensively over the summer. In the opening days of September, the currency weakened further. A 1.75 point increase in the Banca d'Italia's discount rate on September 4 (which brought the rate to 15 percent) and the government's decision to seek emergency powers bought a brief respite, but within a week the lira had crashed through its Exchange Rate Mechanism floor.

Britain's exchange rate was also showing disturbing symptoms. In the second week of July, sterling fell to its lowest level against the DM since the April 1992 election.[14] The currency's weakness deepened in August. Britain reportedly expended at least $1.3 billion of reserves that month to keep sterling from falling through its floor against the DM. The first week in September, the Bank of England borrowed $14.5 billion of foreign reserves to finance further intervention, news of which allowed sterling to recover temporarily.[15]

On September 16, the Bank of England engaged in massive intervention in support of the pound, reportedly expending as much as $20 billion, or half its total foreign exchange reserves.[16] Its discount rate was raised from 10 to 12 percent and a second increase to 15 percent was announced. None of these measures sufficed. Hemorrhaging reserves forced the government to withdraw sterling from the ERM at the end of the day. Italy pulled out later that night, and Spain devalued the peseta by 5 percent. Portugal devalued by 6 percent on November 22. (Simultaneously, Spain shifted its ERM band a second time, also by 6 percent, although no discontinuous devaluation of the peseta occurred.) Ireland devalued in January, and Spain and Portugal again in May.

Thus a period of nearly five years distinguished by the absence of realignments came to an ignominious end, imparting a painful lesson to central bankers and politicians who had thought that the preconditions for European monetary union were already in place.

Pegged But Adjustable Exchange Rates: The Necessary Conditions

When the EMS was launched in 1979, few economists gave it much chance of surviving. It not only survived but grew and prospered. It is worth considering, therefore, what this experience reveals about the preconditions for maintaining pegged exchange rates. We focus on three: the capacity to undertake relative price adjustments, robust monetary rules, and ability to contain market pressures.

The Capacity to Undertake Relative Price Adjustments

Pegged rate systems face difficulties when significant changes are required in the relative prices of domestic and foreign goods, of traded and nontraded goods, and of labor and commodities. If nominal exchange rate changes are not permitted, the response must occur through the synchronous adjustment of numerous wages and prices. If some wages and prices adjust sluggishly, transitional output losses may result. Exchange rate changes can avert these losses by altering many prices at once. This is the daylight savings time argument for exchange rate adjustments.

This perspective suggests that pegged exchange rates can be sustained only if shocks requiring sizable relative price adjustments are infrequent; if individual wages and prices adjust smoothly; or if changes in nominal exchange rates are permitted in the event of exceptional shocks.

In practice, the first two conditions have not been met, while the third has been a feature of all successful pegged rate systems. Such systems feature escape clauses providing for realignments in the event of exceptional shocks.[17] The EMS as initially designed, for example, explicitly provided for realignments.[18]

The theory of escape clauses emphasizes that realignments can be undertaken without undermining authorities' commitment to pegged rates if they are initiated in response to exceptional shocks that can be directly observed or otherwise independently verified, and if those shocks are not instigated by the authorities themselves—that is, if moral hazard is not a problem. German economic and monetary union is an example of such a shock; as we document below, the German Bundesbank argued that it was possible to realign in response without undermining confidence in the EMS.

In contrast, if the contingencies that trigger the escape clause are private information, the contingent rule may lack credibility.[19] The gains from possessing an escape clause may be outweighed by the losses associated with the expectations of devaluation, higher interest rates, and inflationary pressure engendered by its existence. From this perspective, the new EMS was a gamble in which the authorities traded the third necessary condition for a viable exchange rate system (the escape clause) for the added credibility of a fixed rate, in the hope that one of the other two necessary conditions (infrequent shocks or smooth domestic adjustments) would miraculously arise.

Robust Monetary Rules

Because the credibility of a pegged rate system requires that exchange rate changes should occur only in response to exceptional disturbances, realignments resulting from self-fulfilling speculative attacks must be ruled out. A necessary condition for precluding such attacks is to adopt robust monetary rules.

Later in this chapter, we describe the conditions under which multiple equilibria and self-fulfilling speculative attacks may exist in the foreign exchange market. At this stage, we simply note that there are conditions in which a speculative crisis can occur—even though monetary policy is conspicuously consistent with balance-of-payments equilibrium. If investors anticipate that post-attack monetary policy will be loosened, then capital gains on foreign assets will be rationally anticipated. It is this ex post validation that makes an attack equilibrium possible alongside a no-attack equilibrium.

Under these circumstances, current and past policies do not suffice to rule out balance-of-payments crises; anticipated future policies matter as well. The escape clause feature of pegged rate systems—that the parity may be changed if exceptional shocks occur—is compatible with the credibility of the peg only if changes in monetary and exchange rate policy do not occur under other circumstances. Thus a robust monetary rule is one that precludes a shift to more accommodating policies in the presence of a speculative attack not grounded in fundamentals.

Such rules are our second necessary condition for the viability of a pegged rate system. The EMS prescription that a country wishing to change its parity must obtain the agreement of all other participating countries on both the principle of the parity change and its size functions as a mechanism committing countries to the pursuit of robust monetary rules.[20]

Ability to Contain Market Pressures

A third necessary condition for the viability of a fixed rate system concerns central bank actions in the event of a crisis. If the markets are uncertain as to whether the authorities are prepared to follow a robust monetary policy rule, they may test the authorities' resolve by running on their reserves. A government's commitment to follow a robust policy may not be enough to stabilize the exchange rate if the government is newly constituted and the markets are still uncertain about the government's intention. This is an example of the private information problem emphasized by Matthew B. Canzoneri.[21]

A concerted effort is required to defeat a speculative attack motivated on these grounds. One way of doing so is to raise domestic interest rates to such heights that the capital gains accruing on foreign assets if a realignment occurs are outweighed by the return on interest-bearing domestic assets. Investors then have no further incentive to test the authorities' resolve. But the maintenance of stratospheric interest rates may be painful, as we explain below. Central banks seeking to contain market pressures may have to resort to alternative means.

One alternative is for strong-currency countries to intervene in support of weak currencies. This implies that they should accumulate reserves, which would appear to be painless. But strong-currency countries fear that unlimited intervention threatens price stability because it implies an increase in the monetary base.[22] Central banks that commit to intervene in unlimited amounts may renege when they perceive that domestic price stability is jeopardized. We show below that this problem has arisen under the EMS.

Another way of containing market pressures is to resort to restrictions on capital movements. Capital controls, as an administrative restriction, limit the funds that can be legally and profitably transferred between currencies over short periods.[23] Such administrative controls may be circumvented eventually; however, in the meantime, they prevent the exhaustion of foreign reserves and abandonment of the exchange rate peg. Even if the controls protect the pegged rate for only a few days, this can provide precious scope for organizing an orderly realignment (which under EMS rules requires extensive consultation) and hence for insuring the survival of the system.

To sum up, the three conditions that we cited as necessary for a pegged rate system—the capacity to undertake relative price adjustments, robust monetary rules, and ability to contain market pressures—characterized the European Monetary System as initially designed but were eliminated under the new EMS. Ruling out realignments—whatever the anti-inflationary benefits in weak-currency countries—has made relative price changes more difficult to effect. Eliminating capital controls—whatever the virtues in terms of resource allocation—has left central banks bereft of protection from attacks. The desire to qualify for monetary union provided countries with the incentive to adopt robust policy rules consistent with the maintenance of fixed rates. Once the prospects for European monetary union dimmed, however, speculative attacks proved impossible to rebuff. The EMS became unstable.

Overt Competitiveness Problems

The simplest—and hence most popular—explanation for the September crisis is that it resulted from competitiveness problems. In this view, certain countries experienced persistent inflation and rising labor costs, which undermined the competitiveness of their traded-goods sectors. The markets identified these countries and attacked their currencies once devaluation was overdue.[24]

From this perspective, the countries whose exchange rates have been shaken since September fall into three categories. In the first is Italy, which shows clear signs of deteriorating competitiveness. Strikingly, Italy was the first EMS country to suffer foreign exchange market difficulties in the summer and autumn of 1992. Thus, we conclude that simple competitive problems played a part—but only a limited one—in the September crisis.

The second category includes Spain and the United Kingdom (along with two countries outside the EMS, Sweden and Finland). Although they too suffered foreign exchange crises in September, the evidence on competitiveness is more ambiguous. Some indicators suggest a problem, while others do not. In the third category are the other EMS countries that experienced exchange rate difficulties—France, Belgium, Denmark, and Ireland—none of which showed significant signs of deteriorating competitiveness.[25]

We present three competitiveness measures for each country: bilateral unit labor costs relative to Germany, multilateral relative unit labor costs adjusted for the business cycle, and the ratio of traded to nontraded goods prices.[26]

Figure 7.1 focuses on Italy, the only EMS country that shows unambiguous evidence of deteriorating international competitiveness. The unit labor cost indexes in figure 7.1 indicate a loss of competitiveness of some 20 percent for Italy since 1988. This is confirmed by the decline in the ratio of traded to nontraded goods prices.

Figures 7.2 and 7.3 examine Spain and the United Kingdom, the two other EMS countries that present some indication of competitive difficulties (although the evidence is not clear). In the case of Spain, real exchange rates, whether measured by labor costs or the price ratio between traded and nontraded goods, depict a massive real appreciation from the 1987 trough. One would expect a trend in this direction because of the Balassa-Samuelson effect, however.[27] Because Spain was growing rapidly during the period, this qualification renders the evidence for that country difficult to interpret.

There may also be some evidence of overvaluation for the United Kingdom. Interpretation of that evidence is complicated by the fact that the real appreciation predates Britain's entry into the ERM in October 1990. (Sterling did, however, shadow the ERM from 1987 onward.) The

Index of multilateral relative unit labor costs

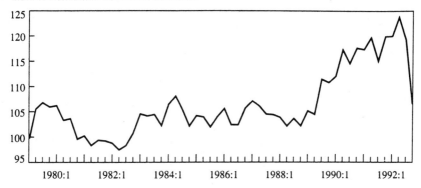

Index of bilateral relative unit labor costs

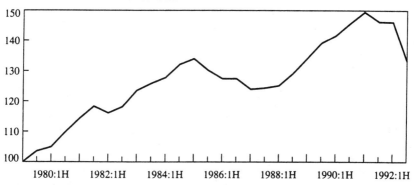

Traded to nontraded goods price index

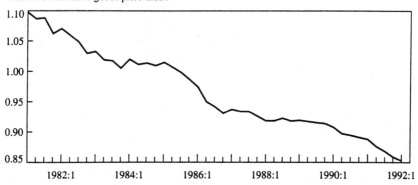

Figure 7.1
Competitiveness measures for Italy, 1979–92.
Source: Multilateral normalized relative unit labor costs are plotted quarterly and are from *International Financial Statistics.* Bilateral unit labor costs are plotted semiannually relative to Germany and are calculated using data from *OECD Economic Outlook,* various issues. Traded to nontraded goods price index is quarterly, from *Main Economic Indicators,* OECD, various issues.

Index of multilateral relative unit labor costs

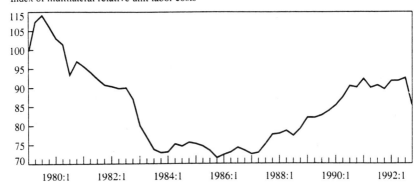

Index of bilateral relative unit labor costs

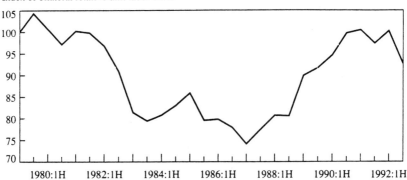

Traded to nontraded goods price index

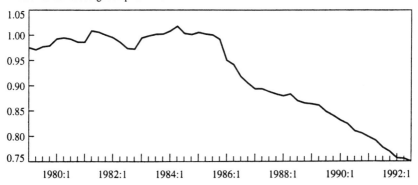

Figure 7.2
Competitiveness measures for Spain, 1979–92.
Source: Same as figure 7.1, except the index of traded to nontraded goods uses data from
International Financial Statistics.

Index of multilateral relative unit labor costs

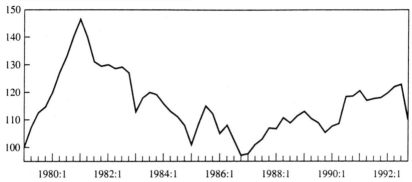

Index of bilateral relative unit labor costs

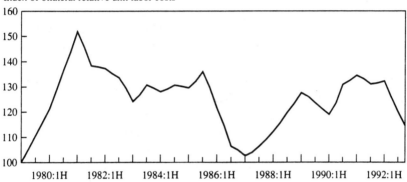

Traded to nontraded goods price index

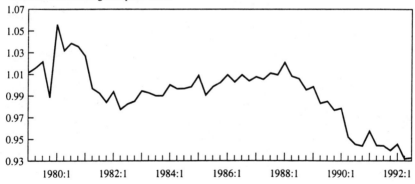

Figure 7.3
Competitiveness measures for United Kingdom, 1979–92.
Source: See figure 7.1.

behavior of relative labor costs suggests that improvements were actually underway since entry. This observation creates some difficulty for those who argue that Britain's crisis was a product of the decision to join the ERM at an overvalued rate.

Sweden and Finland, while not ERM members, can be placed in this category as well. Finland suffered a massive shock because of the collapse of its Soviet trade; this required radical adjustments of the prices and costs of Finnish exports, which had to be redirected toward other markets. Sweden felt the repercussions of problems in neighboring Finland (with which it competed in products such as timber and minerals) and encountered difficulties in other markets, as well.[28] Both countries were grappling with widening budget deficits and serious banking problems. The labor cost indexes for Sweden in Figure 7.4 suggest that a major deterioration had occurred in the late 1980s; however, a reversal was underway starting in 1990, which should have reassured foreign exchange market participants. In contrast, the price ratio of traded to nontraded goods shows no sign of recovery.

Figure 7.5 for Finland makes clear that a dramatic adjustment of wages and costs had taken place by 1992. But the magnitude of the Soviet shock makes it difficult to know whether these adjustments sufficed.

Figures 7.6 through 7.8 show these same competitiveness measures for Denmark, France, and Ireland, which also suffered attacks on their exchange rates starting in September. No sign of competitive difficulties appears in any of these countries, aside from the disquieting behavior of Danish unit labor costs. And the rise in Danish unit labor costs, centered around the mid-1980s, leveled off after 1986. There is little evidence of deterioration since that time.

On balance, we conclude that the divergent movement of prices and labor costs played a part—but a limited one—in the September crisis. This is an indictment of the no-devaluation policies of the new EMS (or of the macroeconomic policies followed by some of the participating countries). But this indictment is not universal. Aside from Italy and, arguably, Spain and the United Kingdom, support for the simple competitiveness explanation of the crisis is hardly overwhelming.

German Unification and Hidden Competitiveness Problems

Even if relative unit labor costs in Germany and its EMS partner countries diverged only slightly, the latter still could have suffered competitive difficulties because of the asymmetric GEMU shock. German unification

Index of multilateral relative unit labor costs

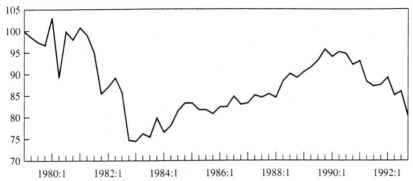

Index of bilateral relative unit labor costs

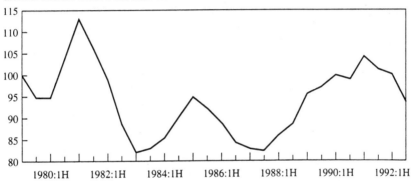

Traded to nontraded goods price index

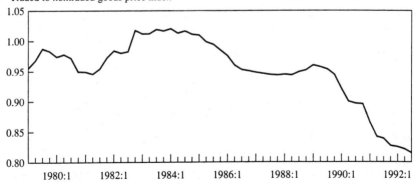

Figure 7.4
Competitiveness measures for Sweden, 1979–92.
Source: See figure 7.1.

Index of multilateral relative unit labor costs

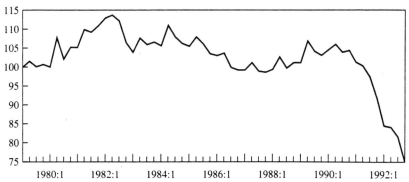

Index of bilateral relative unit labor costs

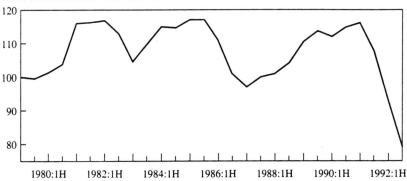

Traded to nontraded goods price index

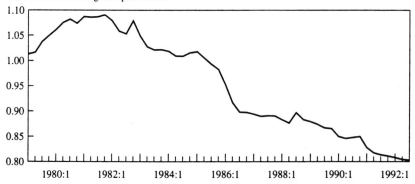

Figure 7.5
Competitiveness measures for Finland, 1979–92.
Source: See figure 7.2.

Index of multilateral relative unit labor costs

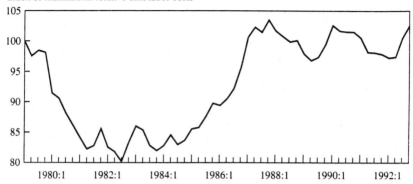

Index of bilateral relative unit labor costs

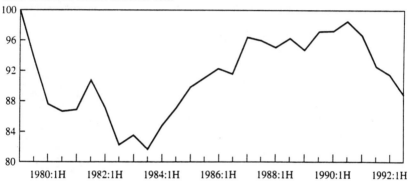

Traded to nontraded goods price index

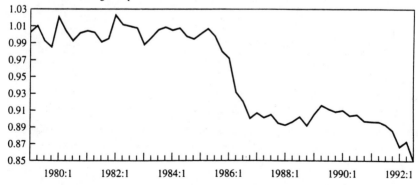

Figure 7.6
Competitiveness measures for Denmark, 1979–92.
Source: See figure 7.1.

Index of multilateral relative unit labor costs

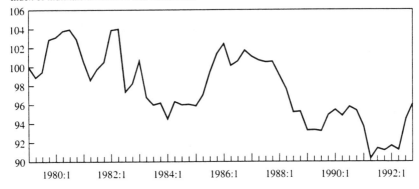

Index of bilateral relative unit labor costs

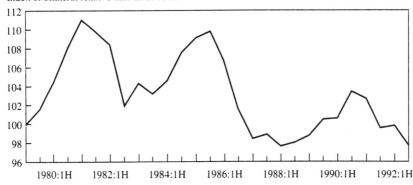

Figure 7.7
Competitiveness measures for France, 1979–92.
Source: See figure 7.1.

necessitated a decline in prices and costs in other EMS countries relative to those prevailing in Germany. That prices and costs evolved in parallel in Germany and other EMS countries does not therefore absolve other EMS members of the charge of inadequate competitiveness.

We develop this point with a simple model of the relative-price effects of German economic and monetary unification, and show how the requisite changes can be brought about under different exchange rate arrangements.

Modeling German Unification

The instantaneous absorption by the Federal Republic of another country almost half its geographical size and one-quarter of its population was

Index of multilateral relative unit labor costs

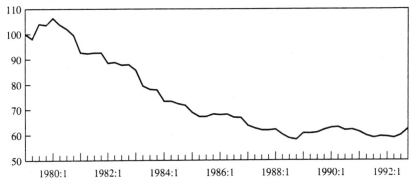

Index of bilateral relative unit labor costs

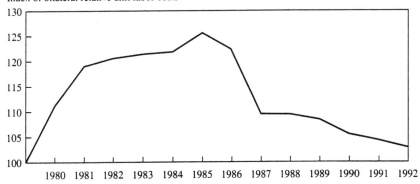

Traded to nontraded goods price index

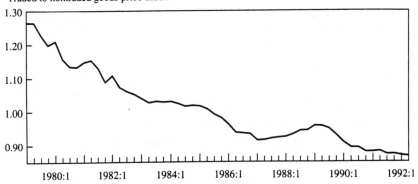

Figure 7.8
Competitiveness measures for Ireland, 1979–92.
Source: See figure 7.1. Irish bilateral unit labor costs are plotted annually.

bound to affect economic conditions profoundly. Most early analyses concluded that an appreciation of the DM (a fall in prices and costs in other EMS countries relative to those prevailing in Germany) would be required in response to the shock.[29] A demand-side view noted that public and private spending rose considerably in the wake of unification.[30] Public spending was spurred by the need for investment in infrastructure and the rise in unemployment compensation. The surge in private spending in the East reflected consumption smoothing in anticipation of real wage gains. In the absence of a commensurate supply-side response, the pressure on home goods could only be accommodated by a real appreciation. A complementary supply-side approach stressed the existence of high-return investments in the East.[31] This placed upward pressure on real interest rates in Germany, attracting capital inflows and inducing a real appreciation.

Standard textbook models correctly predicted the macroeconomic consequences of the shock and pointed to the requisite adjustments. To drive home this point, we employ a simple two-country model in the tradition of Mundell-Fleming:

Germany	Other EMS Countries	
$m - p = ay - bi$	$m^* - p^* = ay^* - bi^*$	(1)
$y = hq - kr + \mu$	$y^* = -hq^* - kr^*$	(2)
$r = i - \dot{p}$	$r^* = i^* - \dot{p}^*$	(3)
$\dot{p} = cy$	$\dot{p}^* = cy^*$	(4)

$$q = e + p^* - p \tag{5}$$

$$i = i^* + \dot{e}, \tag{6}$$

where all variables are in logs except for the real and nominal interest rates (r and i respectively). Asterisks denote foreign countries (for current purposes, the rest of the EMS), and dots over variables represent derivatives with respect to time. Equations 1 and 2 describe money and goods market equilibria where m is the money supply, p is the price level, q is the real exchange rate, and a, b, h and k are parameters. Output y denotes the deviation from trend. The unification shock (equivalently, a positive demand or negative supply shock) is represented by μ; for analytical simplicity, we model μ as permanent.[32] Equation 3 defines the real interest rate in Germany and the rest of the EMS. Equation 4 is a naive

Phillips curve, where c is a parameter.[33] Equation 5 defines Germany's real exchange rate relative to the other EMS countries. Equation 6 represents full capital mobility, as in the new EMS (where e is the domestic currency price of a unit of foreign exchange).

If $z = p - p^*$ is the difference between price levels in Germany and the rest of EMS, then the system simplifies to

$$\dot{q} = \beta[2hq(a - bc) + z - (m - m^*) + \mu(a - bc)], \text{ and} \tag{7}$$

$$\dot{z} = \beta[2hbcq - kcz + kc(m - m^*) + bc\mu], \tag{8}$$

where the coefficient β is assumed to be positive.[34]

If in response to the unification shock (when μ becomes positive) money supplies m and m^* remain unchanged, the long-run equilibrium is reestablished when q falls by $\mu/2h$ with $z = 0$. When exchange rates are allowed to float, this is also the short-run equilibrium as the deutsche mark appreciates by $\mu/2h$ on impact. Price levels in Germany and other countries do not have to move. Output rises in the same proportion in both countries, perfectly spreading the unification shock across them. (If Germany reduces m to prevent its price level from rising, with m^* unchanged, a stronger initial appreciation will occur, followed by a decline of prices in Germany relative to those in the rest of the EMS.)

The same outcome can be achieved within the EMS so long as the deutsche mark is revalued at the time of unification. Thereafter, prices and output evolve in parallel in Germany and other EMS countries. Exchange rate flexibility is needed only once, when the shock occurs. If the new parity is chosen correctly, there is no need for further realignment.

The Conflict

Aware of market pressures for an appreciation of its currency, the Bundesbank apparently desired a realignment of the DM as early as 1989. Revaluing the DM within the EMS requires the unanimous agreement of ERM countries, however. France, pledged to its *franc fort*, vetoed any change in its parity relative to the DM. Britain, which had just entered the ERM, argued that a downward realignment against the DM would undermine the credibility of its monetary strategy. The Bundesbank's preference for a realignment was rejected, apparently repeatedly.

Assuming that the commitment not to realign was credible, domestic and foreign interest rates should have been equalized. (This is not far-fetched for the main EMS countries in 1990–91; Figure 7.9 shows that by

Percent per year

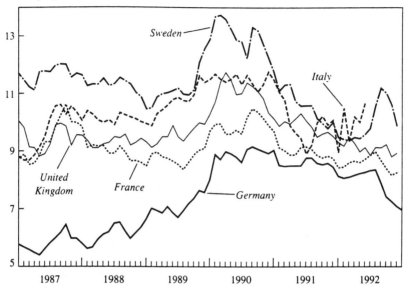

Figure 7.9
Long-term interest rates in Europe, 1987–92.
Source: International Financial Statistics.

1991, French and German long-term interest rates had more or less converged.) With $i = i^*$, equation 7 simplifies to

$$(1 - kc)\dot{q} = -2hcq - c\mu. \tag{9}$$

Although realignment was ruled out, the real appreciation (which still had to ultimately equal $\mu/2h$) could only be achieved by increasing the level of German prices relative to price levels in other EMS countries. It is worth noting that, according to equation 9, the evolution of the real exchange rate and therefore relative inflation rates is independent of the monetary policies pursued by Germany and the rest of the EMS. Similarly, equation 10 shows that the ratio of output in Germany and the rest of the EMS does not depend on the policies chosen:

$$y - y^* - [\beta/(1 - \beta ak)][2bhq + b\mu]. \tag{10}$$

Yet output and price *levels* are affected by policy actions, creating an unavoidable conflict of interest. The real appreciation required to accommodate unification can be achieved with many different combinations of price inflation in Germany and the rest of the EMS. Feasible options include a burst of inflation in Germany and stable prices elsewhere, a constant price level in Germany and a burst of deflation elsewhere, and moderate inflation in Germany combined with moderate deflation elsewhere. But, as in any fixed rate system, monetary policies in Germany and in the rest of the EMS cannot be set independently.

France and other countries may have thought that, by denying the Bundesbank its request for a realignment, they could force it to adopt a more expansionary monetary policy, thereby eliminating the need for contractionary policies elsewhere in the EMS.[35] For its part, the Bundesbank did not conceal its desire to check inflation at home even if doing so implied disinflation elsewhere. If we model Germany as the Stackelberg leader and assume that the rest of the EMS adjusts monetary policy to peg its DM rate, we can combine equation 9 with equations 1 through 4 to obtain

$$\dot{p} = c\beta(bhq - kp + km + b\mu). \tag{11}$$

The implications of equations 9 and 11 are shown in figure 7.10.[36] The real exchange rate must appreciate from q_0 to q_1 in the long run. If Germany's money supply remains unchanged, the system moves over time from A to B: the required real appreciation is achieved through inflation in Germany caused by excess demand (or, equivalently, inadequate supply). The price level in the rest of the EMS may rise or fall.[37] If instead Germany uses its leadership to insure domestic price stability, the new long-run equilibrium is D. The real appreciation is now accomplished through disinflation and recession in the rest of the EMS. Because other EMS countries peg their currencies to the DM, they import Germany's tight monetary policy.[38] A conflict was thus unavoidable once the Bundesbank reaffirmed its commitment to check inflation and the other EMS countries confirmed their unwillingness to realign.

The Outcome

The implication of this model is that stable relative prices were not enough. Prices and costs in other EMS countries had to decline relative to those prevailing in Germany. As shown in figure 7.11, the other EMS countries in fact succeeded in reducing their inflation rates relative to Germany's.

Without an empirically calibrated version of the model, it is difficult to say whether the observed changes in relative prices were enough. A way

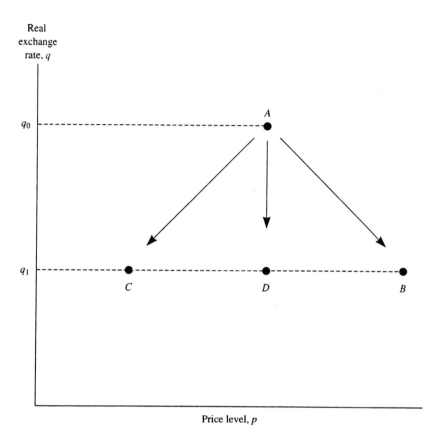

Figure 7.10
The long-run German real exchange rate and monetary policy options.

around this problem is to focus on the quantities that relative prices affect.
The GEMU shock, as an increase in German spending, should have driven
up the prices of goods produced and consumed in Germany relative to
those produced and consumed abroad. As an increase in German investment relative to German saving, it should have weakened Germany's current account and strengthened those of its EMS trading partners. As an
increase in German demand for the goods of its EMS trading partners, it
should have enhanced profitability in other EMS countries. If other countries' current accounts in fact weakened, then the prices of their goods
must have fallen insufficiently (or risen excessively) relative to the price of
German goods. Similarly, if the profitability of their manufacturing sectors
deteriorated rather than strengthened, price discipline outside Germany
must have been inadequate. Absent the requisite relative price move-

Percent per year

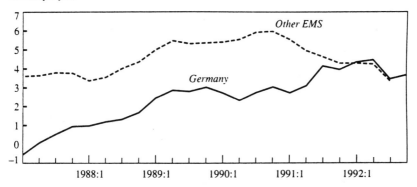

Figure 7.11
Inflation in EMS countries, 1987:1–1992:4.
Source: Authors' calculations using consumer price index data in *International Financial Statistics*. The Other EMS line is a weighted average of EMS countries, excluding Germany, with weights based on 1987 GDP data.

ments, other countries would have had to push up their nominal rates along with Germany's in order to restrict domestic demand and maintain external balance, reinforcing the negative trend in domestic profitability.

We therefore examined the profit share in manufacturing (where available) and the current account of the balance of payments. Italy's deteriorating current account and business profitability confirm our hypothesis of a competitiveness problem. The evidence for the United Kingdom is as ambiguous as before; while the profitability measure suggests an improvement in competitiveness since ERM entry, the current account shows a relapse in 1992. In the case of Spain, the profit share holds up nicely after 1988 despite the rise in labor costs, consistent with the arguments of those who would minimize competitive difficulties. For Finland and Sweden, profits and the current account both suggest that, by 1992, adjustment to earlier difficulties was underway. In none of the other countries experiencing an attack (France, Belgium, Denmark, and Ireland) does evidence of serious problems appear.

By the fall of 1992, then, adjustment to the GEMU shock was well underway. Competitive disequilibria were being corrected. Even taking into account the effects of the GEMU shock on equilibrium relative prices and costs, we conclude—like Richard Portes[39]—that while competitiveness problems cannot be dismissed (aside from Italy and possibly Spain and the United Kingdom) it is difficult to find firm support for them, even when one focuses on data that take into account the asymmetric GEMU shock.

In addition, there is the troubling fact of timing. German unification occurred in 1990, but the EMS crisis occurred in 1992. Markets are forward-looking; traders make profits if they succeed in anticipating events. It seems peculiar that the imbalances set in motion by German unification should have destabilized EMS parities more than two years after the fact, and not earlier. The Spanish peseta, for one, was at the top of its EMS band only days before it was attacked. If the markets perceived that competitiveness problems were evolving over time, traders should have begun to sell pesetas in anticipation of future difficulties, driving the currency toward the bottom of its band before the fact. This did not occur.

Inevitable Policy Shifts

In fact, markets may have been more sophisticated—not less—than we have so far given them credit. Even if current policies were consistent with the maintenance of ERM parities, the markets could have been anticipating a shift in future policies. The policies of austerity required to defend prevailing parities gave rise to growing unemployment, as shown in figure 7.12. As unemployment rose, the political or economic cost of maintaining those policies may have grown too heavy for governments

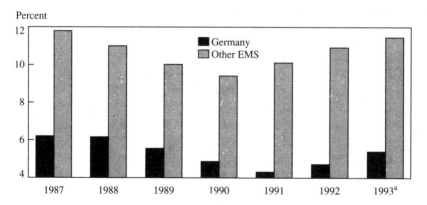

Figure 7.12
Unemployment rates in EMS countries, 1987–93.
Source: Authors' calculations using *OECD Economic Outlook*, December 1992, and 1987 GDP numbers from *International Financial Statistics* to weight EMS countries excluding Germany.
[a] Based on OECD projections.

and their constituencies to bear. Anticipating the inevitable, traders may have sold the currencies of these countries before the policy shift occurred.

Considerable informal evidence is consistent with this view. European unemployment was high and rising on the eve of the crisis. The budgetary austerity required to meet the convergence criteria forced governments to implement painful measures of fiscal austerity, which elicited howls of protest. The Spanish government proposed reductions in the rate of unemployment benefits, for example, provoking labor unrest. In Britain, intense criticism was levied against the decision to maintain high interest rates in the face of an incipient recession.

To analyze this explanation more systematically, we use a one-country version of the model presented above (with no unification shock). All variables are defined as before.

$$m - p = ay - bi, \tag{12}$$

$$y = h(e - p) - kr, \tag{13}$$

$$i = r + \dot{p}, \tag{14}$$

$$\dot{p} = cy, \text{ and} \tag{15}$$

$$i = i^* + \dot{e}. \tag{16}$$

Because we assume that the country is small, the foreign price level and interest rate are taken as constant and normalized to zero. The model reduces to

$$\dot{e} = \beta[ah(e - p) + (1 - kc)(p - m)], \text{ and} \tag{17}$$

$$\dot{p} = \beta c[bh(e - p) - k(p - m)]. \tag{18}$$

Figure 7.13 represents the long-run equilibrium with a money supply m_0 and an associated stable convergence path $S_0 S_0$.[40] The money supply remains unchanged so long as no disturbance occurs. The system rests at point A with a pegged exchange rate $e_0 = m_0$ if policy is not expected to change. In this equilibrium, the exchange rate corresponds to the fundamental m_0.

In contrast, the expectation that at a future date monetary policy will be relaxed from m_0 to m_1 implies long-run equilibrium at point D. When the markets realize that policy will change, they attack the currency. This attack exhausts the authorities' foreign exchange reserves, forcing them to abandon the exchange rate peg. This attack occurs before the shift in

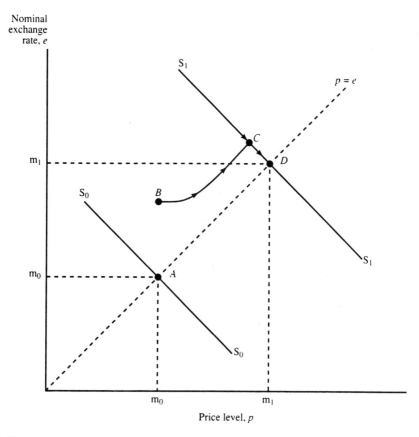

Figure 7.13
Long-run equilibria as a result of central bank monetary policy.

monetary policy itself. Indeed, it may occur as soon as the markets become aware that monetary policy will change; otherwise unexploited profit opportunities would exist. The period of floating begins with a depreciation that causes a jump from A to B. Although the monetary authorities initially keep the money supply unchanged at m_0, the knowledge that it will be raised subsequently to m_1 weakens the exchange rate immediately. Following the jump depreciation, the exchange rate continues to depreciate along the path BC. Point C represents the instant when the money supply is increased to m_1, just preceding the last phase in the transition along the path CD.

Our third model of the September crisis thus considers it a consequence of market anticipations of an inevitable shift in monetary policies provoked by rising unemployment. A complete analysis of this explanation must recognize that governments, in deciding whether to shift to less restrictive policies, weighed the benefits as well as the costs of the prevailing regime. The costs were associated with unemployment; the benefits were associated with qualifying for monetary union. Thus anything that reduced the likelihood that these benefits would still exist in the future should have influenced the calculations of monetary authorities and governments.

An implication of this trade-off is that the stability of exchange rates should be correlated with the prospects for European monetary union. This was clearly the case in 1992. The weakness of the lira dated from the day the negative outcome of the Danish referendum was known. The lira, the British pound, the Danish krone, and the French franc all fell on June 3, the first trading day after the referendum. The Danish *nej* was a surprise; it had not been forecast by the opinion polls. Initially, reports stated that legal experts saw no way that the Maastricht Treaty, or even parts of it, could be approved and enacted by only eleven EC member states.[41] Doubts were compounded by press reports that confusion about the treaty's viability would stoke German concerns about the wisdom of pressing ahead with European monetary union. Italian businessmen voiced fears that the Danish rejection would undermine Italy's resolve to comply with the convergence criteria laid down at Maastricht.[42]

Ireland's ratification of the treaty on June 18 did little to change the outlook. The lira did strengthen slightly once the Irish results were known. But uncertainty remained about the outcome of the French referendum in September and the implications of the Danish *nej*.[43] Until these questions were resolved, traders pondered three possible outcomes: that Maastricht would collapse, that eleven of the twelve EC states would go ahead with EMU, or that there would be a two-speed Europe in which some states would unite their currencies and others would not.[44]

In August, French opinion polls perturbed the markets on a regular basis. On Wednesday the fifth, for example, the DM rose against other European currencies as traders anticipated the release of a negative polling result later in the day. As it turned out, the poll indicated that a slim majority of French voters favored the treaty, "but the result proved too inconclusive for most dealers, and the German currency drifted further upwards."[45]

The turnaround occurred on Tuesday, August 25, when for the first time a poll predicted a slim rejection of the treaty, by a margin of 51 to 49 percent.[46] Sterling fell to within one-half pfennig of its floor against the

DM as "the prospect of European monetary union collapsing has become a strong incentive for investing in D-Marks."[47] Another poll on August 28, with an even larger negative margin (53 percent), pushed the lira through its floor against the DM and led to weakness in other EMS currencies.[48] On August 31, Commission President Jacques Delors threatened to resign if the French rejected the treaty, warning that a negative vote would jeopardize European unity itself; the pound, lira, and French franc continued to slide.[49]

We can more systematically analyze the impact of these events on expectations by examining the behavior of forward exchange rates. Figure 7.14 displays daily data on spot rates, one-year-ahead forward rates, and EMS bands. The data for Italy are graphic reminders of the shaky credibility of the lira's EMS peg. From 1987 through early 1989, the forward rate was consistently below the bottom of the band. In contrast to other EMS currencies, the forward rate was again below the bottom of the band at the beginning of 1992. This is consistent with our conclusion that the markets perceived Italy as having more competitiveness problems than other EMS countries. The forward discount then grew to sizable proportions during the summer.

The behavior of the British pound and the Spanish peseta (as shown in figure 7.14) is strikingly different. Following the two countries' entry into the ERM, their forward rates consistently remained within the band. Even in the days leading up to the lira devaluation (September 14), the two currencies' forward rates did not drop out of the band. Again, this is consistent with our conclusion that Britain's and Spain's competitiveness problems were less pronounced than Italy's.

Figure 7.14 also plots forward rates for four other countries for which there is even less evidence of competitive difficulties: Ireland, France, Denmark, and Sweden. It is striking that these countries saw their forward rates drop out of the band after the Danish referendum and before September 14. (For comparison, we also provide data on the rock-solid Dutch guilder.)

To a considerable degree, the data support the explanation for the crisis based on deterministic shifts in future policies. In particular, this explanation is supported by the correlation between obstacles to ratifying the Maastricht Treaty and difficulties in foreign exchange markets. As these obstacles mounted, the balance of costs and benefits shifted away from policies that would support the exchange rate in order to qualify for EMU and toward more expansionary policies that would respond to rising unemployment.

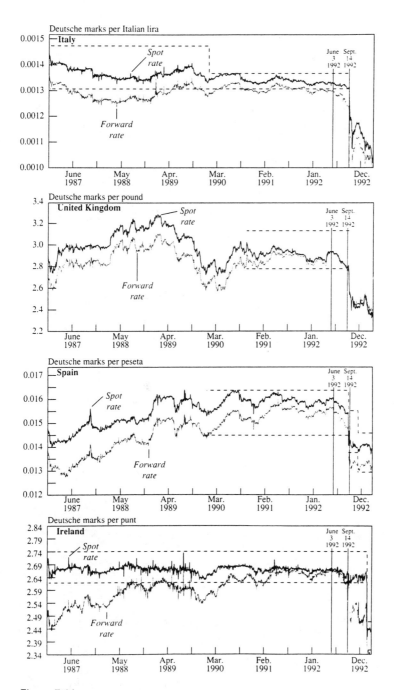

Figure 7.14
Spot and forward exchange rates in EMS countries, 1987–92.
Source: Data Resources Inc. (DRI) and Sveriges Riksbank.
[a] Dashed lines are EMS currency bands for each currency plotted vis-à-vis the deutsche mark. The forward rate is the one-year-ahead forward exchange rate. Tic marks are 115 trading days apart for all panels except Sweden.

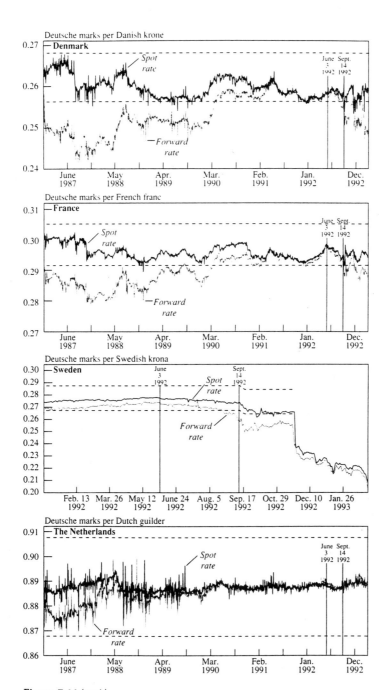

Figure 7.14 (cont.)

Nonetheless, certain facts sit uneasily with this interpretation. Unemployment was rising everywhere, not only in those countries that were attacked. Incumbent governments were weak throughout Europe, not just where speculative crises erupted. While some countries that were attacked shifted their policies in more stimulative directions subsequently, others did not. All this leads us to believe that a fourth and final explanation is required based on multiple equilibria and self-fulfilling speculative attacks.

Self-Fulfilling Speculative Attacks

The idea that a pegged exchange rate can be successfully attacked in the absence of any problem with fundamentals, either expected or future, rests on the principle of self-fulfilling attacks that arbitrarily shift the foreign exchange market between alternative equilibria. That multiple equilibria can exist in foreign exchange markets was pointed out by Flood and Garber[50] and Obstfeld.[51] An attack can occur even if the stance of policy is consistent with balance-of-payments equilibrium and the pegged exchange rate is sustainable indefinitely. Yet if investors anticipate that monetary policy will be modified as the result of an attack—becoming looser than the preattack policy—then capital gains on foreign assets will be rationally anticipated. It is this ex post validation that makes attack and no-attack equilibria viable simultaneously.

This model must be clearly distinguished from that of Krugman[52] and Flood and Garber,[53] described above. That model has a unique equilibrium: the exchange rate is attacked only if a balance-of-payments problem already exists, implying the eventual exhaustion of reserves. Equally, the model of multiple equilibria we develop in this section should be distinguished from the model developed in the previous section. There, equilibrium is unique: the exchange rate is attacked only if an anticipated future balance-of-payments problem exists, inevitably implying the eventual exhaustion of reserves.

Self-fulfilling attacks are different. In the preceding models, the markets merely anticipate the crisis; in models of self-fulfilling attacks, they provoke it. The policy shift is contingent; it occurs if and only if an attack occurs. In the absence of the attack, no balance-of-payments problem exists and the current exchange rate can be maintained indefinitely. But if an attack occurs because market participants rationally anticipate that, if (and only if) attacked, policy will be modified in a more expansionary direction, then the attack can succeed, shifting the economy to a different equilibrium.

To illustrate these points, we again use the single-country model of the preceding section. But we now assume that central bank policy remains invariant in the absence of an attack. How events evolve in the event of an attack depends on the central bank's reaction. We explore two alternatives, under the assumption of perfect foresight. The first alternative is the case of a "wet" central bank that, in the event of an attack, increases the money supply from m_0 to m_1. The corresponding long-run equilibrium is at point B in figure 7.15. Should a speculative attack unfold, depreciation would occur immediately as the economy jumps from A to C on the new stable path $S_1 S_1$. Over time the system converges to B along that stable path.[54] The attack is self-fulfilling. The currency is weak because of the monetary authorities' lack of credibility in reacting to the attack.

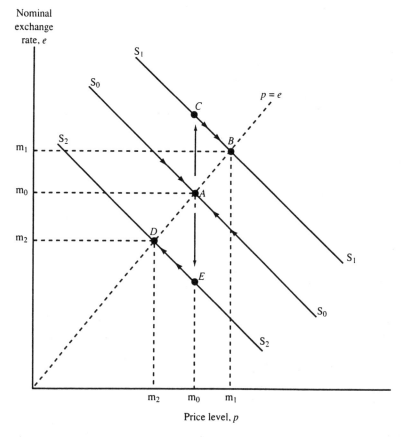

Figure 7.15
Long-run equilibria after a central bank reacts to a speculative attack.

The second equilibrium describes the case of a "dry" central bank that credibly commits to react to an attack by decreasing the money supply from m_0 to m_2. The corresponding path is shown by the jump from A to E followed by convergence to the long-run equilibrium point D along the stable path S_2S_2. This second equilibrium will not be observed because, under the perfect foresight assumption, a speculative attack will not occur when the exchange rate is expected to appreciate.

For this model of multiple equilibria to be compelling, there must be specific grounds for supposing that it applied to the events of September. In other words, there must be an intrinsic reason to have anticipated a shift in policy if and only if an attack occurred. In fact, incentives for just such a shift were built into the Maastricht Treaty.

The relevant provisions of the treaty are summarized in the appendix. For current purposes what matter are the so-called "convergence criteria" that must be met by countries seeking to qualify for monetary union—particularly the condition requiring a country to maintain a stable exchange rate (within the normal, narrow EMS fluctuation band) for the two preceding years without "severe tensions." The downside of this rule is that tensions provoked by the market may disqualify a country from European monetary union and thereby introduce scope for self-fulfilling attacks. This in turn would remove the government's incentive to maintain the current policies whose principal benefits resulted from qualifying the country for EMU. A rational government would shift toward more accommodating monetary policies only if attacked. But the knowledge that it had this incentive to change policy in the event of an attack provides foreign exchange traders with the incentive to undertake it. While the treaty can be interpreted as precluding EMU membership only by countries that actively sought to devalue, as opposed to those that did so involuntarily, it seems unlikely in practice that countries that experienced crises forcing them to realign would be regarded favorably by the European Monetary Institute (EMI) and the European Commission when it came time for them to evaluate conformance with the convergence criteria.[55]

"Severe tensions" in 1992 would be more likely to lead a government to conclude that its prospects for participating in EMU had been significantly damaged if two additional conditions were met: first, that EMU is likely to begin relatively early, giving devaluing countries little time to repair their reputations; and second, that countries missing the boat when it leaves the dock will find it difficult to board later. The timing of Stage

III, the formal start of EMU, is uncertain. The European Commission and the European Monetary Institute must indicate to the Council no later than the end of 1996 which countries meet the convergence criteria. If only a minority of EC countries do so, Stage II may continue until January 1, 1999, the last possible date for the inauguration of EMU. Again, the Commission and the EMI must report in 1998 as to which countries satisfy the conditions and thus can form the initial nucleus of the monetary union. Other countries may be admitted once it is determined that they satisfy the conditions.

But if a majority of EC countries meet the convergence criteria, Stage III may start earlier. Most commentators have interpreted the provision that the European Monetary Institute and the Commission must report no later than the end of 1996 as implying that Stage III will not commence before that point (that is, the beginning of 1997). In fact, nothing in the treaty prevents the EMI and the Commission from reporting earlier in Stage II if they believe that a majority of countries satisfy the convergence criteria. In theory, they could report on January 2, 1994, the second day of Stage II, using the performance of countries during Stage I as their basis for concluding that the convergence criteria were satisfied. Theoretically, nothing prevents Stage III from beginning as early as next year.[56]

Moreover, an implication of the convergence criteria is that the conditions applied to the first group of participants may be looser than those applied later. This argument is spelled out by Alberto Alesina and Vittorio Grilli.[57] They show that once a subset of EMS countries that share a preference for relatively low inflation forms a monetary union, they may resist enlarging it to include other countries preferring higher inflation, because this may push up the union's common inflation rate, making things worse for the initial members. This can be true even when every country would be better off with a Community-wide monetary union than with no monetary union at all.[58]

In summary, this section's model shows that self-fulfilling attacks can occur in theory. The events of the summer of 1992 confirm that they can occur in practice. In particular, the Maastricht Treaty's provisions regarding membership and starting date for EMU created scope for self-fulfilling attacks. Whether certain EMS countries also had competitiveness problems will continue to be debated. Our point here is that there were good reasons to anticipate a speculative crisis even in the absence of such problems.

A Survey of Foreign Exchange Markets

Given the four interpretations we have presented to explain the September crisis—overt or hidden competitiveness problems, anticipated policy shifts, and speculative attacks unrelated to competitiveness—it seems natural to ask market participants which ones informed their actions. In the second half of February 1993, we therefore mailed a questionnaire to all European traders listed in the *Currency and Instrument Directory*.[59] Although some dealers are not listed in this directory, it represents nearly the entire population of foreign exchange traders. We sent out 560 questionnaires and received 132 responses, a respectable response rate for a mail survey. The results are tabulated in tables 7.3 through 7.7.

The survey responses provide some support for all four interpretations. However, we would argue, the balance of sentiment supports anticipated future policy shifts and self-fulfilling attacks. In table 7.3 we tabulate answers to the question, "What in your opinion was the most important factor in making changes in ERM currencies likely?" Many respondents checked more than one alternative. Yet inflation—the source of speculative attacks in models emphasizing current fundamentals—is not one of the most popular answers.

An exception to this generalization is the view of German inflation. The response that German inflation made a realignment likely must be

Table 7.3
Reasons for the Crisis
(Percent)

Question and response	Very important	Important	Not important
What in your opinion was the most important factor in making changes in ERM currencies likely?			
Lack of public support for the Maastricht Treaty	33.1	44.4	15.0
Persistent inflation in:			
Italy	27.8	39.1	22.6
Spain	21.8	37.6	28.6
UK	15.0	40.6	32.3
Germany	38.3	35.3	18.0
High German interest rates	68.4	21.1	6.0
Realignment was overdue anyway	39.8	27.1	24.1
Instability of Swedish and Finnish currencies	10.5	33.8	42.9

Source: Authors' calculations based on their February 1993 survey of European foreign-exchange traders.

Table 7.4
Why Did Central Banks Give Up?
(Percent)

Question and response	Very important	Important	Not important
In September, central banks ultimately gave up defending certain European currencies. What explains this decision?			
Central banks' reserves are always insufficient	23.3	40.6	30.8
Central banks' reserves are insufficient now that most exchange controls in Europe have been removed	28.6	38.3	28.6
Central banks worried that further interest rate increases would destabilize banking systems	21.8	47.4	24.1
The Bundesbank worried that further intervention would threaten price stability	22.6	45.1	26.3
Central banks worried that further interest rate increases would worsen domestic economic conditions	64.7	23.3	3.8

Source: Authors' calculations based on their February 1993 survey of European foreign-exchange traders.

Table 7.5
Expectation of Imminent Changes in ERM Parities
(Percent)

Question and response	
When did you first begin to think that changes in ERM exchange rates were imminent?	
Before the Danish referendum in June	21.8
Just after the Danish referendum	46.6
Upon hearing about public opinion polls in France during the run-up to the referendum	15.1
Around the time of the Finnish crisis and devaluation	6.8
Around the time of the Swedish crisis in September	6.8
Other	9.1

Source: Authors' calculations based on their February 1993 survey of European foreign-exchange traders.

Table 7.6
Devaluation Contagion within the ERM
(Percent)

Question and response	
Did the weakness of some ERM currencies late in the summer lead you to anticipate weakness of other ERM currencies?	
The 90.2 percent responding yes gave these reasons:	
Devaluing countries are able to undercut competitors	53.4
Markets "tasted blood" (realized that there were profits to be made)	76.7
Other	4.5

Source: Authors' calculations based on their February 1993 survey of European foreign-exchange traders.

Table 7.7
Devaluation Contagion from Outside the ERM
(Percent)

Question and response	
Did the weakness of non-ERM countries (those of Finland, Sweden, and Norway, for example) lead you to anticipate weakness of ERM currencies?	
The 50.4 percent responding yes gave these reasons:	
Devaluing countries are able to undercut competitors	23.3
Markets have "tasted blood" (realize that there are profits to be made)	42.9
Other	3.8
The 49.6 percent responding no gave these reasons:	
ERM central banks can borrow from one another	22.6
EC countries mostly trade with one another	24.8
EC countries' financial markets are deeper	36.1
Other	1.5

Source: Authors' calculations based on their February 1993 survey of European foreign-exchange traders.

interpreted differently than concern about inflation in other countries because the DM, rather than one of the currencies attacked, was the strong currency against which the others were devalued. Emphasis on German inflation is properly interpreted as an indication that traders anticipated high interest rates and tight money, which would exacerbate unemployment in other EMS countries. This interpretation is supported by the emphasis respondents placed on the high level of German interest rates, which heightened deflationary pressure and unemployment in other countries, again increasing the likelihood of a future policy shift.

Only 22 percent of the respondents claim to have been expecting a realignment before the Danish referendum.[60] This confirms our point that the timing of the 1992 attacks does not fit well with interpretations emphasizing current fundamentals. The importance respondents attached to the two referenda supports our third interpretation, which emphasizes rising unemployment and future policy shifts.

Once the initial attacks occurred, the relative importance traders attached to different factors could have changed. Fundamentals could have become increasingly important in countries such as Ireland that traded heavily with the first EMS countries forced to devalue.[61] Alternatively, lack of confidence in EMS currencies could have spread contagiously. Responses that "the markets had 'tasted blood' (realized that there were profits to be made)" are consistent with this view. Tables 7.6 and 7.7 suggest that factors other than fundamentals outweighed considerations of trade and competitiveness. Not surprisingly, competitiveness played a larger role in spillovers within the EMS than in spillovers from the Nordic countries to the EC.

This survey sheds considerable light on what happened during the September crisis. The emphasis respondents placed on inflation suggests that fundamentals played some role; it is no coincidence, in other words, that the Italian lira was first to be attacked, followed by sterling and the peseta. But fundamentals do not explain the timing or course of the attacks. Whether the markets forced a change in policy or simply anticipated it remains an open question. One fact points in the direction of the former explanation: in enumerating what factors they consider when assessing the prospects for a particular currency, dealers gave a low ranking to unemployment, suggesting that they attached relatively little weight to the possibility that a deteriorating employment situation would inevitably force a government to abandon its defense of the currency.

Life without Capital Controls

The removal of capital controls has changed the European monetary environment in two significant ways. First, the absence of controls renders official foreign exchange reserves redundant—or nearly so. Reserves are dwarfed by the resources that markets can bring to bear. This in turn implies the need for very high interest rates to defend an exchange rate when the markets attack it. Second, these high interest rates can seriously and negatively affect economic activity, the government budget, the housing market, and the stability of the financial system if they are maintained for extended periods. And in a foreign exchange market with multiple equilibria, they may have to be maintained at high levels indefinitely.

Table 7.8
Interest Rate Required to Render Investors Indifferent between Holding Domestic and Foreign Assets
(Percent per Year)

	Event	
Probability of event	5 percent devaluation in 10 days	10 percent devaluation in 10 days
50 percent	85	238
70 percent	136	442
90 percent	201	762

Source: Authors' calculations.

Market Pressures

Daily turnover on foreign exchange markets exceeds $1 trillion—more than the total official foreign reserves of all IMF member countries combined—according to the Bank for International Settlements.[62] These numbers dwarf the otherwise-impressive quantities of intervention in which the EC countries engaged during the crisis: $46 billion in July and August, and $228 billion in September and October.[63]

Relative to reserves, then, the supply of speculative capital is in effect perfectly elastic. Under these circumstances, only very high short-term interest rates may prevent the exhaustion of foreign exchange reserves. Table 7.8 illustrates this point for various devaluation expectations. To offset a 10 percent devaluation with a 90 percent likelihood of occurring in ten days, risk-neutral investors will require annualized interest rates of 762 percent.[64] In this light, it is not surprising that Sweden was forced to raise its overnight rate to an annualized rate of 500 percent at the peak of its crisis.

Are countries at the mercy of the markets, or can capital controls increase their room for maneuver? As table 7.4 reports, survey respondents attached surprisingly little importance to the presence or absence of controls: nearly half the respondents listed as unimportant the fact that reserves are insufficient now that controls have been removed. Yet there is at least circumstantial evidence that capital controls play a significant role. Of the countries subjected to the fiercest attacks, none of those that were forced to leave the ERM maintained capital controls. In contrast, all of those countries that managed to realign and remain within the ERM still had controls in place. Moreover, Ireland removed its controls on January 1, 1993, and was forced to realign shortly thereafter.

Further evidence is provided by deviations from covered interest parity, a standard measure of the magnitude of controls. In figure 7.16, speculative attacks are easily identifiable in France and Italy before January 1990 and July 1990, respectively, when controls were lifted; the data confirm that countries that maintained controls enjoyed very substantial insulation between onshore and offshore interest rates on comparable assets.[65] Ireland, one of the few EMS countries to retain significant capital controls in 1992, provides a recent example. At the time of the crisis, Irish controls allowed domestic interest rates to be nearly 80 (annualized) percentage points lower than they would have been without controls, measured by the deviation from covered interest parity shown in figure 7.17.

In response to our argument that controls play an important role in supporting pegged exchange rates, it might be argued that France and Denmark, which did not have controls, were also attacked but were not forced to devalue. It is not as difficult as it might seem to reconcile this objection with our conclusion because there is an alternative to controls: unlimited intervention by other countries. Both Denmark and France were recipients of massive (effectively unlimited) support by the Bundesbank, as we analyze below.

Costs of Defense

Sufficiently high interest rates should be capable of rebuffing even the most concerted speculative attack. If so, then understanding the crisis requires an explanation of why some governments refused to hold interest rates at high levels. Market participants clearly recognized that high interest rates were painful, as responses to our survey showed in table 7.4. The question is through what channels this pain was experienced.

In this section, we consider four areas that high interest rates might affect: economic activity, the housing market, the banking system, and the budget. In all four cases, even stratospheric interest rates—like Sweden's 500 percent overnight rates—have relatively small effects as long as they are maintained for short periods. Only when high rates are maintained for extended periods does the pain prove intolerable.

Critically, however, when the potential source of instability is multiple equilibria in the foreign exchange market, it may be necessary to maintain high rates for extended periods. This is what governments concluded was intolerable in the final months of 1992.

Percent deviation

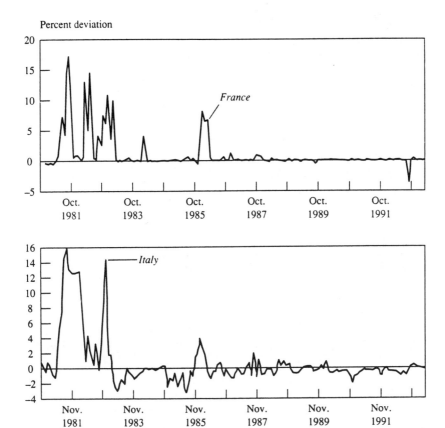

Figure 7.16
Spread between offshore and onshore interbank rates for France and Italy.
Source: Authors' calculations using DRI bid rates.
ᵃ The figure shows the difference between interest rates for one-month maturities in London, where interest rate parity holds, and in Paris and Milan, respectively, where controls are applied.

Percent deviation

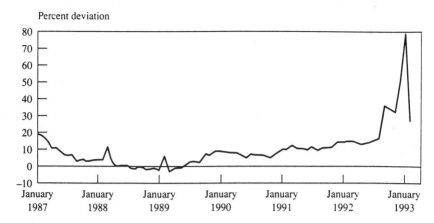

Figure 7.17
Deviations from covered interest rate parity for the Irish punt.
Source: Authors' calculations using DRI data on one-month maturities.

Impact on economic activity. Criticism of high interest rates on the grounds that they depressed economic activity was rampant in the fall of 1992.[66] Of course, this is the standard reason that governments are thought to dislike high rates.

Starting in 1990, the upward pressure on short-term interest rates was considerable. But in terms of the determinants of investment activity and other macroeconomic aggregates, long-term interest rates are likely to matter more. The upward movement of long-term nominal rates was minimal, as shown in figure 7.9. Because there was little reason to expect a change in inflationary expectations over long horizons, the figure provides a reasonable picture of the evolution of long-term real rates. Thus insofar as changes in interest rates exercise their real effects through standard macroeconomic channels, it would appear that their effect on the European economy remained minimal. Only if the rise in interest rates was expected to be long-lived and thereby to affect the entire term structure would one expect to see activity dramatically affected.

Impact on mortgage interest rates. In the United Kingdom and Ireland, mortgage interest payments are indexed to money market rates.[67] Hence higher money market rates can impose a significant cost on homeowners. Assume a mortgage rate of 10 percent. If the money market rate increases to 20 percent for two weeks, then the annual mortgage rate (computed as a geometric average of monthly rates and adjusted yearly) increases to

10.4 percent. If the overnight rate increases to 100 percent for two weeks, the annual mortgage rate rises to 12.8 percent. These are significant but not intolerable costs.

If, however, defense of the currency requires high money market rates to be maintained for longer periods, the impact on mortgage rates can be dramatic. Even a relatively "modest" money market rate of 20 percent maintained for three months raises the annual mortgage rate to 12.4 percent, while a 100 percent interest rate lifts it to a punishing 27.7 percent. Higher mortgage rates can in turn have a predictable negative effect on the housing market. Unless the authorities believe that high interest rates will succeed in quickly repelling a speculative attack, they may hesitate to pursue this option because of the screams of homeowners.[68]

Impact on the budget. Equally important for some countries is a third channel through which high interest rates affect the economy: the government budget. Interest rate increases can have a significant impact on the budgetary position in countries with high debt-to-GDP ratios. In Italy, for example, where the debt-to-income ratio exceeds 100 percent and significant amounts of debt are short term, every percentage point increase in the Banca d'Italia's discount rate adds 13 trillion lire to the budget deficit.[69]

In addition, there is the danger that higher interest rates will transform the exchange rate crisis into a debt crisis. The average maturity of the Italian public debt is three years. Gross debt issues amount to more than half of GDP each year.[70] Any hint that the budget deficit is about to widen significantly because of increased debt-service costs could alarm bondholders and make the next round of financing perilous.[71]

But again, the duration of the interest rate increases is critical. If rates rise only temporarily, the increased debt-service burden is relatively modest. Indeed, assuming a manageable debt-service burden, a temporary increase in rates can make absorbing new issues more attractive because of their temporarily high yield.

Impact on the banks. A final channel through which high interest rates can adversely affect the economy is by destabilizing the banking system. High central bank lending rates increase the cost of credit to commercial banks. This undermines bank profitability and capital adequacy, in the worst case requiring the government to bail out the banks. Bailouts shift the cost of stabilizing the banking system onto the government balance sheet, with negative implications for inflation, the current account, and

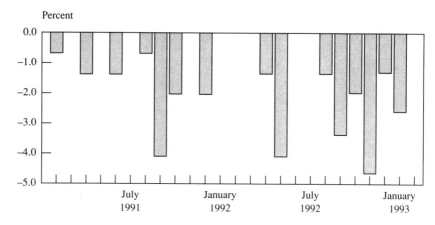

Figure 7.18
Changes in ratings of banks in Europe, 1991–93.
Source; International Bank Corporate Analysis, 1993.
^aDifference between the number of banks with rankings that are upgraded and those that are downgraded, as a percentage of all rated banks. Countries included are Belgium, Denmark, Finland, France, Germany, Ireland, Italy, the Netherlands, Portugal, Spain, Sweden, and the United Kingdom. No bar signifies that there were no changes in bank ratings for that particular month.

ultimately exchange rate stability. When asked why central banks gave up defending certain currencies, about two-thirds of survey respondents ranked as important or very important worries that further interest rate increases would destabilize banking systems; this is shown in table 7.4.

Evidence of the difficulties of European banks is provided in figure 7.18. It reports the difference between the number of banks whose financial status is upgraded and downgraded by International Bank Corporate Analysis, a rating agency based in London. The deteriorating financial condition of European banks is evident in the fact that the numbers are consistently negative. The difference in numbers of downgradings and upgradings peaks in September 1991; in May 1992, immediately before the first phase of the crisis; in the subsequent September, following the rise in discount rates; and again in the following November. This suggests a correlation between the interest rate policies pursued to defend EMS parities and the difficulties of the banks.

Again, however, that impact is likely to be powerful only if rates are held at high levels for extended periods. Furthermore, both commercial and central banks found ways to soften the effects. In Sweden, for example, where overnight rates were raised to an annualized rate of 75 and then 500 percent, the Riksbank employed a graduated ladder of interest rates. Each bank has its own interest rate scale, which is set according to its capital. In September only Swedish Kr 1.6 billion of the Swedish Kr 46.6 billion of bank borrowings from the central bank bore the highest ("marginal") interest rate. The average overnight lending rate was 23 percent for banks borrowing from the central bank when the marginal rate was 75 percent, and 50 percent when the marginal rate was 500 percent.[72]

In France as in Sweden, resident commercial banks were spared the full blow of the increase in short-term rates to more than 20 percent. They enjoy privileged access to the Bank of France's biweekly allotments, on which the rate was not raised. This—along with strong moral suasion by the authorities—explains the differential between the London and Paris rates on the franc. (The London rate soared relative to that prevailing in Paris; a differential of nearly five percentage points opened up at the height of the crisis.[73])

Another way high interest rates may destabilize the banking system is through their impact on the property market. If high interest rates are maintained for an extended period, the consequences can include weak demand for loans, an increase in the number of foreclosures, and a further decline in property prices—all of which would be bad news for the banks. Again, none of these effects is likely to operate powerfully if the increase in interest rates is short-lived.

Implication

Our analysis of the four channels through which high interest rates affected the economy points to the same conclusion; stratospheric rates are tolerable for short periods but become impossible to bear if maintained for long. If European central banks stopped defending their exchange rates, they must have grown convinced that their high interest rates would prove impossible to reduce quickly.

The Swedish case supports this conjecture. Toward the beginning of the crisis, the Riksbank raised its marginal rate to 500 percent. But the reserves that had been lost during the crisis did not flow back in as soon as the crisis passed, even after turbulence in other markets died down. When capital again flowed out in November (the total outflow during one week reached Swedish Kr 158 billion, in comparison with an outflow of Swedish Kr 60 billion in September), it would have been necessary to ratchet interest rates back up, without any assurance that it would stop the hemorrhage of reserves that had continued after the first rate increase.[74] At this point the Riksbank stopped defending the krona.

That a short period of high interest rates would not permanently curtail adverse speculation is an implication of the existence of multiple equilibria. High rates could defer the speculative attack so long as they are maintained, as we explained in the discussion surrounding table 7.8 above. But as soon as rates are lowered, the markets have the same incentive as before to attack. Once they do, the exchange rate depreciates as the government shifts to a more accommodating policy. In the presence of multiple equilibria, interest rates therefore have to be maintained indefinitely at high levels to stabilize the exchange rate.[75] This is what central banks were unwilling to tolerate in 1992.

The Political Economy of the Crisis

Stratospheric interest rates could be used to defend exchange rate pegs at best to a limited extent. The only means available to defend the pegs was therefore unlimited foreign support.

Did Countries Expect Unlimited Support?

Foreign support, after all, was supposed to be what distinguished the EMS from other fixed exchange rate arrangements. It featured a very short-term financing facility (VSTF) (first established in 1972 as part of the Snake, the failed attempt to stabilize intra-European exchange rates that had preceded the EMS). The VSTF exists because of the obligation to intervene when a currency reaches the edge of its fluctuation band.[76] When a bilateral exchange rate reaches the maximum permissible distance from its declared central parity (2.25 percent in the normal EMS band, and 6 percent in the case of the wider band temporarily given to some new entrants to the system), both central banks concerned are required to intervene. While the strong-currency country might in principle purchase third currencies in exchange for its own currency, it was agreed when the EMS was established that interventions should be conducted in the currencies concerned. According to the EMS Act of Foundation, "interventions shall in principle be effected in currencies of the participating central banks. These interventions shall be unlimited at the compulsory intervention rates."[77]

Moreover, the EMS agreement gave countries reason to expect unlimited support when their currencies fell to the bottom of the band. Again, the Act of Foundation is unambiguous: "To enable interventions to be made in Community currencies, the participating central banks shall open each other very short-term credit facilities, unlimited in amount."[78]

The VSTF worked to the satisfaction of all concerned until 1992. Many of the eleven realignments that took place between 1979 and 1987 occurred in the midst of incipient crises that were contained temporarily by large-scale intervention organized under the, provisions of the VSTF until an orderly realignment could be arranged.[79]

Why Countries Should Have Known Better

With hindsight, it is obvious that no central bank would ever commit unconditionally to unlimited lending.[80] The question is how a presumption to the contrary could have come about. Otmar Emminger, the Bundesbank governor who signed the EMS Act, had obtained beforehand from the government of the Federal Republic of Germany a clause permitting the Bundesbank to opt out from these responsibilities. Emminger apparently saw nothing peculiar about this arrangement, as he recalls in his memoirs.

Of particular importance for us were the agreements between the Government and the Bundesbank, especially concerning the underpinning of the Bundesbank's autonomy with regard to monetary policy. These agreements have been summarized in a letter written by me and addressed to the Federal Government in November 1978. Its essence was as follows:
'The autonomy of the Bundesbank in monetary policy would particularly be put in jeopardy if strong imbalances with the future EMS resulted in extreme intervention obligations which would then threaten the value of the currency. This would make it impossible for the Bundesbank to carry out its legal obligations. Referring to repeated assurances from the Chancellor and the Finance Minister, the Bundesbank is starting from the premise that, if need be, the German government will safeguard the Bundesbank from such a situation of constraint, either by a correction of the exchange rate in the EMS or, if necessary, by discharging the Bundesbank from its intervention obligations.'
The decisive factor regarding the policy of stability was without a doubt the intention to keep the Bundesbank's intervention obligations to an acceptable minimum.[81]

The government acquiesced. Economics Minister Otto von Lambsdorff went to the Bundestag on December 6, 1978, and stated, "The adjustment of the exchange rate has always been the responsibility of the Government and not of the Bundesbank. The Bundesbank has the responsibility to intervene, and the option not to intervene if it is its opinion that it is not able to do so."[82]

For many years this distinction was incompletely appreciated. Through the early years of the EMS, capital controls and realignments obviated the need for unlimited intervention. Things were different in 1992, when neither capital controls nor the realignment option remained. What happened once the crisis started building in June necessarily remains a matter of speculation (no pun intended). There is no question that the Bundesbank initially responded by intervening in support of the lira, acquiring some $4 billion of foreign exchange. It then grew worried over its ever-growing reserves (some DM 92 billion in September 1992 alone). By early September, its target monetary aggregate M3 was rising at an annual rate of nearly 10 percent (far above the target range of 3.5 to 5.5 percent).

The Bundesbank's Objectives

Accurately characterizing the Bundesbank's objectives is crucial to understanding the political economy of the crisis. Those objectives have always been clearly and consistently stated. As early as 1990, it was the Bundesbank's view that:

To the extent that the stability of exchange rates or even the pronounced strength of a number of partner currencies that do not belong to the "hard core" of the EMS can be explained essentially by inflation-induced higher rates of interest, it can basically be justified only if it is consolidated by a domestic economic policy that is durably geared to stability. If success is not achieved in coping with the structural causes of inflation within a reasonable period of time, it will probably become increasingly difficult over the long term to avoid having recourse to exchange rate adjustments.[83]

German economic and monetary unification brought these conflicts to a head. The Bundesbank dutifully asked for a DM appreciation. When rebuffed, it correctly warned that exchange rate adjustments were unavoidable. As pressure built in the summer of 1992, it responded initially by fulfilling its intervention obligations. But doing so heightened the conflict between two of its priorities: safeguarding the EMS and maintaining price stability. On Friday, September 11, after a day of massive and unprecedented Bundesbank purchases of lira, Chancellor Helmut Kohl traveled to Frankfurt to meet with Bundesbank officials and discuss the dilemma. Given the 1978 agreement with the Federal Government, it is plausible that the Bundesbank, meeting the Chancellor in the midst of a concerted attack, invoked its right to limit its intervention on the grounds that doing otherwise—given foreign resistance to realignment—might threaten price stability.[84]

This conjecture is supported by the fact that, over the following weekend, Bundesbank President Helmut Schlesinger sought to arrange a general realignment of EMS currencies in return for a reduction in German interest rates.[85] The Italians are known to have been reluctant to devalue, as were the British and the Spaniards when sounded out a couple of days later. Notwithstanding their recalcitrance, unlimited nonsterilized interventions and loans through the VSTF could have, in principle, succeeded in supporting the existing parities. But by denying its request for a DM revaluation, the other ERM member countries subjected the Bundesbank to demands for intervention incompatible with its commitment to monetary stability.

With hindsight, common sense suggests that a commitment to unlimited intervention is not time consistent.[86] The September crisis simply brought to the surface an obvious fact: with no realignments and no capital controls, the new EMS was insupportable.

Why, of all the currencies attacked, did only two—the Danish krone and the French franc—escaped unscathed? One interpretation is that the Bundesbank provided more extensive support for these than for other EMS currencies. The Bundesbank has long been a strong supporter of the coronation theory, according to which monetary union is the last step in a long process of convergence of national monetary policies. A possible implication of the coronation theory is that France and Denmark had already established their commitment to convergence and hence were worthy of support. As members of the "convergence club," France and Denmark had inflation rates even lower than Germany's. Other countries that had made less progress toward convergence may have been deemed less worthy of support.

In light of its commitment to domestic price stability, the Bundesbank simply did not have the latitude to provide unlimited support to all EMS currencies. It logically attached priority to the defense of certain currencies such as the franc and the krone. In addition to their membership in the convergence club, France and Denmark were pivotal countries politically. France's participation in the monetary union was essential to prevent the latter from degenerating into a DM area and denying Germany the political and diplomatic concessions (such as a Community foreign policy) it desired as its quid pro quo for European monetary union.[87] Denmark remained (along with the United Kingdom) one of only two EC countries that had not yet ratified the Maastricht Treaty. To withdraw support for the krone at a time when the Danish government had initiated a second campaign to secure ratification might have torpedoed the entire EMU process.

In contrast, Italy, Spain, and Portugal neither played such a critical role politically nor clearly belonged to the EMS's hard core. The first statement also applies to Ireland; the second applies to the United Kingdom. Thus it is logical that the Bundesbank would have devoted its scarce resources to other currencies first.

There is a further hypothesis: that the Bundesbank saw in the crisis the opportunity to shape a monetary union more to its liking—specifically, one purged of its weaker members. Supporting this view is a disquieting pattern of public statements by Bundesbank officials.[88]

On August 25, Reimut Jochimsen, a member of the Bundesbank's policymaking council, suggested that a realignment could be in the offing. On August 28, Johann Wilheim Gaddum, a member of the seven-man permanent directorate, expressed the view that there was no reason to cut German interest rates. On September 10, anonymous sources within the Bundesbank suggested that the pound should be devalued. On September 15, newspapers reported sources in the Bundesbank as suggesting that a sterling devaluation could not be ruled out. And on September 16, Helmut Schlesinger was widely quoted as saying that Europe's financial difficulties remained unresolved. Each of these statements worked to destabilize weak EMS currencies.

Until the relevant memoirs and records are published, this hypothesis cannot be tested. The comments above could be dismissed simply as ill-advised statements in the heat of battle. What is clear, in any case, is that it was not realistic to expect adequate support, given the size of the attacks made possible by fully liberalized markets. Equally clear is that governments should not expect to receive unlimited and unconditional support in future EMS crises.

The Way Forward

The September 1992 crisis confirmed an elementary but strangely neglected principle of international economics: the incompatibility of pegged exchange rates, monetary policy independence, and full capital mobility. In drawing implications for the transition to EMU, it is essential to bear in mind that the ideal solution of simultaneously achieving all three of these desiderata is ruled out. Any workable solution will have to sacrifice at least one of them, and thus will inevitably meet with objections. In this last section, we present six options for the future, proceeding from the least to the most likely.

Attempting to Proceed as Before

The first alternative is to attempt to proceed as before, in the belief that future disturbances as severe as German economic and monetary unification are unlikely. In this view, EMS countries can simply rededicate themselves to harmonizing their macroeconomic policies, and exchange rate stability will follow. Our analysis makes clear that the events of September were more than a delayed reaction to a onetime shock. In addition, they reflect intrinsic sources of instability that are still very much present. Ample scope remains for self-fulfilling speculative attacks to repeatedly destabilize the EMS. Neither the absence of extraneous shocks nor policy convergence can rule out self-fulfilling attacks. If this is the correct way of viewing the events of September, then proceeding as before is not feasible.

Proceeding as Before But with More Realignments

The Bundesbank's own preference would be to proceed as before but with more realignments to compensate for policy divergences. But, as we explained in our discussion of escape clauses and robust monetary rules, periodic realignments are problematic when capital markets are free of controls. If there is one clear lesson to be drawn from the September crisis, it is that markets anticipate events. Central banks that believe they can peg the exchange rate for significant periods and then change it discretely overlook this elementary fact.

A variant of this approach is more continuous realignments—that is, shifting the band without discretely changing the exchange rate and thereby allowing the rate to fluctuate over wider range. As we explained in the third section, this is likely to aggravate credibility problems because the markets will have reason to doubt that the authorities are committed to supporting the exchange rate when it approaches the edge of the existing band. Insofar as more frequent shifts of the band allow the exchange rate to fluctuate over a wider range, this option creates the same objections as generalized floating, which we consider below.

A Shotgun Wedding between Germany and France

Marginally more likely is a shotgun wedding (perhaps the better analogy would be an elopement) between Germany and France. If the two countries credibly commit to close harmonization of monetary policies and to unlimited intervention of whichever currency weakens, the DM-franc rate could provide a stable core to which other northern European currencies could attach themselves.

The idea of a de facto monetary union centered on Germany is not unprecedented. For ten years, the Netherlands has forsaken monetary sovereignty in order to peg the guilder to the franc. More recently, Belgium, Denmark, and Austria (not yet an EC member) have adopted Dutch-style policies. Once France and Germany establish a pact, Belgium, Denmark and the Netherlands could quickly join. In much the same way that the EC grew from a core group of six countries to its current membership of twelve, what started as an alliance between two of the leading monetary powers of Europe could eventually encompass most of the continent.

The problem with this scenario is that, in contrast to the de facto monetary union between Germany and the Netherlands (and the more formal union between Belgium and Luxembourg), a Franco-German marriage would not be a union of one large and one small country, where the latter delegated all control of household finances to the dominant marital partner.[89] Germany is unlikely (to put it mildly) to grant seats on the Bundesbank's board to officials from the Bank of France. France will not soon give Germany control of its macroeconomic policies, in the absence of which unlimited intervention is unacceptable to the Bundesbank. The Maastricht Treaty creates a broader institutional framework and safeguards within which some such compromises and trade-offs should be palatable. Outside of it they remain unacceptable, as Helmut Schlesinger made clear in a speech on March 30, 1993.[90] Absent institutional innovations of this sort, a commitment to stabilize the DM-franc rate can always be abandoned or reversed. Under these circumstances, statements that the two governments "desire" or "intend" to stabilize the rate, however earnest, will not be regarded as credible.

An Early Two-Speed EMU

Credibility requires an institutional framework like that attempted by the Maastricht Treaty. But revising that treaty would require several years of intergovernmental conferences and yet more years for ratification. If the timetable is to be accelerated, therefore, this must be done within the confines of the existing treaty. The treaty is commonly read as preventing the initiation of Stage III (full monetary union) before January 1, 1997. But as we explained above, nothing in principle prevents the EMI and the Commission, which must report before the end of 1996, from reporting as early as the beginning of 1994. The treaty only states that Stage III must begin after Stage II, and that Stage II begins on January 1, 1994.

That a majority of EC countries must satisfy the convergence criterion requiring two years of exchange rate stability might seem to be the binding constraint on an early start. Of the twelve, only six—France, Germany, Belgium, the Netherlands, Luxembourg, and Denmark—will have displayed two years of exchange rate stability at the beginning of 1994 (assuming no additional unforeseen events). Greece, a non-EMS country, is not a candidate, while Italy and the United Kingdom would first have to reenter the ERM and then wait two years. Whether a majority of EC countries can be said to satisfy this criterion therefore hinges on the evaluation of Ireland, Portugal, and Spain. The relevant protocol to the treaty states that "the Member State [must have] respected the normal [2.25 percent] fluctuation margins ... without severe tensions for at least the last two years before the examination."[91] This would appear to rule out Ireland's participation before early 1995 and Spain and Portugal's for at least two years (because they have both retained the wider margins of fluctuation). However, the protocol continues, "In particular, the Member State shall not have devalued its currency's bilateral central rate against any other Member State's currency *on its own initiative* for the same period."[92] The on-its-own-initiative proviso might provide a loophole through which Ireland could slip and deliver the required majority.[93]

But strong-currency countries like Germany would allow this loophole to determine the starting date of EMU only if it were crystal clear that the member-state(s) in question satisfied the other convergence criteria. Projections for 1993, assuming no GDP growth in EC countries, show no country satisfying both the debt and deficit requirements. Unless these positions change dramatically, it seems unlikely that the on-its-own-initiative loophole would be allowed to determine the outcome.

More Exchange Rate Flexibility

Monetary policy independence, widely regarded as useful for policy purposes, and full capital mobility, as mandated by the Single European Act, can be reconciled with one another by flexible exchange rates. This is why generalized floating is sometimes advanced as a natural response to the EC's monetary dilemma. Italy and the United Kingdom have shown the way and evince little regret.

This proposal, most popular in U.S. academic circles, is heretical in the European context. For historical reasons—competitive devaluation and related monetary conflicts in the 1930s are believed to have soured the European political climate—aversion to floating in Europe is intense.[94] European countries are more open to trade than the United States, which means that exchange rate fluctuations are more disruptive and give rise to stronger political objections. The Common Agricultural Policy (CAP), designed to stabilize domestic currency prices of certain agricultural products, is disrupted by floating rates.

These problems become more acute with the progress of the Single European Act. As intra-European trade expands and substitutability between the products of competing suppliers grows, exchange rate fluctuations will give rise to even more import penetration, intensifying the pain experienced by import-competing producers. The Common Agricultural Policy will become more difficult to operate in the face of exchange rate changes. Exchange rate fluctuations have always created strong incentives for illicit cross-border shipments of agricultural goods whose domestic currency prices are supported. But while this has long been a problem, it becomes intractable with the removal of border controls and inspections as a consequence of the Single European Act.[95]

Finally, there is the objection that floating will prevent Europe from reaping the benefits of the Single Market. How, it is asked, could meaningful commodity and factor market linkages be created in the presence of a dozen (or, following enlargement, fifteen) national currencies fluctuating against one another? One answer is that firms and traders can hedge exchange rate risk. Unfortunately, protection is expensive. In particular, investors in plant and equipment with a long service-life have little protection available at an affordable price.[96] R.L.A. Morsink and Willem Molle report some evidence that exchange rate variability depresses direct foreign investment among EC countries.[97]

The single most damning objection is political. Once European markets become more integrated because of the Single European Act, wide exchange rate swings may become unbearable for firms confronted by a surge of competing imports suddenly sold at bargain prices because of the exchange rate change. That they would seek political redress is predictable. Fluctuations within a wide target zone could be interpreted as the intended result of beggar-thy-neighbor policies. Political pressure would mount in strong-currency countries to offer some form of protection from members engaging in "exchange dumping." Countries such as the United Kingdom, if thought to be manipulating their exchange rates in order to steal a competitive advantage, would be given a choice between participating in the monetary union project or being expelled from the Single Market. What is ultimately at stake, therefore is the Single Market Project itself.[98]

The United States and Canada offer a puzzling contrast. They have pursued economic integration over the years without yet prompting calls for exchange rate stabilization, much less currency unification.[99] This remains true despite very pronounced fluctuations in Canada's effective real exchange rate (which mainly reflects movements relative to the United States). These fluctuations, on the order of 25 percent, as shown in figure 7.19, would be regarded as unbearable in Europe. Why this has not been true of Canada remains an open question. A plausible conjecture is that as North American economic integration proceeds, political pressures for exchange rate stabilization will intensify. They may spread to the United States as integration with Mexico goes forward and certain U.S. industries find themselves at a competitive disadvantage because of a depreciation of the peso.

A compromise between pegged and freely floating rates for Europe might be wider fluctuation bands. If bands are sufficiently wide to remove the need for realignments, there will be no incentive for speculative attacks. If parity adjustments are sufficiently frequent, the band can be

Index, 1985 = 100

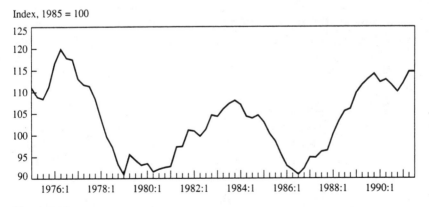

Figure 7.19
Canadian real effective exchange rate, 1971:1–1991:3.
Source: International Financial Statistics.

adjusted around the exchange rate without requiring the rate itself to move discretely.

Unfortunately, such arrangements tend to pose credibility problems. If the exchange rate is allowed to fluctuate widely and the band is shifted frequently, it will be difficult for observers to determine whether the authorities are adjusting the parity only in response to exceptional disturbances or in fact reverting to preexisting inflationary tendencies. Capital might not flow in stabilizing directions when the rate moved to the edge of the band, and the target zone honeymoon would be lost. A high probability of realignment when the exchange rate drifted toward the edge of the band could destabilize the entire arrangement, replacing the target zone honeymoon with a target zone divorce.[100] For all these reasons, however appealing they are in theory, floating exchange rates are not feasible in Europe in practice.

Throwing Sand in the Wheels of Speculation

This leaves only one alternative, which itself has significant disadvantages. This is an explicit or implicit tax on foreign exchange transactions. One option is a Tobin tax of, say, 1 percent on each purchase or sale of foreign exchange (a 2 percent tax on a roundtrip transaction). Such a tax would discourage speculators from taking one-way bets. It could not support weak currencies permanently, but it would provide time to organize orderly realignments. Because it is not an administrative (that is, a quantitative) restriction, it would be permissible under the provisions of the Maastricht Treaty and the Single European Act.

Our preferred option is an implicit tax. This would require financial institutions purchasing foreign exchange with domestic currency for their own account or on behalf of customers to make non-interesting-bearing deposits with the central bank. The Banca d'Italia pioneered such policies in the 1970s. Countries could emulate the specific measures adopted by the Spanish government during the September crisis, when it required institutions purchasing foreign currency against the peseta to deposit a sum equivalent to the transaction, interest-free, with the Bank of Spain for one year. Again, because deposit requirements are not an administrative prohibition, they do not violate either the letter or the spirit of the Maastricht Treaty or the Single European Act.

Both measures work by raising the cost of cross-border capital flows. An appealing feature is that they penalize short-term capital movements more heavily than long-term investments. A 1 percent tax on each transaction (2 percent on a roundtrip transaction) represents an annualized cost of nearly 8,000 percent on a one-day shift, 180 percent over a week, 27 percent over a month, but only 0.2 percent over 10 years. Because speculative attacks are based on short-term positions, such a tax would limit the amount of intervention required to support currencies and, where necessary, provide time to arrange orderly realignments.

The strength of the Tobin tax is its transparency. Deposit requirements, while more opaque, have the advantage that the implicit tax increases with the interest rate. In normal times, when interest rates are low, so is the opportunity cost of the funds deposited in non-interest-bearing accounts. Under the Bank of Spain's measure, the implicit tax is an annualized 5 percent if the interest rate is 5 percent. The violation of interest parity is modest. But if it becomes necessary to raise interest rates in response to speculative pressure, the opportunity cost increases accordingly. If interest rates are raised to triple-digit levels, as in Sweden and Ireland during their crises, the implicit tax rises to triple-digit levels. The wedge between domestic and foreign interest rates widens accordingly, reducing the dislocations to the domestic economy caused by policies of exchange rate support.

If the point of the policy is merely to provide enough time to arrange an orderly realignment, then a modest Tobin tax would do. But in the presence of multiple equilibria, the authorities may wish to resist the pressure to realign. Then it may be necessary to raise interest rates for an extended period, in which case deposit requirements have a comparative advantage.

These measures have disadvantages, as we explain momentarily. But it is not enough for critics to point to their disadvantages. They must offer an alternative. And they must show that their alternative is feasible, unlike those we have listed above.

It might be thought that deposit requirements would thwart the creation of an integrated financial market. Recall, however, that a deposit requirement is not an administrative control. No one would be prevented from undertaking any financial transaction. Such a measure would no more prevent the development of a single financial market than modest national taxes on carrots prevent the development of a single carrot market.

A second invalid objection is that, to work, such measures would have to be coordinated internationally. Those who invoke this view note that foreign exchange is traded all over the world. But this fact is irrelevant: deposit requirements work by reducing the cost to the government in question of supporting its exchange rate. By creating a wedge between domestic and foreign interest rates analogous to the capital-control wedges documented in the eighth section, they would limit the domestic dislocations caused by policies of defense.

Other objections carry more weight. Deposit requirements could discourage the development of local financial markets. When Spain introduced them in September 1992, for example, the blow to its burgeoning financial market was severe. To minimize these costs, the measure should be applied only for a transitional limited period and ideally by all ERM countries simultaneously.

A related danger is that, by reducing the liquidity of financial markets, such a measure discourages long-term as well as short-term inward investment. Foreign investment might be depressed, not by the fact that investors would have to pay 1 percent to repatriate their funds, but by the tendency to discourage the development of local financial centers, which would increase bid-ask spreads and related thin-market problems.

A further danger is that the imposition of deposit requirements would weaken monetary discipline and jeopardize the convergence process. Aware that they provide additional room for maneuver for national policymakers, these officials might utilize their newfound freedom recklessly. While this danger is real, the same objection applies to widening or eliminating fluctuation margins. For all these reasons, a deposit requirement is not the best of all worlds. Our point is that it is the best of all *possible* worlds.

Conclusion

A basic axiom of international economics is the incompatibility of fixed exchange rates, full international capital mobility, and national policy autonomy. From this perspective, the instability of the EMS is no surprise. Between 1987 and 1990, realignments were spurned and capital mobility was perfected by the removal of capital controls, but the option of independent policies was not abandoned. Given this incompatibility and some time, an EMS crisis was all but inevitable. The only mystery is how its outbreak was deferred for so long.

We have distinguished four explanations for what triggered the 1992 crisis: overt competitiveness problems in certain high-inflation countries; hidden competitiveness problems associated with German economic and monetary union; anticipated future competitiveness problems caused by a predictable backlash against policies pursued to maintain competitiveness; and speculative crises of a purely self-fulfilling nature. As our discussion of the various national experiences makes clear, we believe that all four explanations apply to the 1992 crisis, although to extents that vary across countries. But for those concerned with future options, the final explanation is key.

Those who remain optimistic about the prospects for the EMS[101] and about the viability of the existing blueprint for European monetary union fail to appreciate how the very structure of the Maastricht Treaty is conducive to multiple equilibria and self-fulfilling speculative attacks. To salvage the Maastricht blueprint, it is not sufficient for governments to rededicate themselves to policies of austerity or to raise interest rates to high levels for limited periods. Neither step will necessarily succeed in fending off speculative attacks. In addition, the structure of the European Monetary System and the blueprint for European monetary union must be changed.

The options for resolving this dilemma are a forced march to European monetary union or taxing foreign exchange transactions. In practice the first option—a Franco-German alliance or an early two-speed EMU—is not feasible for political reasons. This makes us reluctant advocates of the last alternative: throwing sand in the wheels of international finance.

Appendix: A Brief Overview of Monetary Aspects of the Maastricht Treaty

The Maastricht Treaty laid down four convergence criteria that had to be met by countries that qualified to participate in European monetary union.[102] Countries would have to have achieved a high degree of price stability; their average rate of CPI inflation during the twelve months preceding the initiation of monetary union could be no more than 1.5 percentage points higher than the inflation rates of the three EC member states with the lowest inflation. Countries would have to have maintained stable exchange rates (within their normal EMS fluctuation bands) for the two years preceding entry without devaluing their currencies. Their long-term interest rates during the year preceding entry could be no more than 2 percentage points higher than those of the three member states that best controlled inflation. Countries would have to have achieved a "sustainable fiscal position"; their budget deficit could be no more than 3 percent of GDP, and their gross public debt could not exceed 60 percent of GDP.[103]

The treaty specified a transition to take place in stages. Stage I, beginning with the removal of capital controls in 1990, was to be marked by the reduction of inflation and interest rate differentials and by a stabilizing of exchange rates. Stage II, to begin on January 1, 1994, would prepare actively for monetary union. Domestic laws would have to be changed to conform to all aspects of the Maastricht Treaty. In particular, national central banks would have to be made fully independent, as specified in the treaty. A transitional entity, the European Monetary Institute (EMI), would be created at the beginning of Stage II. It would coordinate member countries' monetary policies in the final phases of the transition and plan the move to monetary union.

Stage III would inaugurate monetary union and establish the European Central Bank (ECB). National central banks would continue to exist as subsidiaries of the ECB, mostly to take charge of bank supervision and provide hospitality for academic conferences.

Notes

For help with data, we thank Samuel Bentolila, Menzie Chinn, Jeffrey Frankel, Lars Jonung, Philippe Moutot, Francesco Papadia, and the following organizations: International Bank Corporate Analysis, Data Resources Inc., and Morgan Guaranty. For comments and suggestions we thank—without implicating—Patrick Artus, Michael Bordo, William Branson, Michael Burda, Matthew Canzoneri, Georges de Menil, Rudi Dornbusch, Michele Fratianni, Peter Garber, Alexander Italianer, Peter Kenen, Harmen Lehment, Jacques Melitz, Stefano Micossi, Maury Obstfeld, Richard Portes, Andre Sapir, Robert Shiller, Horst Siebert, Jürgen von Hagen, and Brookings Panel members. Officials from central banks and treasuries also provided comments, although they sometimes disagreed strongly with our conclusions. We thank Lorenzo Bini-Smaghi, Pierluigi Ciocca, Erik Hoffmeyer, Lars Hörngren, Otmar Issing, Patrick Le Nain, Francesco Papadia, Philippe Moutot, and José Vinals. Barry Eichengreen's research was supported by the Center for German and European Studies of the University of California and the Institute for Advanced Study in Berlin. Charles Wyplosz's work has benefited from INSEAD research and development funding: Brigitte Pernet efficiently processed our survey and provided valiant secretarial support. Able research assistance was provided by Ansgar Rumler and Miriam Guzy. Ansgar died tragically in a skiing accident just as this research was completed; we dedicate the chapter to him.

1. The Irish punt joined the list in early 1993.

2. Ivo Dawnay and Robert Graham, "Major Calls for ERM Reform," *Financial Times*, September 20, 1992, p. 1.

3. Krugman (1979).

4. Flood and Garber (1984a).

5. Flood and Garber (1984b).

6. Obstfeld (1986a).

7. One seemingly logical option—floating exchange rates—is strongly opposed by Europeans, a fact that is not always adequately appreciated. Their resistance results in part from the extent of intra-European trade, which renders exchange rate fluctuations costly. Previous experiences with floating rates, like that of the 1930s, have left a particularly bitter taste in the mouths of European policymakers. Moreover, Europeans fear that manipulation of exchange rates would represent a threat to the common market itself, for reasons we explain below. History also explains why Europe feels the need to firmly anchor Germany in an open trade and payments area; to achieve this goal, a common market and fixed exchange rates are viewed as essential.

8. The term "new EMS" was coined by Giavazzi and Spaventa (1990). Portes (1993) presents an analysis of these developments that parallels our own account.

9. A twelfth realignment on January 8, 1990 replaced the Italian lira's wide band with the narrow EMS band by leaving the upper limit unchanged and raising the lower limit, thereby effectively raising the central rate against the DM by 3.5 percent. No change in the actual lira-DM rate was involved. Giavazzi and Giovannini (1989) and Gros and Thygesen (1992) provide short histories of the circumstances surrounding each realignment.

10. De Grauwe (1994).

11. Whether this change reflected a conscious policy decision is open to question. In any case, there were notable dissenters from the no-realignment strategy, including the German Bundesbank. See for example Deutsche Bundesbank (1991, p. 66). We return to these issues in footnote 12 and in the fifth and tenth sections below.

12. The Basle-Nyborg Agreement, while liberalizing access to financing facilities for use in supporting weak exchange rates, in fact called for undertaking small realignments more frequently, perhaps by shifting the band without changing the exchange rate discretely, as with the 1990 realignment of the lira. How this recommendation came to be discarded remains an important subject for research.

13. The Single European Act allows all EC countries to resort to emergency controls for a period of no more than six months. The Maastricht Treaty, however, rules that out completely from the beginning of Stage II on January 1, 1994. See the appendix for more information.

14. The dominant explanation in the press was that the decline of the dollar rendered British goods uncompetitive against their U.S. substitutes. See, for example, *Economist*, September 19, 1992, p. 31.

15. Peter Norman, James Blitz, and Tracy Corrigan, "UK Will Borrow D-Marks to Aid £," *Financial Times*, September 4, 1992, p. 1, and Peter Norman, "Positive Response to Currency Plan," *Financial Times*, September 4, 1992, p. 22.

16. "A Ghastly Game of Dominoes," *Economist*, September 19, 1992, p. 89.

17. The theory of escape clauses has been revived recently by Grossman and van Huyck (1988), De Kock and Grilli (1989), Flood and Isard (1989), Obstfeld (1992), and Giovannini (1993).

18. This observation raises an important question about life after European monetary unification: what will substitute for exchange rate changes in the event of exceptional shocks? By now, an extensive literature exists on the prospective effects of EMU. Horn and Persson (1988) suggest that EMU, by increasing the credibility of policymakers' commitment to price stability, might enhance wage flexibility. Similarly, the Commission of the European

Communities (1990) argues that EMU, by increasing the credibility of fiscal authorities' commitment not to bail out depressed regions, will encourage workers in such areas to moderate wage demands. Bertola (1988) argues that once exchange rates are immutably fixed, workers will respond by adjusting on other margins, enhancing wage flexibility and interregional migration. While the costs and benefits of monetary unification are not the subject of this chapter, in the final sections we discuss the implications of our analysis for European monetary union.

19. Canzoneri (1985).

20. This collective decisionmaking rule was in fact adopted to avert beggar-thy-neighbor policies, but evolved into a way of imposing discipline on inflation-prone countries. Naturally, it was abandoned by the United Kingdom and Italy when they suspended their ERM memberships.

21. Canzoneri (1985).

22. This is not the case when intervention is sterilized, but sterilized intervention is widely regarded as ineffectual; see Obstfeld (1990). For a recent view to the contrary, however, see Catte, Galli, and Rebecchini (1992).

23. This is formally analyzed in Wyplosz (1986). With capital controls, a speculative attack is of bounded size per unit of time. Hence, there exists a volume of foreign exchange reserves (possibly augmented by foreign loans) that is sufficient to support the fixed rate regime. As we explain below, it would also be possible to use nonadministrative measures such as taxes on foreign exchange transactions to achieve the same effect.

24. For an official expression of this view, see Commission of the European Communities (1993).

25. Limitations of the data for Portugal prevented us from undertaking a comparable analysis, but the data that exist suggest that Portugal also falls into this last category.

26. We measure bilateral unit labor costs by converting each country's unit labor costs in domestic currency into deutsche marks using the period average exchange rate. We prefer this measure to the multilateral one on the grounds that the latter is dominated by fluctuations in the U.S. dollar. The multilateral unit labor cost measure is based on the IMF index. In that index, the trade weights are a function of the shares of the sixteen foreign countries in the subject country's imports and exports, their relative shares in third markets, and the openness of their manufacturing sectors. It would not be appropriate, therefore, to construct bilateral unit labor cost comparisons relative to Germany by dividing the IMF index for the subject country by the IMF index for Germany because the two use different weights. As a measure of the relative price of traded and nontraded goods, we use the ratio of wholesale price to consumer price indexes.

27. The Balassa-Samuelson effect is the tendency for the price level to be higher in high-income countries because of the relatively high price of nontraded goods. The same point applies to Italy, albeit to a lesser extent.

28. As the *Financial Times* reported, "Many investors also consider the krona heavily overvalued against the D-Mark. Sweden's export performance in recent years has been poor and there are no signs of an immediate improvement." James Blitz, "Central Banks Move to Ease Strain of the D-Mark," *Financial Times*, August 21, 1992, p. 2.

29. Typically these studies focused on the exchange rate change needed in the short run, largely neglecting long-run aspects. An exception is a paper by Begg and others (1990),

which suggested that it might be necessary in the long run for the DM to depreciate to create a market for the additional German exports needed to service the foreign debt accumulated in the short run. The point is formally developed in Wyplosz (1991). Given our concern with the events of 1992, we focus here on the short run.

30. See Burda (1990).

31. See Siebert (1991) and Neumann (1992).

32. The shock might also be modeled as temporary, as in Wyplosz (1991). But this extension would not alter in any significant way the short-run responses upon which we focus here. Similarly, we neglect feedbacks through net exports without loss of generality.

33. Adding expectations would enrich the dynamics and complicate the presentation without substantively affecting the conclusions.

34. The coefficient $\beta = [b + k(a - bc)]^{-1}$ must be positive for the system comprised of equations 7 and equation 8 to be saddle-path stable. We assume this to be the case in the following discussion. As usual, we treat the exchange rate as the nonpredetermined variable and the price level as the sticky predetermined variable.

35. An attempt to do so was made in October 1991. French short-term interest rates were brought below German levels in the hope that the Bundesbank would respond by adjusting German rates in the same direction. This did not occur; the French move had to be reversed as capital began to flow out.

36. The system is dynamically stable. Once the exchange rate is fixed, dynamics are provided by the sluggish adjustment of domestic currency prices.

37. Here the behavior of prices depends on the sign of $(bh - k)$ alone. This would not be the case in a model with output spillovers factored into equation 2.

38. Indeed, the Bundesbank might pursue an even more contractionary policy, forcing more radical disinflation on other EMS countries and shifting the new long-run equilibrium to a point such as C.

39. Portes (1993).

40. As in the case of the German unification shock, we assume that $\beta = [b + k(a - bc)]^{-1}$ is positive so that the system is saddle-path stable. We treat the exchange rate as the nonpredetermined variable and the price level as the predetermined variable. The convergence path is shown as downward-sloping, which occurs if $1 > kc + ah$. None of the conclusions is affected in the case in which $1 < kc + ah$ and the convergence path is upward-sloping.

41. The main factor disturbing the lawyers was that the Maastricht agreement is an amendment to the Treaty of Rome and is bound by Article 236 of that treaty, which requires unanimous approval by all member states.

42. On German doubts, see Quentin Peel, "Bonn Anxious that German Doubts on EMU May Grow," *Financial Times*, June 4, 1992, p. 4. On Italian concerns, see Robert Graham, "Italian Business Fears Loss of Resolve," on p. 5 of the same issue. As Robert Graham reported, "Ever since the Danes rejected the treaty in a referendum at the beginning of the month, businessmen and bankers have been concerned that the process of closer European integration would be slowed and the resolve of the Italian authorities to tackle the country's deteriorating public finances would be weakened." "Italian Banks Increase Prime Rate to 14 Percent," *Financial Times*, June 23, p. 2.

43. France's referendum was called by President Mitterrand in the aftermath of the Danish rejection. He calculated (incorrectly) that a strong *oui* would relaunch the process.

44. See James Blitz, "D-Mark Firm Despite EMU Vote," *Financial Times*, June 20–21, 1992, p. 13.

45. James Blitz, "Sterling/D-Mark Hits New Low," *Financial Times*, August 6, 1992, p. 28.

46. Alice Rawsthorn, "French Support for Union Drops," *Financial Times*, August 26, 1992, p. 1.

47. James Blitz, "Close Shave for Sterling," *Financial Times*, August 26, 1992, p. 26. See also Peter Marsh and James Blitz, "EC Ministers Rule Out Realignment of ERM," *Financial Times*, August 29–30, 1992, p. 1.

48. Alice Rawsthorn, "French Doubts on Maastricht Grow," *Financial Times*, August 29–30, 1992, p. 3.

49. Lionel Barber and William Dawkins, "French No Vote Would Destabilize Europe, EC Warns," *Financial Times*, September 1, 1992, p. 1.

50. Flood and Garber (1984b).

51. Obstfeld (1986a).

52. Krugman (1979).

53. Flood and Garber (1984a).

54. This trajectory resembles Rudiger Dornbusch's overshooting result. (Undershooting would occur if the convergence path slopes upward.) Here, however, the money increase is the perfectly anticipated endogenous response of the central bank to the speculative attack and not, as in Dornbusch (1976), an exogenous change in the money supply.

55. We return to this point in the eleventh section. Also see the appendix of this chapter.

56. The dominant view in 1992 was that the earliest date of real importance was January 1, 1997. The procedure for early start-up was seen as a diplomatic gesture toward France, with little chance of activation. If this view is correct, it tends to weaken the explanation of self-fulfilling attacks but can be used to winnow scenarios for the future of EMU that we discuss in our concluding sections.

57. Alesina and Grilli (1993).

58. Alesina and Grilli's model is based on strong assumptions, notably that the common inflation rate of the EMU will be chosen by the median voter, with one vote per country. It nonetheless makes a useful point that the early entrants may reap most of the benefits of EMU without admitting the laggards, and that, insofar as the latter have different character-istics, the former may erect barriers to subsequent accession.

59. Citibank (1990). We sent questionnaires only to the heads of trading rooms or to senior traders, not to each individual in the same financial institution. Nonetheless, in more than half the cases, we sent two or more questionnaires to a particular financial institution.

60. Some respondents may have exaggerated their foresight. This bias supports our argu-ment by suggesting that even less than the 22 percent of respondents who claimed to have anticipated a realignment before the Danish referendum really did so.

61. Forty percent of Ireland's exports went to EMS countries that had been forced to realign by the end of 1992. These and the following figures on 1991 trade shares are from the IMF's *Direction of Trade Statistics* (1992).

62. See "Realignment Merchants," *Economist*, September 26, 1992, p. 90.

63. Alogoskoufis (1993). The figures refer to estimates of gross intervention.

64. These rates are calculated with the simplifying assumption that foreign assets do not bear interest. Because interest rates on DM bank deposits were on the order of 7 percent, this approximation changes the results very little.

65. Note that covered interest differentials can remain even in the absence of controls because of transactions costs, information costs, differential default risk on assets denominated in different currencies, and expectations that capital controls may be reimposed before the interest-bearing assets mature, as Frankel and MacArthur (1988) have argued. However, their magnitude should be relatively small.

66. For example, for commentary on Ireland, see "Down the Fast Track to a Pot of Gold," *Financial Times*, October 14, 1992, p. 2.

67. Arrangements are similar in Sweden. When the Swedish central bank raised its marginal lending rate from 16 to 75 percent in the second week of September, the banks announced that they were raising home loan rates by 5 percentage points to 22.5 percent and short-term property loans by 3.5 points to 21 percent. But because approximately 85 percent of the loans are not indexed, the blow was quite limited.

68. In the United Kingdom, mortgage lenders welcomed sterling's departure from the ERM on the grounds that it heralded lower interest rates; they therefore begged the government not to reenter the mechanism. See David Owen and Chris Tighe, "Tory MPs Fight Shy of the ERM," *Financial Times*, September 18, 1992, p. 5.

69. See James Blitz, "Italian Lira: The Sick Currency of Europe," *Financial Times*, July 22, 1992, p. 2. See also estimates that every point of short-term interest rates (as opposed to the discount rate) adds 15 trillion lire. (Edward Balls, "The Delicate Art of Persuasion," *Financial Times*, August 4, 1992, p. 14.) These estimates assume that the higher interest rate is maintained for at least two years; Pierluigi Ciocca of the Banca d'Italia confirmed this in private communication.

70. *La Lettre du C.E.P.I.I.* (January 1993, p. 1).

71. For models of debt runs, see Alesina, Prati, and Tabellini (1990) and Giavazzi and Pagano (1990).

72. See Sara Webb, "Sweden Awaits Return of the 'Hot Money,'" *Financial Times*, September 11, 1992, p. 2. For an excellent analysis of the Swedish crisis, see Hörngren and Lindberg (1993). The Riksbank also provided its banks and financial institutions with a large number of special facilities at much lower rates (Sveriges Riksbank, *Annual Report* 1992:4, p. 20).

73. Still, there is no doubt that banks suffered. The Association of French Banks asserts that holding the prime rate to 10 percent when overnight money and even three-month interest rates commanded 12 percent was costing the bankers Ffr 300 million ($54 million) a month, a substantial sum compared to the value of the commercial banks' demand and time deposits (about Ffr3.9 billion). It has been suggested that the banks, rather than incurring the wrath of the government by raising lending rates, refused to lend at all. See William Dawkins, "French Banks Seeking Base Rate Rise," *Financial Times*, October 3, 1992, p. 2.

74. Sveriges Riksbank (1993).

75. Insofar as reserves have fallen in the course of previous crises, it may be necessary to ratchet domestic rates up to even higher levels.

76. Amounts lent under the provisions of the VSTF must be repaid with interest within seventy-five days of the end of the month in which the intervention took place, but the loan can be renewed automatically for three months, and conditionally for another three months. More details on the mechanics of these operations are provided by Giavazzi and Giovannini (1989, pp. 38–39). Prior to the Basle-Nyborg Agreement of 1987, the repayment period was forty-five days. Central banks can also use the VSTF for intramarginal intervention, but in this case, access is not automatic.

77. The act is formally known as the European Council Brussels Resolution, Article 3.7, and was passed on December 5, 1978. This passage appears in Article 2.2, Section I, Document 8. See Commission of the European Communities (1984, p. 130).

78. European Council Brussels Resolution, Article 6.1, Section II, Document 8. See Commission of the European Communities (1984, p. 130).

79. Mastropasqua, Micossi, and Rinaldi (1988).

80. The analogy with the domestic lender-of-last-resort function suggests that a central bank will demand the right to choose whether to bail out an insolvent or illiquid institution, and will insist on oversight privileges in return.

81. Emminger (1986, pp. 361–62).

82. Emminger (1986, pp. 361–62).

83. Deutsche Bundesbank (1991, p. 66). We thank Otmar Issing for bringing this quotation to our attention.

84. It might be the second time that this clause has been used. Neumann and von Hagen (1992) report that the Bundesbank already invoked it in 1983 when the French franc was under attack.

85. For a detailed account of these negotiations see Peter Norman, "The Day Germany Planted a Currency Time Bomb," *Financial Times*, December 12–13, 1992, p. 2.

86. While a central bank might commit to this before the fact, it would have strong incentives to renege afterwards. A few early commentators on the EMS Act, such as Vaubel (1980) emphasized this point. For further discussion, see Begg and Wyplosz (1993).

87. For further analysis of this issue-linkage interpretation of the political economy of European monetary union, see Garrett (1993) and Eichengreen and Frieden (1993).

88. Ivo Dawnay and Andrew Fisher, "Britain Points Finger at Germany," *Financial Times*, September 17, 1992, p. 1.

89. Luxembourg openly delegates control of its monetary policy to Belgium, while the Netherlands does so de facto with Germany. This asymmetry in the size of cooperating countries may imply that exchange rate stabilization can be effected in North America without resorting to monetary union, assuming such stabilization eventually becomes necessary in conjunction with the North American Free Trade Agreement, as we suggest below.

90. Christopher Parks, "Schlesinger Warns on EMU Shortcuts," *Financial Times*, March 30, 1993, p. 2.

91. Treaty on European Union (the Maastricht Treaty). See Commission of the European Communities (1992, Article 109; p. 41, and Protocol, Article 3, p. 185).

92. Treaty on European Union (the Maastricht Treaty). Emphasis added. See Commission of the European Communities, 1992, Protocol, Article 3, pp. 185–86).

93. The prospective expansion of the Community cannot relax this constraint. Austria comes close to satisfying the convergence criteria, but its application is being processed in parallel with those of Finland and Sweden, which do not. EC procedures make it virtually impossible to expedite the admission of one country but not the others.

94. The importance of this historical legacy in conditioning European attitudes is emphasized by Giavazzi and Giovannini (1989). Recall that initiatives to stabilize intra-European exchange rates after the breakdown of the Bretton Woods System started immediately with the establishment of the Snake.

95. For details, see Eichengreen (1993b). Many economists—ourselves included—would argue that economic efficiency would be enhanced by eliminating the CAP, and that if the trade-off is between flexible rates and the CAP, Europe is better off sacrificing the latter to secure the former. But there is good reason to conclude that this trade-off is not politically feasible in the short run, as recent demonstrations against agricultural liberalization in France underscore. Over a longer horizon, one can imagine that the CAP could be transformed into a system of lump-sum income supports for European farmers, which would reduce its distortionary effects and remove one obstacle to greater exchange rate flexibility in Europe without creating political resistance.

96. Even three-month contracts in excess of $1 million can cost 2 percent or more. Options running more than five years to maturity are virtually unknown; 80 percent run less than one year.

97. Morsink and Molle (1991).

98. "L'affaire Hoover" illustrates the point. The Hoover Company stopped producing vacuum cleaners in France in early 1993 in favor of expanding its operations in Scotland, partly in response to sterling's depreciation against the franc. The decision elicited heated French and EC-level complaints.

99. Schott and Smith (1988) note that the AFL-CIO argued at an early stage in Canadian-U.S. free trade negotiations that an undervalued Canadian dollar conferred on producers north of the border an unfair competitive advantage; the union pressed for eventual one-to-one parity. But Schott and Smith conclude that this argument was an isolated exception to general neglect of the exchange rate issue. Similarly, Harris (1991) argues for the desirability of exchange rate management to prevent persistent misalignments, but does not link the need for stabilization to integration. For further discussion, see Bayoumi and Eichengreen (1994).

100. Bertola and Caballero (1992).

101. See, for example, the Commission of the European Communities (1993).

102. The treaty followed the recommendations of the Delors Committee (Committee for the Study of Economic and Monetary Union, 1989).

103. Unlike the first three conditions, the fourth is subject to significant qualifications. For analysis and discussion see Kenen (1992), Buiter, Corsetti, and Roubini (1993), and Eichengreen (1992c).

8

The Political Economy of Fiscal Restrictions: Implications for Europe from the United States

8.1 Introduction

The Maastricht Treaty's provisions regarding fiscal policy are among its most controversial. Signatories commit to limiting their public-sector debts and deficits to levels generally not exceeding 60 and 3 percent of GDP, respectively.[1] Whatever the merits of the arguments for these "excessive deficit procedures," there is also the question of their effects. In other words, do self-imposed fiscal restrictions really restrain behavior, or can governments circumvent them? And if fiscal restrictions restrain, do they also inhibit certain positive functions of fiscal policy?

One source of evidence on these issues is the United States, all of whose state governments, with the exception of Vermont, function under self-imposed fiscal restraints. Since the severity of these provisions differs significantly, it may be possible to draw inferences about their effects from cross-state comparisons.

In this paper we summarize some of the findings of a research program in which we have been analyzing, jointly and in collaboration with other investigators, the operation of fiscal restrictions in the United States as a way of shedding light on the likely effects of the excessive deficit provisions of the Maastricht Treaty. We consider the impact of fiscal restrictions on the levels of debts and deficits, on the cost of borrowing, and on stabilization function of fiscal policy.

8.2 Deficit Restrictions and the Size of Deficits

The self-avowed purpose of fiscal restrictions on U.S. states is to limit their public-sector debts and deficits. Some balanced-budget requirements

Originally published in *European Economic Review* 38 (1994): 783–91, with Tamim Bayoumi. Reprinted with permission.

seek to limit the deficits of state governments by requiring the governor to submit a balanced budget or the legislature to pass a balanced budget. Others prohibit the state from carrying over a deficit into the next fiscal year, from carrying it over for more than a year, or from carrying it over into the next biennium. Constitutional and statutory debt limits are designed to restrain governments from issuing public obligations. While a number of previous studies have dismissed such provisions as ineffectual, others (Advisory Commission on Intergovernmental Relations, 1987) have concluded that they have some effect.

Table 8.1 reports results from what is perhaps the simplest approach to this question. It displays linear regressions designed to explain the size of the state budget surplus or deficit.[2] The specification follows the Advisory Commission on Intergovernmental Relations (1987); here the regressions are estimated using pooled time-series–cross-section data for 1985–89. The per capita surplus is related to agricultural output per capita, the percent of state population aged 54 or older, federal aid per capita, and a dummy variable for states in the South, plus fixed effects for years and three measures of the severity of fiscal restrictions.[3] *Restraint* is the ACIR index, ranging from one to ten, of the relative stringency of state balanced budget requirements. *Restraint2* is a dummy variable equalling one for states prohibited from carrying over a deficit into the next fiscal year. *Restraint3* is a dummy variable for states whose governors must sign a balanced budget by statutory or constitutional law.

The coefficients on *Restraint2* and *Restraint3* differ from zero at the 95 percent confidence level (one tail test). Their positive signs suggest that states whose governors must sign balanced budgets and states that cannot carry over deficits run larger surpluses. The coefficient on *Restraint*, the ACIR index, although also positive is not significantly different from zero. Since *Restraint* is an increasing function of *Restraint2*, *Restraint3* and other weaker fiscal restrictions as well, its insignificance suggests that it is mainly more stringent restrictions that affect behavior. Thus, these results suggest that fiscal restraints affect the size of budget deficits.

8.3 The Cost of Borrowing and Credit Rationing

The impact of fiscal restraints on debt issuance can in principle be investigated in analogous fashion. Models of credit rationing (e.g., Stiglitz and Weiss, 1981) suggest, however, that the relationship between debt and yields may be nonlinear, since a rise in yields and hence in debt service may so increase default risk that at some point potential borrowers are

Table 8.1
The Effect of Fiscal Restraints on the General-Fund Budget Balance[a]

	(1)	(2)	(3)
Constant	25.30	46.23	41.93
	(0.52)	(1.02)	(1.10)
Restraint	3.16	—	—
	(1.63)	—	—
Restraint2	—	23.43	—
	—	(2.06)	—
Restraint3	—	—	19.65
	—	—	(2.13)
Elders	−1.48	−2.08	−5.01
	(−0.53)	(−0.74)	(−2.05)
Grant	0.02	0.02	0.12
	(0.46)	(0.37)	(3.15)
South	−36.45	−40.38	−28.38
	(−2.67)	(−2.91)	(−2.55)
Agripc	0.01	0.01	0.01
	(1.18)	(1.31)	(1.56)
1986	−11.12	−10.92	−12.94
	(0.66)	(−0.56)	(−0.92)
1987	0.17	−2.92	−9.21
	(0.03)	(−0.17)	(−0.64)
1988	19.60	18.53	2.37
	(1.16)	(1.10)	(0.17)
1989	26.74	29.21	15.56
	(1.56)	(1.71)	(1.10)
N	250	250	242
R-squared	0.08	0.09	0.14
F-statistic	2.39	2.58	5.34

Source: Eichengreen (1994).
[a] *t*-statistics are in parentheses.

quantity constrained. The question is how, if at all, self-imposed fiscal restrictions affect this credit constraint.

Here we extend the results of Bayoumi, Goldstein, and Woglom (BGW) (1995), who have used a similar framework to examine these questions. (Their approach differs in its specification of the determinants of default.[4]) Consider the arbitrage equation

$$(1 + R + s)P(H) = (1 + R), \tag{1}$$

where s is the premium over the risk free rate R, and $P(H)$ is the probability P of total default H. Letting H be linear in its determinants,

$$H = d(R + s)(B + \beta X), \tag{2}$$

where β and d are parameters to be estimated, B is the ratio of debt to gross state product, and X is a vector of other factors affecting the default probability. $R + s$ is interacted with B and X on the assumption that a given correlate of default (the size of the debt burden, for instance) has a more powerful effect the higher are interest costs.

Assuming $P(H) = \exp(-H)$, we can substitute (2) into (1) and solve for s, obtaining[5]

$$s = dR(B + \beta X)/[1 - d(B + \beta X)]. \tag{3}$$

We estimate the following variant of this equation:

$$s_{it} = [(a_0 + a_1 B_{it} + a_2 TAX_{it} + a_3 UNEM_{it-1} + a_4 RESTRAINT_{it})/$$

$$\{1 - a_5(a_1 B_{it} + a_2 TAX_{it} + a_3 UNEM_{it-1} + a_4 RESTRAINT_{it})\}] + \varepsilon_t,$$

where $UNEM_{-1}$, the level of state unemployment lagged one period, and $RESTRAINT$, the ACIR index of the severity of fiscal restrictions, are included in the X vector. ε_t is the error term, and the a_i are coefficients to be estimated. a_1 measures the effect of the level of debt on yields, a_5 the nonlinear interaction between yields and interest payments. If a_5 is positive the supply curve bends back.

The dependent variable is the differential between the yield on the general obligation bonds of each state relative to the lowest yielding general obligation bond, based on the Chubb Relative Value Study. The equation was estimated on data for the 37 states for which yield data were available, pooling annual observations for 1981 through 1990. To account for possible endogeneity of some of the regressors, estimation was by instrumental variables. Instruments were the index of the severity

Table 8.2
Parameter Estimates for Yield Equation[a]

a_0	a_1	a_2	a_3	a_4	a_5
25.48	18.16	−8.33	4.88	−3.04	0.007
(1.28)	(2.10)	(1.98)	(2.48)	(2.23)	(1.62)

[*] t-statistics in parentheses. $R^2 = 0.22$.

of fiscal restrictions and measures of underlying state characteristics, including the percentage of the population under 18 and over 65, average number of persons per household, the rate of growth of the population, and the 1991 state population.

The estimated equation appears in Table 8.2. The coefficient on the fiscal restraints, a_4, suggests that, for average levels of B, TAX and $UNEM_{-1}$, moving from no restraints to the most severe restraints reduces interest costs by nearly 50 basis points. An interpretation of this result is that fiscal restraints lower the required return on general obligation bonds by reducing the likelihood of future surges of borrowing and hence the likelihood of default. The positive value of a_5 suggests that this effect grows with the level of debt. The parameter estimates also suggest that a state with no fiscal restrictions is rationed out of the capital market when its ratio of debt to gross state product reaches 8.7 percent. (This compares to the estimate of 8.9 percent obtained by BGW.) But the presence of restrictions relaxes the credit-rationing constraint: moving from no restrictions to the most severe restrictions raises the maximum debt permitted by the market from 8.7 to 10.8 percent of gross state product. Again, an interpretation is that the presence of restrictions which reduces the likelihood of future borrowing also reduces the probability of future default, encouraging the markets to engage in additional current lending despite the tendency for more lending, by driving up current interest costs, to raise default probabilities, ceteris paribus.[6]

8.4   The Extent of Stabilization

These findings concerning the impact of fiscal restraints suggest that such measures can discourage deficit spending on the part of state governments, which would be viewed as desirable by those who believe in forces biasing deficits toward the excessive. Working in the other direction, however, is the possibility that binding fiscal restrictions may weaken the automatic stabilization function of fiscal policy. We investigate this possibility in our 1993 paper, again using data for the states. Assume that fiscal balance depends on the rate of change of output and on its own lagged value:

$$(BAL/GDP)_t = \alpha + \beta\Delta \log(Y_t) + \tau(BAL/GDP)_{t-1} + \varepsilon_t, \tag{4}$$

where (BAL/GDP) is the ratio of the fiscal surplus to output, Y is real GDP, Greek letters are estimated coefficients, Δ is the difference operator, and β measures the sensitivity of the fiscal balance to the cycle. (For local governments the lagged dependent variable was replaced by a time trend.) A positive β indicates that the balance varies countercyclically, providing automatic stabilization.

State fiscal balance is defined as total government revenues minus total expenditures. Local government fiscal balance is defined as total revenues less direct expenditures.[7] The data for state and local governments, covering the period 1971–90 and 1975–90, respectively, are normalized by the nominal gross state product of the previous year and aggregated into the eight standard regions used by the Bureau of Economic Analysis. The results (Table 8.3) indicate that state rather than local governments stabilize over the cycle. When the equations are estimated as a system with β constrained to be equal across regions, its estimated value is 0.054 and highly significant. By contrast, the coefficient in the local government regressions is 0.003 and insignificantly different from zero.[8]

We also report the estimated β coefficients for each region when they are not constrained to be equal. For state governments the likelihood ratio statistic rejects the hypothesis of equality at the 10 percent level. State budgets in New England, the Mid East and the Far West display relatively large cyclical offsets, on the order of 0.09–0.20. The South East and Rocky Mountains have slightly lower values (0.06–0.09), while the Great Lakes, Plains and South West have the smallest offsets, ranging from 0.02 to 0.05. Most of the β coefficients are significantly different from zero, confirming that state governments provide significant regional stabilization. The results for local governments are very different. The constraint of equality cannot be rejected, and only one of the freely estimated values differs significantly from zero.

Regional differences in behavior of state governments correspond to differences in fiscal controls. Many New England states have particularly weak fiscal restraints: California, which dominates the Far West economically, has relatively lax state fiscal controls; in the Plains region, in

Table 8.3
Regional Results for State Governments and Local Governments[a]

	State government		Local government	
	β	R^2	β	R^2
All regions	0.054 (0.009)	0.18–0.80	0.003 (0.004)	0.16–0.76
New England	0.154** (0.046)	0.24	0.16 (0.011)	0.22
Mid-East	0.095** (0.025)	0.83	0.035* (0.016)	0.40
Great Lakes	0.049** (0.013)	0.67	−0.005 (0.007)	0.45
Plains	0.020 (0.015)	0.67	−0.003 (0.014)	0.40
South East	0.064** (0.012)	0.79	0.002 (0.009)	0.54
South West	0.042* (0.017)	0.50	0.013 (0.009)	0.50
Rocky Mountains	0.086** (0.017)	0.74	−0.005 (0.010)	0.76
Far West	0.198** (0.028)	0.67	0.015 (0.013)	0.60
Likelihood ratio test of constraint ($\chi^2(7)$)	2.5*		9.0	

[a] The equations were estimated using multivariate least squares. The first row shows the results when all of the β coefficients were constrained to be the same. The last row shows the result from testing this constraint using a likelihood ratio test. The state government equations were estimated over FY 1971–90, those for local government on data for FY 1975–90. The estimated coefficients on constant terms, lagged dependent variables and time trends are not reported. * and ** indicate the coefficient is significant at the 10 and 1 percent level, respectively. The likelihood ratio statistic is a test that all of the coefficients are equal in a multivariate least squares estimation.

contrast, all of the states have relatively stringent restraints. To investigate this connection further, the regressions were repeated on a state-by-state basis. Estimated values of β were then related to the ACIR index of the stringency of fiscal restraints, which as explained in Section 8.2 ranges from 1 to 10. This produced the following result:

$$\beta = 0.1129 - 0.0045 RESTRAINT, \ R^2 = 0.04.$$
$$\quad (0.0221) \ (0.0024)$$

The coefficient on fiscal restraints differs from zero at the ten percent level. It suggests that moving from no fiscal restraints to the most stringent level of controls lowers the cyclical offset by 0.045. Given the estimated intercept, this indicates that restraints reduce the cyclical variance of the fiscal balance by about 40 percent of its original value. When the sample is limited to states with fiscal indices of 6 or more, which covers over four fifths of the sample, the estimated impact of fiscal restraints is even larger, indicating that the full-sample results are if anything a lower-bound estimate.[9]

Which component of the surplus is affected by restraints? We reestimated Eq. (4) state by state for revenues and expenditures separately, and again regressed the coefficients on the fiscal index.[10] Most of the difference in behavior associated with fiscal restraints is on the expenditure side. The coefficient on the fiscal index in the expenditure equation is -0.0043, as opposed to 0.0002 in the revenue equation. Over 90 percent of the reduction in automatic stabilizers caused by fiscal restraints occurs through reducing the cyclical sensitivity of expenditures.

A significant share of stabilization in the United States thus appears to be carried out at the state level. In the 1970s and 1980s, over 5 percent of fluctuations in state income was offset through fiscal stabilization by state and local governments.

8.5 Implications for Europe

What are the implications for the European Community? If U.S. experience is any guide, the fiscal restraints of the Maastricht Treaty are enforceable. But if vigorously enforced, they could significantly diminish the stabilization capacity of national budgets. Given their openness and the consequent small size of their fiscal multipliers, EC member states should no more assume principal responsibility for fiscal stabilization in Europe than do state governments in the United States. But advocates of Maastricht cannot have it both ways: while there is no question that fiscal stabilization is more appropriately undertaken at the EC level, the treaty makes no provision for expanding the Community's fiscal role. Given that in post-EMU Europe the EC budget will in all likelihood remain small by U.S. standards, providing little scope for automatic stabilization at the Community level, vigorously applying the Excessive Deficits Procedures of the treaty to the national budgets of member states would leave post-Maastricht Europe with significantly less automatic stabilization than the U.S. economic and monetary union.

Notes

Work on this chapter was begun during Eichengreen's visit to the International Monetary Fund. We gratefully acknowledge the contributions of coauthors—Morris Goldstein and Geoffrey Woglom in particular—on whose collaborative research we draw this chapter. Helpful comments were provided by Jürgen von Hagen, Torsten Persson and Guido Tabellini. Views expressed are not necessarily those of the IMF.

1. More precisely, excessive deficits will be said to exist if the deficit of all levels of government exceeds 3% of GDP and if in addition either the deficit ratio has not declined "substantially and continuously" to a level "close" to the 3% reference value, or that ratio cannot be regarded as "exceptional and temporary and...close to" the 3% threshold. The ratio of government debt to GDP will be excessive if it is greater than 60% and is not "sufficiently diminishing and approaching the 60% level at a satisfactory pace...."

2. According to the Bureau of the Census, spending financed out of rainy day funds is included in the budgetary data we analyze here. Hence, the deficit and the change in debt can differ. (Expenditures financed out of rainy day funds can show up as deficits without causing a commensurate increase in debt.) Von Hagen (1992) considers stocks rather than flows (debts and debt limits rather than deficits and balanced-budget provisions as here), finding some evidence that states with debt limits finance more of their debt with instruments other than full-faith-and-credit obligations. On this issue, see also footnote 6 below.

3. Additional regressions analyzed the effects of whether or not the state governor possessed a line-item veto, whether there existed tax or expenditure limitations, the year in which statehood was granted, and gross state product per capita. These changed none of the results.

4. Their model does not interact $r + s$ with X. It provides more precise estimates of the point where credit rationing occurs but does not test for a shift in that point as a result of fiscal restraints.

5. In deriving this equation, BGW approximate $\log(1 + x)$ by x.

6. These results are strengthened if the true level of debt for states with fiscal restrictions is understated due to the use of off-balance items. States with strong restrictions would have estimated debt which was too low; hence, the increase in the interest spread due to debt and the reduction in the spread due to the existence of fiscal restrictions would both be understated.

7. Despite the fact that state unemployment insurance trust funds are administered by the federal government, our consolidated state-level data were constructed to include them since they are likely to be especially sensitive to the cycle.

8. At 0.080, the sum of the coefficients on state and local governments is very similar to that produced by regression analysis using National Income and Product Accounts data for the U.S. as a whole. See Bayoumi and Eichengreen (1995).

9. Similar results are obtained by Poterba (1994).

10. The log of real state product was also included, since state governments administer more programs directly in smaller states, which may affect the cyclical behavior of revenues and expenditures. This variable was not significant in the regressions using the overall surplus.

9 Fiscal Policy and Monetary Union: Is There a Tradeoff between Federalism and Fiscal Restrictions?

9.1 Introduction

A prominent feature of the Maastricht Treaty on European Union is the restrictions it places on fiscal policy. Under the provisions of its Excessive Deficit Procedure (or EDP), governments of EU member states are required to avoid "excessive deficits." Article 104c empowers the European Commission to monitor deficits and debts and to assess their compliance with the reference values of 3 and 60 percent of GDP defined in a protocol of the treaty. If the Commission concludes that a government is running an excessive deficit, it registers its opinion with the European Council. The Council, if it agrees, recommends steps to eliminate the problem. It may require the member state to publish additional information before issuing bonds and securities, invite the European Investment Bank to "reconsider" its lending policy, require the country to make non-interest-bearing deposits with the European Union and impose unspecified fines. In an attempt to strengthen these procedures still further, the German finance minister, Hans Waigel, has proposed a "stability pact" that would oblige EMU member states to limit their budget deficits to one percent of GDP and impose harsh penalties on violators.

One justification for this approach invokes the advantages of fiscal policy coordination in an integrated Europe. A counterargument is that even if fiscal policy in one country affects interest rates in others, there is no need for policy coordination, since such spillovers are purely pecuniary externalities that operate through the price system.[1] This reasoning

Originally appeared as NBER Working Paper no. 5517 (March 1996), under the title "Fiscal Policy and Monetary Union: Is There a Tradeoff between Federalism and Budgetary Restrictions," with Jurgen von Hagen. (This chapter is a slightly expanded version of "Fiscal Restraints, Federalism and European Monetary Union: Is the Excessive Deficit Procedure Counterproductive?" *American Economic Review* 86 (May 1996): 134–38, with Jürgen von Hagen.) Reprinted with permission.

breaks down if other distortions exist, in which case fiscal policy coordination may be desirable both in the preparatory stages to monetary union and during monetary union itself. Even then, however, numerical debt and deficit limits like those specified in the treaty are not an ideal basis for macroeconomic policy coordination. By limiting the flexibility of national fiscal policies, they may actually impede efforts to coordinate stabilization policies.[2] The Maastricht Treaty acknowledges this point by providing an entirely different mechanism for fiscal policy coordination, the "Mutual Surveillance Procedure" of Art. 103 under which the Council develops guidelines for the economic policies of member states, monitors their performance and issues recommendations.

Another motivation for the EDP is the fear that unfettered fiscal policies will be a source of inflationary pressure that the European Central Bank (ECB) will be unable to resist. The argument is that monetary union requires restrictions on member states to prevent the latter from over-borrowing, because excessive debt may lead to a bailout by the Union and threaten the stability of the single currency. The response may take two forms: an ex post bailout involving monetization of government debt, or an ex ante bailout entailing policies of keeping interest rates artificially low. Either policy could give rise to inflation and threaten the stability of the single currency. This is in contrast to a situation in which each country issues its own currency and each central therefore has the capacity to act as its own lender of last resort, which will encourage governments to internalize bailout risk.

In this chapter we challenge the view that borrowing restraints are an appropriate institutional means for preventing the members of a monetary union from overborrowing and forcing the common central bank to extend a bailout. We begin in section 9.2 by describing the bailout scenario in more detail. Section 9.3 then considers the international incidence of borrowing restraints. Using data for a cross section of federal states, we show that in fact there is no association between monetary union and restrictions on borrowing by subcentral governments.

There is, however, an association between fiscal restraints on subcentral governments and the tax base under the control of subnational authorities. Fiscal restraints appear where subcentral governments finance only a small share of their expenditures out of their own taxes.[3] We demonstrate this association using a sample of 45 countries.

The intuition for this association is straightforward. When a subnational jurisdiction retains significant control of taxation, the central government can reasonably ask it to use tax policy to deal with any debt problems it creates for itself. But when the tax base is controlled by the national government, raising its own taxes is not an option: the only alternatives for subnational jurisdictions will be to default or obtain a bailout. In many circumstances, central governments will perceive the political costs of default as high. They will find it difficult to refuse the request for a bailout. This, it can be argued, creates the need for fiscal restraints on subnational governments to minimize such requests.

Section 9.4 turns to the long-term consequences of borrowing restraints. Prohibiting borrowing by subcentral governments will not eliminate their demand for current expenditures financed from sources other than current revenues. Governments whose spending ambitions are restricted by newly imposed borrowing restraints may step up pressure on the central government to borrow for them. The financial position of the central government may deteriorate, therefore, when borrowing by subcentral governments is restricted.

Section 9.5 summarizes the implications of our analysis for the European Union.

9.2 The Bailout Scenario

The scenario the framers of the treaty had in mind presumably runs as follows.[4] Imagine that the government of a member state experiences a revenue shortfall and finds it difficult to service its debt. Investors concerned about the interruption of debt service sell their bonds, forcing the affected government to raise interest rates when rolling over maturing issues. The rise in rates further widens the gap between government revenues and expenditures, compounding budgetary difficulties. Problems in the bond market spill over to other markets, because for example higher interest rates depress equity prices. In the worst case scenario, the collapse of asset prices and the impact of higher interest rates on corporate profitability and the performance of outstanding loans destabilize the banking system.[5]

Faced with this crisis, a government's first recourse may be to the printing press. It may pressure the central bank to purchase debt sold by private investors to prevent bond prices from falling and to limit the danger that equity markets and the banking system will be destabilized. McKinnon (1995) argues that this capacity of the central bank to backstop the market in government debt is critical to the stability of the financial sector in high-debt economies.

Monetary union deprives participating governments of the ability to counter a bond market crisis with autonomous central bank intervention. Member governments faced with a bond market crisis may, however, request a bailout from their common central bank. In the European context, the question then becomes whether the ECB can resist such demands. At first glance, there are reasons to be optimistic. The Maastricht Treaty provides for the independence of the European Central Bank (ECB) and makes its mandate the pursuit of price stability. In conjunction with Art. 21 of the Protocol on the European System of Central Banks, which states that the ECB cannot acquire any public debt directly from the issuer, this provides some assurance that the ECB will not monetize public debts. This presumption is strengthened by Art. 104b, which holds that neither the Union nor any member state shall be responsible for the debt of other EU members.

But there are also grounds to doubt that the ECB will be able to resist demands for a bailout. A basic principle of the European Union, stated in the Preamble and in Art. A of the Treaty, is that members pursue policies of solidarity and coherence leading to the convergence of their economies. Leaving a member state to suffer a fiscal crisis on its own may be regarded as a breach of these principles; invoking EU solidarity may therefore be a way to solicit financial assistance, including the monetization of bad debts.[6] The knowledge that such pressure will be applied and that the ECB's "commitment technology" is less than completely effective gives rise to a moral hazard problem for the governments of member states. The rationale for the EDP then becomes to prevent them from indulging in hazardous behavior.

9.3   The Incidence of Borrowing Restrictions

If limits on freedom to borrow are essential for the stability of a common currency, then one would expect such restrictions to be prevalent in existing monetary unions. In fact, this is not the case. The Belgium-Luxembourg Monetary Union imposes no borrowing limits on its members. In the East Caribbean Currency Area and the West and Central African Monetary Unions, limits exist on governments' ability to borrow from the central bank but not on borrowing from other sources (Boughton 1993, Nascimento 1994). The monetary union between the United States and the Federated States of Micronesia (FSM) is an exception in that the FSM are subject to a strict balanced-budget provision. This is a product of national legislation, however, and is not mentioned in the Compact Agreement between the United States and the FSM (although the monetary union is).[7] Neither did the important historical examples of monetary unions, the Latin Monetary Union and the Scandinavian Monetary Union, impose borrowing restraints on their member states. In sum, fiscal restraints are the exception rather the rule in monetary unions.

The generality of this evidence is less than clear because actual monetary unions are few and most are comprised of low-income developing economies. We can expand the sample by considering federal states, since the typical federation has a common currency but devolves significant fiscal functions to subnational governments, in this sense resembling the typical monetary union. We therefore gathered data for sixteen federations. We coded as a fiscal restraint any restriction other than a "weak golden rule." (A weak golden rule requires deficits to be no larger than public investment. A "strong golden rule" reinforces this provision by formally separating the current and capital budgets and limiting the fungibility of funds.)

Of the sixteen countries in our sample, two feature self-imposed balanced-budget rules or borrowing limits, five require central government approval for borrowing, and one (Nigeria) imposes an outright ban on subcentral government borrowing.[8] But eight impose no restrictions on subcentral governments. Given an odds ratio of $1:1$, limits on the freedom to borrow of subcentral governments cannot be regarded as a general feature of federations.[9]

The results are different for thirty-three unitary states.[10] Of these, only four leave subcentral governments free of borrowing restraints. Ten impose strict golden rules or require the approval of the national parliament for subcentral government borrowing, twelve require central government approval, and seven prohibit subcentral government borrowing outright. But the contrast between unitary and federal states is hardly comforting to those who insist that restraints are needed to safeguard a common currency from fiscal abuses by subcentral governments, since the budgetary powers of the latter and hence their capacity to undermine monetary stability are presumably larger in federations. By this argument, borrowing limits should be more prevalent in federal than unitary states, but the opposite is true.

9.4   Borrowing Restraints and the Vertical Structure of the Fiscal System

How then can the incidence of borrowing restraints across countries be understood? In analyzing the pressure for the monetary authorities to respond to a debt run, the discussion in section 9.2 ignores the extent to which a state experiencing a borrowing crisis has other instruments at its command. Most obviously, the authorities can promise to raise taxes or cut spending to make available the resources needed to service and retire their debts. While changes in fiscal policy take time to deliver revenues, a government that takes fiscal steps now that promise to raise revenues later should be able to borrow against its expected future income.[11] Fiscal actions, in other words, should have the capacity to address debt problems.

The important question is therefore the extent to which a state facing a borrowing crisis can control its receipts. A critical determinant of this capacity is the vertical structure of the fiscal system, and in particular the distribution of the tax base between central and subcentral governments. At one extreme, a country's entire tax base is owned by the central government, which pays grants to subcentral governments to enable them to carry out their functions. At the other extreme, subcentral governments own a sufficiently large share of the tax base to finance their expenditures, leaving them financially independent of the central government.[12]

In the first case, a heavily indebted subcentral government may face bankruptcy due to a small shock to its economy. The only choices then left to the central government are to let the subcentral jurisdiction go bankrupt or to provide a bailout. Under many circumstances, the bankruptcy option will not be palatable. Anticipating this, subcentral governments have an incentive to adopt risky financial policies. In contrast, when subcentral governments possess tax resources of their own, there exists a third option: the central government can demand that they use these to service and restructure their debts. The implication is that borrowing limits designed to safeguard the central government's financial stability will exist in countries where subcentral governments command only a small portion of the tax base.

We characterize the vertical structure of a country's fiscal system in terms of the share of subcentral government spending financed by revenues from own tax resources.[13] In our data set, the share of own taxes varies from 3.2 percent in Trinidad and Tobago and 5.2 percent in the Netherlands, on the one hand, to 79 percent in Mexico and 67 percent in Germany, on the other. Micronesia (8.5 percent) and Australia (27.8 percent) have the lowest shares of own tax revenues among the federal states. Of unitary states, Guatemala (73.7 percent), and Sweden (57.4 percent) have the largest shares. For the countries with a federal structure, own taxes as a share of spending average 53 percent, compared to 34 percent for the states with a unitary structure, a difference that is statistically significant at the one-percent level.[14] Thus, federal states tend to have more balanced vertical fiscal structure than unitary states.

We test the hypothesis that borrowing restraints on subcentral governments are a function of the vertical structure of the fiscal system by estimating a probit regression on cross-country data for 1985–87.[15] The dependent variable is coded as zero if a country has no restrictions on subcentral government borrowing or only a weak golden rule, and unity otherwise. The independent variable of interest is our measure of the vertical structure of the fiscal system (denoted STRUCTURE). We also include 1987 GDP per capita in U.S. dollars (denoted PCGDP) to control for stage economic development. The estimated equation (with standard errors in parentheses) confirms that countries whose central governments control a small share of the tax base are less likely to restrict borrowing by subcentral governments.

Restrictions = 0.25 – 3.51 Structure – 0.04 PCGDP
        (0.65) (1.16)   (0.04)

$X^2 = 8.00$, Number of observations = 45, $p = 0.045$ (1)

Adding a dummy for federal states does not significantly improve the fit of be regression. Nor does dropping the insignificant per capita income variable.

Restrictions = 1.91 – 3.53 Structure
        (0.57) (1.16)

$X^2 = 7.80$, Number of observations = 45, $p = 0.005$ (2)

Thus, the results support our hypothesis that the incidence of borrowing restraints can be explained by the vertical structure of the fiscal system.

9.5   Long-Run Effects of Fiscal Restrictions

Government borrowing is a mechanism for distributing over time the burden of adjustment to transitory shocks and for spreading the tax burden associated with public investment. The desire to have government provide these services will not disappear when borrowing restraints are imposed. Restricting the ability of subcentral governments to borrow may therefore lead them to demand that the central government engage in the borrowing necessary to provide those functions.

In addition to using their political leverage to encourage the central government to undertake additional borrowing, subcentral governments can encourage this outcome by spending more than they take in, in the hope that the central government will make good the difference. Indeed, in some situations in which subcentral governments are legally prohibited from borrowing, the central government will have no other choice. Italy illustrates these dynamics. Although (or, one may argue, precisely because) Italian regions and municipalities are barred from borrowing, a large part of Italy's huge public debt reflects deficits of the regional and local jurisdictions absorbed by the central government.

Some economists (viz. Sala-i-Martin and Sachs 1992) suggest that the smooth operation of a monetary union requires a system of fiscal federalism to provide interregional transfers in response to shocks. The pressure for the central government to provide these services will presumably be greater where restrictions on borrowing by subcentral governments prevent the latter from providing those services themselves. For Europe this means that the EDP may spur the creation of a system of fiscal federalism in which Brussels collects taxes and provides transfers to member states in amounts that increase with, say, the level of unemployment. Insofar as the member states resist giving up their tax revenues as quickly as they begin demanding additional services from the EU, the financial position of the latter is likely to deteriorate.

These considerations lead us to conjecture that restraints on the budgetary freedom of subcentral governments will encourage the transfer of fiscal authority to the center and increase the demand for central government borrowing, ultimately weakening the financial stability of the center. The central government's financial position should be more fragile in countries where subcentral governments face stringent borrowing restraints than in countries where subcentral governments are free to borrow.

Testing this hypothesis requires a measure of the central government's financial position. The ratio of government debt to GDP is problematic because a given ratio may be high or low depending on the size of the public sector, which is a matter of national preference. Instead, we measure debt exposure as the ratio of central government debt to central government tax revenues, again in 1985–87. Our index of the stringency of borrowing restraints equals zero for no restrictions, one for a strict golden rule or congressional approval, two for self-imposed restraints, three where central government approval is required, and four for outright bans on subcentral borrowing. Self-imposed restrictions are weaker than those applied by the central government, since revoking the latter requires the concurrence of an outside authority. Congressional approval is a weaker restraint than approval by the Executive, since a region is sure to have representation in the national congress.

Debt exposure may also depend on country-specific preferences affecting the propensity to finance central government expenditures with future taxes. We therefore include in our regression a proxy for the preference for tax financing, namely the ratio of central government tax revenues to GDP (lagged to minimize simultaneity). Estimation yields the following result (with standard errors in parentheses):

Debt exposure $= 2.79 + 0.41$ Restrictions
                         (0.69) (0.15)

$- 7.77$ Tax Financing Preference
(2.60)

$R^2 - 0.31$, Number of observations $= 36$, $F = 7.31$, $p = 0.001$ (3)

The central governments of countries with tight borrowing restraints on subcentral jurisdictions are thus more heavily exposed to debt. An interpretation is that subcentral governments whose freedom to borrow is limited pressure the central government to undertake activities that give rise to additional borrowing, leading to a deterioration in the financial position of the central authorities.

9.6   Implications for Europe

Our results suggest that the more dependent subcentral governments are on financing by the central government, the more likely is a bailout in the event of a financial crisis, and the greater is the incentive for subcentral jurisdictions to engage in excessive borrowing. They suggest that the credibility of a prohibition against bailouts of subcentral governments thus depends on the vertical fiscal structure of the public sector.

The implications for the European Union are clear. So long as national governments continue to control their own tax bases, they can raise taxes to deal with debt crises and will be expected to do so. The existence of these instruments for coping with crises should help the European Commission and the ECB resist the pressure for a bailout. That the cost of coping with the crisis will be borne by the member state itself, in the form of higher taxes, will limit moral hazard.

One day a decision may be taken to transfer control of Europe's tax base from EU member states to the Union itself. There will then be a case for fiscal restraints to contain moral hazard problems. But not even steadfast proponents of political integration see this as a realistic possibility for the foreseeable future. In any case, this issue is logically independent of EMU, since fiscal centralization may or may not occur in a monetary union.

Our finding that the debt exposure of central governments increases with the stringency of borrowing restraints on subcentral jurisdictions means that the EDP will not necessarily enhance the stability of the single European currency. Member states with a taste for tax-smoothing services but unable to provide them themselves will press the EU to supply them. The EU possesses the capacity to respond. Although the Commission's budget must be balanced, the EU can borrow off-budget through the European Investment Bank. An unanticipated consequence of the EDP may therefore be to augment the fiscal powers of Brussels. As the latter provides tax-smoothing services and undertakes additional responsibilities, it may accumulate larger debts than if member states were free to borrow. The consequent increase in the financial fragility of the European Union may ultimately be a stronger source of inflationary pressures than the debt exposure individual member states would acquire in the absence of borrowing restraints.

Notes

1. See Buiter, Corsetti, and Pesenti (1995).

2. This point is made, inter alia, by Hughes-Hallett and Vines (1991), Goodhart and Smith (1993), and De Grauwe (1994).

3. While there is a negative association, as one would expect, between federal structure and the share of the tax base under the control of the national authorities, that association is less than perfect, leading to different correlations with the cross-country incidence of fiscal restraints.

4. See for example Commission of the European Communities (1990).

5. The most influential model of debt runs is Calvo (1988). For models applied to the European context, see Alesina, Prati, and Tabellini (1990) and Giavazzi and Pagano (1990).

6. In a sense, such concerns are unrelated to the issue of EMU; solidarity, coherence, and convergence are principles of the European Union regardless of whether or not it adopts a common currency.

7. In any case, it is hard to believe that borrowing limits on the FSM states flow from concern for the stability of the U.S. dollar.

8. Our sample, dictated by data availability, includes Argentina, Australia, Austria, Brazil, Canada, Germany, India, Malaysia, Mexico, the FSM, Nigeria, Pakistan, Switzerland, the United Arab Emirates, the United States, and Venezuela.

9. Pakistan and Nigeria moved from no restrictions to limits on state government borrowing in their transition from the strongly federal postcolonial constitutions to their current, more

centralized constitutions. Brazil, in contrast, recently moved to borrowing limits on state governments imposed by the federal government and voted in the federal parliament. These limits, however, effectively apply only to foreign currency loans that are guaranteed by the federal government.

10. The sample consists of Belgium, the Bahamas, Bolivia, Chile, Colombia, Costa Rica, Denmark, the Dominican Republic, Ecuador, El Salvador, Finland, France, Greece, Guatemala, Honduras, Indonesia, Ireland, Italy, Japan, Korea, Luxembourg, the Netherlands, New Zealand, Nicaragua, Norway, Panama, Peru, Portugal, Spain, Sweden, Trinidad and Tobago, Uruguay, and the United Kingdom.

11. Even if the government raises taxes now, it may take a year before the impact on revenues materializes. To the extent that income taxpayers pay estimated taxes quarterly or the authorities raise sales taxes and VAT, results may materialize faster, but it is still the case that time will have to pass before a significant increase in net revenues eventuates.

12. Actual fiscal systems can be described as combinations of these limiting cases. The German Reich from 1871 to 1918 is an example of a third model, where the central government is largely deprived from own tax resources and is therefore financially dependent on the subcentral governments.

13. For a discussion of the measurement of the fiscal capacity of subcentral governments, see Levin (1991). While in principle one might also include own revenues from nontax resources, such data do not exist for all countries in our sample.

14. The t-test for equal means is $t = 7.47$.

15. In a few cases, problems of availability forced us to substitute figures for earlier or later periods; a data appendix is available upon request.

10

A More Perfect Union? On the Logic of Economic Integration

This chapter is about the connections between three types of union—customs union, monetary union, and political union. The first section asks whether monetary integration is a concomitant of commercial integration.[1] The second asks whether political integration is a concomitant of monetary integration.

I use the ambiguous word "concomitant" to indicate that I am actually looking at several questions. One is whether monetary integration must accompany commercial integration before efficiency advantages can be obtained from the latter. Another is whether commercial integration delivers a larger increase in efficiency and welfare when accompanied by monetary integration, and whether the welfare improvement from monetary integration is greater when accompanied by political integration. A third question asks what combination of commercial, monetary, and political integration is Pareto optimal. And a fourth, and different, question—concerned with the political equilibrium rather than the social optimum—asks whether monetary union is necessary to maintain political support for commercial integration and whether political integration is necessary to assemble support for monetary union.

My answer to the first question is that neither a common currency nor measures to limit fluctuations of exchange rates are essential to derive efficiency advantages from a customs union, assuming that the union is "natural"—that the benefits of trade creation dominate the costs of trade diversion (Krugman, 1991b). No strictly economic obstacle prevents countries from removing trade barriers and restructuring along lines of comparative advantage while retaining national, potentially fluctuating, currencies. Although one can argue, along the lines of the European

Originally appeared in *Princeton Essays in International Finance* (Princeton: International Department of Economics, Princeton University, 1996), under the title "A More Perfect Union? The Logic of Economic Integration." Reprinted with permission.

Commission (1990), that the complete integration of product markets requires eliminating the transactions costs and uncertainties associated with separate currencies, few would question that the approximation possible in the absence of monetary integration is still an improvement over the status quo. For example, most would agree that the member states of the European Union (EU) benefit from their common market despite the fact that they lack a common currency.

Similarly, it is possible to obtain efficiency advantages from a single currency while maintaining separate, sovereign, political jurisdictions. There is no strictly technical obstacle, for example, to constructing an optimal contract for the future European Central Bank (ECB), as in Walsh (1995), while allowing other policies to be determined at the national level by separate, sovereign, political entities. In particular, there is no economic obstacle to appointing members of the executive board of the ECB at the national level while continuing to formulate fiscal policy in national capitals.

From the standpoint of political equilibrium, however, there are reasons to think that these three forms of integration should go hand in hand. Swings in the exchange rates of the currencies of customs-union members inflict costs on concentrated interests; when a currency appreciates, the profit squeeze on producers of tradables may lead them to lobby for import restraints. Cooperative exchange-rate management and even a common currency may be needed to alleviate this threat; otherwise, beyond some point, commercial integration without monetary integration may be politically infeasible.

Similarly, there are reasons to worry that monetary integration without political integration is problematic. Different interest groups—debtors and creditors, laborers and capitalists, producers of traded and nontraded goods—are differently affected by monetary policy. They will need reassurance that the ECB's implicit contract weighs their preferences appropriately and that a mechanism exists to enforce that contract. In the United States, the Congress is such a mechanism; the threat of a bill compromising the independence of the Federal Reserve System is its ultimate sanction. A European monetary union comprising separate sovereign states, and an ECB the statute of which can be changed only by renegotiating an international treaty, will face no such sanction. The implication is that steps toward political union that vest significant power in the hands of the European Parliament may be needed to render the ECB politically acceptable.

This is the point in the introduction when I am supposed to anticipate my conclusions. Unfortunately, it is hard to offer a statement such as "monetary union is necessary for economic union," or "political union is needed for monetary union." Although it is not unusual for an economist's conclusions to depend on the assumptions adopted, the results in the present case are especially sensitive. In the interest of being provocative, let me offer a conjecture. I suggest that economic integration without monetary integration is not a political equilibrium, but that political integration is not needed to render monetary integration politically acceptable.

10.1 Commercial Integration and Monetary Integration

The argument that economic union without monetary union is not a political equilibrium can be set forth using Europe as an example.[2] The more integrated European economies become, the more pronounced will be the distributional consequences of intra-EU currency swings. With the perfection of the Single Market, EU countries that let their currencies depreciate will flood other member states with exports. Those countries that experience import surges will, in response, demand the imposition of voluntary export restraints by their EU trading partners or the granting of subsidies for their own affected industries. Thus, exchange-rate instability may be fatally corrosive to the Single Market.

The corrosive effect of currency fluctuations was clearly evident in the wake of the 1992 depreciation of the lira, which caused a sharp depreciation of Italy's real exchange rate and an appreciation of the real exchange rates of France and Germany.[3] Given Europe's increasingly integrated market, this boosted Italian exports, strengthened Italy's current account, and helped to moderate its recession. The repercussions abroad, however, were strongly negative. The EU commissioner for the internal market, Mario Monti, warned of "growing concern among industrialists that the lira's devaluation is giving Italian companies an advantage over their European competitors," reflecting the fact that inflation had not risen to match the depreciation of the currency (*Financial Times*, February 28, 1995, p. 6). "It was impossible to have a guaranteed single market in a situation where currency fluctuations remained unchecked," Mr. Monti maintained, adding that "the continuing devaluation of the lira would in the long run lead to prolonged disruption in the internal market."

That Monti was not merely blowing smoke is evident from the French government's demand that Brussels extend subsidies to affected industries. In addition, Helmut Werner, president of the Mercedes-Benz automotive group, warned, on April 26, 1995, that "unpredictable exchange rate fluctuations are threatening the European single market with dis-integration, ..." and he appealed "for political action to restore cohesion and the introduction of a single European currency to stabilise industry's cost and price structure" (Parkes, 1995, p. 1). Similarly, *Corriere Della Sera* reported on May 24, 1995, that Alain Juppé, the new French prime minis-ter, warned that France would "react against" those countries that play "out of the [Maastricht] rules," making it clear that "French irritation against the depreciation of the lira and the peseta has reached the top level: the government level ... that which until yesterday seemed the position of some sectors of the French economy (like the automobile and textile industries, which see Italian competition as unfair) is now the offi-cial position of France." The implication is that countries cannot support the internal market and at the same time oppose the single currency. The conflict between market integration and exchange-rate fluctuations points to the need for, as Monti suggests, "some sort of monetary arrangement ... to complement the single market." If the gains from completing the Single Market are large, it follows that Europe must achieve monetary union.

It is revealing that no one accused the Italian government of deliber-ately manipulating the lira. The currency's weakness reflected the failure of the Italian parliament to adopt a 1995 budget that would hold the defi-cit to its original target of 8 percent of GDP. The fiscal problem implied debt-service difficulties and, in the eyes of the market, the possibility that the Bank of Italy might be forced to monetize budget deficits or backstop the market for public debt. It was believed, in other words, that inflation might accelerate in the future, and the lira's depreciation in January and February reflected market anticipations of this outcome. Yet the deprecia-tion gave rise to strenuous objections elsewhere in Europe despite the fact that (1) the lira's value had not been manipulated and (2) there was good reason to believe that the impact on competitiveness would eventually die out. Imagine the complaints if the government of Italy—or of Greece or the United Kingdom—were perceived as *deliberately* manipulating its currency to steal market share from European competitors.

This danger has, in fact, been emphasized by some observers. On February 11, 1995, *The Economist* (p. 14) wrote that "as long as Europe's currencies are free to move against one another, the single market will never be secure. The risk will remain that national governments will seek to protect their countries' firms against rivals in countries that have just devalued. The greater the volatility, the greater the pressure for national protection, and the greater the danger to all the past achievements of the common market." On March 4, 1995, *The Economist* (p. 59) told its U.K. audience that "the benefits we now gain from the European single market will come under threat and a question may arise over our very membership of the EU. If the pound is the only major EU currency outside the Ecu bloc, it is likely to come under frequent pressure. The Ecu countries may well regard progressive devaluation of a weak pound as unfair competition. It is very possible that they will retaliate, and there are a variety of ways in which single-market rules can be changed to our disadvantage. The pressure to raise trade barriers could be considerable. Meetings of the European Council could become increasingly acrimonious."

The argument that monetary union is required to reap the benefits from the Single Market is sometimes rebutted by the assertion that Europe can have stable exchange rates without attaining monetary union. I am skeptical that this is so. The liberalization of capital movements has made intermediate exchange-rate arrangements like the pegged-but-adjustable rates of the narrow-band European Monetary System (EMS) more difficult to sustain. The elimination of capital controls, a corollary of the Single Market project, strips governments of the insulation they need to defend pegged-but-adjustable rates and removes the breathing space they require to organize orderly realignments. The interest-rate hikes that governments must impose when their currencies come under attack may so aggravate unemployment, raise the costs of servicing the public debt, inflate mortgage payments, and destabilize the banking system as to be insupportable. In such an environment, a government that would have been willing otherwise to maintain an exchange-rate peg might be induced to abandon it in the face of speculative pressure; in other words, speculative attacks could become self-fulfilling.[4] As it becomes more difficult to operate pegged-but-adjustable rates, governments will have to choose between some form of floating, on the one hand, and permanently fixed rates, on the other, with the second alternative achievable only through monetary union. And there is by now considerable evidence that since the shift from fixed to floating currencies, the volatility of exchange rates has increased much more than the volatility of fundamentals, a fact convincingly demonstrated by Andrew Rose (1994). This is the basis for arguing that economic integration requires monetary integration.

Having presented this argument, I now want to challenge it and suggest that the connections between commercial integration and exchange-rate stability are not so straightforward as is sometimes supposed. Today, when there is so much discussion of the effect of exchange-rate volatility on trade, it is easy to forget that the presumption for many years was that

currency fluctuations and trade restraints were substitutes, not complements. "The ossification of exchange rates," as Peter Kenen (1994) puts
it, was widely lamented in the 1960s; the difficulty of dismantling trade
barriers was attributed to the reluctance of deficit and surplus countries
to alter their exchange rates. More freely adjustable currencies, many
observers believed, were needed to repel the protectionist threat.[5]

Observers were predisposed to this interpretation because of the fre-
quency with which governments had resorted to trade restrictions to balance the external accounts over the years. During World War II, countries
had used exchange and trade controls in lieu of currency depreciation.
After the war, they had retained exchange and trade restrictions for fear
of the inflationary consequences of currency depreciation; the Bretton
Woods Agreement allowed for the transitional use of controls on current-
account transactions precisely in order to support the par values established in 1946, although it turned out that even stringent current-account
restrictions did not obviate the need to devalue in 1949 (Polak, 1951). In
the 1950s, European countries established the European Payments Union
(EPU), which authorized them to use exchange and trade restrictions,
again in order to support the maintenance of pegged rates. Observers at
the time emphasized this connection between pegged exchange rates and
the survival of trade restrictions. Milton Friedman's famous 1953 essay on
floating rates is properly interpreted as advocating floating exchange
rates in lieu of the pegged rates supported by the EPU, which he saw as
encouraging the retention of exchange and trade restrictions. Policymakers also acknowledged the connection. In 1952, the British pondered
floating the pound in order to permit the immediate resumption of
current-account convertibility, but they retreated instead into the trade
and monetary controls of the EPU (Cairncross, 1992).

Some observers, casting their gaze back further, blamed the rigid
exchange rates of the gold standard for the protectionism of the 1930s.
Having emerged from World War I with their competitive positions transformed, countries experienced persistent payments surpluses and deficits.
Those in deficit, beholden to gold-standard ideology and reluctant to
devalue, used tariffs to limit their reserve losses and to support their gold-
standard parities (Eichengreen, 1992b, chaps. 11–12). The conflict between
trade liberalization and exchange-rate stability sharpened with the onset of
the Great Depression. Tariff protection became the only way of reconciling the gold standard with the desire to reflate.[6] In the United States, the
deflation associated with the fixed exchange rates of the gold standard

heightened support for the very high duties of the Hawley-Smoot Tariff.[7] In Britain, where free trade had been the hegemonic ideology for nearly a century, Keynes's arguments for a general tariff to reconcile interest-rate cuts with sterling's gold-standard parity fell on increasingly sympathetic ears (Balogh, 1976; Eichengreen, 1984).

One year after abrogating the gold standard, the United States was able to move back toward freer trade and adopt the Reciprocal Trade Agreements Act. The United Kingdom did not revoke its general tariff, but it did negotiate preferences with the members of the Commonwealth and British Empire beginning with the Ottawa Conference in 1932. The remaining gold-standard countries found their currencies overvalued. To stem their reserve losses, they raised tariffs and tightened quantitative restrictions. Only when the last members of the gold bloc devalued in 1936 did the vicious spiral of trade destruction end. In 1985, Jeffrey Sachs and I published an article in which we argued that the "competitive devaluations" of the 1930s were by no means as incompatible with macro-economic stability as has sometimes been asserted by recent scholars. In so stating, we were merely resurrecting an interwar argument to the effect that greater willingness to alter exchange rates was needed to solidify the commitment to open markets.[8]

If this was the state of the debate in the early postwar period, it has subsequently been turned on its head. Economists now argue that exchange-rate *variability* jeopardizes the commitment to free trade. Ronald McKinnon (1996) blames the exchange-rate fluctuations associated with the post-1973 system of floating rates for the "new protectionism" of the 1970s. Fred Bergsten and John Williamson (1983) blame erratic currency movements, particularly between the dollar and the yen, for the trade-conflicts of the 1980s. Enzo Grilli (1988) offers statistical evidence connecting exchange-rate fluctuations with trade protection in the United States and Europe.

This perspective reflects the strains placed by the post-1973 float on the global trading system. The failure of the dollar to depreciate against the European currencies in the mid-1970s and its subsequent overvaluation were perceived as jeopardizing free trade; the combination led the United States to adopt the trigger-price mechanism for steel and to restrict imports of sugar and shoes. The dollar's appreciation in the first half of the 1980s squeezed the profits of American producers and generated a protectionist ground swell in the U.S. Congress. Only the Plaza Agreement and Louvre Accord, which brought the dollar back to earth, rescued the multilateral trading system.

Similarly, when sterling depreciated against the franc starting in September 1992, and the Hoover vacuum cleaner manufacturing company moved 200 jobs from Dijon to Scotland (no more than a little "sucking sound" by Ross Perot's standards), politicians in Paris and Brussels were led to ask whether a country that failed to play by the monetary rules of the EU game should be accorded the privileges of the Single Market. When the Mexican peso lost half its value against the dollar starting in December 1994, U.S. producers complained of "cut-rate" Mexican competition, swelling the ranks of those opposing the North American Free Trade Agreement (NAFTA). Finally, talk of a transatlantic free-trade area in 1995 was thwarted by European politicians who complained that the dollar's decline was enabling Boeing to undercut Airbus unfairly. The presumption was that floating rates, not fixed rates, were incompatible with commercial integration.

There is no real inconsistency among these arguments about the protectionist effects of fixed and floating rates. Their common elements are that *misaligned* exchange rates fan protectionist flames and that currencies may become misaligned both when they are pegged and when they are floating. The question then becomes, would monetary unification prevent real misalignments? Imagine that monetary union were to begin in Europe without the emission of euros or the withdrawal of the national currencies from circulation; the ECB would simply exchange national currencies at par, just as the currency notes issued by the district reserve banks in the United States are exchanged at par by the Federal Reserve System.[9] Real exchange rates could be computed as before, by converting an index of national prices or wages into one national currency, say, deutsche marks, using the fixed exchange rates. It would still be possible for real exchange rates to be misaligned in a meaningful sense if their levels were to give rise to large unemployment differentials across countries.[10] If this is what we mean by misalignment, it is entirely possible for misalignments to occur within monetary unions, whether they pertain to Spain in EMU or to New Jersey in the United States. The likelihood that unemployment will foster resistance in the affected region to economic and monetary union is precisely what I mean by the political repercussions of misalignment.

What grounds, then, are there for thinking that monetary unification will eliminate resistance to economic integration? That conclusion may still follow if one believes that eliminating the exchange rate as an instrument of adjustment will induce changes in labor-market structure and performance that enhance wage flexibility and labor mobility. In fact, there is some empirical support for this application of the Lucas Critique (which says that the very structure of an economy may be affected by changing or even fixing one of the variables functioning within it). It can be argued that Italian unions gave up indexation and agreed to other policies enhancing wage flexibility in recognition of the fact that labor-market reform was needed to prepare for monetary union. And Olivier Blanchard and Pierre-Alain Muet (1993) find some evidence that wage flexibility has increased in France as the *franc fort* has gained credibility. I would argue that the flexibility of wages in New Jersey and the willingness of workers to move to neighboring states should be understood, at least in part, as reflecting the absence of any prospect of an exchange-rate change that would raise the demand for labor.

This was also true internationally during the classical gold standard era. In the countries at the core of that pegged-rate system, wages were flexible and workers migrated in unprecedented numbers, partly because they realized that there would be no change in the exchange rate to improve labor-market conditions.[11] Tamim Bayoumi and I (1996b) present evidence that the labor- and product-market response to shocks was faster under the gold standard than under monetary regimes characterized by greater exchange-rate variability. This was at least in part an endogenous consequence of the monetary regime.

I am not suggesting, of course, that wages and prices will become perfectly flexible once exchange-rate changes are a thing of the past. As a partly reconstructed Keynesian, I believe that nominal inertia will persist, and so will unemployment. My hypothesis is that wage and price setters will adapt so as to avoid increases in unemployment sufficient to provoke resistance to continued participation in the economic and monetary union.

If one wishes to argue that labor markets will adapt to a fixing of the exchange rate, one must also argue that they will adapt to currency volatility if currencies continue to float. When exchange rates fluctuate, workers demand wage indexation, the frequent renegotiation of wage contracts, and other mechanisms to prevent real wages from being disturbed by exchange-market shocks. Insofar as a depreciation of the currency then causes money wages to rise, the impact on international competitiveness will be minimal. The export surge to other EU markets that jeopardizes economic and monetary union in the scenario described above will thus be averted or at least moderated. Again, I would not go so far as to argue that this de facto or de jure indexation can eliminate the real effects of exchange-market shocks, only that movement in this direction will attenuate the conflict between exchange-rate variability and market integration.

What should we conclude about whether monetary unification is necessary to maintain political support for market integration? It is not possible to mount a general argument that monetary union is either essential or irrelevant. If exchange rates are locked, labor markets will adapt to prevent the emergence of persistent pockets of high unemployment. If exchange rates continue to fluctuate, markets will adapt to moderate their impact on competitiveness. Neither adjustment will be complete, however, and political problems will remain. My own instinct is that monetary unification is the more stable long-run solution. If currency fluctuations persist, complaints about competitive depreciation and exchange dumping will be an enduring problem. Markets have already adjusted about as far as they can to accommodate fluctuating rates, and they have not neutralized completely the effects of fluctuations on competitiveness, at least not enough to eliminate serious complaints about competitive depreciation. If exchange rates are locked once and for all, however, we can expect to see considerable additional adjustment in market structure and response. Although asymmetric shocks will remain a problem in the immediate future, because labor and product markets will adapt only gradually to the new regime, market institutions and arrangements will evolve in the long run to compensate more effectively for the absence of the exchange-rate instrument. Few Princeton professors would argue that New Jersey's unemployment rate would be lower or more stable if Governor Whitman controlled a separate currency. Given sufficient time for institutions to adapt, I submit that the same will be true of Belgium. The phrase "sufficient time," however, is crucial; it is intended to emphasize that the first years will be difficult.

10.2 Monetary Integration and Political Integration

Michael Mussa is fond of describing how, each time he walks to the IMF cafeteria, down the corridor where the currency notes of the member states are arrayed, he rediscovers one of the most robust regularities of monetary economics: the one-to-one correspondence between countries and currencies. If monetary unification precedes political unification in Europe, it will be an unprecedented event.

There is much historical evidence consistent with this view. In virtually all of today's advanced industrial countries, political unification has preceded monetary unification. When the United States was a loose confederation of former British colonies, individual states retained the right to issue their own money-like liabilities. State governments issued bills of credit, certificates of interest, and special indents that circulated as money, and state legal-tender laws required that these be accepted at par in settlement of tax and other obligations (Schweitzer, 1989). Given the states' divergent demands for seigniorage, the separate monies led to fluctuating exchange rates. Only with the decision to form a political union and the adoption of the U.S. Constitution in 1788 was the right to issue legal tender limited to the federal government.[12]

In Germany, economic unification began with the creation of the Zollverein in 1834. Its constituent states initially had separate systems of coinage. Although they eventually negotiated treaties designed to standardize their coinage and fix the exchange rates between their currencies, this was not a monetary union in the strict sense. The individual German states refused to allow their right to issue paper money to be regulated by treaty. Governments created note-issuing development banks and otherwise subordinated monetary policy to the goal of state-led development. They were willing to agree to a uniform currency and common central bank only after political unification in 1871 (Holtfrerich, 1989, pp. 226–228).

Similarly, Italy had several currency systems in place at the time of political unification in 1861. The states brought together in the Kingdom of Italy each depended on bank notes issued by a single institution (often private, or semiprivate), except for Sardinia, which had two banks of issue. Although the newly created government of the Kingdom of Italy saw the merit of creating a single central bank, it had difficulty limiting the prerogatives of the local banks.[13] The creation of a true central bank, by the Banking Act of 1893, required political integration that subordinated regional interests to the national interest. Thus, although political integration preceded monetary integration in Italy, other forms of economic integration preceded political integration, in the sense that regional political interests disintegrated as a result of the creation of a more integrated Italian economy.

Why have nations been so reluctant to cede control of the central bank's printing press? One reason is that monetary sovereignty has historically been essential for the national defense (Goodhart, 1995). Because a credible defense presupposes the ability to resist attack, certain tax instruments, prominent among them the inflation tax, are assigned to the national authorities. Money can then be printed to pay soldiers and purchase war materiel when other revenues are insufficient or interrupted.

National defense helps to explain why Germany and France resisted early postwar proposals for European monetary integration.[14] It cannot, however, account for the present resistance to European monetary unification. French and German opponents of monetary unification do not seriously believe that war between the two countries is possible. If a revenue of last resort is needed for defense against a common external threat, it can be provided by the ECB.

More typically, economists understand Mussa's observation about countries and currencies in terms of optimal taxation. Jurisdictions differ in the value they attach to different taxes and public spending programs. The structures of national economies differ; where nonmonetary demands and supplies are more elastic, for example, optimal tax rates will be lower. Furthermore, those who bear the burden of taxes other than the inflation tax are more powerful in some countries than in others. They prefer different levels for the inflation tax, and in the absence of a political process to reconcile their views, they agree implicitly to retain a national currency.[15] The problem with this argument is that seigniorage typically accounts for only a small share of government revenues; this is certainly true of the high-income, low-inflation nations of Europe. It is hard to imagine that such countries attach much value to the inflation tax.

Another argument, put forward by James Ingram (1959) and popularized in the current European context by Xavier Sala-i-Martin and Jeffrey Sachs (1992), is that a monetary union requires fiscal federalism to operate efficiently. Fiscal federalism on the American scale, however, requires the centralization of national tax revenues and expenditure decisions, and European nations are unlikely to cede control of taxes and spending in the absence of political integration. It is conceivable that the EU budget could be rigged to mimic the shock-absorber role of the federal fiscal systems in the Canadian and U.S. monetary unions; Alexander Italianer and Jean Pisani-Ferry (1992) have suggested how this might be done. There remains considerable resistance, however, to expanding the EU budget by even the modest amounts required to activate such a scheme, and there are worries that a system in which the distribution of intra-EU transfers becomes a function of national unemployment rates might give rise to problems of moral hazard.

Not everyone agrees that fiscal federalism is essential for monetary union. To the extent that national fiscal policies remain free of the constraint that would be imposed by strict enforcement of the Maastricht Treaty's Excessive Deficit Procedure, stabilization—automatic and otherwise—can be provided by adjusting fiscal policies at the national level. In other words, there may be several ways of organizing the stabilization provided by fiscal federalism.

A different argument—one that dominates discussion in Europe today—is that monetary unification requires political unification, because only with political unification will it be possible to prevent reckless fiscal policies from destabilizing the common currency. The Germans argue that high debts and deficits threaten the stability of the single currency because they raise the specter of debt runs, which will force the ECB to bail out countries in financial distress. This view must confront the fact that the Maastricht Treaty includes a "no-money-financing rule" that states that the ECB may not monetize public debt. The fear must be that the ECB cannot really stand by while a member state experiences a debt run (like large commercial banks, national governments will be "too big to fail"). Knowing that the no-money-financing rule will not be enforced, member states will be tempted to incur excessive deficits, a temptation they will resist only if inhibited by stronger restraints on their fiscal autonomy. Effective restraints, however, imply transferring power and authority to the EU level—that is, they imply political integration.

The stability pact among EMU countries that was recently proposed by Germany's finance minister, Theo Waigel, illustrates the point. It would commit members of the monetary union to keep deficits below 1 percent of GDP under ordinary circumstances, would require a deposit of 0.25 percent of GDP by countries violating the 3 percent upper limit on deficits, and would create an EU stability council to monitor compliance and to issue (presumably binding) guidelines for fiscal policy. These measures are stronger than the Excessive Deficit Procedure of the Maastricht Treaty, which requires member states to keep their deficits below 3 percent of GDP and imposes only weak sanctions on violators once they have entered the monetary union. There is reason to doubt, however, that a European Union already plagued by an inability to force its members to abide by the rules of the Single Market could actually collect substantial fines. Sovereign nations are unlikely to agree to transfer a significant fraction of national income on the word of an ad hoc EU entity. Only within formal federations, the argument runs, are subnational jurisdictions prepared to turn over significant fiscal autonomy to the center. Political unification is, consequently, a prerequisite for the credible fiscal restraints that monetary union requires.

In work with Jürgen von Hagen (see chapter 8), I have suggested that this logic is flawed, because it fails to consider what determines the credibility of the ECB's commitment to avoid a bailout. It ignores the extent to which a government experiencing a fiscal crisis has other instruments at its command. Most obviously, a government can employ fiscal policy. In particular, it can raise taxes to make available the resources needed to service and redeem its debts. The implication for the European Union is that, so long as national governments continue to control their tax bases, they can raise taxes to deal with fiscal crises and should be expected to do so. The existence of these instruments will help the European Commission and the European Central Bank resist pressure to intervene. The cost of coping with the crisis will thus be borne by the member state in question, minimizing moral hazard. There will be no need to transfer control of fiscal policies from national capitals to the European Union and no need to strengthen the political powers of the EU.[16]

In today's Europe, then, none of the arguments mentioned above explains why monetary union requires political union. Each view acknowledges that fiscal policy is at the core of sovereignty. Each recognizes that national governments are reluctant to cede their fiscal prerogatives. But it is a non sequitur to infer that monetary unification requires significant limits on fiscal autonomy. There is no necessary conflict between monetary integration and national political autonomy.

The argument that monetary integration requires political integration must therefore rest on the politics of monetary policy itself. A central bank's statutes should encourage the monetary authorities to formulate policies that optimize a social welfare function defined in terms of inflation, unemployment, and other variables. Typically, the central bank is given a mandate that reflects the value that society attaches to these outcomes. To shield the bank from problems of time inconsistency and interest-group pressure, it is granted independence, but oversight is still exercised by a congress or parliament capable of applying penalties if the central bank abuses its independence. These institutional arrangements may be regarded as mechanisms to simulate the kind of optimal contracts for central bankers that are modelled by Carl Walsh (1995). In the case of monetary union, political integration may be needed to emulate these arrangements. In particular, effective oversight, with credible sanctions, may require that there be a congress and president or a parliament at the union level. A national central bank is accountable to a national parliament, which can abrogate the central bank's statutory independence or eject from office central bankers whose agendas are incompatible with its own. But the European Parliament lacks the power to modify the ECB's statute, which can be changed only by renegotiating an international treaty. The "democratic deficit," to use the popular European term, is severe. Although the ECB is required to submit a report annually on its conduct of monetary policy, and members of its board may be called before the European Parliament to testify, it is not clear what difference this will make, absent any potential sanction. If the ECB is inadequately accountable to its constituents, its constituents will challenge its authority and perhaps even prevent it from coming into being.

We should ask, however, whether there are ways of lending legitimacy to an independent central bank other than by forcing members of its board to testify beneath the hot lights of a committee hearing room. Max Weber, from whose work the literature on legitimacy derives, does not attach much weight to democratic legitimacy. He emphasizes, instead, three other sources of legitimacy: charisma, tradition, and law.[17] Weber notes that legitimate authority has often been enjoyed by a charismatic leader—the "Colin Powell syndrome," in which the victorious general, the spell-binding parliamentary orator, or the captain of industry commands respect in the political realm. Although tall central bankers who smoke big cigars may enjoy unusual respect, I am not inclined to attach much weight to charisma as a source of legitimacy. It is difficult to imagine that doubts about the legitimacy of the ECB will be allayed by the appointment of a charismatic ECB president.

Weber's second consideration, tradition, is more clearly applicable to central banking. Weber notes that princes and patriarchs gain legitimacy by the very act of governing. One might thus imagine that a central bank's authority will acquire legitimacy simply because it has been responsible for monetary policy for a long time. Another central bank might command respect, however, because of its admirable record of guarding the stability of its currency. It is not clear whether Weber's argument hinges on reputation—that experience breeds respect only if the authority demonstrates its capacity for benign and effective rule—or whether experience elicits compliance in and of itself. Either way, however, the ECB cannot inherit this source of legitimacy quickly.

Weber's third factor, the law, is where the hopes of the framers of the Maastricht Treaty clearly lay.[18] In this view, individuals respect authority, because they are legally obligated to do so. This respect is rational because legal rules are efficient. To quote Weber (1984, p. 34), the legitimacy of legal rules derives from a belief "in the validity of legal statute and functional 'competence' based on *rationally* created rules" (italics added).[19] Viewed from this standpoint, the legitimacy of the ECB derives from a statute that is designed to insure its "functional competence." In other words, Europe's citizens value price stability and will respect the authority of the ECB if they believe that its structure and mandate—that is, the rules it follows—will lead it to guard the stability of the currency. That mandate, and the laws that establish the bank's constitution and composition—prohibiting board members from taking advice from national governments, for example, a practice that might lead them to disregard the bank's statutory mandate—may compensate for the ECB's lack of democratic legitimacy.

Essentially, this view suggests that democratic legitimacy—accountability to an EU government that provides national constituencies with a voice in the formulation of monetary policy—is superfluous, because the ECB statute prevents the bank from deviating from its mandate and because the various interest groups all attach priority to price stability. Both assumptions may be questioned. Some observers worry that ECB board members will be unduly responsive to special interest groups. In particular, they worry that representatives from high-debt countries will accommodate the desire of their national governments for low interest rates to help with debt-servicing problems, preventing the ECB from delivering price stability. Its "functional competence" being inadequate, its authority will be dismissed as illegitimate.

Careful readers will detect a shift in the argument, a change that is emphasized in the work of the political philosopher John Schaar (1969). Weber depicted the law as an objective, external set of incentives and constraints that lends legitimacy to authority because it leads to the pursuit of socially desirable policies. Modern definitions introduce an intervening variable—expectations—between law and legitimacy.[20]

As is often the case when expectations are introduced, multiple equilibria are possible. In one equilibrium, observers have confidence in the functional competence of the ECB. They believe that its statute protects the bank from partisan pressures, allowing it to pursue its mandate. Because they are content to let the bank pursue those policies, their expectations are self-fulfilling. In the other equilibrium, observers are skeptical of the ECB's functional competence, believing that its statute leaves it exposed to partisan pressures that will lead it to disregard its mandate. Those who value various goals will therefore lobby the ECB to pursue them, making the ECB more likely to succumb to pressure and validating the expectations of those who doubted its functional competence in the first place.

This interpretation of the rule of law is featured in the recent work of Barry Weingast (1995). Weingast argues that viable laws must be self-enforcing and that they must be enforced in democracies by the collective will of the masses. This gives rise to a coordination problem that, in the present context, runs as follows. If sufficient numbers of European citizens believe in the efficacy of the ECB statute, none of them will have an incentive to lobby the ECB, because lobbying is costly and not likely to succeed unless many citizens engage in it simultaneously. If sufficient numbers of citizens lose confidence in its efficacy and independence simultaneously, however, they may coordinate on a lobbying equilibrium that erodes the autonomy of the ECB.

We can depict this situation using the simple diagrammatic apparatus in Figure 10.1, where L represents the level of lobbying by special interest groups and π is the level of inflation. The figure shows two reaction functions, one for the lobbyists and one for the ECB. The ECB's reaction function slopes upward on the assumption that more intense lobbying leads it to adopt more inflationary policies. The lobbyists' reaction function slopes upward to capture the idea that at low levels of inflation,

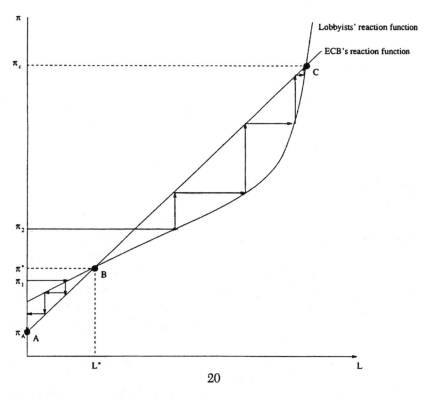

Figure 10.1
Lobbying and inflation: The possibility of multiple equilibria.

special-interest groups do not doubt the ECB's commitment to price stability and thus refrain from lobbying, but that they come to doubt the ECB's resolve as inflation rises and therefore engage in increasingly intense lobbying activities. The ECB's reaction function intersects the vertical axis at the low inflation rate it would prefer in the absence of outside pressure. The lobbyists' reaction function intersects the vertical axis at a higher level and is more elastic, capturing the idea that inflation must hit a certain threshold before interest groups begin to doubt the ECB's resolve and initiate lobbying, after which lobbying increases rapidly. A rationale for drawing the lobbyists' function as convex to the origin is that the capacity for lobbying activity is limited.

Assume that the ECB opens for business by setting the inflation rate at π_A. There will then be no lobbying. It is evident that A, like C, is a stable equilibrium. If the inflation rate rises to π_1 as a result of a disturbance, it then falls back to π_A. But, if for any reason inflation rises above the threshold π^*, it then rises further to π_C.

With time, the ECB may succeed in acquiring a reputation for pursuing stable and desirable policies and may earn the respect of its constituents. Weber's second factor, a long record of successful rule, will then enhance its legitimacy. It will do so, however, only it enjoys insulation from political pressures, and that will be true only if its constituents are sufficiently confident in its commitment to its mandate to resist the temptation to engage in lobbying. A newly established central bank for which the commitment to price stability and insulation from political pressures are not yet clearly established may never have a chance.

10.3 Conclusion

In Europe, the EMU debate centers on whether completing the Single Market requires monetary unification and whether monetary integration is feasible without political integration. The Anglo-American view is that there is no connection between economic and monetary unification, whereas the French and the German governments insist that economic integration without monetary integration cannot provide a political equilibrium. German leaders further insist that monetary integration requires political integration in order to lend credibility to the governments' commitments to pursue fiscal policies consistent with price stability and to endow the EU with adequate enforcement powers.

I conclude that monetary integration is not essential to realize the efficiency gains from economic integration, and political integration is not essential to derive efficiency gains from monetary integration. Indeed, I am so confident of these conclusions—along with the rest of the economics profession—that I have hardly discussed them at all! Still, monetary integration may be needed to make economic integration a political equilibrium, and political integration may be needed to render monetary integration politically acceptable. The emphasis in this sentence, however, should be on the word "may," because neither case is clear cut.

My personal feeling is that currency fluctuations, if allowed to persist, will give rise to repeated charges of competitive depreciation and exchange dumping and to a political response, in the form of restraints on competition, that will severely hinder the operation of the Single Market. The alternative, monetary unification, will give rise in the short run to pockets of unemployment and political problems of its own. In the longer run, however, factor and product markets will adapt, reducing the costs of operating a currency union. Eventually, the absence of internal exchange-rate adjustments and of restraints on interstate commerce will become nonissues, as they are in the United States. The initial years will be difficult, however, and success is uncertain.

A corollary is that other regional integration initiatives—NAFTA for example—need not imply monetary integration, because they are more limited in scope. The lesser importance of Mexican exports to the United States, compared, say, to Italian exports to France, limits the political backlash from exchange-rate fluctuations. And the retention of limited capital controls by many developing countries strengthens their ability to limit exchange-rate fluctuations. At the same time, the importance of intraregional trade is likely to grow with time as a result of regional integration initiatives—as it has in Europe since the 1950s—and technological change in financial markets will continue to undermine the effectiveness of capital controls. This suggests that there will be an increasing need to buttress economic integration with monetary integration in other parts of the world, as there has been in Europe.

I find unconvincing the argument that Europe needs political integration to give teeth to the Maastricht Treaty's fiscal sanctions, because the fiscal restrictions in the treaty are redundant so long as national governments retain the power to tax, a power that gives them a relatively low-cost alternative to default and lends credibility to the treaty's no-bailout rule. Indeed, in the event that political integration proceeds and the power to tax is shifted to Brussels, the ability of member states to raise their own taxes to deal with inherited debt problems will be constrained. This will, in turn, intensify the pressure for a bailout in the event of a debt run. Political integration may therefore be the problem rather than the solution.

A stronger justification for political integration is to render the ECB accountable to the European citizenry or, alternatively, to hope that the ECB's legal legitimacy will substitute for its lack of democratic legitimacy. It is possible that the Europeans will come to respect the authority of the ECB because they are confident of its dedication to its legal mandate.

The element of confidence—expectations—is critical, however. If the ECB's constituents lack confidence in its policies, they will be reluctant to hold its liabilities, and the resulting high interest rates will make it much more difficult for the central bank to pursue its mandate. The costs of pursuing price stability, which take the form of unemployment, will also be greater, in turn intensifying the pressure on the ECB to divert its attention to other targets. Skepticism may thus prove self-fulfilling. If the ECB gets off to a good start, however, and acquires a reputation for faithfulness to its mandate, Weber's second source of legitimacy—tradition grounded in a record of good policies—will kick in. Again, this means that the first years will be critical.

Notes

This chapter was delivered as the Frank D. Graham Memorial Lecture at Princeton University. Portions of it owe much to my teachers, Sheldon Wolin and John Schaar, whose influence it gives me pleasure to acknowledge. Ron Rogowski instructed me on the literature on legitimacy. Jeffrey Frieden's council clarified my thinking on matters political. Fabio Ghironi generously allowed me to draw on joint work and critiqued my analysis. Finally, I thank Max Corden for helpful comments; in a sense, this chapter is a sequel to his Graham Lecture on the same subject.

1. Throughout this chapter, I use the term "commercial integration" to refer to movement toward the establishment of free-trade areas and customs unions, and "economic integration" to denote more far-reaching initiatives, such as the European Union's effort to establish an integrated internal market both in goods and services and in factors of production.

2. Space and time constraints lead me to neglect two complications, both of which have to do with the politics and economics of alternative exchange-rate regimes. One is that Economic and Monetary Union (EMU) will not necessarily lock all intra-EU exchange rates, because countries that do not meet the preconditions for entry or possess an opt-out clause may not participate. The other is that, regardless of the number of EU countries participating in the monetary union, there will still be scope for exchange-rate movements and independent monetary policies insofar as the euro can fluctuate against the dollar, the yen, and other foreign currencies.

3. Some months earlier, in July 1992, the Italian government, industrialists, and trade-union leaders had agreed to eliminate the country's existing system of wage indexation. This agreement, which was renewed in July 1993, prevented nominal depreciation from being passed through into wages and prices.

4. For models of this situation, see Maurice Obstfeld (1986a, 1994) and F. Gulcin Ozkan and Alan Sutherland (1994). Although the point is controversial, I would argue that this model fits the 1992 attack on sterling quite well (Eichengreen and Wyplosz, 1993). The lira presents a more complicated ease insofar as there exists considerable evidence that it was overvalued in the first half of 1992. But no one would claim that this overvaluation reached 35 percent—the magnitude of the depreciation that occurred subsequently. Thus, it can be argued that subsequent events led to a policy shift that was itself contingent on the speculative attack—that the lira crisis both depended on fundamentals and had self-fulfilling features.

5. In the words of one contemporary: "The removal of the balance-of-payments is an important positive contribution that the adoption of flexible exchange rates could make to the achievement of the liberal objective of an integrated international economy" (Johnson, 1972, p. 210).

6. Textbook treatments emphasize the tendency for exchange-rate variability to fan protectionist flames following the collapse of the gold-exchange standard in the early 1930s. My point here is that much of the literature contemporary to the collapse argued the opposite: that overvaluation in the countries that remained on gold posed a problem for free trade. Charles Feinstein, Peter Temin, and Gianni Toniolo (1995) provide a recent restatement of this view.

7. A debate about how much capacity the United States could muster to offset the depression without threatening the dollar's fixed gold-standard parity arrays Milton Friedman and Anna Schwartz (1963) against Elmus Wicker (1966) and the present author (1992b). But even those who would deny that a fixed exchange rate inhibited monetary-policy activism would probably agree that the ideology of the gold standard was a significant constraint.

8. The evidence Douglas Irwin and I (1995) present on the trade-creating and trade-diverting effects of the currency blocs of the 1930s also supports this view. We estimate gravity equations explaining the volume of bilateral trade in 1928, 1935, and 1938. In addition to the standard arguments of the gravity model (national incomes, per capita incomes, distance between the trading partners, and contiguity), we include measures of membership in the leading commercial and financial blocs of the period. We find that the different currency blocs of the 1930s had very different implications for trade. Sterling-bloc countries traded more among themselves and with the rest of the world than was predicted by the gravity model, suggesting that policies followed by the members of the bloc did, on balance, create trade. Gold-bloc countries, by contrast, did not trade disproportionately with one another or with the rest of the world, possibly because they used tariffs and quotas to prop up overvalued currencies.

9. The Maastricht Treaty does not require the ECB to issue the single currency immediately, although national central banks will immediately lose all right to issue national currencies on their own initiative and will become mere operating arms of the ECB. Nothing essential changes if we assume, instead, that national currencies are replaced with euros immediately, but the case in the text is the easiest one to consider.

10. What is a misalignment, after all, if not a wage explosion that prices workers out of employment, or a failure of wages to fall in response to a decline in local labor demand? Clearly, this is only one possible definition of the term, although I would argue that it is the relevant one here. For alternative definitions, see Jeffrey Frankel (1985).

11. To be precise, workers migrated in unprecedented numbers *relative to the size of the world economy*. Note that I characterize the gold standard as a pegged- rather than fixed-rate system. As Michael Bordo and Finn Kydland (1995) have emphasized, the gold standard

featured an escape clause that allowed for exchange-rate changes in the event of exceptional shocks. This provision was rarely, however, invoked in the countries at the core of the international gold standard in the final decades before 1913.

12. Arthur Rolnik, Bruce Smith, and Warren Weber (1993) tell this story in reverse. They suggest that the inefficiencies of separate currencies created pressure for the creation of a single currency and that this required political unification. By implication, the U.S. Constitution was the product of floating exchange rates!

13. Only in 1874, thirteen years after political unification, did Italy succeed in limiting banknote issues (by tying them to historical market shares). Gold convertibility was established in 1884, when the discount rates of the leading banks were brought under government control, and banks were allowed to increase their issue only if they obtained 100 percent backing for the excess (Sannucci, 1989). The local Italian banks had developed to serve the distinctive financial needs of the regional economies, and the local populace defended them against attempts to limit their prerogatives.

14. Helge Berger and Albrecht Ritschl (1995) argue, for example, that enthusiasm for the EPU rested in large part on the ability of this form of European monetary integration to lock Germany into the European economy.

15. The Keynesian version of this argument is that countries will resist monetary integration if they prefer different positions on the Phillips Curve tradeoff between output and inflation (Corden, 1972).

16. We test this hypothesis by estimating a probit regression on cross-country data for 1985–87. The dependent variable is zero if a country has no restrictions on subcentral government borrowing or only a weak golden rule, and unity otherwise. The independent variable represents the vertical structure of the fiscal system by the share of subcentral government spending financed by its own tax revenues. We also include 1987 GDP per capita in U.S. dollars (PCGDP) to control for the stage of economic development. The estimated equation (with standard errors in parentheses) confirms that countries where subcentral governments control a large share of the tax base are significantly less likely to restrict borrowing by their subcentral governments:

$$\text{Restrictions} = 0.25 - 3.51\ \text{Structure} - 0.04\ \text{PCGDP}$$
$$\phantom{\text{Restrictions} = }(0.65)\quad(1.16)\phantom{\ \text{Structure}}\quad(0.04)$$

$$X^2 = 8.00,\ \text{Number of observations} = 45,\ p = 0.045$$

The implications for EMU are clear. The vertical structure of taxes in the European Union is controlled almost completely by national governments. (The EU's own resources are limited to tariff revenues, a 1 percent value-added tax collected by national governments, and a modest levy on national governments.) The equation predicts that a political entity having these characteristics will not impose borrowing restrictions. Given the scope for the governments of EU member states to use their own taxes to deal with financial difficulties, the Excessive Deficit Procedure would appear to be redundant.

17. A convenient introduction to Weber's writings on this subject is the selection of his work in William Connolly (1984). The literature on democratic legitimacy goes back further, of course, to Rousseau and Locke, among others.

18. It is not surprising that this is the factor most relevant to our case: Weber himself suggests that modernization entails a progression from charismatic leadership to leadership grounded in law (Wolin, 1981).

19. This is an argument Seymour Martin Lipset has pursued. Lipset (1960) suggests that there are two sources of support for a governmental arrangement: belief in its legitimacy and belief in its efficiency, and he implies that these two beliefs may be causally linked, presumably with causality running from the latter to the former.

20. Schaar (1969, p. 284) states that "if a people holds the belief that existing institutions are 'appropriate' or 'morally proper,' then those institutions are legitimate. That's all there is to it." The point appears in Weber (quoted in Rosen, 1979, p. 76), who writes: "The basis of every system of authority, and correspondingly of every kind of willingness to obey, is a *belief*, a belief by virtue of which persons exercising authority are lent prestige." Other examples of the line of thought cited by Schaar are, from Lipset (1960, p. 77): "Legitimacy involves the capacity of the system to engender and maintain the belief that the existing political institutions are the most appropriate ones for the society"; from Bierstedt (1964, p. 386): "Legitimacy has been defined as 'the degree to which political institutions are valued for themselves and considered right and proper'"; and from Merelman (1966, p. 548): "That government is legitimate which is viewed as morally proper for a society." The dates of these citations reflect the upsurge of interest in this topic associated with the civil disobedience of the 1960s.

11   How Will Transatlantic Policy Interactions Change with the Advent of EMU?

11.1   Introduction

European monetary unification will alter interactions not just between members of the monetary union but between those countries and the rest of the world. In the language of the literature on policy coordination, the monetary policy game involving Europe's national central banks and the Federal Reserve Board will become a two-player game between the European Central Bank and the Fed.[1] It may be obvious that creating a European Central Bank that internalizes monetary policy externalities within Europe will have implications for strategic interactions between monetary authorities in Europe and the rest of the world, but it is not clear in which direction those changes will run. The implications become even less clear when one observes that changes in the responsiveness of Europe's monetary policy may affect the behavior not just of monetary authorities elsewhere in the world but also of fiscal authorities both inside and outside Europe.

In this chapter we make a start at analyzing these questions. We specify a simple model—the closest thing to a consensus model in the policy coordination literature—and analyze strategic interactions before and after EMU. Following Canzoneri and Henderson (1991) we use a three-country Mundell-Fleming model in which policymakers minimize quadratic loss functions. But we extend their framework by modeling fiscal as well as monetary policies.[2]

Adding fiscal policy raises issues that are particularly contentious in the current European setting. In standard textbook models, fiscal retrench-

Prepared for the CEPR workshop on Options for the Future Exchange Rate Policy of the European Monetary Union, Brussels, February 5–6, 1997, with Fabio Ghironi. We thank the participants, Olivier Jeanne, and participants in a seminar at the IMF for their comments.

ment reduces output and employment. In the current European context, however, the possibility has been raised that fiscal contractions can be expansionary.[3] Fiscal contraction may increase aggregate supply by reducing distortionary taxes; it may stimulate demand (consumption in particular) by reducing expectations of distortionary future taxes.[4] This uncertainty about the own-country impact of fiscal initiatives renders the cross-border effects, and the nature of strategic interactions, even less clear.

In this chapter we analyze policymakers' response to aggregate supply disturbances in both the Keynesian and anti-Keynesian cases.[5] For the anti-Keynesian case we obtain three surprising results.

EMU may enhance fiscal discipline outside Germany and stabilize employment in the face of supply shocks. The change in the responses of monetary and fiscal authorities that comes with the advent of Stage III may stabilize European output and employment. EMU may stabilize European fiscal policy outside Germany. Thus our results contrast with popular fears that EMU will encourage governments to pursue unstable fiscal policies. Also, the ECB's monetary policy turns out to be quite similar to the Bundesbank's under the EMS, and European inflation under EMU is lower than German inflation under the EMS, contrary to current German fears. Nonetheless, inflation rises elsewhere in Europe and the average European inflation rate is higher than under the EMS (if for reasons different from those usually invoked to argue that the ECB will be subject to inflationary pressure).

The ECB and central banks outside Europe will have little incentive to coordinate their response to supply shocks.[6] Governments (the fiscal authorities) will wish central banks to coordinate, but the latter will not share their interest. This points to conflicts in a situation where ministers are entitled to provide "general orientations" for exchange-rate policy (under the provisions of the Maastricht Treaty) but the ECB is not obliged to accept them.

Fiscal coordination can be counterproductive under EMU. Governments and central banks on both sides of the Atlantic are worse off when the French and German governments cooperate. This is because there remain other externalities in the model: the transatlantic fiscal externality arising from the failure of the U.S. and European governments to coordinate their tax and spending policies, the transatlantic monetary externality arising from the failure of the Fed and the ECB to coordinate, and externalities resulting from the failure of fiscal *and* monetary policymakers to cooperate. Absent fiscal coordination, governments cut spending and taxes too aggressively in an effort to export unemployment; cooperation between

France and Germany reduces this bias in Europe but reinforces it in the United States (the United States has an incentive to cut taxes even more aggressively).[7] When there is no fiscal coordination in Europe, the expansionary bias of European fiscal policies reduces inflation; fiscal cooperation is thus harmful for inflation stabilization, and central banks react by contracting more, thereby raising unemployment. Fed-ECB cooperation causes the central banks to resist exporting inflation and encourages them to use monetary policy more cautiously. This stabilizes employment but aggravates inflation. It is widely presumed that EMU requires intra-EU fiscal coordination; we find that there are cases where this is undesirable. Moreover, global fiscal cooperation would not be beneficial because the externalities that monetary and fiscal policymakers impose on one another inside each country play an important role.[8]

The results for the Keynesian case are different.

EMU may reduce monetary discipline in Europe. Our findings for the Keynesian case are thus more consistent with the presumption that EMU weakens monetary discipline. But the reason is not lack of fiscal discipline—in fact, the transition to EMU continues to stabilize fiscal policy relative to the EMS (both French and German fiscal policies are less expansionary than under the EMS). As before, EMU removes the intra-European monetary externality; this reduces unemployment in both France and Germany and enhances welfare for both the French and German governments. As before, European inflation is higher than under the EMS, and the ECB is worse off than the Bank of France, but better off than the Bundesbank. Both German authorities prefer EMU to the EMS because of the effects of increased fiscal discipline. Both the Fed and the U.S. government are better off under EMU; this is in contrast to the anti-Keynesian case, where EMU leaves their welfare basically unchanged.

The ECB and central banks outside Europe will wish to coordinate their response to supply shocks. Inflation is higher when monetary policies are coordinated, but the employment gains more than offset the inflation loss for central banks. The conflict of interest between central banks and governments in the anti-Keynesian case evaporates here.

The ECB will want European governments to coordinate their policies. In the anti-Keynesian case, European and U.S. governments wanted their central banks to cooperate but the central banks did not. Now the reverse is true in Europe: in the Keynesian case, the ECB wants European governments to cooperate but the latter do not. This accords with the policy debate in which European central banks are insisting on mutual surveillance of fiscal policies but national governments are resisting.

These results are derived from a specific model.[9] In the Barro-Gordon (1981) tradition, wages are set at the start of each period, a convenience that allows nominal variables to have real effects. But in contrast to most previous treatments (e.g., Canzoneri and Henderson 1991), interest rates help determine money-market equilibrium.[10] Due to this and due to the introduction of fiscal policy, the reduced forms of the model are complicated functions of the structural parameters. We therefore assign numerical values to the structural parameters and simulate the stabilization game.

11.2   The Anti-Keynesian Case

We start by describing the structure of the model before considering alternative policymaking regimes.

The Model

The world is divided into three countries: France, Germany, and the United States. Their three outputs are imperfect substitutes in consumption. To focus on international interactions, we assume no time inconsistency problem and that all disturbances are unexpected. All variables denote deviations from zero-disturbance values and are expressed in logarithms.[11]

Output in each country (y^{US}, y^{G}, y^{F}) is an increasing function of employment (n^{US}, n^{G}, n^{F}) and a decreasing function of a world productivity disturbance (x):

$$y^{j} = (1 - \alpha)n^{j} - x \qquad j = US, G, F, \tag{1}$$

where $(1 - \alpha)$, with $0 < \alpha < 1$, the elasticity of output with respect to employment is the same in all countries. The productivity disturbance is identically and independently distributed with zero mean.

Labor demand is derived from the profit maximization condition for firms, where τ indicates the rate of taxation of revenues:[12]

$$w^{j} - p^{j} = -\alpha n^{j} - \tau^{j} - x \qquad j = US, G, F. \tag{2}$$

The anti-Keynesian effects of fiscal policy in our model come through this equation. For plausible parameter values, the supply-side distortion associated with (non-lump-sum) taxes dominates the effect on aggregate demand of the associated increase in public spending.[13]

Consumer price indices (q^{US}, q^{G}, q^{F}) are weighted averages of the prices of U.S., German, and French goods. American consumers allocate a fraction β of their spending to European goods (half to each) so the U.S. CPI is

$$q^{US} = (1 - \beta)p^{US} + \frac{1}{2}\beta(p^G + e^G) + \frac{1}{2}\beta(p^F + e^F). \tag{3}$$

Exchange rates e^G and e^F are the dollar prices of the deutsche mark (DM) and the French franc (FF). Equation (3) can be rewritten as

$$q^{US} = p^{US} + \frac{1}{2}\beta(z^G + z^F), \tag{4}$$

where z^G and z^F are the relative prices of the two European goods in terms of the U.S. good:

$$z^G = e^G + p^G - p^{US}, \\ z^F = e^F + p^F - p^{US}. \tag{5}$$

z^G is the dollar-DM real exchange rate, z^F the dollar-FF real exchange rate. If the dollar depreciates in real terms against one of the other currencies, the dollar real exchange rate rises.

European consumers allocate a fraction β of their spending to the U.S. good and divide the rest equally between the two European goods. The European CPIs are

$$q^G = \frac{1}{2}(1 - \beta)p^G + \frac{1}{2}(1 - \beta)(p^F + e^F - e^G) + \beta(p^{US} - e^G),$$

$$q^F = \frac{1}{2}(1 - \beta)p^F + \frac{1}{2}(1 - \beta)(p^G + e^G - e^F) + \beta(p^{US} - e^F), \tag{6}$$

or

$$q^G = p^G - \beta z^G - \frac{1}{2}(1 - \beta)(z^G - z^F),$$

$$q^F = p^F - \beta z^F - \frac{1}{2}(1 - \beta)(z^F - z^G). \tag{7}$$

The relative price of German goods in terms of French goods (the FF-DM real exchange rate) is $(z^G - z^F)$.

Demands for all goods increase with output. Residents of all countries increase their spending by the same fraction ($0 < \varepsilon < 1$) of increases in output. The marginal propensity to spend is equal to the average propensity to spend for all goods for residents of all countries. The German propensity to import from France is one-half of one minus the German propensity to import from the United States. Thus, if the German propensity to import from the United States is one-third, the German propensity to import from France is one-third, and the total German propensity to import is two-thirds.

Demands for all goods fall with ex ante real interest rates (r^{US}, r^G, r^F). Residents of each country decrease spending by the same amount ($0 < v < 1$) for each percentage point increase in the ex ante real interest rate facing them.

Denoting government spending as g, we have equilibrium conditions for the three goods:

$$2y^{US} = \delta z^G + \delta z^F + 2(1-\beta)\varepsilon y^{US} + \beta\varepsilon(y^G + y^F) - 2(1-\beta)vr^{US}$$

$$- \beta v(r^G + r^F) + 2\eta g^{US} + (1-\eta)(g^G + g^F) + 2u,$$

$$y^G = -\delta z^G - \frac{1}{2}\delta(z^G - z^F) + \beta\varepsilon y^{US} + \frac{1}{2}(1-\beta)\varepsilon(y^G + y^F) - \beta vr^{US}$$

$$- \frac{1}{2}(1-\beta)v(r^G + r^F) + (1-\eta)g^{US} + \frac{1}{2}\eta(g^G + g^F) - u, \qquad (8)$$

$$y^F = -\delta z^F + \frac{1}{2}\delta(z^G - z^F) + \beta\varepsilon y^{US} + \frac{1}{2}(1-\beta)\varepsilon(y^G + y^F) - \beta vr^{US}$$

$$- \frac{1}{2}(1-\beta)v(r^G + r^F) + (1-\eta)g^{US} + \frac{1}{2}\eta(g^G + g^F) - u.$$

Ex ante real interest rates are

$$r^j = i^j - E(q^j_{+1}) + q^j \qquad j = US, G, F, \qquad (9)$$

where i^{US}, i^G, and i^F are nominal interest rates on bonds denominated in dollars, DM's, and FF's, respectively, and $E(\bullet_{+1})$ indicates the expected value of a variable tomorrow on the basis of information available today. Depreciation of a currency shifts world demand toward that country's good.[14,15]

The government budget constraints are

$$g^j = \tau^j \qquad j = US, G, F. \qquad (10)$$

Government spending falls entirely on goods (transfers are considered negative taxes and are included in τ); g^j defines the ratio $G^j/(P^j Y^j)$ and government j's budget constraint is $G^j = \tau^j P^j Y^j, j = US, G, F.$[16]

Each country issues domestic-currency-denominated bonds. Investors regard bonds denominated in different currencies as perfect substitutes and hold positive amounts of all three bonds only when their expected returns measured in a common currency are equal:

$$i^{US} = i^G + E(e^G_{+1}) - e^G,$$
$$i^{US} = i^F + E(e^F_{+1}) - e^F.$$
(11)

Each country's currency is held only by its residents. Demands for real money balances are

$$m^j - p^j = y^j - \lambda i^j \qquad j = US, G, F.$$
(12)

Firms' labor demands can be rewritten as

$$p^j = w^j + \alpha n^j + \tau^j + x \qquad j = US, G, F.$$
(13)

Substituting (1) and (13) into the demands for real money balances and solving for employment, we obtain

$$n^j = m^j - w^j - \tau^j + \lambda i^j, \qquad j = US, G, F.$$
(14)

At the beginning of each period, competitive unions and firms sign contracts specifying nominal wages. Unions choose wages to minimize a linear convex combination of expected deviations of employment and the real wage from equilibrium values. They minimize:

$$L^{u^j} = \frac{1}{2}\{\omega E_{-1}[(n^j)^2] + (1-\omega)E_{-1}[(w^j - q^j)^2]\}$$
(15)

$$0 < \omega < 1, \quad j = US, G, F.$$

Unions take into account the constraints given by the labor demands of firms. They solve:

$$\min_{w^j} \frac{1}{2}\{\omega E_{-1}[(m^j - w^j - \tau^j + \lambda i^j)^2] + (1-\omega)E_{-1}[(w^j - q^j)^2]\}$$

$$j = US, G, F.$$

The first-order condition leads to the wage-setting rule:

$$w^j = \omega E_{-1}(m^j + \lambda i^j - \tau^j) + (1-\omega)E_{-1}(q^j) \qquad j = US, G, F.$$
(16)

Nominal wages are a weighted average of expected total labor costs of firms (because $m^j + \lambda i^j - \tau^j = w^j + n^j$) and of the expected CPI.[17] To focus on international interactions, we assume that all disturbances are random and unexpected and that there are no time inconsistency problems. The endogenous variables are shown in the appendix to be linear functions of the policy instruments and the shocks. Expected values of the instruments and the endogenous variables at the beginning of the period therefore coincide with their no-disturbance equilibrium values, that is, zero.[18] The wage-setting rule simplifies to

$$w^j = 0 \qquad j = US, G, F. \tag{17}$$

Plugging these results into the expressions for employment and prices, we obtain

$$n^j = m^j - \tau^j + \lambda i^j, \tag{18}$$

$$p^j = \alpha n^j + \tau^j + x \qquad j = US, G, F.[19] \tag{19}$$

Under flexible exchange rates, each central bank chooses its money supply to minimize:

$$L^{cb^j} = \frac{1}{2}[a(q^j)^2 + (1-a)(n^j)^2] \qquad 0 < a < 1, \quad j = US, G, F, \tag{20}$$

where a measures the weight central bankers attach to inflation relative to employment.

The government chooses taxes to minimize a quadratic loss function that depends on deviations of inflation, employment, and taxation from their equilibrium values. We assume that the volatility of taxation is a cost for fiscal authorities (to capture the idea that fiscal policy is difficult to fine tune relative to monetary policy and the fact that governments may care about the distortions they impose on the economy when actively using their instruments). Thus, country j's government minimizes:

$$L^{fa^j} = \frac{1}{2}\{b_1[b_2(q^j)^2 + (1-b_2)(n^j)^2] + (1-b_1)(\tau^j)^2\} \tag{21}$$

$$0 < b_1, b_2 < 1, \quad j = US, G, F.$$

b_1 measures the degree of activism in the management of fiscal policies. b_2 measures the relative weight attached to inflation and employment by the fiscal authorities. The higher b_1, the higher the degree of fiscal activism.

Endogenous variables in the United States depend on the stance of U.S. monetary and fiscal policies, on the aggregate stance of European policies, and on the productivity and demand shocks. Since there are no intra-U.S. policy spillovers, except for the externalities that the Fed and the American fiscal authority impose on each other, only the relative position of U.S. versus aggregate European policies matters. U.S. inflation and employment are

$$q^{US} = Am^{US} - B\left(\frac{m^G + m^F}{2}\right) + E\tau^{US} + \Gamma\left(\frac{\tau^G + \tau^F}{2}\right) + Ku + Hx; \qquad (22)$$

$$n^{US} = (1 - \lambda\Lambda)m^{US} + \lambda\Theta\left(\frac{m^G + m^F}{2}\right) - (1 - \lambda\Omega)\tau^{US}$$

$$+ \lambda\Psi\left(\frac{\tau^G + \tau^F}{2}\right) + \Phi u - \Xi x. \qquad (23)$$

The German CPI and employment depend on the German money supply and taxation, on how policy affects the position of Europe relative to the United States, and on how they affect the position of Germany relative to France. German and French inflation and employment are given by

$$q^G = \alpha m^G + (A - \alpha)\left(\frac{m^G + m^F}{2}\right) - Bm^{US} + (1 - \alpha)\tau^G$$

$$+ [E - (1 - \alpha)]\left(\frac{\tau^G + \tau^F}{2}\right) + \Gamma\tau^{US} + M(m^F - m^G)$$

$$- N(\tau^F - \tau^G) - Ku + Hx; \qquad (24)$$

$$q^F = \alpha m^F + (A - \alpha)\left(\frac{m^G + m^F}{2}\right) - Bm^{US} + (1 - \alpha)\tau^F$$

$$+ [E - (1 - \alpha)]\left(\frac{\tau^G + \tau^F}{2}\right) + \Gamma\tau^{US} - M(m^F - m^G)$$

$$+ N(\tau^F - \tau^G) - Ku + Hx; \qquad (25)$$

$$n^G = m^G - \lambda\Lambda\left(\frac{m^G + m^F}{2}\right) + \lambda\Theta m^{US} - \tau^G + \lambda\Omega\left(\frac{\tau^G + \tau^F}{2}\right)$$

$$+ \lambda\Psi\tau^{US} + \lambda O(m^F - m^G) - \lambda Z(\tau^F - \tau^G) - \Phi u - \Xi x; \qquad (26)$$

$$n^F = m^F - \lambda\Lambda\left(\frac{m^G + m^F}{2}\right) + \lambda\Theta m^{US} - \tau^F + \lambda\Omega\left(\frac{\tau^G + \tau^F}{2}\right)$$

$$+ \lambda\Psi\tau^{US} - \lambda O(m^F - m^G) + \lambda Z(\tau^F - \tau^G) - \Phi u - \Xi x. \qquad (27)$$

Table 11.1
Structural Parameters and Target Weights

$\alpha = .34$	$\beta = .1$	$\delta = .8$	$\varepsilon = .8$	$v = .4$
$\eta = .9$	$\lambda = .6$	$a = .9$	$b_1 = .2$	$b_2 = .1$

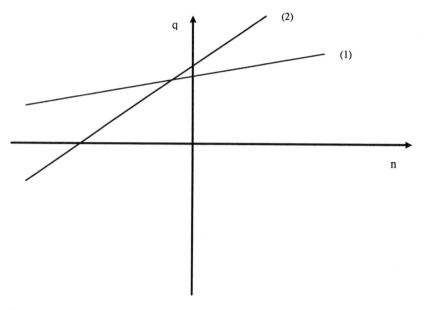

Figure 11.1
Central banks' trade-offs
(1) Faced by: Fed, irrespective of exchange-rate regime in Europe; Bundesbank under EMS; ECB.
(2) Faced by: Bundesbank under flexible exchange rates in Europe; Bank of France under flexible exchange rates in Europe and under EMS.

When simulating the interactions among policymakers, we impose "consensus" values for the structural parameters and the weights in the loss functions. The parameters we use are shown in table 11.1.[20]

The reduced forms above are derived assuming that exchange rates are freely flexible. Ghironi and Giavazzi (1997a) obtain a set of general results about how the trade-offs faced by policymakers change under different assumptions about the prevailing exchange-rate regime. Following their approach, we define the employment-inflation trade-offs of the authorities as follows. Central banks face trade-offs given by

$$(\partial q^j / \partial n^j)^{CB^j} = (\partial q^j / \partial m^j)/(\partial n^j / \partial m^j) \qquad j = US, G, I$$

Table 11.2
The Players' Trade-offs in an Anti-Keynesian World

	Federal Reserve	Bundesbank	Bank of France	ECB
Flexible rates	.3534	.5449	.5449	
EMS	.3534	.3534	.5449	
EMU	.3534			.3534

	U.S. government	German government	French government
Flexible rates	−1.3393	−.5542	−.5542
EMS	−1.3393	−.5122	−.3084
EMU	−1.3393	−.4872	−.4872

These trade-offs are positively sloped (see figure 11.1), a steeper trade-off being more favorable for inflation-averse central bankers (it allows the central bank to achieve a larger reduction in inflation at the cost of a smaller employment loss).[21] The results obtained by Ghironi and Giavazzi (1997a) allow us to argue that the German and French central banks face more favorable trade-offs than the U.S. monetary authority.[22] Numerical values of the trade-offs are summarized in table 11.2.

Governments face trade-offs given by

$$(\partial q^j / \partial n^j)^{Gov^j} = (\partial q^j / \partial \tau^j)/(\partial n^j / \partial \tau^j) \qquad j = US, G, F.$$

These are negatively sloped in the anti-Keynesian case we consider first.[23] For unemployment-averse governments, a flatter trade-off will be more favorable, as the economy will move closer to the situation of zero unemployment for any given decrease in CPI inflation. Consistent with Ghironi and Giavazzi (1997b), the German and the French governments face more favorable trade-offs than the U.S. government under flexible rates (see figure 11.2).

Employment-Inflation Trade-offs under Alternative Exchange-Rate Regimes

The EMS We characterize the EMS, following Giavazzi and Giovannini (1989), as a regime in which the Bundesbank sets its money supply and the Bank of France sets the DM/franc rate.[24] Since it effectively sets the money supply for all of Europe (and since the United States and Europe are symmetric), the Bundesbank faces the same employment-inflation trade-off as the Fed. (The trade-off facing the German fiscal authority differs from that of the American government, for reasons explained below.)

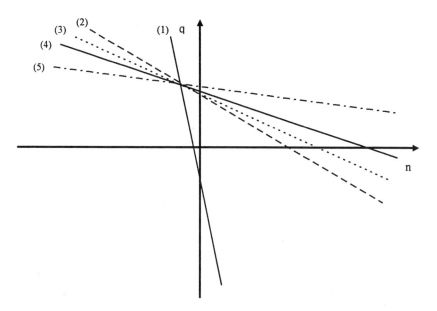

Figure 11.2
Governments' trade-offs
(1) Faced by U.S. government, irrespective of exchange-rate regime in Europe.
(2) Faced by both German and French governments under flexible exchange rates in Europe.
(3) Faced by German government under EMS.
(4) Faced by both German and French governments under EMU.
(5) Faced by French government under EMS.

The reduced form for the DM/FF exchange rate is shown in the appendix to be

$$e^G - e^F = \phi(m^F - m^G) - \xi(\tau^F - \tau^G). \tag{28}$$

Solving for m^F produces the constraint on the French money supply:

$$m^F = m^G + \frac{1}{\phi}(e^G - e^F) + \frac{\xi}{\phi}(\tau^F - \tau^G). \tag{29}$$

Reduced forms for employment and the CPI are obtained by plugging this equation into the previously obtained reduced forms. For the United States:

$$q^{US} = Am^{US} - Bm^G - \frac{B}{2\phi}(e^G - e^F) - \frac{B\xi}{2\phi}(\tau^F - \tau^G) + E\tau^{US}$$

$$+ \Gamma \frac{\tau^G + \tau^F}{2} + Ku + Hx; \tag{30}$$

$$n^{US} = (1 - \lambda\Lambda)m^{US} + \lambda\Theta m^G + \frac{\lambda\Theta}{2\phi}(e^G - e^F) + \frac{\lambda\Theta\xi}{2\phi}(\tau^F - \tau^G)$$

$$- (1 - \lambda\Omega)\tau^{US} + \lambda\Psi\frac{\tau^G + \tau^F}{2} + \Phi u - \Sigma x. \tag{31}$$

The asymmetry between the instruments controlled by the two European central banks makes U.S. prices and employment sensitive to movements of the French franc against the deutsche mark and to differences between French and German fiscal policies.

Making use of definitions in the appendix, German and French CPIs and employment become

$$q^G = Am^G - Bm^{US} + (1 - \alpha)\tau^G + [E - (1 - \alpha)]\frac{\tau^G + \tau^F}{2} + \Gamma\tau^{US}$$

$$+ \left(\frac{A - \alpha}{2\phi} + \frac{M}{\phi}\right)(e^G - e^F) + \left[\frac{\xi(A - \alpha)}{2\phi} + \frac{M\xi}{\phi} - N\right](\tau^F - \tau^G)$$

$$- Ku + Hx; \tag{32}$$

$$q^F = Am^G - Bm^{US} + (1 - \alpha)\tau^F + [E - (1 - \alpha)]\frac{\tau^G + \tau^F}{2} + \Gamma\tau^{US}$$

$$+ \left(\frac{A + \alpha}{2\phi} - \frac{M}{\phi}\right)(e^G - e^F) + \left[\frac{\xi(A + \alpha)}{2\phi} - \frac{M\xi}{\phi} + N\right](\tau^F - \tau^G)$$

$$- Ku + Hx;$$

$$n^G = (1 - \lambda\Lambda)m^G + \lambda\Theta m^{US} - \tau^G + \lambda\Omega\frac{\tau^G + \tau^F}{2} + \lambda\Psi\tau^{US}$$

$$+ \frac{\lambda}{2}\left(1 - \frac{\Lambda}{\phi}\right)(e^G - e^F) - \frac{\lambda\Lambda\xi}{2\phi}(\tau^F - \tau^G) - \Phi u - \Sigma x;$$

$$n^F = (1 - \lambda\Lambda)m^G + \lambda\Theta m^{US} - \tau^F + \lambda\Omega\frac{\tau^G + \tau^F}{2} + \lambda\Psi\tau^{US} \tag{33}$$

$$+ \left[\frac{1}{\phi} - \frac{\lambda}{2}\left(1 + \frac{\Lambda}{\phi}\right)\right](e^G - e^F) + \frac{\xi}{\phi}\left(1 - \frac{\lambda\Lambda}{2}\right)(\tau^F - \tau^G)$$

$$- \Phi u - \Sigma x.$$

Under the EMS, the employment-inflation trade-off faced by the Bank of France is $(\partial q^F/\partial n^F)^{BoF} = [\partial q^F/\partial(e^G - e^F)]/[\partial n^F/\partial(e^G - e^F)]$. The trade-offs facing the Fed and the U.S. government do not depend on the European exchange-rate regime.[25] The trade-off facing the Bundesbank worsens (relative to the flexible-rate case) and equals that of the Fed, while the trade-off facing the Bank of France remains unchanged.[26] The German and French governments face more favorable trade-offs than before, but the French government's gain is larger.[27]

EMU Under EMU, the DM/franc nominal exchange rate is locked. France and Germany's monetary policies are managed subject to this constraint by a European Central Bank with preferences defined over aggregate European variables. The ECB chooses m^{Eu}, the European money supply, to minimize:

$$L^{ECB} = \frac{1}{2}[.9(q^{Eu})^2 + .1(n^{Eu})^2]. \tag{34}$$

With some algebra:

$$q^{Eu} = \frac{q^G + q^F}{2} = Am^{Eu} - Bm^{US} + E\frac{\tau^G + \tau^F}{2} + \Gamma\tau^{US} + Ku + Hx;$$

$$n^{Eu} = \frac{n^G + n^F}{2} = (1 - \lambda\Lambda)m^{Eu} + \lambda\Theta m^{US} - (1 - \lambda\Omega)\frac{\tau^G + \tau^F}{2} \tag{35}$$

$$+ \lambda\Psi\tau^{US} - \Phi u - \Sigma x.$$

The reduced form equations for U.S. variables can be rewritten as

$$q^{US} = Am^{US} - Bm^{Eu} + E\tau^{US} + \Gamma\left(\frac{\tau^G + \tau^F}{2}\right) + Ku + Hx;$$

$$n^{US} = (1 - \lambda\Lambda)m^{US} + \lambda\Theta m^{Eu} - (1 - \lambda\Omega)\tau^{US} + \lambda\Psi\left(\frac{\tau^G + \tau^F}{2}\right) \tag{36}$$

$$+ \Phi u - \Sigma x.$$

Since the Maastricht Treaty does not require European governments to cooperate in the sense of jointly minimizing their loss functions, the French and German governments can still play Nash and have preferences defined over national variables. Therefore:

$$q^G = p^G - \beta z^G - \frac{1}{2}(1 - \beta)(z^G - z^F),$$

and

$$q^F = p^F - \beta z^F - \frac{1}{2}(1 - \beta)(z^F - z^G) = p^F - \beta z^F + \frac{1}{2}(1 - \beta)(z^G - z^F).$$

Subtracting q^G from q^F:

$$q^F - q^G = p^F - p^G + z^G - z^F. \tag{37}$$

The definitions of the real exchange rates imply:

$$z^G - z^F = e^G - e^F + p^G - p^F. \tag{38}$$

Because the DM-FF nominal exchange rate is fixed ($e^G - e^F = 0$):

$$z^G - z^F = p^G - p^F. \tag{39}$$

Plugging (39) into (37), we have that $q^G = q^F = q^{Eu}$. Locking the nominal exchange rate between European currencies thus implies that French and German inflation rates are equalized ex ante. Differences in fiscal policies across European countries only affect employment. This can be shown by deriving the reduced forms for n^G and n^F. Recalling the reduced form for the nominal exchange rate between the French franc and the deutsche mark, we see that $e^G - e^F = 0$ implies

$$m^F - m^G = \frac{\xi}{\phi}(\tau^F - \tau^G). \tag{40}$$

Another consequence of $e^G - e^F = 0$ is $i^F - i^G = 0$. Equation (18) therefore implies

$$n^F - n^G = m^F - m^G - (\tau^F - \tau^G) = -\left(1 - \frac{\xi}{\phi}\right)(\tau^F - \tau^G). \tag{41}$$

From (41), differences between τ^G and τ^F imply differences in employment. Solving for n^F and plugging the result into $n^G = 2n^{Eu} - n^F$ yields

$$n^G = n^{Eu} - \frac{1}{2}\left(1 - \frac{\xi}{\phi}\right)(\tau^G - \tau^F). \tag{42}$$

Finally, plugging the reduced form equation for n^{Eu} into this equation, we obtain reduced forms for employment:

$$n^G = (1 - \lambda\Lambda)m^{Eu} + \lambda\Theta m^{US} - \frac{1}{2}\left(2 - \lambda\Omega - \frac{\xi}{\phi}\right)\tau^G$$

$$- \frac{1}{2}\left(\frac{\xi}{\phi} - \lambda\Omega\right)\tau^F + \lambda\Psi\tau^{US} - \Phi u - \Sigma x. \tag{43}$$

$$n^F = (1 - \lambda\Lambda)m^{Eu} + \lambda\Theta m^{US} - \frac{1}{2}\left(2 - \lambda\Omega - \frac{\xi}{\phi}\right)\tau^F$$

$$- \frac{1}{2}\left(\frac{\xi}{\phi} - \lambda\Omega\right)\tau^G + \lambda\Psi\tau^{US} - \Phi u - \Sigma x. \tag{44}$$

The Fed's employment-inflation trade-off under EMU is the same as under the EMS (because it is independent of the DM/franc exchange-rate regime). The ECB now faces the same trade-off as the Bundesbank previously.[28]

The German government's trade-off improves with the shift from EMS to EMU, while the French government's trade-off worsens. Say that the French fiscal authorities want to stimulate employment under the EMS; they cut government spending. But the cut in French government spending must be coupled with an increase in the French money supply for any exchange rate chosen by the Bank of France, reinforcing the expansionary employment effect and improving the French government's trade-off.[29]

With the transition to EMU, a cut in French spending now provokes both an increase in the French money supply and a reduction in the German money supply (leaving the Europewide money supply unchanged). Because the induced change in the French money supply is smaller than under the EMS, the trade-off faced by the French government is worse (a given change in taxes and spending produces smaller employment gains). The same logic runs in reverse for the German fiscal authority: the trade-off between its policy objectives improves following the transition to EMU.[30,31]

The behavior of the trade-offs under different regimes provides insight into the strategic interaction of policymakers, as we now show.

The Stabilization Game in an Anti-Keynesian World

We analyze the response of policymakers to a positive realization of x (a symmetric negative global productivity shock) in the absence of demand disturbances.

The Flexible Exchange-Rate Solution Here, all policymakers play non-cooperatively and take other players' actions as given.

Reduced forms for the United States and Germany are shown in table 11.3.[32] Solving the central banks' minimization problem yields the first-order conditions:

$$.9q^j \frac{\partial q^j}{\partial m^j} + .1n^j \frac{\partial n^j}{\partial m^j} = 0 \qquad j = US, G, F. \tag{45}$$

Table 11.3
Reduced Form Equations in an Anti-Keynesian World

(a) Flexible exchange rates

$$q^{US} = .26m^{US} - .02\frac{m^G + m^F}{2} + .75\tau^{US} + .22\frac{\tau^G + \tau^F}{2} + .93x;$$

$$n^{US} = .75m^{US} - .03\frac{m^G + m^F}{2} - .56\tau^{US} + .49\frac{\tau^G + \tau^F}{2} - .21x;$$

$$q^G = .39m^{US} - .13m^F - .02m^{US} + .46\tau^F + .22\tau^{US} + .93x;$$

$$n^G = .72m^G + .03m^F - .03m^{US} - .83\tau^G + .27\tau^F + .49\tau^{US} - .21x.$$

(b) EMS

$$q^{US} = .26m^{US} - .02m^G - .02(e^G - e^F) + .75\tau^{US} + .11\tau^G + .11\tau^F + .93x;$$

$$n^{US} = .75m^{US} - .03m^G - .03(e^G - e^F) - .56\tau^{US} + .24\tau^G + .25\tau^F - .21x;$$

$$q^G = .26m^G - .02m^{US} + .42\tau^G + .33\tau^F + .22\tau^{US} - .24(e^G - e^F) + .93x;$$

$$q^F = .26m^G - .02m^{US} + .42\tau^G + .33\tau^F + .22\tau^{US} - .75(e^G - e^F) + .93x;$$

$$n^G = .75m^G - .03m^{US} - .82\tau^G + .26\tau^F + .49\tau^{US} + .06(e^G - e^F) + .21x;$$

$$n^F = .75m^G - .03m^{US} + .51\tau^G - 1.07\tau^F + .49\tau^{US} + 1.38(e^G - e^F) - .21x.$$

(c) EMU

$$q^{US} = .26m^{US} - .02m^{Eu} + .75\tau^{US} + .22\frac{\tau^G + \tau^F}{2} + .93x;$$

$$n^{US} = .75m^{US} - .03m^{Eu} - .56\tau^{US} + .49\frac{\tau^G + \tau^F}{2} - .21x;$$

$$q^{Eu} = .26m^{Eu} - .02m^{US} + .75\frac{\tau^G + \tau^F}{2} + .22\tau^{US} + .93x;$$

$$n^{Eu} = .75m^{Eu} - .03m^{US} - .56\frac{\tau^G + \tau^F}{2} + .49\tau^{US} - .21x;$$

$$n^G = .75m^{Eu} - .03m^{US} - .94\tau^G + .38\tau^F + .49\tau^{US} - .21x;$$

$$n^F = .75m^{Eu} - .03m^{US} + .38\tau^G - .94\tau^F + .49\tau^{US} - .21x.$$

Solving the fiscal authorities' minimization problems yields their reaction functions:

$$.2\left(.1q^j\frac{\partial q^j}{\partial \tau^j} + .9n^j\frac{\partial n^j}{\partial \tau^j}\right) + .8\tau^j = 0 \qquad j = US, G, F. \tag{46}$$

These six conditions comprise a system of six linear equations in six unknowns. Symmetry between France and Germany implies equal settings for the French and German instruments, reducing the system to four equations in four unknowns.

Central banks, concerned mainly with inflation, respond to the supply shock with a monetary contraction. (Results for the anti-Keynesian case are displayed in tables 11.4–11.6). Fiscal authorities, concerned mainly with employment, adopt expansionary policies (in this context, by cutting

Table 11.4
Optimal Values of the Policy Instruments in an Anti-Keynesian World

	Flexible rates	EMS	EMU	Post-EMU (A)	Post-EMU (B)	Post-EMU (C)	Post-EMU (D)
m^{US}	$-1.4443x$	$-1.4280x$	$-1.4335x$	$-1.4086x$	$-1.5000x$	$-1.4717x$	$-1.7329x$
m^G	$-1.6941x$	$-1.4174x$					
m^F	$-1.6941x$						
m^{Eu}			$-1.4023x$	$-1.3759x$	$-1.5000x$	$-1.4717x$	$-1.7329x$
τ^{US}	$-.1671x$	$-.1668x$	$-.1668x$	$-.1646x$	$-.1676x$	$-.1652x$	$-.0348x$
τ^G	$-.2588x$	$-.2269x$	$-.2488x$	$-.2451x$	$-.1676x$	$-.1652x$	$-.0348x$
τ^F	$-.2588x$	$-.3055x$	$-.2488x$	$-.2451x$	$-.1676x$	$-.1652x$	$-.0348x$
$e^G - e^F$		$-.1217x$					

Table 11.5
Endogenous Variables in Anti-Keynesian World

	Flexible rates	EMS	EMU	Post-EMU (A)	Post-EMU (B)	Post-EMU (C)	Post-EMU (D)
q^{US}	$.3988x$	$.3911x$	$.3979x$	$.4064x$	$.3999x$	$.4091x$	$.4730x$
q^G	$.2789x$	$.3973x$					
q^F	$.2789x$	$.2577x$					
q^{Eu}			$.3633x$	$.3730x$	$.3999x$	$.4091x$	$.4730x$
n^{US}	$-1.2685x$	$-1.2660x$	$-1.2657x$	$-1.2474x$	$-1.2719x$	$-1.2519x$	$-1.4475x$
n^G	$-1.3675x$	$-1.2065x$					
n^F	$-1.3675x$	$-1.2637x$					
n^{Eu}			$-1.1554x$	$-1.1375x$	$-1.2719x$	$-1.2519x$	$-1.4475x$

Table 11.6
Values of the Loss Functions in an Anti-Keynesian World

	Flexible rates	EMS	EMU	Post-EMU (A)	Post-EMU (B)	Post-EMU (C)	Post-EMU (D)
L^{Fed}	$.1520x^2$	$.1514x^2$	$.1514x^2$	$.1521x^2$	$.1529x^2$	$.1537x^2$	$.2055x^2$
L^{Buba}	$.1285x^2$	$.1375x^2$					
L^{BoF}	$.1285x^2$	$.1097x^2$					
L^{ECB}			$.1261x^2$	$.1273x^2$	$.1529x^2$	$.1537x^2$	$.2055x^2$
$L^{US\,govt.}$	$.1576x^2$	$.1569x^2$	$.1569x^2$	$.1525x^2$	$.1584x^2$	$.1536x^2$	$.1913x^2$
$L^{G\,govt.}$	$.1959x^2$	$.1530x^2$	$.1462x^2$	$.1419x^2$	$.1584x^2$	$.1536x^2$	$.1913x^2$
$L^{F\,govt.}$	$.1959x^2$	$.1817x^2$	$.1462x^2$	$.1419x^2$	$.1584x^2$	$.1536x^2$	$.1913x^2$

public spending). European monetary policies are more contractionary than American monetary policy, while European fiscal policies are more expansionary. The asymmetry reflects the different trade-offs facing policymakers on the two sides of the Atlantic.[33] Each European central bank contracts more because the two European economies are smaller and more open. The exchange-rate appreciation induced by domestic monetary contraction, ceteris paribus, does more to damp down inflation in more open economies. Compared to that of the United States, the monetary contraction reduces inflation more, at lower cost in employment, encouraging the more active use of the instrument. Tax and spending cuts raise employment and further damp down inflation; because governments care mainly about employment, the more active use of monetary policy by their national central banks encourages them to use fiscal policy more actively.[34]

The EMS Solution Reduced forms for the EMS scenario are shown in table 11.3. The Bank of France now minimizes its loss function with respect to $e^G - e^F$, yielding:

$$.9q^F \frac{\partial q^F}{\partial(e^G - e^F)} + .1n^F \frac{\partial n^F}{\partial(e^G - e^F)} = 0. \tag{47}$$

U.S. policies differ little from the case of flexible exchange rates.[35] But French and German policies are significantly different. Under flexible rates the Bank of France could not successfully export inflation by appreciating the franc against the DM (since France and Germany were symmetric). Now the Bank of France can push up the franc relative to the deutsche mark, exporting inflation.[36] The French central bank still faces the same trade-off as under flexible rates, but the Bundesbank faces a less favorable trade-off (the same as the Fed). The German inflation rate is now higher than under flexible rates. The Bundesbank's optimal policy is less contractionary than before: the fact that it faces the same employment-inflation trade-off as the Fed damps its incentive to appreciate its currency relative to the dollar.

Both European governments face better trade-offs than the U.S. government, and this gives them a chance to export unemployment to the other side of the Atlantic. This time, European governments are successful at achieving a better stabilization of employment than their U.S. counterpart, being helped by the reduced degree of monetary contraction in Europe.[37] The French government faces a more favorable trade-off than the German. French fiscal policy is more expansionary than German fiscal policy because of this and to counteract the contractionary consequences of the appreciation of the franc. Nonetheless, unemployment is higher in France than in Germany. Thus, while the Bank of France is better off than the Bundesbank, the French government is worse off than the German. Even if the latter faces a more favorable trade-off under the EMS regime than under the symmetric regime, German fiscal policy is less aggressive when the intra-European regime is asymmetric. This is a consequence of the reduced monetary contraction by the Bundesbank, which lowers the need for fiscal expansion to sustain employment.

The EMU Solution   Under EMU the first-order condition for the ECB is

$$.9q^{Eu}\frac{\partial q^{Eu}}{\partial m^{Eu}} + .1n^{Eu}\frac{\partial n^{Eu}}{\partial m^{Eu}} = 0. \tag{48}$$

The system of reaction functions can be simplified by observing that there are no asymmetries between the European countries.[38]

In contrast to the fears of inflation expressed by EMU critics in Germany, the ECB's policy is quite similar to the Bundesbank's under the EMS.[39] The Bank of France adopted an aggressive anti-inflationary policy under the EMS because it faced a more favorable trade-off than the Bundesbank; this allowed the French authority to export inflation to Germany via exchange-rate appreciation. The Bundesbank was less aggressive because it controlled the money supply for all of Europe and thus faced an unfavorable employment-inflation trade-off. Since the ECB now makes monetary policy for all of Europe, like the Bundesbank under the EMS, it faces the Bundesbank's trade-off. Hence, the fact that the ECB attaches the same weights to inflation and employment as the Bundesbank explains why its choice is similar to that of the German central bank. But the ECB selects a less contractionary point on its trade-off. Under EMU, the ECB does not have to cope with the inflationary consequences of the aggressive French monetary policy that the Bundesbank was facing. Because there is no Bank-of-France-like monetary contraction under EMU and the relevant trade-off is worse, the French government's employment-friendly tax cut is smaller. That smaller tax cut does less to damp down inflation. Nonetheless, German fiscal policy becomes more expansionary, reflecting the German government's improved trade-off, and this helps to stabilize inflation.[40] The ECB therefore adopts a more contractionary monetary policy than the Bundesbank previously.

Because EMU removes the intra-European monetary externality, unemployment is lower in both European countries. This leaves both European governments, which care mainly about unemployment, better off with the transition from the EMS to EMU. European inflation is lower under EMU than German inflation under the EMS. Intuitively, since the ECB's response lies between those of the two European central banks under the EMS, Europewide (and German) inflation lies between the French and German rates under the EMS. Thus, the Bundesbank's successors are left better off by the transition to EMU. Only the Bank of France's successors are left worse off (because Europewide inflation is higher than French inflation under the EMS).

This is our first important result. The change in the responses of monetary and fiscal authorities with the advent of Stage III may stabilize European output and employment. EMU may stabilize fiscal policy in Europe. And the ECB's monetary policy is likely to be quite similar to the Bundesbank's. Thus, results obtained using an approach that focuses on strategic interactions contrast with popular fears that EMU will encourage governments to pursue unstable fiscal policies and destabilize employment. They also contrast with German fears about the inflationary consequences of EMU for the German economy. Eliminating the contractionary bias of monetary policies under the EMS actually benefits Germany. At the same time, inflation rises elsewhere in Europe, driving the average European inflation rate above its level under the EMS.[41,42]

Although there are no asymmetries between the two European countries, the fact that intra-European fiscal externalities are not internalized makes the U.S.-Europe equilibrium asymmetric. Both European governments still enjoy better trade-offs than the U.S. government. Hence, fiscal policies in Europe are more active than U.S. fiscal policy and European governments successfully export some unemployment to the United States. Inflation is higher in the U.S. than in Europe (bigger European tax and spending cuts do more to damp down inflation).[43]

EMU and Policy Coordination in the Anti-Keynesian World

We consider a number of possible scenarios in the post-EMU era.

Cooperation Between Central Banks In previous cases, European central banks were able to take advantage of the asymmetry between the United States and Europe to achieve lower levels of inflation than in the United States.[44] This may be interpreted to provide an argument for transatlantic cooperation. Under this scenario, the dollar/Euro exchange rate is free to float, and fiscal authorities play Nash. But now the Fed and the ECB jointly minimize a weighted average of their loss functions. Symmetry motivates setting the weights to one half.[45] Central banks solve:

$$\min_{m^{US},m^{Eu}} \frac{1}{2}L^{Fed} + \frac{1}{2}L^{ECB}. \tag{49}$$

The first-order conditions are

$$.9q^{US}\frac{\partial q^{US}}{\partial m^{US}} + 0.1n^{US}\frac{\partial n^{US}}{\partial m^{US}} + .9q^{Eu}\frac{\partial q^{Eu}}{\partial m^{US}} + .1n^{Eu}\frac{\partial n^{Eu}}{\partial m^{US}} = 0; \tag{50}$$

$$.9q^{US}\frac{\partial q^{US}}{\partial m^{Eu}} + 0.1n^{US}\frac{\partial n^{US}}{\partial m^{Eu}} + .9q^{Eu}\frac{\partial q^{Eu}}{\partial m^{Eu}} + .1n^{Eu}\frac{\partial n^{Eu}}{\partial m^{Eu}} = 0. \tag{51}$$

Monetary policies become less contractionary since central banks no longer have an incentive to manipulate the exchange rate to export inflation across the Atlantic.[46] In turn, this induces the fiscal authorities to respond more moderately in all three countries. The equilibrium is still asymmetric because of the existence of intra-European fiscal externalities. France and Germany continue to cut taxes and spending more aggressively than does the United States (in the effort to export unemployment to one another and to the United States by depreciating the Euro relative to the dollar). Because tax cuts damp down European inflation relative to U.S. inflation, the ECB is still less contractionary than the Fed.

Transatlantic monetary cooperation is undesirable from the standpoint of central banks because less contractionary monetary policies coupled with smaller reductions in taxation cause both U.S. and European inflation to rise. It is desirable from the standpoint of governments, however, because preventing central banks from manipulating exchange rates raises equilibrium output and employment. This is our second important result. Though the fiscal authorities will want central banks to cooperate, the Fed and the ECB will not.

One can imagine how this could give rise to conflicts. Article 109 of the Maastricht Treaty empowers the Council of Ministers, acting by qualified majority, to adopt "general orientations" for exchange-rate policy vis-à-vis non-EU currencies. A purpose of this provision is presumably to facilitate the negotiation of Louvre-like intervention agreements. Article 109 states that such orientations must not jeopardize the pursuit of price stability, although it does not indicate who will determine whether this is the case. Nor does it provide a mechanism that would make the Council's general orientations binding on the ECB.[47]

That monetary cooperation can be counterproductive is not a new result. Canzoneri and Henderson (1991) show that cooperation limited to a subset of central banks can be counterproductive. Rogoff (1985) shows that cooperation can be counterproductive when it aggravates time inconsistency. Ghironi and Giavazzi (1997b) show that cooperation can be counterproductive when it prevents a central banker from optimally exploiting a favorable trade-off. Here the result derives from the fact that cooperation encompasses central banks but not governments (that fiscal authorities cooperate with neither one another nor with their central banks).

Cooperation between European Governments We now assume that the French and German governments cooperate but the ECB and Fed do not. The two European governments minimize the average of their respective loss functions, solving:

$$\min_{\tau^G, \tau^F} \frac{1}{2} L^{fa^G} + \frac{1}{2} L^{fa^F}. \tag{52}$$

The first order conditions are

$$.2\left(.1q^{Eu}\frac{\partial q^{Eu}}{\partial \tau^G} + .9n^G\frac{\partial n^G}{\partial \tau^G}\right) + .8\tau^G + .2\left(.1q^{Eu}\frac{\partial q^{Eu}}{\partial \tau^G} + .9n^F\frac{\partial n^F}{\partial \tau^G}\right) = 0; \tag{53}$$

$$.2\left(.1q^{Eu}\frac{\partial q^{Eu}}{\partial \tau^F} + .9n^F\frac{\partial n^F}{\partial \tau^F}\right) + .8\tau^F + .2\left(.1q^{Eu}\frac{\partial q^{Eu}}{\partial \tau^F} + .9n^G\frac{\partial n^G}{\partial \tau^F}\right) = 0. \tag{54}$$

The system can be further simplified by noting that intra-European fiscal cooperation under EMU renders European policymakers' incentives identical to those of American policymakers.[48]

Again, policy coordination is counterproductive. This is our third important result. Both central banks and all three governments are worse off than when neither central banks nor governments cooperate. Neither France nor Germany cuts taxes as aggressively (since they refrain from trying to export unemployment to the other). This induces the ECB to contract more aggressively. Because policy instruments are set identically in the United States and Europe, European governments no longer manage to depreciate the Euro against the dollar. In the absence of the favorable effect of the appreciation of the dollar on U.S. prices, the Fed contracts more aggressively to damp down inflation, inducing the U.S. government to respond more actively. This notwithstanding, U.S. inflation and unemployment rise, leaving the U.S. government and the Fed worse off. Inflation and unemployment also rise in Europe, rendering all three European policy authorities worse off too.[49]

Thus, intra-EU fiscal policy coordination is counterproductive under EMU when the policy has anti-Keynesian effects. Governments and central banks on both sides of the Atlantic are worse off when the French and

German governments cooperate.[50] This is because there remain other externalities in the model: the transatlantic fiscal externality arising from the failure of the U.S. and European governments to coordinate their tax and spending policies, the transatlantic monetary externality arising from the failure of the Fed and the ECB to coordinate, and the externalities associated with the failure of central banks and governments to coordinate. Absent fiscal cooperation, all three governments cut taxes too aggressively to export unemployment; cooperation between France and Germany reduces this bias in Europe but reinforces it in the United States (the United States has an incentive to cut taxes even more aggressively). The two central banks react by contracting more. Inflation nevertheless remains high, and unemployment worsens.

The presumption in Europe is that EMU requires intra-EU fiscal coordination. The Maastricht Treaty provides a Mutual Surveillance Procedure (Article 103) that instructs the Council to develop guidelines for the economic policies of member states, to monitor their economic policies, and to issue recommendations should policies be inconsistent with its guidelines. The rationale for this procedure is to encourage fiscal policy coordination. Our analysis suggests that there are cases where this is undesirable.

Cooperation between Central Banks and Cooperation between European Governments   If the French and German governments cooperate and the Fed and the ECB cooperate as well, only policy externalities associated with the absence of transatlantic fiscal cooperation and with cooperation between monetary and fiscal authorities remain. Relative to where the two European governments cooperate but the Fed and the ECB do not, all three governments are better off, but both central banks are worse off. Governments will want their central banks to cooperate, but their central banks will resist. This is the same result we obtained in the absence of intra-EU fiscal coordination.

Cooperation between Central Banks plus Global Fiscal Cooperation   When all three fiscal policymakers cooperate, they jointly minimize a weighted sum, with weights equal to one half, of the U.S. government's loss function and of an average of the German and French governments' losses. The problem is

$$\min_{\tau^{US},\tau^G,\tau^F} \frac{1}{2}L^{fa^{US}} + \frac{1}{2}\left(\frac{L^{fa^G} + L^{fa^F}}{2}\right). \tag{55}$$

The first-order conditions are

$$.2\left(.1q^{US}\frac{\partial q^{US}}{\partial \tau^{US}}+.9n^{US}\frac{\partial n^{US}}{\partial \tau^{US}}\right)+.8\tau^{US}+.5\left[.2\left(.1q^{Eu}\frac{\partial q^{Eu}}{\partial \tau^{US}}+.9n^{G}\frac{\partial n^{G}}{\partial \tau^{US}}\right)\right.$$

$$\left.+.2\left(.1q^{Eu}\frac{\partial q^{Eu}}{\partial \tau^{US}}+.9n^{F}\frac{\partial n^{F}}{\partial \tau^{US}}\right)\right]=0; \tag{56}$$

$$.2\left(.1q^{US}\frac{\partial q^{US}}{\partial \tau^{G}}+.9n^{US}\frac{\partial n^{US}}{\partial \tau^{G}}\right)+.5\left[.2\left(.1q^{Eu}\frac{\partial q^{Eu}}{\partial \tau^{G}}+.9n^{G}\frac{\partial n^{G}}{\partial \tau^{G}}\right)\right.$$

$$\left.+.8\tau^{G}+.2\left(.1q^{Eu}\frac{\partial q^{Eu}}{\partial \tau^{G}}+.9n^{F}\frac{\partial n^{F}}{\partial \tau^{G}}\right)\right]=0; \tag{57}$$

$$.2\left(.1q^{US}\frac{\partial q^{US}}{\partial \tau^{F}}+.9n^{US}\frac{\partial n^{US}}{\partial \tau^{F}}\right)+.5\left[.2\left(.1q^{Eu}\frac{\partial q^{Eu}}{\partial \tau^{F}}+.9n^{G}\frac{\partial n^{G}}{\partial \tau^{F}}\right)\right.$$

$$\left.+.2\left(.1q^{Eu}\frac{\partial q^{Eu}}{\partial \tau^{F}}+.9n^{F}\frac{\partial n^{F}}{\partial \tau^{F}}\right)+.8\tau^{F}\right]=0. \tag{58}$$

These can be combined with (50) and (51) to obtain values for the policy instruments.

When governments no longer attempt to export unemployment, fiscal policies become dramatically less expansionary. This fuels inflation and central banks respond with sharp monetary contraction (even though the Fed and the ECB, now playing cooperatively, no longer seek to export inflation to one another). The employment loss is larger than before. Smaller tax cuts end up destabilizing inflation. Consequently, central banks as well as governments suffer larger losses.[51]

Global fiscal cooperation together with global monetary cooperation leads to the worst possible outcome due to the absence of cooperation between monetary and fiscal authorities. The main impact of monetary policy is on the variable that is most important for fiscal policymakers— employment—while the main impact of fiscal policy is on the variable that is most important for central banks—inflation. Our result is consistent with the familiar finding that, when multiple externalities tend to offset each other, internalizing only some of them can be counterproductive.

11.4   The Keynesian Case

In the Keynesian case we eliminate the distortionary tax in equation (2), assuming instead that taxes are lump sum. Two features of the specification

Table 11.7
Reduced Form Equations in a Keynesian World

(a) Flexible exchange rates

$$q^{US} = .26m^{US} - .02\frac{m^G + m^F}{2} + .18g^{US} + .19\frac{g^G + g^F}{2} + .93x;$$

$$n^{US} = .75m^{US} - .03\frac{m^G + m^F}{2} + .64g^{US} + .43\frac{g^G + g^F}{2} - .21x;$$

$$q^G = .39m^G - .13m^F - .02m^{US} + .09g^G + .09g^F + .19g^{US} + .93x;$$

$$n^G = .72m^G + .03m^F - .03m^{US} + .32g^G + .32g^F + .43g^{US} - .21x.$$

(b) EMS

$$q^{US} = .26m^{US} - .02m^G - .02(e^G - e^F) + .18g^{US} + .19\frac{g^G + g^F}{2} + .93x;$$

$$n^{US} = .75m^{US} - .03m^G - .03(e^G - e^F) + .64g^{US} + .43\frac{g^G + g^F}{2} - .21x.$$

$$q^G = .26m^G - .02m^{US} + .09g^G + .09g^F + .19g^{US} - .24(e^G - e^F) + .93x;$$

$$q^F = .26m^G - .02m^{US} + .09g^G + .09g^F + .19g^{US} + .75(e^G - e^F) + .93x;$$

$$n^G = .75m^G - .03m^{US} + .32g^G + .32g^F + .43g^{US} + .06(e^G - e^F) - .21x;$$

$$n^F = .75m^G - .03m^{US} + .32g^G + .32g^F + .43g^{US} + 1.38(e^G - e^F) - .21x.$$

(c) EMU

Reduced forms for q^{US} and n^{US} are as in (a), with m^{Eu} replacing $(m^G + m^F)/2$.
Reduced forms for q^{Eu} and n^{Eu} can be recovered by symmetry.

are important for the results. Because European governments are assumed to divide their spending evenly between French and German goods (paralleling the behavior of French and German households), European fiscal policies do not affect the intra-European exchange rate once we remove the distortionary tax.[52] And international cooperation will not generally be superior to other regimes because of the existence of other distortions (associated with the lack of cooperation between monetary and fiscal authorities within countries). As in the anti-Keynesian case, global cooperation between monetary or fiscal authorities will not be optimal.

Reduced forms for the Keynesian case are in the appendix. Numerical values of the reduced forms are displayed in table 11.7.

The Stabilization Game

Now that government spending has Keynesian effects (operating through the balanced-budget multiplier), governments concerned mainly to offset the rise in unemployment respond by raising spending (though that increase will be damped because the sign of their trade-off has changed, additional government spending increasing inflation).[53]

Table 11.8
Optimal Values of Economic Policy Instruments in a Keynesian World

	Flexible rates	EMS	EMU	Post-EMU (A)	Post-EMU (B)	Post-EMU (C)	Post-EMU (D)
m^{US}	−2.1332x	−2.1112x	−2.0907x	−2.0461x	−2.1671x	−2.1212x	−2.3374x
m^G	−2.5075x	−2.1531x					
m^F	−2.5075x						
m^{Eu}			−2.0804x	−2.0363x	−2.1671x	−2.1212x	−2.3374x
g^{US}	.2166x	.2160x	.2156x	.2115x	.2165x	.2124x	.3566x
g^G	.1307x	.1126x	.1087x	.1067x	.2165x	.2124x	.3566x
g^F	.1307x	.1260x	.1087x	.1067x	.2165x	.2124x	.3566x
$e^G - e^F$		−.1382x					

Table 11.9
Endogenous Variables in a Keynesian World

	Flexible rates	EMS	EMU	Post-EMU (A)	Post-EMU (B)	Post-EMU (C)	Post-EMU (D)
q^{US}	.4806x	.4794x	.4783x	.4880x	.4804x	.4901x	.4901x
q^G	.3748x	.4997x					
q^F	.3748x	.3615x					
q^{Eu}			.4826x	.4921x	.4804x	.4901x	.4901x
n^{US}	−1.5284x	−1.5247x	−1.5213x	−1.4930x	−1.5281x	−1.4997x	−1.4997x
n^G	−1.8380x	−1.5892x					
n^F	−1.8380x	−1.7729x					
n^{Eu}			−1.5348x	−1.5064x	1.5281x	−1.4997x	−1.4997x

The Flexible Exchange-Rate Solution Under flexible rates, central banks concerned mainly with inflation cut back the money supply, while governments concerned more with unemployment increase spending. (Results for Keynesian case are shown in tables 11.8–11.10.) As was the case before, European central banks continue to tighten more than the Fed because the two European economies are more open than the United States and face more favorable trade-offs. The French and German governments, in contrast, increase spending less than the United States because they fail to internalize the employment-creating effects of their spending on the other European country. (This contrasts with the anti-Keynesian case, where European governments adjusted their spending more radically than the United States because they faced more favorable trade-offs and intra-European fiscal spillovers were negative.)[54]

Table 11.10
Values of the Loss Functions in Keynesian World

	Flexible rates	EMS	EMU	Post-EMU (A)	Post-EMU (B)	Post-EMU (C)	Post-EMU (D)
L^{Fed}	$.2207x^2$	$.2196x^2$	$.2187x^2$	$.2186x^2$	$.2206x^2$	$.2205x^2$	$.2205x^2$
L^{Buba}	$.2321x^2$	$.2386x^2$					
L^{BoF}	$.2321x^2$	$.2160x^2$					
L^{ECB}			$.2226x^2$	$.2225x^2$	$.2206x^2$	$.2205x^2$	$.2205x^2$
$L^{US\,govt.}$	$.2313x^2$	$.2302x^2$	$.2292x^2$	$.2209x^2$	$.2312x^2$	$.2229x^2$	$.2557x^2$
$L^{G\,govt.}$	$.3123x^2$	$.2349x^2$	$.2191x^2$	$.2112x^2$	$.2312x^2$	$.2229x^2$	$.2557x^2$
$L^{F\,govt.}$	$.3123x^2$	$.2905x^2$	$.2191x^2$	$.2112x^2$	$.2312x^2$	$.2229x^2$	$.2557x^2$

The EMS Just as in the anti-Keynesian case, the Bundesbank contracts less dramatically with the shift from floating to the EMS; as before, it sees itself as possessing less opportunity to export inflation because it sets the money supply for all of Europe. And as before, the Bank of France manages to export inflation to Germany by appreciating the exchange rate. German monetary policy being less contractionary, German fiscal policy can be less expansionary (limiting the cost to the government from changing spending). The French government now expands less than under flexible exchange rates. Even if the Bank of France manages to appreciate the franc, French money supply still decreases by less than under flexible rates.[55] This reduces the need for expansion to stabilize employment. However, since French monetary policy is more contractionary than German monetary policy, the French government expands more than the German. As in the anti-Keynesian case, the French government and central bank are better off now that they have the exchange rate to manipulate. While the Bundesbank is worse off, the German government is better off due to the smaller fall in German employment and the need to alter the level of public spending by less.

Thus, while the signs of the fiscal responses differ from the anti-Keynesian case, the consequences for welfare are little affected.

EMU In the anti-Keynesian case, the ECB followed a policy quite similar to the Bundesbank's under the EMS. Now the ECB is significantly less restrictive than the Bundesbank under the EMS.[56] Since there is no radical monetary contraction by the Bank of France, the French government increases spending by less. Because that smaller spending increase contributes less to inflation, the ECB contracts the money supply by less.[57]

Thus, the results in the Keynesian case are consistent with the popular presumption that EMU weakens monetary discipline. The reason is not lack of fiscal discipline—to the contrary, the transition to EMU continues to stabilize fiscal policy relative to the EMS (both French and German fiscal policies are less expansionary than under the EMS). As before, EMU removes the intra-European monetary externality and the incentive for the Bank of France to tighten excessively; this produces less unemployment in both France and Germany and an improvement in welfare for both the French and German governments. As before, average European inflation is higher than under the EMS, and the ECB is worse off than the Bank of France but better off than the Bundesbank under that regime. The transition continues to benefit the German authorities because of the increase in fiscal discipline.

Both the Fed and the U.S. fiscal authority are better off due to EMU. That there is no Bank-of-France-like contraction driving up U.S. import prices means that a less radical monetary contraction is required of the Fed, and a less pronounced (and costly) increase in public spending is required of the U.S. government. This is in contrast to the anti-Keynesian case, in which both the Fed and the U.S. government were basically unaffected by EMU. Then the move from EMS to EMU induced the Fed to adopt a more contractionary policy but had little impact on U.S. fiscal policy. Policy changes in the United States and Europe had roughly offsetting effects on U.S. variables, which remained close to their levels under the EMS.

EMU and Policy Coordination in the Keynesian World

We focus on the same four scenarios as before.

Cooperation between Central Banks As before, monetary policy becomes less contractionary now that central banks resist the incentive to export inflation. As before, this allows governments to respond more moderately (now this means that they increase spending by less). While unemployment is lower and inflation is higher, now central banks as well as governments are better off. The conflict over cooperation that arose in the anti-Keynesian case (where governments wanted central banks to cooperate but central banks did not) evaporates here. Even if inflation is higher, the employment gains associated with the removal of the contractionary bias of noncoordinated monetary policies offset the inflation loss and induce the central banks to cooperate.

Cooperation between European Governments   In the anti-Keynesian case, European and U.S. governments wanted central banks to cooperate but central banks did not. Now the ECB wants European governments to cooperate but governments do not. This seems to accord with the policy debate in which European central banks are insisting on mutual surveillance of fiscal policies but national governments are resisting. When European governments cooperate, they increase their spending much more dramatically (internalizing the stimulus to employment in the rest of Europe). Central banks respond by contracting more. Both inflation and unemployment are lower in Europe, although the French and German governments are left worse off because they pay an additional cost from changing their policy instruments.[58]

Cooperation between Central Banks and Cooperation between European Governments   When fiscal cooperation in Europe is coupled with transatlantic monetary cooperation, monetary policies become less contractionary. Governments adopt less expansionary fiscal policies to stimulate employment. Inflation rises in both Europe and the United States; unemployment falls. Now there is no conflict over the desirability of monetary cooperation. Though inflation rises, the employment gain suffices to induce central banks to cooperate.

Cooperation between Central Banks and Global Fiscal Cooperation   As in the anti-Keynesian case, cooperation among central banks together with cooperation among governments is counterproductive. When the transatlantic employment-creating effect of fiscal policies is internalized, fiscal expansions increase sharply (in contrast to the anti-Keynesian case, where internalization of fiscal externalities reduced the degree of fiscal activism). This fuels inflation and induces central banks to react with more contractionary policies (as in the anti-Keynesian world). Although the effects on endogenous variables are negligible (inflation and unemployment remain basically unchanged with respect to the previous policy regime), governments are significantly worse off because of the more active use they make of their instrument.

11.5   Conclusion

We have addressed the question of how EMU will affect U.S.-Europe policy interactions and the prospects for transatlantic cooperation, focusing on optimal reactions to a common supply disturbance in both Keynesian and anti-Keynesian settings. The anti-Keynesian case could prevail in the early years of Stage III, when European countries are still seeking to move away from unsustainable fiscal trajectories. The Keynesian case may be a more accurate depiction of subsequent years.

In the anti-Keynesian scenario, EMU may enhance monetary and fiscal discipline outside Germany and stabilize employment in Europe. This contrasts with fears that EMU will encourage governments to pursue unstable fiscal policies and with current German fears about EMU. But the ECB and central banks outside Europe will have little incentive to coordinate their response to supply shocks. Governments may want central banks to coordinate, but the latter will not share their interest. And fiscal coordination can be counterproductive under EMU because there remain other externalities in the model even when intra-European fiscal externalities are internalized. It is widely presumed that EMU requires intra-EU fiscal coordination; we find that there are cases where this is undesirable.

Things change when fiscal policy has Keynesian effects. In this case, EMU may reduce monetary discipline, the ECB's policy being less restrictive than the Bundesbank's under the EMS. But the reason is not lack of fiscal discipline—to the contrary, the transition to EMU continues to stabilize fiscal policy relative to the EMS. Along with the German authorities, the Fed and the U.S. government are made better off by EMU. This is in contrast to the anti-Keynesian case, where both the Fed and the U.S. government are left basically indifferent. Finally, when fiscal policy has standard textbook effects, the ECB and central banks outside Europe will wish to coordinate their response to supply shocks. The conflict between central banks and governments in the anti-Keynesian setting evaporates, but a new conflict arises. The ECB will want European governments to coordinate their policies, but governments will not. This result seems consistent with the current policy debate, in which European central banks are insisting on mutual surveillance of fiscal policies but national governments are resisting.

Our conclusions do not encourage hopes for transatlantic monetary cooperation in the early years of Stage III when anti-Keynesian conditions may prevail. This confirms Kenen's (1995) skepticism about the prospects for monetary cooperation and reinforces cautions expressed in Eichengreen and Ghironi (1996a).

At the same time, the arrangements central banks prefer may not be optimal either. Governments in both Europe and the U.S. would prefer the ECB and Fed to cooperate. But this is not sufficient to argue in favor of monetary cooperation if we regard central bank independence as a

Table 11.11
Average Losses in an Anti-Keynesian World

	EMU	Post-EMU (A)	Post-EMU (B)	Post-EMU (C)	Post-EMU (D)
United States	$.15415x^2$	$.1523x^2$	$.15565x^2$	$.15365x^2$	$.1984x^2$
Germany	$.13615x^2$	$.1346x^2$	$.15565x^2$	$.15365x^2$	$.1984x^2$
France	$.13615x^2$	$.1346x^2$	$.15565x^2$	$.15365x^2$	$.1984x^2$

Table 11.12
Average Losses in a Keynesian World

	EMU	Post-EMU (A)	Post-EMU (B)	Post-EMU (C)	Post-EMU (D)
United States	$.22395x^2$	$.21975x^2$	$.2259x^2$	$.2217x^2$	$.2381x^2$
Germany	$.22085x^2$	$.21685x^2$	$.2259x^2$	$.2217x^2$	$.2381x^2$
France	$.22085x^2$	$.21685x^2$	$.2259x^2$	$.2217x^2$	$.2381x^2$

"good" to be preserved. There is a need for another solution to the problem of choosing the optimal post-EMU policymaking regime.

Suppose no cooperation exists among monetary and fiscal authorities, so that central bank independence (in the sense we have defined it) is preserved. Suppose also that citizens in each country care about both the central bank and government's loss functions and value monetary regimes according to an arithmetic average of the losses after optimal policies are implemented. Table 11.11 suggests that residents of all countries prefer EMU coupled with ECB-Fed cooperation. However, while the choice criterion summarized in table 11.11 does not require the central banks to cooperate with governments, the scenario that is preferred by citizens in all countries is not what central banks prefer.[59] We are left with the problem of how to implement the optimal arrangement without violating the independence of central banks. This points to the importance of the institutional design as a means for dealing with conflicts that might arise among policymakers.[60]

There are several other lines along which our research could be extended and improved. An interesting one has to do with the interactions between monetary and fiscal policy and with the potential presence of asymmetries across countries in the way fiscal policy affects the economy. Empirical observation seems to suggest that a model in which cross-country asymmetries in the impact of fiscal policy are allowed could be a better depiction of reality in the short as well as in the long run. For example, it may be argued that the U.S. economy and the core European economies are indeed more likely to be in a Keynesian environment also in the short run, while the anti-Keynesian case would better apply to peripheral European economies. Other sources of cross-country asymmetry that are not explored in this chapter may be relevant.[61] Exploring the consequences of alternative dollar-Euro exchange-rate regimes could also be interesting. The abundance of potentially interesting extensions of our analysis makes it even more apparent that our results have been obtained within the framework of a model which, as all models, is an extremely simplified picture of reality. Therefore, we do not claim too much for their generality.[62] However, the results we have obtained for a sensible parameterization of the model seem to point to interesting phenomena, which do deserve further exploration. Finally, on the sensitivity of the findings to our assumptions about parameter values, although some sensitivity analysis would be appropriate, we believe that the consistency of the numerical results with theoretical results presented in the chapter lends some robustness to the conclusions of our exercise.

Appendix A: Solution of the Model under Flexible Exchange Rates

This appendix presents the solution of the model under flexible exchange rates for the case of anti-Keynesian fiscal policies.

We use the following simplified notation. For any variable f, we define

$$\bar{f} = \frac{f^G + f^F}{2}; \quad \tilde{f} = f^{US} - \frac{f^G + f^F}{2}; \quad \hat{f} = f^G - f^F.$$

With these definitions in mind, subtracting the sum of equations (8G) and (8F) from equation (8US), rearranging, and dividing by two yields

$$-[1 - (1 - 2\beta)\varepsilon]\tilde{y} - (1 - 2\beta)v\tilde{r} - (1 - 2\eta)\tilde{g} + 2\delta\tilde{z} + 2u = 0, \qquad (A.1)$$

where we assume that β and ε are such that $1 - (1 - 2\beta)\varepsilon > 0$.
Subtracting (8) for France from (8) for Germany and rearranging gives

$$-\hat{y} - 2\delta\hat{z} = 0. \qquad (A.2)$$

Subtracting $(r^G + r^F)/2$ from r^{US}, multiplying by two, eliminating $(i^{US} - i^G)$ and $(i^{US} - i^F)$ using the uncovered interest parity conditions, and using the definitions of CPIs and real exchange rates allows us to write:

$$\tilde{r} = \frac{1}{2}(1 - 2\beta)\{[E(z_{+1}^G) - z^G] + [E(z_{+1}^F) - z^F]\}. \qquad (A.3)$$

To simplify this expression, recall that static expectations are rational in our model. Expected values of all disturbances for tomorrow and beyond based on today's information are zero, and expected real exchange rates for tomorrow and beyond based on today's information are independent of expected future money supplies because expected nominal wages and output prices are flexible. We can therefore impose a no-speculative-bubble condition such that

$$E(z_{+1}^g) = E(z_{+1}^f) = 0.$$

Equation (A.3) can now be rewritten as

$$\tilde{r} = -(1 - 2\beta)\bar{z}. \tag{A.4}$$

Equation (1), together with equation (18), allows us to write

$$\tilde{y} = (1 - \alpha)\{\tilde{m} - \tilde{\tau} + \lambda\tilde{i}\}. \tag{A.5}$$

Imposing the no-speculative-bubbles condition on the nominal exchange rate and summing the uncovered interest parity conditions, we obtain

$$\tilde{i} = -\bar{e}. \tag{A.6}$$

Solving the equations defining the dollar-DM and dollar-FF real exchange rates for the nominal exchange rates and plugging the results into the previous equation, we have

$$\tilde{i} = -\bar{z} - \tilde{p}. \tag{A.7}$$

Equation (19) allows us to write

$$\tilde{p} = \alpha\tilde{m} + \alpha\lambda\tilde{i} + (1 - \alpha)\tilde{\tau}. \tag{A.8}$$

Substituting this result into (A.7) and rearranging:

$$\tilde{i} = -\frac{1}{1 + \alpha\lambda}\{\bar{z} + \alpha\tilde{m} + (1 - \alpha)\tilde{\tau}\}. \tag{A.9}$$

Plugging (A.9) into (A.5), we obtain

$$\tilde{y} = \frac{1 - \alpha}{1 + \alpha\lambda}\{\tilde{m} - (1 + \lambda)\tilde{\tau} - \lambda\bar{z}\}. \tag{A.10}$$

We can now derive a reduced form for $\bar{z} = (z^G + z^F)/2$. Substituting (A.4) and (A.10) into (A.1), taking the governments' budget constraints into account and rearranging, we have

$$\bar{z} = \frac{\rho}{\gamma}\,\tilde{m} - \frac{\mu}{\gamma}\,\tilde{\tau} - \frac{2}{\gamma}\,u, \tag{A.11}$$

where the parameters are

$$\gamma = \frac{\lambda(1-\alpha)[1-(1-2\beta)\varepsilon]}{1+\alpha\lambda} + (1-2\beta)^2 v + 2\delta;$$

$$\rho = \frac{(1-\alpha)[1-(1-2\beta)\varepsilon]}{1+\alpha\lambda};$$

$$\mu = \frac{(1-\alpha)(1+\lambda)[1-(1-2\beta)\varepsilon]}{1+\alpha\lambda} - (1-2\eta),$$

which are all positive given our assumptions.

In the case of monetary union in Europe, the previous equation defines the reduced form for the real exchange rate between the dollar and the Euro.[63] Since public expenditures coincide with tax revenues, an increase in taxes is also an increase in expenditure and induces a real appreciation.[64]

Using (18) for France and Germany together with (1) for those same countries yields

$$\hat{y} = (1-\alpha)[\hat{m} - \hat{\tau} + \lambda\hat{\imath}]. \tag{A.12}$$

From the uncovered interest parity conditions:

$$\hat{\imath} = \hat{e}. \tag{A.13}$$

However, it is also true that

$$\hat{z} = \hat{e} + \hat{p}. \tag{A.14}$$

Making use of (18) and (19) for France and Germany, we get

$$\hat{e} = \hat{z} - \alpha\hat{m} - (1-\alpha)\hat{\tau} - \alpha\lambda\hat{\imath}. \tag{A.15}$$

Since equation (A.13) holds:

$$\hat{\imath} = \frac{1}{1+\alpha\lambda}[\hat{z} - \alpha\hat{m} - (1-\alpha)\hat{\tau}]. \tag{A.16}$$

Plugging (A.16) into (A.12) and substituting into (A.2), we obtain

$$-(1-\alpha)\left\{\hat{m} - \hat{\tau} + \lambda\left[\frac{1}{1+\alpha\lambda}[\hat{z} - \alpha\hat{m} - (1-\alpha)\hat{\tau}]\right]\right\} - 2\delta\hat{z} = 0. \tag{A.17}$$

The world demand disturbance does not appear in expressions for differences between German and French variables since it affects both countries in the same way.

Equations (A.11) and (A.17) can be solved for z^G and z^F to obtain

$$z^G = \frac{\rho}{\gamma}\tilde{m} - \frac{\mu}{\gamma}\tilde{\tau} - \frac{2}{\gamma}u - \frac{1-\alpha}{2[\lambda(1-\alpha) + 2\delta(1+\alpha\lambda)]}[\hat{m} - (1+\lambda)\hat{\tau}]; \quad (A.18G)$$

$$z^F = \frac{\rho}{\gamma}\tilde{m} - \frac{\mu}{\gamma}\tilde{\tau} - \frac{2}{\gamma}u + \frac{1-\alpha}{2[\lambda(1-\alpha) + 2\delta(1+\alpha\lambda)]}[\hat{m} - (1+\lambda)\hat{\tau}]. \quad (A.18F)$$

Subtracting (A.18F) from (A.18G) gives the reduced form for the FF-DM real exchange rate:

$$\hat{z} = -\frac{1-\alpha}{\lambda(1-\alpha) + 2\delta(1+\alpha\lambda)}[\hat{m} - (1+\lambda)\hat{\tau}]. \quad (A.19)$$

If m^G increases, the FF tends to appreciate with respect to the DM, further weakening the DM relative to the dollar. Thus, the model captures the so-called dollar-DM polarization, with European currencies other than the DM strengthening with respect to the German currency when the latter weakens against the dollar.[65]

Plugging (A.11) into (A.9) gives the reduced form for the U.S.-Europe nominal interest differential:

$$\tilde{i} = -\varphi\tilde{m} + \upsilon\tilde{\tau} + 2\kappa u, \quad (A.20)$$

where $\varphi = \dfrac{\rho + \alpha\gamma}{\gamma(1+\alpha\lambda)} > 0; \quad \upsilon = \dfrac{\mu - \gamma(1-\alpha)}{\gamma(1+\alpha\lambda)} > 0 \Leftrightarrow \mu > \gamma(1-\alpha);$

$$\kappa = \frac{1}{\gamma(1+\alpha\lambda)} > 0.$$

Together with the uncovered interest parity conditions, (A.20) implies the reduced form for the nominal exchange rate between the dollar and the European currency:

$$\tilde{e} = \varphi\tilde{m} - \upsilon\tilde{\tau} - 2\kappa u. \quad (A.21)$$

A monetary expansion in the U.S. causes the dollar to depreciate against the European currency.

Plugging the reduced form for the FF-DM real exchange rate into (A.16), we obtain the reduced form for the FF-DM nominal rate:

$$\hat{e} = -\phi\hat{m} + \xi\hat{\tau}, \quad (A.22)$$

where $\phi = \dfrac{1-\alpha}{1+\alpha\lambda}\dfrac{1}{\lambda(1-\alpha)+2\delta(1+\alpha\lambda)} + \dfrac{\alpha}{1+\alpha\lambda};$

$$\xi = \frac{(1+\lambda)(1-\alpha)}{1+\alpha\lambda}\frac{1}{\lambda(1-\alpha)+2\delta(1+\alpha\lambda)} - \frac{1-\alpha}{1+\alpha\lambda}.$$

Holding the German money supply and taxation constant, a higher money supply in France depreciates the FF against the DM. The same effect is produced by an increased taxation in France if $\xi < 0$.

To find reduced form equations for interest rates, it is useful to use Aoki's technique of reasoning in terms of averages and differences. Define the world nominal and real interest rates as averages of the U.S. and (aggregate) European values:

$$i^W = \frac{1}{2}(i^{US} + i); \tag{A.23}$$

$$r^W = \frac{1}{2}(r^{US} + \bar{r}). \tag{A.24}$$

We know that $\tilde{r} = -(1-2\beta)\bar{z}$. Also, $i = 2i^W - i^{US}$. Plugging this into $\tilde{\imath} = -\bar{e}$ and rearranging, we have

$$i^{US} = i^W - \frac{1}{2}\bar{e}. \tag{A.25}$$

Using (A.23), we find

$$i = i^W + \frac{1}{2}\bar{e}. \tag{A.26}$$

Substituting $\bar{r} = 2r^W - r^{US}$ into $\tilde{r} = -(1-2\beta)\bar{z}$ and rearranging:

$$r^{US} = r^W - \frac{1}{2}(1-2\beta)\bar{z}. \tag{A.27}$$

Given (A.24), we have

$$\bar{r} = r^W + \frac{1}{2}(1-2\beta)\bar{z}. \tag{A.28}$$

Imposing the no-speculative-bubble condition on the world consumer price index:

$$r^W = i^W + q^W. \tag{A.29}$$

Since real exchange-rate movements cancel on a world scale, the world CPI coincides with the world PPI:

$$q^W = \frac{1}{2}[p^{US} + \beta\bar{z} + \frac{1}{2}p^G - \frac{1}{2}\beta z^G - \frac{1}{4}(1-\beta)\hat{z} + \frac{1}{2}p^F - \frac{1}{2}\beta z^F + \frac{1}{4}(1-\beta)\hat{z}]$$

$$= \frac{1}{2}(p^{US} + \bar{p}) = p^W. \tag{A.30}$$

Thus, (19) yields

$$q^W = p^W = \frac{1}{2}[\alpha m^{US} + (1-\alpha)\tau^{US} + \alpha\lambda i^{US} + \alpha\bar{m} + (1-\alpha)\bar{\tau} + \alpha\lambda\bar{i} + 2x]. \tag{A.31}$$

Or

$$q^W = p^W = \alpha m^W + (1-\alpha)\tau^W + \alpha\lambda i^W + x. \tag{A.32}$$

Plugging this result into (A.29):

$$r^W = (1 + \alpha\lambda)i^W + \alpha m^W + (1-\alpha)\tau^W + x. \tag{A.33}$$

World interest rates are obtained by summing $(8US, G, F)$ and dividing by two:

$$y^{US} + \bar{y} = \varepsilon y^{US} + \varepsilon\bar{y} - v(r^{US} + \bar{r}) + g^{US} + \bar{g}. \tag{A.34}$$

This can be rewritten as

$$(1 - \varepsilon)y^W = -vr^W + g^W, \tag{A.35}$$

and solved for the world real interest rate:

$$r^W = \frac{1}{v}g^W - \frac{1-\varepsilon}{v}y^W. \tag{A.36}$$

Observing that

$$y^W = (1-\alpha)n^W - x, \quad n^W = m^W - \tau^W + \lambda i^W, \text{ and } g^W = \tau^W,$$

(A.36) can be rewritten as

$$r^W = \frac{1}{v}\tau^W - \frac{1-\varepsilon}{v}(1-\alpha)(m^W - \tau^W + \lambda i^W) + \frac{1-\varepsilon}{v}x. \tag{A.37}$$

Finally, equating the right-hand sides of (A.33) and (A.37) and solving for i^W, we have

$$i^W = -\frac{\chi}{\vartheta}m^W + \frac{\sigma}{\vartheta}\tau^W - \frac{\varsigma}{\vartheta}x, \tag{A.38}$$

where $\chi = \alpha + \dfrac{(1-\alpha)(1-\varepsilon)}{\nu} > 0;$ $\sigma = \dfrac{1}{\nu} - 1 + \alpha + \dfrac{(1-\alpha)(1-\varepsilon)}{\nu} > 0;$

$\varsigma = 1 - \dfrac{1-\varepsilon}{\nu} > 0 \Leftrightarrow \varepsilon + \nu > 1;$ $\vartheta = 1 + \alpha\lambda + \dfrac{\lambda(1-\alpha)(1-\varepsilon)}{\nu} > 0.$

Since $\chi > 0$, an increase in the world money supply leads to a lower world nominal interest rate. An increase in world public expenditure induces a higher world nominal interest rate.

Substituting (A.38) and (A.21) into (A.25) and (A.26), we have the reduced forms for the U.S. and the "European" nominal interest rates:[66]

$$i^{US} = -\frac{\chi + \varphi\vartheta}{2\vartheta}\,m^{US} + \frac{\varphi\vartheta - \chi}{2\vartheta}\,\bar{m} + \frac{\sigma + \upsilon\vartheta}{2\vartheta}\,\tau^{US} + \frac{\sigma - \upsilon\vartheta}{2\vartheta}\,\bar{\tau} + \kappa u - \frac{\varsigma}{\vartheta}\,x;$$

(A.39)

$$\bar{i} = -\frac{\chi + \varphi\vartheta}{2\vartheta}\,\bar{m} + \frac{\varphi\vartheta - \chi}{2\vartheta}\,m^{US} + \frac{\sigma + \upsilon\vartheta}{2\vartheta}\,\bar{\tau} + \frac{\sigma - \upsilon\vartheta}{2\vartheta}\,\tau^{US} - \kappa u - \frac{\varsigma}{\vartheta}\,x,$$

(A.40)

where

$$\frac{\chi + \varphi\vartheta}{2\vartheta} > 0; \quad \frac{\varphi\vartheta - \chi}{2\vartheta} > 0 \Leftrightarrow \chi < \varphi\vartheta; \quad \frac{\sigma + \upsilon\vartheta}{2\vartheta} > 0; \quad \frac{\sigma - \upsilon\vartheta}{2\vartheta} > 0 \Leftrightarrow \sigma > \upsilon\vartheta.$$

In order to find reduced forms for the German and French nominal interest rates, observe that the uncovered interest parity conditions and (A.22) imply

$$\hat{i} = \hat{e} = -\phi\hat{m} + \xi\hat{\tau}.$$

(A.41)

Equation (A.41) provides the reduced form for the FF-DM nominal exchange rate.[67]

Equation (A.40) and (A.41) allow us to obtain reduced forms for German and French nominal interest rates:

$$i^{G} = -\frac{\chi + \varphi\vartheta}{2\vartheta}\,\bar{m} + \frac{\varphi\vartheta - \chi}{2\vartheta}\,m^{US} + \frac{\sigma + \upsilon\vartheta}{2\vartheta}\,\bar{\tau} + \frac{\sigma - \upsilon\vartheta}{2\vartheta}\,\tau^{US}$$

$$-\frac{\phi}{2}\,\hat{m} + \frac{\xi}{2}\,\hat{\tau} - \kappa u - \frac{\varsigma}{\vartheta}\,x;$$

(A.42)

$$i^{F} = -\frac{\chi + \varphi\vartheta}{2\vartheta}\,\bar{m} + \frac{\varphi\vartheta - \chi}{2\vartheta}\,m^{US} + \frac{\sigma + \upsilon\vartheta}{2\vartheta}\,\bar{\tau} + \frac{\sigma - \upsilon\vartheta}{2\vartheta}\,\tau^{US}$$

$$+\frac{\phi}{2}\,\hat{m} - \frac{\xi}{2}\,\hat{\tau} - \kappa u - \frac{\varsigma}{\vartheta}\,x.$$

(A.43)

With these reduced forms for nominal interest rates, we can derive reduced forms for employment and CPI in the United States, Germany, and France. Using (18) and (19), and the reduced forms for the real exchange rates, some algebra allows us to obtain:

$$q^{US} = \left[\alpha + \frac{\beta\rho}{\gamma} - \frac{\alpha\lambda(\chi + \varphi\vartheta)}{2\vartheta}\right]m^{US} - \left[\frac{\beta\rho}{\gamma} - \frac{\alpha\lambda(\varphi\vartheta - \chi)}{2\vartheta}\right]\bar{m}$$

$$+ \left[1 - \alpha - \frac{\beta\mu}{\gamma} + \frac{\alpha\lambda(\sigma + \upsilon\vartheta)}{2\vartheta}\right]\tau^{US} + \left[\frac{\beta\mu}{\gamma} + \frac{\alpha\lambda(\sigma - \upsilon\vartheta)}{2\vartheta}\right]\bar{\tau}$$

$$+ \left(\alpha\lambda\kappa - \frac{2\beta}{\gamma}\right)u + \left(1 - \frac{\alpha\lambda\varsigma}{\vartheta}\right)x$$

$$= Am^{US} - B\frac{m^G + m^F}{2} + E\tau^{US} + \Gamma\frac{\tau^G + \tau^F}{2} + Ku + Hx; \qquad (A.44)$$

$$n^{US} = \left[1 - \frac{\lambda(\chi + \varphi\vartheta)}{2\vartheta}\right]m^{US} + \frac{\lambda(\varphi\vartheta - \chi)}{2\vartheta}\bar{m} - \left[1 - \frac{\lambda(\sigma + \upsilon\vartheta)}{2\vartheta}\right]\tau^{US}$$

$$+ \frac{\lambda(\sigma - \upsilon\vartheta)}{2\vartheta}\bar{\tau} + \lambda\kappa u - \frac{\lambda\varsigma}{\vartheta}x$$

$$= (1 - \lambda\Lambda)m^{US} + \lambda\Theta\frac{m^G + m^F}{2} - (1 - \lambda\Omega)\tau^{US}$$

$$+ \lambda\Psi\frac{\tau^G + \tau^F}{2} + \Phi u + \Sigma x; \qquad (A.45)$$

$$q^G = \alpha m^G + (A - \alpha)\frac{m^G + m^F}{2} - Bm^{US} + (1 - \alpha)\tau^G$$

$$+ [E - (1 - \alpha)]\frac{\tau^G + \tau^F}{2} + \Gamma\tau^{US} + M(m^F - m^G)$$

$$- N(\tau^F - \tau^G) - Ku + Hx; \qquad (A.46)$$

$$n^G = m^G - \lambda\Lambda\frac{m^G + m^F}{2} + \lambda\Theta\, m^{US} - \tau^G + \lambda\Omega\frac{\tau^G + \tau^F}{2}$$

$$+ \lambda\Psi\tau^{US} + \lambda O(m^F - m^G) - \lambda Z(\tau^F - \tau^G) - \Phi u - \Sigma x; \qquad (A.47)$$

$$q^F = \alpha m^F + (A - \alpha)\frac{m^G + m^F}{2} - Bm^{US} + (1 - \alpha)\tau^F$$

$$+ [E - (1 - \alpha)]\frac{\tau^G + \tau^F}{2} + \Gamma\tau^{US} - M(m^F - m^G)$$

$$+ N(\tau^F - \tau^G) - Ku + Hx; \tag{A.48}$$

$$n^F = m^F - \lambda\Lambda\frac{m^G + m^F}{2} + \lambda\Theta\, m^{US} - \tau^F + \lambda\Omega\frac{\tau^G + \tau^F}{2}$$

$$+ \lambda\Psi\tau^{US} - \lambda O(m^F - m^G) + \lambda Z(\tau^F - \tau^G) - \Phi u - \Sigma x; \tag{A.49}$$

where M, N, O, and Z are defined by

$$M = \frac{\alpha\lambda\phi}{2} - \frac{1 - \alpha}{2[\lambda(1 - \alpha) + 2\delta(1 + \alpha\lambda)]};$$

$$N = \frac{\alpha\lambda\xi}{2} - \frac{(1 + \lambda)(1 - \alpha)}{2[\lambda(1 - \alpha) + 2\delta(1 + \alpha\lambda)]};$$

$$O = \frac{\phi}{2};$$

$$Z = \frac{\xi}{2}.$$

Summing the reduced-form equations for German and French variables and dividing by two, we obtain the reduced forms for European variables (which are symmetric to the reduced form equation for the U.S. variables). When we sum these reduced form equations, the intra-European cross-country externalities cancel.

Appendix B: The Keynesian World

In the Keynesian-case, government spending g is financed with lump-sum taxes, so that the τ-term in equation (2) cancels. The solution procedure of the model under flexible exchange rates is exactly as in appendix A. Here we highlight some of the consequences of having nondistortionary taxation and present the main reduced forms for the cases of flexible exchange rates, EMS, and EMU.

Equations (18) and (19) in the text become

$$n^j = m^j + \lambda i^j, \tag{B.1}$$

$$p^j = \alpha n^j + x \qquad j = US, G, F. \tag{B.2}$$

The reduced form for $\bar{z} = (z^G + z^F)/2$ is now

$$\bar{z} = \frac{\rho}{\gamma}\tilde{m} - \frac{2\eta - 1}{\gamma}\tilde{g} - \frac{2}{\gamma}u, \tag{B.3}$$

where γ and ρ are as above and $\eta > 1/2$ by assumption. z^G and z^F become

$$z^G = \frac{\rho}{\gamma}\tilde{m} - \frac{2\eta - 1}{\gamma}\tilde{g} - \frac{2}{\gamma}u - \frac{1-\alpha}{2[\lambda(1-\alpha) + 2\delta(1+\alpha\lambda)]}\hat{m}; \tag{B.4G}$$

$$z^F = \frac{\rho}{\gamma}\tilde{m} - \frac{2\eta - 1}{\gamma}\tilde{g} - \frac{2}{\gamma}u + \frac{1-\alpha}{2[\lambda(1-\alpha) + 2\delta(1+\alpha\lambda)]}\hat{m}. \tag{B.4F}$$

As a result, the reduced form for the FF-DM real exchange rate is

$$\hat{z} = -\frac{1-\alpha}{\lambda(1-\alpha) + 2\delta(1+\alpha\lambda)}\hat{m}. \tag{B.5}$$

Having removed the distortionary effect of taxes on domestic PPIs implies that fiscal policies do not affect the intra-European exchange rate. This is because the pattern of government spending is identical across European countries. Instead, asymmetry in the pattern of government spending across the Atlantic ensures that fiscal policies do affect the transatlantic exchange rates.

The U.S.-Europe nominal interest differential becomes

$$\tilde{i} = -\varphi\tilde{m} + v'\tilde{g} + 2\kappa u, \tag{B.6}$$

where φ and κ are defined above and

$$v' = \frac{2\eta - 1}{\gamma(1+\alpha\lambda)} > 0.$$

Hence

$$\bar{e} = \varphi\tilde{m} - v'\tilde{g} - 2\kappa u. \tag{B.7}$$

The FF-DM nominal rate does not depend on fiscal policies:

$$\hat{e} = -\phi\hat{m}; \tag{B.8}$$

where ϕ is unchanged.

Going through the same steps as before, we obtain the following reduced form for the world nominal interest rate:

$$i^W = -\frac{\chi}{\vartheta} m^W + \frac{1}{\vartheta v} g^W - \frac{\varsigma}{\vartheta} x, \tag{B.9}$$

where the new parameters are as in appendix A.

Hence, the reduced forms for the United States, German, and French nominal interest rates are

$$i^{US} = -\frac{\chi + \varphi\vartheta}{2\vartheta} m^{US} + \frac{\varphi\vartheta - \chi}{2\vartheta} \bar{m} + \frac{1 - v'\vartheta v}{2\vartheta v} g^{US} + \frac{1 + v'\vartheta v}{2\vartheta v} \bar{g} + \kappa u - \frac{\varsigma}{\vartheta} x; \tag{B.10}$$

$$i^G = -\frac{\chi + \varphi\vartheta}{2\vartheta} \bar{m} + \frac{\varphi\vartheta - \chi}{2\vartheta} m^{US} + \frac{1 - v'\vartheta v}{2\vartheta v} \bar{g} + \frac{1 + v'\vartheta v}{2\vartheta v} g^{US}$$

$$- \frac{\phi}{2} \hat{m} - \kappa u - \frac{\varsigma}{\vartheta} x; \tag{B.11}$$

$$i^F = -\frac{\chi + \varphi\vartheta}{2\vartheta} \bar{m} + \frac{\varphi\vartheta - \chi}{2\vartheta} m^{US} + \frac{1 - v'\vartheta v}{2\vartheta v} \bar{g} + \frac{1 + v'\vartheta v}{2\vartheta v} g^{US}$$

$$+ \frac{\phi}{2} \hat{m} - \kappa u - \frac{\varsigma}{\vartheta} x. \tag{B.12}$$

Fiscal policies do not affect the intra-European exchange rate. As a consequence, differences in European fiscal policies no longer affect European interest rates.

With these reduced forms for nominal interest rates, we can derive reduced forms for employment and CPI in the United States, Germany, and France. Using (B.1) and (B.2) and the reduced forms for the real exchange rates, some algebra allows us to obtain:

$$q^{US} = \left[\alpha + \frac{\beta\rho}{\gamma} - \frac{\alpha\lambda(\chi + \varphi\vartheta)}{2\vartheta} \right] m^{US} - \left[\frac{\beta\rho}{\gamma} - \frac{\alpha\lambda(\varphi\vartheta - \chi)}{2\vartheta} \right] \bar{m}$$

$$+ \left[\frac{\alpha\lambda(1 - v'\vartheta v)}{2\vartheta v} - \frac{\beta(2\eta - 1)}{\gamma} \right] g^{US} + \left[\frac{\alpha\lambda(1 + v'\vartheta v)}{2\vartheta v} + \frac{\beta(2\eta - 1)}{\gamma} \right] \bar{g}$$

$$+ \left(\alpha\lambda\kappa - \frac{2\beta}{\gamma} \right) u + \left(1 - \frac{\alpha\lambda\varsigma}{\vartheta} \right) x$$

$$= Am^{US} - B\frac{m^G + m^F}{2} + E'g^{US} + \Gamma'\frac{g^G + g^F}{2} + Ku + Hx; \tag{B.13}$$

$$n^{US} = \left[1 - \frac{\lambda(\chi + \varphi\vartheta)}{2\vartheta}\right]m^{US} + \frac{\lambda(\varphi\vartheta - \chi)}{2\vartheta}\bar{m} + \frac{\lambda(1 - v'\vartheta v)}{2\vartheta v}g^{US}$$

$$+ \frac{\lambda(1 + v'\vartheta v)}{2\vartheta v}\bar{g} + \lambda\kappa u - \frac{\lambda\varsigma}{\vartheta}x$$

$$= (1 - \lambda\Lambda)m^{US} + \lambda\Theta\frac{m^G + m^F}{2} + \lambda\Omega'g^{US}$$ (B.14)

$$+ \lambda\Psi'\frac{g^G + g^F}{2} + \Phi u - \Sigma x;$$

$$q^G = \alpha m^G + (A - \alpha)\frac{m^G + m^F}{2} - Bm^{US} + E'\frac{g^G + g^F}{2}$$

$$+ \Gamma'g^{US} + M(m^F - m^G) - Ku + Hx;$$ (B.15)

$$n^G = m^G - \lambda\Lambda\frac{m^G + m^F}{2} + \lambda\Theta m^{US} + \lambda\Omega'\frac{g^G + g^F}{2}$$

$$+ \lambda\Psi'g^{US} + \lambda O(m^F - m^G) - \Phi u - \Sigma x;$$ (B.16)

$$q^F = \alpha m^F + (A - \alpha)\frac{m^G + m^F}{2} - Bm^{US} + E'\frac{g^G + g^F}{2}$$

$$+ \Gamma'g^{US} - M(m^F - m^G) - Ku + Hx;$$ (B.17)

$$n^F = m^F - \lambda\Lambda\frac{m^G + m^F}{2} + \lambda\Theta m^{US} + \lambda\Omega'\frac{g^G + g^F}{2}$$

$$+ \lambda\Psi'g^{US} - \lambda O(m^F - m^G) - \Phi u - \Sigma x.$$ (B.18)

The parameters defining the impact of monetary policies on endogenous variables are unchanged relative to the case of anti-Keynesian fiscal policies. Instead, having removed the distortionary effect of taxation affects the parameters defining the impact of fiscal policies and cancels the impact of differences in European fiscal policies on German and French variables.

Solution of the model under the EMS regime follows the same steps as in the text. The EMS-constraint now implies

$$m^F = m^G + \frac{1}{\phi}(e^G - e^F).$$ (B.19)

Plugging this equation into the previous reduced forms gives

$$q^{US} = Am^{US} - Bm^{G} - \frac{B}{2\phi}(e^{G} - e^{F}) + E'g^{US} + \Gamma'\frac{g^{G} + g^{F}}{2} + Ku + Hx;$$

$$(B.20)$$

$$n^{US} = (1 - \lambda\Lambda)m^{US} + \lambda\Theta m^{G} + \frac{\lambda\Theta}{2\phi}(e^{G} - e^{F}) + \lambda\Omega'g^{US}$$

$$+ \Lambda\Psi'\frac{g^{G} + g^{F}}{2} + \Phi u - \Sigma x; \qquad (B.21)$$

$$q^{G} = Am^{G} - Bm^{US} + \left(\frac{A - \alpha}{2\phi} + \frac{M}{\phi}\right)(e^{G} - e^{F}) + E'\frac{g^{G} + g^{F}}{2}$$

$$+ \Gamma'g^{US} - Ku + Hx; \qquad (B.22)$$

$$n^{G} = (1 - \lambda\Lambda)m^{G} + \lambda\Theta m^{US} + \frac{\lambda}{2}\left(1 - \frac{\Lambda}{\phi}\right)(e^{G} - e^{F})$$

$$+ \lambda\Omega'\frac{g^{G} + g^{F}}{2} + \lambda\Psi'g^{US} - \Phi u - \Sigma x; \qquad (B.23)$$

$$q^{F} = Am^{G} - Bm^{US} + \left(\frac{A + \alpha}{2\phi} - \frac{M}{\phi}\right)(e^{G} - e^{F}) + E'\frac{g^{G} + g^{F}}{2}$$

$$+ \Gamma'g^{US} - Ku + Hx; \qquad (B.24)$$

$$n^{F} = (1 - \lambda\Lambda)m^{G} + \lambda\Theta m^{US} + \left[\frac{1}{\phi} - \frac{\lambda}{2}\left(1 + \frac{\Lambda}{\phi}\right)\right](e^{G} - e^{F})$$

$$(B.25)$$

$$+ \lambda\Omega'\frac{g^{G} + g^{F}}{2} + \lambda\Psi'g^{US} - \Phi u - \Sigma x.$$

The solution under EMU is extremely simple in the Keynesian world. $(e^{G} - e^{F}) = 0$ implies the constraint $m^{G} = m^{F}$. Once this is taken into account, not only are q^{G} and q^{F} equalized ex ante under EMU, but also $n^{G} = n^{F} = n^{Eu}$. Reduced forms for U.S. variables become

$$q^{US} = Am^{US} - Bm^{Eu} + E'g^{US} + \Gamma'\frac{g^{G} + g^{F}}{2} + Ku + Hx; \qquad (B.26)$$

$$n^{US} = (1 - \lambda\Lambda)m^{US} + \lambda\Theta m^{Eu} + \lambda\Omega'g^{US} + \lambda\Psi'\frac{g^{G} + g^{F}}{2} + \Phi u - \Sigma x.$$

$$(B.27)$$

Reduced forms for q^{Eu} and n^{Eu} can be easily recovered by symmetry between the United States and Europe. Note that $n^G = n^F = n^{Eu}$ ex ante does not imply the absence of intra-European fiscal externalities. These come indirectly through the impact of European fiscal policies on transatlantic exchange rates.

Notes

1. In this chapter we follow the literature on strategic aspects of monetary policy in Europe, which focuses on interactions between the Bundesbank and other European central banks. In our model, the Bank of France should be thought of as representing these other central banks. European central banks will become operating arms of the ECB with the advent of Stage III. We abstract from interactions between the EMU insiders and outsiders (a topic that is the subject of Ghironi and Giavazzi 1997b). Similarly, the Federal Reserve should be thought of as representative of non-EU central banks generally.

2. Jensen (1991) presents a two-country model of monetary and fiscal policy interactions. We, in contrast, consider three countries. In addition, our model differs in other respects described below.

3. See, for example, Giavazzi and Pagano (1990b), Bertola and Drazen (1993), and International Monetary Fund (1995).

4. An effect that is not formally captured in our model.

5. Respectively, contractionary and expansionary fiscal contractions.

6. In this chapter, policy coordination and cooperation both mean joint minimization of the players' loss functions.

7. Under the assumption that fiscal policy has anti-Keynesian effects, cutting taxes and public spending is expansionary and stabilizes prices, for reasons we elaborate below.

8. To capture the notion of central bank independence, we assume that each country's central bank and fiscal authority play Nash against one another. Obviously, there is no cooperation between the central bank in one country and any fiscal authority in others.

9. Because of this, we do not claim too much for their generality. But we would argue that this model is a natural point of departure for thinking about these issues.

10. This allows a global aggregate-supply disturbance to affect not just inflation but also output and employment. In addition, the dependence of money-market equilibrium on the interest rate means that stabilizing nominal exchange rates does not automatically stabilize real exchange rates (in contrast to Canzoneri and Henderson 1991). While in their model, employment depends only on own-country money supply, adding interest-rate linkages allows foreign money supplies to affect domestic employment as well.

11. Except in the case of interest rates, public expenditures and taxes. Time subscripts are dropped where possible.

12. Using uppercase letters to denote anti-logs, firms maximize $profit = (1 - \tau)PY - WN$, subject to $Y = N^{1-\alpha}/X$. Each firm is a price taker in the output and in the labor market and is taxed on its total revenues. The first-order condition for maximization with respect to N is $(1 - \tau)P(1 - \alpha)N^{-\alpha}/X = W$. Taking logs, approximating $ln(1 - \tau)$ with $-\tau$, and omitting unimportant constants, we obtain equation (2).

13. We are implicitly assuming that fiscal policies are budget balancing. In the Keynesian case of Section III, we eliminate the tax term from this equation, assuming instead that all taxes are lump sum. In addition, public expenditure is in logs under the assumptions of that case.

14. The increase in demand due to a real depreciation depends on two factors: the common elasticity parameter δ and the size of the country with respect to whose currency the domestic currency is depreciating. Thus, for example, if the deutsche mark depreciates against the dollar, the increase in demand for German goods is twice as much as it would be were the deutsche mark depreciating against the franc, reflecting the fact that the U.S. economy is twice the French one in our model and that, under perfect mobility of goods, "depreciation against a larger market is more profitable." Alternatively, one could think of demand for European goods being more sensitive to changes in the transatlantic real exchange rates than in the intra-European ones because of the characteristics of the goods that are traded and because of the presence of impediments to perfect mobility of goods across the Atlantic.

15. The random disturbance u is identically and independently distributed with zero mean and can shift the world demand from European to U.S. goods.

16. We assume $\eta > 1/2$ to capture the fact that each government is likely to devote a greater fraction of its expenditure to goods produced in its own region. Note that the French and German governments are assumed to have identical spending propensities. This assumption may be justified by noting that the Maastricht Treaty prohibits discrimination in public procurement.

17. If any of these components increases, the nominal wage increases as well, lowering employment. If expected taxation increases, the required nominal wage declines since taxation hits the firms' revenues and does not affect labor income. Higher taxation reduces labor demand by firms; the higher the weight ω of employment in the unions' loss functions, the greater will be the reduction in the nominal wages in response to the decreased labor demand.

18. Zero values for the authorities' instruments are optimal in the absence of disturbances. In Rogoff's (1985) terminology, static expectations are rational.

19. Equation (19) can be rewritten as $p^j = \alpha m^j + (1 - \alpha)\tau^j + \alpha\lambda i^j + x$. From this expression, we see that, leaving aside indirect effects through changes in the nominal interest rate, if $\alpha < 1/2$, fiscal policy has a larger direct impact on the producer price level than monetary policy does. Equation (18) shows that both monetary and fiscal policy have a direct one-to-one impact on employment. As we shall see below, the size of the impact of monetary policy on employment and of fiscal policy on prices is important to our results. In the Keynesian world, the τ-terms disappear from these equations, so that fiscal policy affects employment and producer prices only through changes in the nominal interest rate.

20. The values that we assign to the structural parameters are arbitrary but consistent with intuition and observation. ε can be interpreted as the consumers' marginal propensity to consume out of current income, and a value of 0.8 for this parameter does not seem too far from reality. $a = 0.9$ signals that central banks care much more about inflation that about unemployment in their loss functions, while $b_1 = 0.2$ and $b_2 = 0.1$ signal that governments care more about employment than about inflation but the degree of activism in managing fiscal policy is limited. This last assumption is consistent with the relative rigidity of fiscal policymaking. Ghironi and Giavazzi (1997b) also consider cases in which fiscal activism for stabilization purposes is removed, arguing that this may be consistent with the presence of a strict "fiscal stability pact" in Europe.

21. In figures 11.1 and 11.2, the trade-offs are centered on the disequilibrium point to which the economies are shifted by a negative productivity shock that causes inflation and unemployment.

22. The trade-off faced by a central bank under flexible exchange rates becomes steeper as the size of the economy for which the central bank sets its instrument declines. Germany and France being identical and half the size of the U.S. economy, the Bundesbank and the Bank of France face identical trade-offs that are more favorable than the Fed's.

23. Recall that a decrease in τ is expansionary, raising employment and stabilizing the CPI. As a consequence, the trade-offs faced by the fiscal policymakers are negatively sloped. Starting from the combination of inflation and unemployment induced by a negative supply shock, fiscal policy actually moves both variables in the desired direction.

24. What we have in mind is the choice of the central parity between the two European currencies rather than the choice of the daily exchange rate. In this sense, assuming that realignments are noncooperative—as we are going to do —may be too strong, as realignments are a matter of common discussion under the EMS. However, we believe that the way cooperation is modeled in this chapter also goes beyond what was observed.

25. The reduced-form parameters determining the U.S. authorities' trade-offs are independent of the relative size of the two European countries (Ghironi and Giavazzi 1997b). If Europe consisted of one large country symmetric to the United States and a small open economy with no impact abroad, intra-European exchange-rate arrangements would have no implications for the United States. By implication, since changes in the relative size of European countries do not affect the relevant parameters, the nature of the intra-EU regime must have no impact on U.S. trade-offs also when European countries are identical.

26. The trade-offs are constraints subject to which policymakers optimize their objective functions. The Bank of France's trade-off does not change across regimes because, even if the instrument controlled by the French central bank changes, there is no change in the structural characteristics that determine the trade-off facing the central bank. In particular, there is no change in the size of the economy for which the French authority sets its instrument. This is different from the situation facing the Bundesbank, which now sets the money supply for all of Europe.

27. Under both floating and the EMS, the German and the French governments set taxes only for the domestic economy. But as we move from one intra-European exchange-rate arrangement to another, the structural features of the economies that determine the governments' trade-offs *are* affected. Under flexible rates, the FF-DM exchange rate is endogenous and taxes affect the endogenous variables through their direct supply-and demand-side impacts. But changes in the exchange rate also feed back through prices and employment, providing an *indirect* channel for fiscal impulses. With the transition from floating to the EMS, the French money supply becomes endogenous with respect to not just the German money supply but also both European governments' policies. Instead of having an *indirect* effect on prices and employment via the exchange rate, another *direct* channel for fiscal impulses is added through what was the direct impact of m^F on the economies. Since the French money supply has a larger impact on the French economy under flexible rates, this new channel of direct transmission of fiscal policies is more effective for the French economy, which explains why the French government's trade-off improves more with the transition from flexible rates to the EMS.

28. Since both set the money supply for the whole of Europe. The ECB's trade-off is therefore the same as that facing the Fed.

29. This can be seen from equation (29). Under our assumptions, it is $\phi > 0$ and $\xi < 0$. Recall also note 27.

30. European governments' trade-offs follow from the symmetry of the EMU regime. Consider the change from flexible exchange rates to symmetrically fixed rates under EMU. The endogeneity constraint on monetary policy with respect to taxation is a constraint on the difference of m^G and m^F rather than m^F alone. As a consequence, the improvement in government trade-offs is split evenly between France and Germany: the French government's trade-off does not improve as much as when going from flexible rates to the EMS and the German government's trade-off is better than in that case.

31. Because nominal exchange-rate stability does not imply real exchange-rate stability, in the absence of fiscal cooperation European governments still have an incentive to export unemployment to the United States (via nominal and real movements of the European currencies with respect to the dollar) and to one another (via real FF-DM exchange-rate movements). The United States has a similar incentive to export unemployment.

32. Reduced forms for the French CPI and employment can be obtained by relabeling the corresponding German equations. We report approximate values of the reduced-form parameters—here as in the Keynesian case examined later. Details on the restrictions that hold across parameters are available upon request.

33. The absence of intra-European cooperation is necessary for the asymmetry. If the Bundesbank and the Bank of France cooperated with one another and the same was true of the two European governments, they would act as a single monetary authority and a single government setting instruments for the whole European economy, and different national trade-offs would not induce an asymmetry across the Atlantic.

34. As a result of the policy mix chosen by central banks and governments, European inflation is lower than U.S. inflation, European unemployment higher (the fiscal response only partly offsetting the impact of the monetary contraction on employment because the fiscal authorities pay a cost when changing taxes). The European central banks are better off than the Fed, while both European governments are worse off than the U.S. government. Note that both European currencies depreciate in real terms against the dollar $(z^G + z^F)/2 = -0.0268x$. In appendix A we show that fiscal policies have a larger impact than monetary policies on the U.S.-Europe real exchange rate. Fiscal authorities aim at exporting unemployment via real depreciation, and the impact on the exchange rate of European fiscal expansions dominates that of monetary contractions. But that depreciation is damped by the European central banks' incentive to move along their more favorable trade-offs and to react to its inflationary consequences. Monetary contraction in Europe results in larger employment losses for the two European economies, while the fiscal expansion stabilizes inflation relative to the United States.

35. While the Federal Reserve's optimal reaction to the negative supply shock is less contractionary, the U.S. government's fiscal policy is less expansionary.

36. It is $z^G - z^F = -.0236x$. Note that it is $m^F = -1.6262x$. Although the Bank of France manages to appreciate the franc against the deutsche mark, the fact that the Bundesbank contracts by less causes the French money supply to decrease by less than under flexible rates. There is an analogous result in the Keynesian case.

37. In fact, the real depreciation of the European currencies against the dollar is now given by $(z^G + z^F)/2 = -.0468x$.

38. First-order conditions for the Fed and all three governments remain unchanged. The results for EMU are different from those in Ghironi and Giavazzi (1997b), which distinguishes

EMU insiders and outsiders. Moreover, we allow for the absence of fiscal cooperation in the monetary union, a case not considered by these authors.

39. The ECB's monetary contraction is slightly smaller than the Bundesbank's. It is also less contractionary than those of the French and German central banks under flexible exchange rates for reasons that should be clear.

40. Recall also that, in the EMU scenario, the German and French governments face identical trade-offs. This makes it impossible for them to successfully export unemployment to one another.

41. If for reasons different from those usually invoked to argue that the ECB will be subject to inflationary pressure. Because the ECB faces the same trade-off as the Bundesbank under the EMS, it selects a point on that trade-off closer to the point selected by the Bundesbank under the EMS than to the outcome the Bank of France could achieve.

42. In Eichengreen and Ghironi (1996a) we analyzed political-economy explanations for why Germany might support EMU. The results here provide an *economic* explanation of why the Bundesbank might prefer EMU. As argued by Giavazzi and Giovannini (1989b) (and further explored by Ghironi and Giavazzi 1997a), a managed exchange-rate regime in which peripheral countries are able to export inflation to a core country can survive only so long as the latter is relatively large. In the absence of significant differences in country size and preferences, the core country will prefer a symmetric regime. This would appear to be the increasingly relevant case for Europe. Our results suggest that the political-economy case for EMU may be as important for other countries as for Germany, since the former will no longer enjoy the inflation benefits of an asymmetric regime.

43. The Fed is more contractionary under EMU than under the EMS, since a less active European fiscal stance does less to stabilize U.S. inflation. At the same time, Fed policy is more aggressive than that of the ECB (although this is insufficient to drive U.S. inflation below European levels).

44. Indeed, in all cases, the dollar appreciates in real terms against the European currencies (under EMU, it is: $(z^G + z^F)/2 = -.0495x$) due to the interplay of monetary and fiscal policies, but still U.S. inflation is always higher than in Europe.

45. An alternative, which we do not pursue here, is that the ECB and the Fed bargain over the weights attached to their loss functions.

46. The equilibrium of the monetary-policy game is no longer a Nash equilibrium. This raises the usual implementability problems, which we assume away in what follows. For a survey of the standard reputation arguments on this issue, see Canzoneri and Henderson (1991). The mechanism design approach was first introduced in Persson and Tabellini (1995) and further explored in Morales and Padilla (1995).

47. A decision to establish a system of pegged exchange rates for the industrial countries or a global system of target zones would rest with the Council of Ministers. The Council must act unanimously after consulting with the ECB and attempting to reach a consensus on the compatibility of its decision with price stability. In this case, the Council's decision will bind the ECB.

48. We thus have two equations in two unknowns.

49. Alternatively, consider the comparison with the case where central banks cooperate but fiscal authorities do not. Monetary policy is more contractionary when European fiscal

authorities cooperate but central banks do not (for the reasons described above). Fiscal policies converge to a point between those pursued by the United States and Europe when governments do not cooperate. Neither France nor Germany now cuts taxes as aggressively in an effort to export unemployment to its European neighbor. The U.S. cuts taxes more aggressively to stimulate employment because monetary policy is more contractionary. Strikingly, all three governments and both central banks are worse off than when central banks cooperate but European governments do not. The Fed is worse off because U.S. inflation declines only marginally but unemployment rises significantly. This same rise in American unemployment renders the U.S. government worse off. The European authorities are left worse off because European inflation and unemployment both rise.

50. Regardless of whether or not the Fed and the ECB cooperate.

51. The only authorities that are worse off in an alternative scenario are the European governments in the pre-EMS era: although the outcome in terms of inflation and unemployment in that scenario was more favorable, that outcome was achieved at the cost of more volatile taxation, which kept the European governments' losses above those obtained in the present scenario.

52. In the anti-Keynesian case, European fiscal policies affected the intra-European exchange rate because in addition to changing the demand for European goods, as here, they also affected the supply (through distortionary taxes). Now that the asymmetric supply-side effect has been removed, only the symmetric demand-side effect remains. Note however that European fiscal policies continue to affect the U.S. real exchange rate because of the asymmetries between the United States and the individual European countries.

53. This change in the nature of fiscal policies does not affect the trade-offs facing the central banks. Because fiscal policies do not affect the intra-European exchange rate, changes in the monetary arrangement between European countries no longer affect the trade-off facing governments. All governments' trade-off remains $(\partial q/\partial g)/(\partial n/\partial g) = .0276$. It is positively sloped, fiscal policy having the standard Keynesian effects.

54. In the anti-Keynesian case, a cut in German spending reduced French employment by increasing the supply of German goods, driving down their price, and driving up (appreciating) France's real exchange rate. Now an increase in German spending affects French output mainly by increasing the (German) demand for French goods.

55. It is $m^F = -2.4196x$.

56. Even if it remains less contractionary than the two European central banks under floating, consistent with the changes in incentives due to the different trade-offs facing the monetary authorities.

57. As we show in appendix B, German and French employment is equalized ex ante under EMU (different from the anti-Keynesian case). This is because fiscal policies no longer affect the intra-European exchange rate, removing a distortion in noncooperative fiscal policy-making. Intra-European fiscal externalities still exist due to the impact of European fiscal policies on the U.S./Europe exchange rate, and it is precisely the failure to internalize these employment-creating externalities that causes European fiscal policies to remain less expansionary than U.S. fiscal policy when there is no fiscal cooperation in Europe.

58. The Fed does not share the ECB's desire for European fiscal cooperation. Even if it adopts a more contractionary policy, it cannot fully counteract the inflationary consequences of increased government spending and of the more restrictive policy of the ECB, and its own restrictive policy further aggravates U.S. unemployment.

59. Table 11.12 summarizes the results for the Keynesian case. As expected, EMU coupled with monetary cooperation is first best. In both tables, citizens in Europe and the United States have different views of the second best outcome, Europeans preferring the EMU-no cooperation scenario and Americans favoring EMU coupled with monetary cooperation and intra-European fiscal cooperation. Monetary cooperation with global fiscal cooperation is the worst of all worlds.

60. We make a start at analyzing institutional issues in Eichengreen and Ghironi (1996b).

61. Artis and Gazioglu (1987) analyze the consequences of asymmetries in the wage-setting procedure in a two-country model. Reactions to asymmetric disturbances may be considered, as well as the impact of cross-country differences in the weights attached by policymakers to the targets in their loss functions. We did not consider such asymmetries in order to focus on the impact of strategic interactions in the simplest possible framework.

62. The time frame is another limit of our analysis: monetary and fiscal policy are characterized by different internal and external lags, which we cannot consider in our model. Moreover, a static framework does not allow us to analyze the impact of deficit spending and incomplete pass-through from exchange rates to prices—a commonly observed phenomenon.

63. Summing German and French variables and dividing by two is equivalent to defining "European" variables.

64. Since $\mu > \rho$, fiscal policy always has a greater effect than monetary policy on the U.S.-Europe real exchange rate.

65. Since Germany and France are assumed to be symmetric, U.S. monetary and fiscal policies have no effects on the position of their currencies against each other. Thus, the model captures dollar-DM polarization only when this is caused by German or French economic policies.

66. Plugging (A. 38) into (A.32) gives a reduced form for q^W. The reduced form for the world real interest rate can be found by plugging (A.38) into (A.33). Finally, substituting the reduced form for r^W and (A.17) into (A.27) and (A.28), we obtain reduced-form equations for the U.S. and the "European" real interest rates.

67. If combined with (A.21) and solved for the dollar-DM and dollar-FF nominal exchange rates, it allows us to argue in favor of the presence of a dollar-DM polarization also in nominal terms.

Epilogue: Inconsistent Quartets

International economists regularly refer to the "inconsistent quartet"—to the incompatibility of international capital mobility, pegged exchange rates, monetary autonomy, and free trade. The phrase is frequently invoked in connection with Europe, where the elimination of capital controls by the Single European Act forced governments to choose between stable exchange rates and independent monetary policies. Some go further and argue that this is no choice at all, because exchange rate instability would have a corrosive effect on the freedom of trade within the European Union (EU) and jeopardize the Single Market. Given the difficulty of credibly forswearing monetary autonomy and pegging exchange rates within narrow bands, reconciling free trade and capital mobility in Europe means going all the way to monetary union.

These are controversial propositions. Nearly every link in the causal chain running from the Single Act to monetary unification is challenged by opponents of the European Monetary Union (EMU) project. This makes even the academic literature on European monetary unification contested terrain. Yet modest progress toward a scholarly consensus has resulted from the most recent decade of research. In this final chapter, I summarize the progress made and the questions that remain in the form of a pair of inconsistent quartets.

The first quartet, representing progress made, is comprised of four points that emerge from the academic literature as I have summarized it here.

First, the case for monetary unification must be advanced on political-economy grounds rather than grounds of microeconomic efficiency. While there are efficiency gains from replacing several separate currencies with one, these are likely to be small. Even the European Commission, hardly a disinterested observer, has been forced to acknowledge this fact. This stands in contrast to the Single Market, whose benefits, most economists agree, are certainly large. The political-economy argument for the single currency rests on the importance of avoiding exchange-rate instability and sustaining political support for Europe's internal market, and on the proposition that the only assured way of reaching this goal is by establishing a monetary union. Semifixed exchange rates being intrinsically fragile and easily destabilized by speculative attacks, the only directions for Europe are forward to EMU or backward to floating. And the second option is politically incompatible with the Single Market.

This same logic implies a second point: that the extended transition to monetary union laid out by the framers of the Maastricht Treaty is flawed. The 1992–93 crisis in the European Monetary System (EMS) underscored the difficulty of stabilizing Europe's exchange rates in the face of high capital mobility. In the politicized policymaking environment that is the modern world, any attempt to hold the exchange rate within narrow bands, as the Maastricht Treaty initially required of aspiring candidates for EMU, is easily defeated by speculative attacks, including attacks motivated by self-fulfilling prophecies. The whole point of monetary union is to deliver a degree of currency stability that the attempt to stabilize intra-European exchange rates cannot. It therefore makes no sense to attempt to first achieve a comparable degree of exchange rate and monetary stability before moving to monetary union. The same is true of fiscal policies, which are harder to harmonize before monetary unification (since governments with high debts and deficits must pay an interest rate premium to compensate investors for the possibility of devaluation). If monetary union is to be achieved, Europe will have to take the leap before the nirvana of perfect convergence is reached.

Third, the smoothness of the landing remains uncertain, because Europe is not an optimum currency area. In particular, the EU remains further from this textbook ideal than the United States. Supply and demand disturbances are less symmetric in Europe. Labor mobility and wage flexibility are lower than in America. The EU will therefore find it more difficult to operate a monetary union, especially in its early years. This is not to say that EMU is unwise but that it will not be easy.

Fourth, the imposition of tough budget constraints on governments participating in the monetary union is neither necessary nor desirable. Having given up recourse to an independent monetary response to idiosyncratic shocks, governments will have all the more reason to value their fiscal flexibility. In the early stages of the monetary union, when the European Central Bank is establishing the credibility of its commitment to price stability, automatic fiscal stabilizers will be the only instrument available for coping with macroeconomic shocks. But tight enforcement of the Excessive Deficit Procedure, augmented by a Germanic stability pact, may make this impossible and deactivate Europe's only remaining shock absorbers. It is in any case unnecessary to restrict the fiscal freedom of EU member states on the grounds that the European Central Bank (ECB) must be insulated from the pressure to bail out governments in debt-servicing difficulties, since the Maastricht Treaty already includes a no-bailout rule. That rule is incentive compatible, since national governments continue to collect the bulk of Europe's taxes, and their control of the EU's tax base gives them a third alternative to defaulting and obtaining ECB assistance, namely using their own tax instruments to solve their fiscal problems. Knowledge of this fact should allow the ECB to resist pressure for a bailout. Other concerns about Europe's fiscal policies— that public spending has long been excessive, or that borrowing by one European government drives up interest charges for others—are logically independent of monetary union; using EMU as a pretext for insisting on their solution runs the risk of discrediting the monetary union project.

My second quartet, intended to be complementary rather than incompatible with the first, is made up of four questions still to be answered by researchers.

The first question is how quickly Europe will approach the ideal of an optimum currency area. The European economy will reorganize itself in response to economic and monetary union. As intra-European exchange rates are fixed and then disappear, policymakers will face new constraints, market participants new opportunities. Pensions will become portable and immigrant networks will be established, eventually rendering Europe's labor more mobile. Workers will realize that they cannot be saved from the consequences of excessive wage demands by a depreciation of the exchange rate that restores the country's competitiveness in international markets, and they will allow wages to grow more flexible and responsive to market conditions. Asymmetric demand shocks caused by erratic national monetary policies will disappear. More generally, one can expect aggregate demand conditions to become more closely harmonized across Europe as the process of economic integration proceeds, much as they are more tightly harmonized across regions of the United States.

How quickly this process will unfold is difficult to say. And a fly in the ointment is the possibility of larger asymmetric shocks if industry reorganizes along regional lines. Exchange risk and regulatory barriers to cross-border trade have prevented European industry from concentrating its activities in a small number of locations and exploiting agglomeration economies. As it begins doing so, industry-specific shocks will become region-specific shocks, and supply and demand disturbances will diverge across Europe's regions.[1] Officials may rue the day when they relinquished their macroeconomic independence. On the other hand, the regions in which particular activities are concentrated may not respect national borders, in which case there will be little advantage to retaining national policy autonomy.

How painful remaining divergences from the ideal of the optimum currency area prove will depend on how much fiscal flexibility governments retain. Will officials be convinced of the credibility of the Maastricht Treaty's no-bailout rule and permit member states to shape national fiscal policies to national needs, or will they insist on rigid application of the Excessive Deficit Procedure, disabling even Europe's automatic stabilizers? And if national governments are prevented from exercising fiscal autonomy, will they insist that the EU carry out the requisite public functions, creating political pressure for an EU-wide system of fiscal federalism?

The second question is how the country composition of the monetary union will evolve. Only a subset of member states will be among its founding members. If other countries that aspire to join are forced to meet harsh entry conditions, a project designed to create a truly integrated Europe may instead produce a permanent split. Countries left outside will find it more difficult to join than did their predecessors if they are required to stabilize their exchange rates against the Euro but receive little support from the ECB. If ECB policies result in a high value of the Euro on foreign exchange markets, their competitive difficulties will be further aggravated. They will have to pay high interest charges on their debts if the markets are uncertain about the willingness of the incumbents to admit additional members, making it even harder for the latter to meet the fiscal preconditions for entry.

Then there is the fact that countries like the United Kingdom may prefer to remain outside. One purpose of monetary union is to prevent intra-EU currency fluctuations from eroding political support for the Single Market. A pound sterling whose foreign exchange value fluctuates against the Euro may not be compatible with this imperative. It is even conceivable that countries that prefer to stay outside the monetary union may ultimately be denied access to the Single Market.

A third question is how EMU will affect the evolution of the international monetary system and the prospects for international monetary cooperation. Will the Euro develop into a serious rival to the dollar as a reserve currency? Or will the dollar's international role be strengthened because the ECB cannot hold Euros in its own reserve portfolio? Will monetary cooperation between Europe, the United States, and Japan grow more or less prevalent?

A final question is how the first post-EMU recession will be handled. The ECB will not be inclined to cut interest rates dramatically or let the Euro fall on the foreign exchange markets, for doing so might be seen as calling into question its commitment to price stability. Member states will have little scope for discretionary tax cuts, since they will have just managed to squeeze into the Maastricht Treaty's fiscal trousers, in most cases with their budget deficits right up against the three-percent limit. The eventual increase in wage flexibility and labor mobility will not yet have arrived. Thus, national governments may be helpless in the face of a global business cycle downturn. They may have no choice but to ride it out.

The options then available to Europe's citizens, to invoke Albert Hirschman's famous triad, will be exit, voice, and loyalty.[2] They may voice their objections to this policy of inaction so stridently that monetary and fiscal policymakers spring into action. Loyalty to the European project may force these constituencies to grin and bear it. Hirshman's last option, exit, is not one that has received much study in the literature on monetary unification.[3] One can imagine hard-currency countries like Germany threatening to leave the monetary union if questions arise about the commitment of the ECB to price stability. One can imagine other countries that attach more importance to employment-friendly policies threatening to do so if Europe's fiscal and monetary authorities disregard their pleas. Technically, exit is easy: the government seeking to leave needs only to resume printing its national currency, at which point the ECB will refuse to convert that currency at par. Politically, however, exit would be expensive; it would violate the Maastricht Treaty and jeopardize the entire web of interstate bargains on which the European enterprise is based. That the idea is so explosive may explain why it has yet to be seriously studied.

Europe's monetary unification project is not without risks. And the EU will not put all these behind it with the advent of Stage III. But EMU also holds out the promise of considerable benefits, especially if one believes that monetary unification is needed to solidify political support for the Single Market. The balance of costs and benefits will depend on how the Maastricht Treaty is implemented and on how market structure and performance respond. While these are issues on which the last decade of research has shed some rays of light, many dark corners remain. Those of us who study European monetary unification can take heart in the fact that the next decade will offer as many research opportunities as the last.

Notes

1. Insofar as these disturbances are industry specific.

2. See Hirschman (1970).

3. One notable exception is Cohen (1994).

References

Advisory Commission on Intergovernmental Relations (1987), *Fiscal Discipline in the Federal System*, Washington, D.C.: ACIR.

A'Hearn, B. (1991), "Migration and Economic Convergence in Post-War Italy," unpublished manuscript, University of California, Berkeley.

Alesina, A., and V. Grilli (1993), "On the Feasibility of a One or Multi-Speed European Monetary Union," *Economics and Politics* 5, pp. 145–65.

Alesina, A., A. Prati, and G. Tabellini (1990), "Public Confidence and Debt Management: A Model and Case Study of Italy," in R. Dornbusch and M. Draghi (eds.), *Public Debt Management: Theory and History*, Cambridge: Cambridge University Press, pp. 94–124.

Alogoskoufis, G. (1993), "The Crisis in the European Monetary System and the Future of EMU," paper prepared for the Conference on the Impact of European Monetary Union, Barcelona (March 11–12).

Annual Statistical Abstract of the United Kingdom, (various years), London: HMSO.

Ardy, B. (1988), "The National Incidence of the European Community Budget," *Journal of Common Market Studies* 26, pp. 401–29.

Armstrong, H., and J. Taylor (1985), *Regional Economics and Policy*, London: Philip Allan.

Artis, M., and S. Gazioglu (1987), "A Two-Country Model with Asymmetric Phillips Curves and Intervention in the Foreign Exchange Market," CEPR DP 172.

Atkeson, A., and T. Bayoumi (1993), "Do Private Markets Insure against Regional Shocks in a Common Currency Area? Evidence from the US," *Open Economies Review* 4, pp. 303–24.

Attanasio, O. P., and F. Padoa-Schioppa (1991), "Regional Inequalities, Migration and Mismatch in Italy, 1960–86," in F. Padoa-Schioppa (ed.), *Mismatch and Labor Mobility*, Cambridge: Cambridge University Press, pp. 237–321.

Balogh, T. (1976), "Keynes and the International Monetary Fund," in A. P. Thirlwall (ed.), *Keynes and International Monetary Relations*, London: Macmillan, pp. 66–89.

Barro, R., and D. Gordon (1981), "Rules, Discretion and Reputation in a Model of Monetary Policy," *Journal of Monetary Economics* 12, pp. 101–21.

Barro, R., and X. Sala-i-Martin (1991), "Convergence across States and Regions," *Brookings Papers on Economic Activity* 1, pp. 107–58.

Bartik, T. J. (1985), "Business Location Decisions in the United States: Estimates of the Effects of Unionization, Taxes and Other Characteristics of States," *Journal of Business and Economic Statistics* 3, pp. 14–22.

Bayoumi, T. (1991), "A Note on the Decomposition of Vector Autoregressions," unpublished manuscript, Bank of England.

Bayoumi, T. (1992), "Fiscal Policy and EMU," in C. Goodhart (ed.), *EMU and ESCB after Maastricht*, London: London School of Economics, Financial Markets Group, pp. 242–66.

Bayoumi, T. (1994), "A Formal Model of Optimum Currency Areas," *IMF Staff Papers* 41, pp. 537–58.

Bayoumi, T., and B. Eichengreen (1993a), "Is There a Conflict between EC Enlargement and European Monetary Unification?" *Greek Economic Review* 15, pp. 131–54.

Bayoumi, T., and B. Eichengreen (1993b), "Shocking Aspects of European Monetary Unification," in F. Torres and F. Giavazzi (eds.), *Adjustment and Growth in the European Monetary Union*, Cambridge: Cambridge University Press, pp. 193–229.

Bayoumi, T., and B. Eichengreen (1994), "Monetary and Exchange Rate Arrangements for NAFTA," *Journal of Development Economics* 43, pp. 125–65.

Bayoumi, T., and B. Eichengreen (1995), "Restraining Yourself: The Implications of Fiscal Rules for Economic Stabilization," *IMF Staff Papers* 42, pp. 32–48.

Bayoumi, T., and B. Eichengreen (1996a), "Optimum Currency Areas and Exchange Rate Variability: Theory and Evidence Compared," unpublished manuscript, International Monetary Fund and University of California, Berkeley.

Bayoumi, T., and B. Eichengreen (1996b), "The Stability of the Gold Standard and the Evolution of the International Monetary System," in T. Bayoumi, B. Eichengreen, and M. Taylor (eds.), *Modern Perspectives on the Gold Standard*, Cambridge: Cambridge University Press, pp. 165–88.

Bayoumi, T., M. Goldstein, and G. Woglom (1995), "Do Credit Markets Discipline Sovereign Borrowers? Evidence from U.S. States," *Journal of Money, Credit and Banking* 27, pp. 1046–59.

Bayoumi, T., and P. Masson (1995), "Fiscal Flows in the United States and Canada: Lessons for Monetary Union in Europe," *European Economic Review* 39, pp. 253–74 .

Begg, D., and C. Wyplosz (1993), "The European Monetary System: Recent Intellectual History," in *The Monetary Future of Europe*, London: Centre for Economic Policy Research, pp. 1–78.

Berger, H., and A. Ritschl (1995), "Germany and the Political Economy of the Marshall Plan, 1947–52: A Re-Revisionist View," in B. Eichengreen (ed.), *Europe's Postwar Recovery*, Cambridge: Cambridge University Press, pp. 199–245.

Bergsten, C. F., and J. Williamson (1983), "Exchange Rates and Trade Policy," in W. R. Cline (ed.), *Trade Policy in the 1980s*, Washington, D.C.: Institute for International Economics, pp. 99–120.

Berlin, H. M. (1990), *Handbook of Financial Market Indexes, Averages and Indicators*, Homewood, Ill.: Dow Jones-Irwin.

Bertola, G. (1988), "Factor Flexibility, Uncertainty and Exchange Rate Regimes," in M. de Cecco and A. Giovannini (eds.), *A European Central Bank?* Cambridge: Cambridge University Press, pp. 99—119.

Bertola, G., and R. Caballero (1992), "Target Zones and Realignments," *American Economic Review* 82, pp. 520—55.

Bertola, G., and A. Drazen (1993), "Trigger Points and Budget Cuts: Explaining the Effects of Fiscal Austerity," *American Economic Review* 83, pp. 11—26.

Bianchi, P., and G. Gualtieri (1990), "Emilia-Romagna and its Industrial Districts: The Evolution of Model," in R. Leonardi and R. Y. Nanetti (eds.), *The Regions and European Integration: The Case of Emilia-Romagna*, London: Pinter, pp. 83—108.

Bierstedt, R. (1964), "Legitimacy," in *Dictionary of Social Sciences*, New York: Free Press, pp. 386—87.

Bini-Smaghi, L., and S. Vori (1993), "Rating the EC as an Optimum Currency Area," Bank of Italy Discussion Paper no. 187.

Blanchard, O., and L. Katz (1992), "Regional Evolutions," *Brookings Papers on Economic Activity* 1, pp. 1—61.

Blanchard, O., and D. Quah (1989), "The Dynamic Effects of Aggregate Demand and Supply Disturbances," *American Economic Review* 79, pp. 655—73.

Boltho, A. (1989), "Europe and United States Regional Differentials: A Note," *Oxford Review of Economic Policy* 5, pp. 105—15.

Bordo, M., and F. Kydland (1995), "The Gold Standard as a Rule: An Essay in Exploration," *Explorations in Economic History* 32, pp. 423—64.

Boughton, J. M. (1993), "The Economics of the CFA Franc Zone," in P. R. Mason and M. P. Taylor (eds.), *Policy Issues in the Operation of Currency Unions*, pp. 96—107.

Branson, W. H., and J. Love (1988), "U.S. Manufacturing and the Real Exchange Rate," in R. Marston (ed.), *Exchange Rate Misalignment*, Chicago: University of Chicago Press, pp. 241—70.

Break, G. F. (1967), *Intergovernmental Fiscal Relations in the United States*, Washington, D.C.: Brookings Institution.

Bretzfelder, R. B. (1973), "Sensitivity of State and Regional Income to National Business Cycles," *Journal of Current Business* 53, pp. 22—33.

Bryant, Ralph C. (1987), "Intergovernmental Coordination of Economic Policies: An Interim Stocktaking," in Peter B. Kenen (eds.), *International Monetary Cooperation: Essays in Honor of Henry C. Wallich*, Essays in International Finance no. 169, International Finance Section, Department of Economics, Princeton University.

Buiter, W. H., G. Corsetti, and N. Roubini (1993), "Excessive Deficits: Sense and Nonsense in the Treaty of Maastricht," *Economic Policy* 16, pp. 57—100.

Bulow, Jeremy I., and Kenneth Rogoff (1989), "A Constant Recontracting Model of Sovereign Debt," *Journal of Political Economy* 97, February, pp. 155—78.

Burda, M. C. (1990), "Les conséquences de l'union économique et monétaire de l'Allemagne," *Observations et Diagnostics Economiques* 34, pp. 215—38.

Cairncross, A. (1992), *The British Economy Since 1945*, Oxford: Blackwell.

Calvo, G. (1988), "Servicing the Public Debt: The Role of Expectations," *American Economic Review* 78, pp. 647–61.

Campa, J., and K. Chang (1996), "Arbitrage-Based Test of Target Zone Credibility: Evidence from ERM Cross-Rate Options," *American Economic Review* 86, pp. 726–40.

Canzoneri, M. B. (1985), "Monetary Policy Games and the Role of Private Information," *American Economic Review* 75, pp. 1056–70.

Canzoneri, M. B., and D. W. Henderson (1991), *Monetary Policy in Interdependent Economies: A Game-Theoretic Approach*, Cambridge, Mass.: MIT Press.

Caroleo, F. E. (1990), "Le Cause Economiche Nei Differenziali Regionali Del Tasso Di Disoccupazione," *Economia & Lavoro* 23, pp. 41–53.

Catte, P., G. Galli, and S. Rebecchini (1994), "Concerted Interventions and the Dollar: An Analysis of Daily Data," in P. B. Kenen, F. Papadia, and F. Saccomanni (eds.), *The International Monetary System*, Cambridge: Cambridge University Press, pp. 201–56.

Chapman, P. G. (1991), "The Dynamics of Regional Unemployment in the UK, 1974–89," *Applied Economics* 23, pp. 1059–64.

Citibank (1990), *Currency and Instrument Directory*, London: Bank Research Limited.

Cohen, Benjamin (1994), "Beyond EMU: The Problem of Sustainability," in B. Eichengreen and J. Frieden (eds.), *The Political Economy of European Monetary Unification*, Boulder, Co.: Westview Press, pp. 149–66.

Cohen, D., and C. Wyplosz (1989), "The European Monetary Union: An Agnostic Evaluation," in R. C. Bryant, D. A. Currie, J. A. Frenkel, P. R. Masson, and R. Portes (eds.), *Macroeconomic Policies in an Interdependent World*, Washington, D.C.: IMF, pp. 311–37.

Commission of the European Communities (1984), J. van Ypersele and J. Koeune (eds.), *The European Monetary System*, Luxembourg: Office for Official Publications of the European Communities.

Commission of the European Communities (1990), "One Market, One Money: An Evaluation of the Potential Benefits and Costs of Forming an Economic and Monetary Union," *European Economy* 44, special issue.

Commission of the European Communities (1992), *Treaty on European Union* (Maastricht Treaty), Luxembourg: Office for Official Publications of the European Communities.

Commission of the European Communities (1993), *Annual Economic Report for 1993*, Luxembourg: Office for Official Publications of the European Communities.

Committee for the Study of Economic and Monetary Union (Delors Committee) (1989), *Report on Economic and Monetary Union in the European Community*, Luxembourg: Office for Official Publications of the European Communities.

Connolly, W. (ed.) (1984), *Legitimacy and the State*, Oxford: Blackwell.

Corden, W. M. (1972), "Monetary Integration," Essays in International Finance no. 32, International Finance Section, Department of Economics, Princeton University.

Council of Economic Advisors (1991), *Economic Report of the President*, Washington, D.C.: GPO.

Creedy, J. (1974), "Inter-Regional Mobility: A Cross-Section Analysis," *Scottish Journal of Political Economy* 21, pp. 41–53.

Croxford, G. J., M. Wise, and B. S. Chalkley (1987), "The Reform of the European Regional Development Fund: A Preliminary Assessment," *Journal of Common Market Studies* 26, pp. 25–38.

De Grauwe, P. (1990), "The Cost of Disinflation and the European Monetary System," *Open Economies Review* 1, pp. 147–73.

De Grauwe, P. (1994), *The Economics of Monetary Union*, Oxford: Oxford University Press, 2d edition.

De Grauwe, P. (1996), "The Economics of Convergence towards Monetary Union in Europe," in F. Torres (ed.), *Monetary Reform in Europe*, Lisbon: Universidade Catolica Editoria, pp. 121–48.

De Grauwe, P., and W. Vanhaverbeke (1993), "Is Europe an Optimum Currency Area? Evidence from Regional Data," in P. R. Masson and M. Taylor (eds.), *Policy Issues in the Operation of Currency Unions*, Cambridge: Cambridge University Press, pp. 111–29.

De Kock, G., and V. Grilli (1989), "Endogenous Exchange Rate Regime Switches," NBER Working Paper no. 3066.

Department of Employment and Productivity (1971), *British Labour Statistics: Historical Abstract 1886–1968*, London: HMSO.

Deutsche Bundesbank (1991), *Report of the Deutsche Bundesbank for 1990*, Frankfurt: Deutsche Bundesbank.

Dornbusch, R. (1976), "Expectations and Exchange Rate Dynamics," *Journal of Political Economy* 84, pp. 1161–76.

Dornbusch, R. (1990), "Two-Track EMU, Now!" in K. O. Pohl et al., *Britain and EMU*, London: Centre for Economic Performance, pp. 103–12.

Dornbusch, R., and S. Fischer (1986), *Macroeconomics*, New York: McGraw Hill, 3d ed.

Edwards, S. (1989), *Real Exchange Rates in Developing Countries*, Cambridge, Mass.: MIT Press.

Eichengreen, B. (1984), "Keynes and Protection," *Journal of Economic History* 44, pp. 363–73.

Eichengreen, B. (1990a), "Costs and Benefits of European Monetary Unification," in P. Bérégovoy (ed.), *Vers l'union économique et monétaire européene*, Paris: Ministry of Finance, pp. 15–30.

Eichengreen, B. (1990b), "One Money for Europe? Lessons from the U.S. Currency Union," *Economic Policy* 10, pp. 117–87.

Eichengreen, B. (1991), "Relaxing the External Constraint: Europe in the 1930's," in George Alogoskoufis, Lucas Papademos, and Richard Portes (eds.), *External Constraints on Macroeconomic Policy: The European Experience*, Cambridge: Cambridge University Press, pp. 75–117.

Eichengreen, B. (1992a), "Is Europe an Optimum Currency Area?" in H. Grubel and S. Borner (eds.), *The European Community after 1992: Perspectives from the Outside*, Basingstoke, England: Macmillan, pp. 138–61.

Eichengreen, B. (1992b), *Golden Fetters: The Gold Standard and the Great Depression 1919–1939*, New York: Oxford University Press.

Eichengreen, B. (1992c), "Should the Maastricht Treaty Be Saved?" Princeton Studies in International Finance no. 74, International Finance Section, Department of Economics, Princeton University.

Eichengreen, B. (1993a), "The Crisis in the EMS and the Transition to EMU: An Interim Assessment," in S. Honkapohja (ed.), *Economic Policy Issues in Financial Integration*, Helsinki: University of Helsinki, Institute of International Economic Law, pp. 15–72.

Eichengreen, B. (1993b), "European Monetary Unification," *Journal of Economic Literature* 31, pp. 1321–57.

Eichengreen, B. (1993c), "Labor Markets and European Monetary Unification,"in P. R. Masson and M. Taylor (eds.), *Policy Issues in the Operation of Currency Unions*, Cambridge: Cambridge University Press, pp. 130–62.

Eichengreen, B. (1994), "Fiscal Policy and EMU," in B. Eichengreen and J. Frieden (eds.), *The Political Economy of European Monetary Unification*, Boulder, Co.: Westview Press, pp. 167–90.

Eichengreen, B., and J. Frieden (1993), "The Political Economy of European Monetary Unification: An Analytical Introduction," *Economics and Politics* 5, pp. 85–104.

Eichengreen, B., and F. Ghironi (1996a), "European Monetary Unification: The Challenges Ahead," in F. Torres (ed.), *Monetary Reform in Europe*, Lisbon: Universidade Catholica Editora, pp. 83–120.

Eichengreen, B., and F. Ghironi (1996b): "European Monetary Unification and International Monetary Cooperation," in B. Eichengreen (ed.), *U.S.-European Economic Relations in the Post-Cold War Era* (forthcoming).

Eichengreen, B., and D. A. Irwin (1995), "Trade Blocs, Currency Blocs and the Reorientation of World Trade in the 1930s," *Journal of International Economics* 38, pp. 1–24.

Eichengreen, B., and J. Sachs (1985), "Exchange Rates and Economic Recovery in the 1930s," *Journal of Economic History* 45, pp. 925–46.

Eichengreen, B., and C. Wyplosz (1993), "The Unstable EMS," *Brookings Papers on Economic Activity* 1, pp. 51–143.

Emminger, O. (1986), *D-Mark, Dollar, Währungskrisen*, Stuttgart: Deutsche Verlags-Anstalt.

Engle, R. F., and B. S. Yoo (1987), "Forecasting and Testing in Cointegrated Systems," *Journal of Econometrics* 85, pp. 143–59.

Erdevig, E. (1986), "Federal Funds Flow No Bargain for Midwest," *Economic Perspectives*, January/February, pp. 3–10.

Feinstein, C., P. Temin, and G. Toniolo (1995), "International Economic Organization: Banking, Finance and Trade in Europe between the Wars," in C. Feinstein (ed.), *Banking, Currency and Finance in Europe between the Wars*, Oxford: Clarendon Press, pp. 9–76.

Flood, R. P., and P. M. Garber (1984a), "Collapsing Exchange Rate Regimes: Some Linear Examples," *Journal of International Economics* 17, pp. 1–13.

Flood, R. P., and P. M. Garber (1984b), "Gold Monetization and Gold Discipline," *Journal of Political Economy* 92, pp. 90–107.

Flood, R. P., and P. Isard (1989), "Monetary Policy Strategies," *IMF Staff Papers* 36, pp. 612–32.

Fox, W. F. (1986), "Tax Structure and the Location of Economic Activity Along State Borders," *National Tax Journal* 39, pp. 387–401.

Frankel, J. A. (1985), "Six Possible Meanings of 'Overvaluation': The 1981–85 Dollar," Essays in International Finance no. 159, International Finance Section, Department of Economics, Princeton University.

Frankel, J. A. (1991), "Quantifying International Capital Mobility in the 1980s," in B. D. Bernheim and J. B. Shoven (eds.), *National Saving and Economic Performance*, Chicago and London: University of Chicago Press, pp. 227–60.

Frankel, J. A., and A. T. MacArthur (1988), "Political vs. Currency Premia in International Real Interest Differentials: A Study of Forward Rates for 24 Countries," *European Economic Review* 32, pp. 1083–114.

Frankel, J. A., and A. Rose (1996), "The Endogeneity of the Optimum Currency Area Criteria," unpublished manuscript, University of California, Berkeley.

Fratianni, M., and J. von Hagen (1992), *The European Monetary System and European Monetary Union*, Boulder, Co.: Westview Press.

Friedman, M., and A. J. Schwartz (1963), *A Monetary History of the United States, 1867–1960*, Princeton: Princeton University Press.

Garrett, G. (1993), "The Politics of Maastricht," *Economics and Politics* 5, pp. 105–23.

Ghironi, F., and F. Giavazzi (1997a), "Is Small Beautiful? Currency Unions and the Employment-Inflation Tradeoff," unpublished manuscript, University of California, Berkeley, and Bocconi University, Milan.

Ghironi, F., and F. Giavazzi (1997b), "Out in the Sunshine? Outsiders, Insiders and the United States in 1998," CEPR DP 1547.

Giavazzi, F., and A. Giovannini (1989a), *Limiting Exchange Rate Flexibility: The Case of the European Monetary System*, Cambridge, Mass.: MIT Press.

Giavazzi, F., and A. Giovannini (1989b), "Monetary Policy Interactions under Managed Exchange Rates," *Economica* 56, pp. 199–213.

Giavazzi, F., and M. Pagano (1990a), "Confidence Crises and Public Debt Management," in R. Dornbusch and M. Draghi (eds.), *Public Debt Management: Theory and History*, Cambridge: Cambridge University Press, pp. 125–52.

Giavazzi, F., and M. Pagano (1990b), "Can Severe Fiscal Contractions Be Expansionary? Tales of Two Small European Countries," *NBER Macroeconomics Annual*, pp. 75–111.

Giavazzi, F., and L. Spaventa (1990), "The 'New' EMS," in P. De Grauwe and L. Papademos (eds.), *The European Monetary System in the 1990s*, New York: Longman, pp. 65–85.

Giovannini, A. (1993), "Bretton Woods and Its Precursors: Rules versus Discretion in the History of International Monetary Regimes," in M. D. Bordo and B. Eichengreen (eds.), *A Retrospective on the Bretton Woods System*, Chicago: University of Chicago Press, pp. 109–47.

Goldstein, M., and G. Woglom (1992), "Market-Based Fiscal Discipline in Monetary Unions: Evidence from the US Municipal Bond Market," in M. Canzoneri, V. Grilli, and P. Masson,

Establishing a Central Bank: Issues in Europe and Lessons from the U.S., Cambridge: Cambridge University Press, pp. 228–60.

Goodhart, C. A. E. (1995), "The Political Economy of Monetary Union," in P. B. Kenen (ed.), *Understanding Interdependence: The Macroeconomics of the Open Economy*, Princeton: Princeton University Press, pp. 448–505.

Goodhart, C. A. E., and S. Smith (1993), "Stabilization," in *The Economics of Public Finance*, European Economy Reports and Studies no. 5, pp. 417–56.

Governor of Puerto Rico (1984), *Informe Economica al Gobernador*, San Juan: Office of the Governor.

Greenwood, M. J. (1975), "Research on Internal Migration in the United States: A Survey," *Journal of Economic Literature* 8, pp. 397–433.

Grilli, E. (1988), "Macroeconomic Determinants of Trade Protection," *World Economy* 11, pp. 313–26.

Gros, D., and N. Thygesen (1991), *European Monetary Integration from the European Monetary System to the European Monetary Union*, London: Macmillan.

Grossman, H. I., and J. B. van Huyck (1988), "Sovereign Debt as a Contingent Claim: Excusable Default, Repudiation and Reputation," *American Economic Review* 78, pp. 1088–97.

Group of Ten (1996), "The Resolution of Sovereign Liquidity Crises," abridged version reprinted in Peter Kenen (ed.), "From Halifax to Lyons: What Has Been Done about Crisis Management?" Essay in International Finance no. 200, International Finance Section, Department of Economics, Princeton University, October, pp. 73–77.

Hall, R. (1972), "Turnover in the Labour Force," *Brookings Papers on Economic Activity* 1, pp. 709–56.

Hall, R., and J. Taylor (1988), *Macroeconomics: Theory, Practice and Policy*, New York: Norton.

Harris, R. G. (1991), "Exchange Rates and International Competitiveness of the Canadian Economy," unpublished paper, Simon Fraser University.

Hart, R. A. (1970), "A Model of Inter-Regional Migration in England and Wales," *Regional Studies* 4, pp. 279–96.

Hartland, P. C. (1949), "Interregional Payments Compared with International Payments," *Quarterly Journal of Economics* 63, pp. 392–407.

Helpman E., and P. R. Krugman (1985), *Market Structure and Foreign Trade*, Cambridge, Mass.: MIT Press.

Hewett, R. S., and S. C. Stephenson (1983), "State Tax Revenues under Competition," *National Tax Journal* 36, pp. 95–101.

Hirschman, Albert O. (1970), *Exit, Voice and Loyalty*, Cambridge, Mass.: Harvard University Press.

Holtfrerich, C-L. (1989), "The Monetary Unification Process in Nineteenth-Century Germany: Relevance and Lessons for Europe Today," in M. de Cecco and A. Giovannini (eds.), *A European Central Bank? Perspectives on Monetary Unification after Ten Years of the EMS*, Cambridge: Cambridge University Press, pp. 216–41.

Horn, H., and T. Persson (1988), "Exchange Rate Policy, Wage Formation and Credibility," *European Economic Review* 32, pp. 1621–36.

Hörngren, L., and H. Lindberg (1993), "The Struggle to Turn the Swedish Krona into a Hard Currency," unpublished paper, Sveriges Riksbank, March.

Howard, M. A. (1989), *Fiscal Survey of the States*, Washington, D.C.: National Governors' Association.

Hughes, G., and B. McCormick (1981), "Do Council Housing Policies Reduce Migration between Regions?" *Economic Journal* 91, pp. 919–37.

Hughes-Hallett, A., and D. Vines (1991), "Adjustment Difficulties within a European Monetary Union: Can They Be Reduced?" *Rivista di Politica Economica* 81, pp. 281–322.

Ingram, J. C. (1959), "State and Regional Payments Mechanisms," *Quarterly Journal of Economics* 73, pp. 619–632.

Ingram, J. C. (1962), *Regional Payments Mechanisms: The Case of Puerto Rico*, Chapel Hill: University of North Carolina Press.

Ingram, J. C. (1973), "The Case for European Monetary Integration," Essays in International Finance no. 98, International Finance Section, Department of Economics, Princeton University.

International Bank Corporate Analysis (1993), *Ratings: Financial Institutions and Corporates*, London: IBCA.

International Monetary Fund (1992), *Direction of Trade Statistics*, Washington, D.C.: IMF.

International Monetary Fund (1995), *World Economic Outlook*, Washington, D.C.: IMF, May.

International Monetary Fund (various years), *International Financial Statistics*, Washington, D.C.: IMF.

Istituto Centrale di Statistica (various years), *Annuario di Contabilità Nazionale*, Rome: ISTAT.

Istituto Centrale di Statistica (various years), *Annuario Statistico del Lavoro*, Rome: ISTAT.

Istituto Centrale di Statistica (various years), *Annuario Statistico Italiano*, Rome: ISTAT.

Istituto Centrale di Statistica (various years), *Popolazione e Bilanci Demografici per Sesso, Eta' e Regione*, Rome: ISTAT.

Istituto Centrale di Statistica (various years), *Popolazione e Movimento Anagrafico dei Comuni*, Rome: ISTAT.

Istituto Centrale di Statistica (various years), *Ricostruzione della Popolazione Residente per Sesso, Eta' e Regione*, Rome: ISTAT.

Istituto Centrale di Statistica (various years), *Statistiche Demografiche*, Rome: ISTAT.

Istituto Nazionale per l'Assicurazione Contro gli Infortuni sul Lavoro (various years), *Notiziario Statistico*, Rome: INAIL.

Ishiyama, Y. (1975), "The Theory of Optimum Currency Areas: A Survey," *IMF Staff Papers* 22, pp. 344–83.

Italianer, A., and J. Pisani-Ferry (1992), "Regional Stabilization Properties of Fiscal Arrangements: What Lessons for the Community?" Commission of the European Communities and Centre D'Études Prospectives et D'Informations Internationales (CEPII).

Jensen, Henrik (1991), "Tax Distortions, Unemployment, and International Policy Cooperation," unpublished manuscript, University of Aarhus, Denmark.

Johnson, H. G. (1972), "The Case for Flexible Exchange Rates, 1969," in H. G. Johnson, *Further Essays in Monetary Economics*, London: Allen & Unwin, pp. 198–222.

Kenen, P. B. (1969), "The Theory of Optimum Currency Areas: An Eclectic View," in R. A. Mundell and A. Swoboda (eds.), *Monetary Problems of the International Economy*, Chicago: University of Chicago Press, pp. 41–60.

Kenen, P. B. (1988), *Managing Exchange Rates*, London: Royal Institute of International Affairs.

Kenen, P. B. (1992), *EMU after Maastricht*, Washington, D.C.: Group of Thirty.

Kenen, P. B. (1994), "Ways to Reform Exchange-Rate Arrangements," Reprints in International Finance no. 28, International Finance Section, Department of Economics, Princeton University.

King, R. (1985), *The Industrial Geography of Italy*, London: Croom Helm.

Krugman, P. (1979), "A Model of Balance-of-Payments Crises," *Journal of Money, Credit and Banking* 11, pp. 311–25.

Krugman, P. (1991a), *Economic Geography and International Trade*, Cambridge, Mass.: MIT Press.

Krugman, P. (1991b), "The Move Toward Free Trade Zones," in *Policy Implications of Trade and Currency Zones*, Kansas City, Mo.: Federal Reserve Bank of Kansas City, pp. 7–42.

Krugman, P. (1993), "Lessons of Massachusetts for EMU," in F. Torres and F. Giavazzi (eds.), *Adjustment and Growth in the European Monetary Union*, Cambridge: Cambridge University Press, pp. 241–61.

La Lettre du C.E.P.P.I. (1993), Paris: Centre D'Éstudes et D'Informations Internationales 109, January.

Langley, P. C. (1974), "The Spatial Allocation of Migrants in England and Wales," *Scottish Journal of Political Economy* 21, pp. 259–77.

Levin, J. (1991), "Measuring the Role of Subnational Governments," IMF Working Paper no. 8.

Lippi, M., and L. Reichlin (1993), "The Dynamic Effects of Aggregate Demand and Supply Disturbances," *American Economic Review* 83, pp. 644–52.

Lipset, S. M. (1960), *Political Man*, Garden City, N.Y.: Doubleday.

Marsden, D. (1989), "Occupations: The Influence of the Unemployment Situation," in W. T. M. Molle and A. van Mourik (eds.), *Wage Differentials in the European Community*. Avebury: Gower, pp. 105–39.

Mashek, J. W. (1990), "Governors Vent Ire at Price Tag," *Boston Globe*, July 31, pp. 1, 4.

Massarotto, G., and U. Trivellato (1983), "Un Metodo Per il Raccordo delle Serie Regionali Sulle Forze di Lavoro senza Informazioni Estranee," *Economia & Lavoro* 4, pp. 67–77.

Mastropasqua, C., S. Micossi, and R. Rinaldi (1988), "Interventions, Sterilisation, and Monetary Policy in European Monetary System Countries, 1979–87," in F. Giavazzi, S. Micossi, and M. Miller (eds.), *The European Monetary System*, Cambridge: Cambridge University Press, pp. 252–87.

McGuire, T. J. (1986), "Interstate Tax Differentials, Tax Competition and Tax Policy," *National Tax Journal* 39, pp. 367–73.

McKinnon, R. I. (1963), "Optimum Currency Areas," *American Economic Review* 53, pp. 717–725.

McKinnon, R. I. (1995), "Comment," in P. B. Kenen (ed.), *Understanding Interdependence: The Macroeconomics of the Open Economy*, Princeton: Princeton University Press, pp. 88–97.

McKinnon, R. I. (1996), *The Rules of the Game*, Cambridge, Mass: MIT Press.

Meade, J. (1957), "The Balance of Payments Problems of a Free Trade Area," *Economic Journal* 67, pp. 379–96.

Merelman, R. M. (1966), "Learning and Legitimacy," *American Political Science Review* 60, pp. 548–61.

Miller, E. (1973), "Is Out-Migration Affected by Economic Conditions?" *Southern Economic Journal* 39, pp. 396–405.

Mitchell, B. R. (1988), *British Historical Statistics*, Cambridge: Cambridge University Press.

Morales, Antonio J., and A. J. Padilla (1995), "Designing Institutions for International Monetary Policy Coordination," CEPR DP 1180.

Morgan Guaranty Trust Company (1988), "Financial Markets in Europe: Toward 1992," *World Financial Markets* 5.

Morsink, R. L. A., and W. T. Molle (1991), "Direct Investments and Monetary Integration," *European Economy*, special issue, pp. 36–55.

Mundell, R. A. (1961), "A Theory of Optimum Currency Areas," *American Economic Review* 51, pp. 657–65.

Murphy, K., and R. Hofler (1984), "Determinants of Geographic Unemployment Rates: A Selectively Pooled-Simultaneous Model," *Review of Economics and Statistics* 66, pp. 216–23.

Mussa, M. (1986), "Nominal Exchange Rate Regimes and the Behavior of Real Exchange Rates: Evidence and Implications," *Carnegie-Rochester Conference Series on Public Policy* 25, pp. 117–214.

Myers, M. G. (1970), *A Financial History of the United States*, New York: Columbia University Press.

Nascimento, J-C. (1994), "Monetary Policy in Unified Currency Areas: The Cases of the CAMA and ECCA during 1976–90," Washington, D.C.: IMF.

Neumann, M. J. M. (1992), "German Unification: Economic Problems and Consequences," *Carnegie-Rochester Conference Series on Public Policy* 36, pp. 163–209.

Neumann, M. J. M., and J. von Hagen (1992), "Germany," in M. Fratianni and D. Salvatore (eds.), *Monetary Policy in Developed Economies*, Westport, Conn.: Greenwood Press, pp. 299–334.

Obstfeld, M. (1986a), "Rational and Self-Fulfilling Balance-of-Payments Crises," *American Economic Review* 76, pp. 72–81.

Obstfeld, M. (1986b), "Speculative Attack and the External Constraint in a Maximizing Model of the Balance of Payments," *Canadian Journal of Economics* 19, pp. 1–22.

Obstfeld, M. (1990), "The Effectiveness of Foreign-Exchange Intervention: Recent Experience," in W. H. Branson, J. A. Frenkel, and M. Goldstein (eds.), *International Policy Coordination and Exchange Rate Fluctuations*, Chicago: University of Chicago Press, pp. 197–237.

Obstfeld, M. (1992), "Destabilizing Effects of Exchange-Rate Escape Clauses," CEPR Discussion Paper no. 518.

Obstfeld, M. (1994), "The Logic of Currency Crises," *Cahiers Économiques et Monetaires* 43, pp. 189–213.

Organisation for Economic Cooperation and Development (1986), *Flexibility in the Labour Market*, Paris: OECD.

Ozkan, F. G., and A. Sutherland (1994), "A Model of the ERM Crisis," CEPR Discussion Paper no. 879, January.

Padoa-Schioppa, T., M. Emerson, M. King, J. C. Milleron, J. Paelinck, L. Papademos, A. Pastor, and F. Scharpf (1987), *Efficiency, Stability and Equity: A Strategy for the Evolution of the Economic System of the European Community*, Oxford: Oxford University Press.

Papke, J., and L. Papke (1986), "Measuring Differential State-Local Tax Liabilities and Their Implications for Business Investment Location," *National Tax Journal* 39, pp. 357–66.

Parkes, C. (1995), "EMS Faces Threat of Collapse," *Financial Times*, April 27, p. 1.

Persson, T., and G. Tabellini (1995), "Double Edged Incentives: Institutions and Policy Coordination," in G. Grossman and K. Rogoff (eds.), *Handbook of International Economics*, Vol. III, Amsterdam: North-Holland.

Pissarides, C., and I. McMaster (1990), "Regional Migration, Wages and Unemployment: Empirical Evidence and Implications for Policy," *Oxford Economic Papers* 42, pp. 812–31.

Poehl, K. O. (1988), "A Blueprint for Europe's Central Bank," *The International Economy* 2, pp. 60–64.

Polak, J. J. (1951), "Contribution of the September 1949 Devaluations to the Solution of Europe's Dollar Problem," *IMF Staff Papers* 2, pp. 1–32.

Poloz, S. S. (1990), "Real Exchange Rate Adjustment Between Regions in a Common Currency Area," unpublished manuscript, Bank of Canada.

Poterba, J. (1994), "State Responses to Fiscal Crisis: The Effects of Budgetary Institutions and Politics," *Journal of Political Economy* 102, pp. 799–821.

Portes, R. (1993), "EMS and EMU after the Fall," *The World Economy* 16, pp. 1–16.

Quah, D. (1991), "Identifying Vector Autoregressions: A Discussion of P. Englund, A. Vredin and A. Warne: Macroeconomic Shocks in Sweden 1925–86," unpublished manuscript, London School of Economics, September.

Reed, H. L. (1922), *The Development of Federal Reserve Policy*, Boston: Houghton Mifflin.

Rogoff, K. (1985), "Can International Monetary Policy Cooperation Be Counterproductive?" *Journal of International Economics* 18, pp. 199–217.

Rolnik, A. J., B. D. Smith, and W. E. Weber (1993), "In Order to Form a More Perfect Monetary Union," *Federal Reserve Bank of Minneapolis Review* (Fall), pp. 2–13.

Rose, A. (1994), "Are Exchange Rates Macroeconomic Phenomena?" *Federal Reserve Bank of San Francisco Economic Review* 19, pp. 20–30.

Rose, A., and L. Svensson (1996), "European Exchange Rate Credibility after the Fall," *European Economic Review* 38, pp. 1185–1216.

Rosen, P. L. (1979), "Legitimacy, Domination, and Ego Displacement," in A. J. Vidich and R. M. Glassman (eds.), *Conflict and Control: Challenge to Legitimacy of Modern Governments*, London: Sage, pp. 75–95.

Rousseau, J. (1913), *The Social Contract and Discourses*, New York: Dutton.

Sala-i-Martin, X., and J. Sachs (1992), "Federal Fiscal Policy and Optimum Currency Areas," in M. Canzoneri, V. Grilli, and P. Masson (eds.), *Establishing a Central Bank: Issues in Europe and Lessons from the US*, Cambridge: Cambridge University Press, pp. 195–220.

Salvatore, D. (1981), *Internal Migration and Economic Development: A Theoretical and Empirical Study*, Washington, D.C.: University Press of America.

Sannucci, V. (1989), "The Establishment of a Central Bank: Italy in the Nineteenth Century," in M. de Cecco and A. Giovannini (eds.), *A European Central Bank?* Cambridge: Cambridge University Press, pp. 244–79.

Savvides, A. (1993), "Pegging the Exchange Rate and Choice of a Standard by LDCs: A Joint Formulation," *Journal of Economic Development* 18, pp. 107–25.

Schaar, J. (1969), "Legitimacy in the Modern State," in P. Green and S. Levinson (eds.), *Power and Community: Dissenting Essays in Political Science*, New York: Random House, pp. 276–327.

Schott, J. J., and M. G. Smith (eds.) (1988), *The Canada-United States Free Trade Agreement: The Global Impact*, Washington: Institute for International Economics.

Schweitzer, M. (1989), "State Issued Currency and Ratification of the U.S. Constitution," *Journal of Economic History* 49, pp. 311–22.

Scitovsky, T. (1967), "The Theory of Balance-of-Payments Adjustment," *Journal of Political Economy* 75, pp. 523–31.

Servais, D. (1988), *The Single Financial Market*, Brussels: Commission of the European Communities.

Siebert, H. (1991), "German Unification: The Economics of Transition," *Economic Policy* 13, pp. 287–340.

Stephenson, S. C., and R. S. Hewett (1985), "Strategies for States in Fiscal Competition," *National Tax Journal* 38, pp. 219–26.

Stiglitz, J., and A. Weiss (1981), "Credit Rationing in Markets with Imperfect Information," *American Economic Review* 73, 393–410.

Sveriges Riksbank (1993), *Annual Report 1992*, Stockholm: Sveriges Riksbank.

Tobin, J., W. Donaldson, K. Gordon, W. Lewis, S. Robbins, and W. Treiber (1975), "Report to the Governor: The Committee to Study Puerto Rico's Finances," unpublished manuscript, Yale University.

Topel, R. (1984), "Equilibrium Earnings, Turnover and Unemployment: New Evidence," *Journal of Labor Economics* 2, pp. 500–22.

Townsend, A. R. (1983), *The Impact of Recession*, London: Croom Helm.

United States, President (various years), *Manpower Report of the President*, Washington, D.C.: GPO.

United States Department of Health, Education, and Welfare (various years), *Vital Statistics of the U.S.*, Washington, D.C.: GPO.

United States Department of Labor (various years), *Geographic Profile of Employment and Unemployment*, Washington, D.C.: GPO.

United States Department of Labor (various years), *Employment and Earnings*, Washington, D.C.: GPO.

United States Senate (1980), *Regional Impact of an Economic Slowdown: The Michigan Picture*, Hearings before the Committee on the Budget, 96th Congress, 1st Session, Washington, D.C.: GPO.

Vaubel, R. (1980), "The Return to the New European Monetary System: Objectives, Incentives, Perspectives," *Journal of Monetary Economics* 13, pp. 173–221.

Verway, D. (ed.) (1987), *Michigan Statistical Abstract*, Detroit: Wayne State University Press.

von Hagen, J. (1992), "Fiscal Arrangements in Monetary Union: Evidence from the US," in D. E. Fair and C. de Boissieu (eds.), *Fiscal Policy, Taxation and the Financial System in an Increasingly Integrated Europe*, Dordrecht, the Netherlands: Kluwer Academic Publishers, pp. 337–59.

von Hagen, J. and B. Eichengreen (1996), "Fiscal Restraints, Federalism and European Monetary Union: Is the Excessive Deficit Procedure Counterproductive?" *American Economic Review Papers and Proceedings* 86, pp.134–38.

Walsh, C. (1995), "Optimal Contracts for Central Bankers," *American Economic Review* 85, pp. 150–67.

Weber, A. (1990), "EMU and Asymmetries and Adjustment Problems in the EMS: Some Empirical Evidence," Centre for Economic Policy Discussion Paper no. 448, August.

Weber, M. (1984), "Legitimacy, Politics and the State," in W. Connolly (ed.), *Legitimacy and the State*, Oxford: Blackwell, pp. 32–62.

Weingast, B. R. (1995), "The Political Foundations of Democracy and the Rule of Law," unpublished manuscript, Hoover Institution, February.

Wicker, E. (1966), *Federal Reserve Monetary Policy, 1917–1933*, New York: Random House.

Wigmore, B. (1988), "Was the Bank Holiday of 1933 Caused by a Run on the Dollar?" *Journal of Economic History* 47, pp. 739–55.

Wolin, S. S. (1981), "Max Weber: Legitimation, Method and the Politics of Theory," *Political Theory* 9, pp. 401–24.

Wright, G. (1986), *Old South, New South*, New York: Basic Books.

Wyplosz, C. (1986), "Capital Controls and Balance of Payments Crises," *Journal of International Money and Finance* 5, pp. 167–79.

Wyplosz, C. (1991), "On the Real Exchange Rate Effect of German Unification," *Weltwirtschaftliches Archiv* 127, pp. 1–17.

Index